D0959845

THE MODERN RIFLE

THE MODERN RIFLE

Jim Carmichel

Winchester Press

TO CLARICE
My best pal — who also happens to be my wife

Library of Congress Catalog Card Number: 75-9264
ISBN: 0-87691-206-4

Library of Congress Cataloging in Publication Data

Carmichel, Jim.
The modern rifle.
Includes index.
1. Rifles. I. Title.
TS536.4.C37 683'.42 75-9264
ISBN 0-87691-206-4

Published by Winchester Press
205 E. 42nd St., New York 10017

Printed in the United States of America

Contents

Introduction

Someone once calculated that the world's fund of knowledge doubles every ten years or so. If this is true—and I have no reason to believe it is not—has rifle development kept pace? Is the rifle of today truly a modern tool, or are we still using yesterday's rifle?

Some may claim that the modern rifle appeared centuries ago when spiral grooves were first cut in a gun barrel in order to make the ball fly truer. Since then, it might be argued, there has been no significant alteration of the basic rifle concept, so nothing has really changed all that much. Other firearms buffs might earmark the day of the first self-contained cartridge as the beginning of the era of the modern rifle, while still others will insist the first of today's modern rifles was actually the first repeater.

And, doubtless, there are those who say that there has been no modern rifle in decades, pointing out that the basic Mauser bolt design of 1898 is still very much in use and as popular as ever, perhaps more popular, even after over three-quarters of a century.

But what this reasoning fails to take into account is the *total* rifle built up on one of these actions in a modern shop or plant—the barrel screwed in it, the sights affixed to it, and the ammo fired through it. The Mauser makers of fifty years ago could not have begun to imagine the performance, especially the accuracy, that today's technology and know-how can impart to a *modern* Mauser.

These things don't just happen in good time, but are the result of man's unending quest to better his techniques and his tools. The modern rifle is a perfect example of that spirit. In this book I discuss ways riflemakers have sought to better their product, the ways they proceeded and what they discovered, their successes and their failures.

I also discuss the reasons riflemakers have done what they have. These are not as obvious as one might think. For example, at the beginning of this century, one might have assumed that the main effort of improvement in rifle design would be directed toward increased firepower. But instead, accuracy has been the main motivation, and continues to be.

It is what the shooter wants that determines the course of rifle development—and yet it is not as simple as that, either, for different shooters want different things, and advances provided for one group of shooters may benefit another group that was ignorant of its own needs. An example is the enormous effect that target shooting has had on field shooting—yet how many field shooters, delighted with their fine new rifles, know how or why they are so fine?

Thus the field shooter who really wants to understand the rifles he uses should know something about target shooting—but as it happens, of all the shooting sports the game of target shooting is the least understood. I am constantly amazed at how little the average sport shooter, hunter, or gun collector knows about target shooting and how unaware he is of our debt of gratitude to the target shooters for rifle development which came about at their insistence. Every time a deer hunter levels the cross hairs on a buck, or a kid draws a bead on a tin can, he is enjoying the benefits of developments in ammo, triggers, scopes, and barrelmaking which came about as a direct result of demands first made by target shooters and probably even developed by a target shooter. Yet, the average hunter, gun collector, or gun dealer is far more likely to be able to describe the rules of a basketball game than outline the procedure of the National Match rifle course. The general opinion is that target shooters simply shoot at targets with "funny-looking" guns and that the competitive shooter is more or less the egghead of the shooting world.

In truth, I must admit, this lack of information—call it a breakdown in communication—between target shooters and the rest of the shooting world is largely the fault of persons such as myself who should have been promoting, or at least reporting, the target game. But also, I must confess, most outdoor writers know no more about target shooting than the average Fifth Avenue bra salesman. A few years back I conducted an informal poll among a gathering of some editors of the various shooting magazines, and not one that I queried could describe the standard over-the-course program of a State Championship Big Bore Rifle Tournament. Similarly, one can find any number of magazine articles and books describing, say, the design and function of an Israeli UZI machine gun, an item which very few people have any business with or are legally allowed to possess, but articles or books on target rifles and match shooting, which can be owned and enjoyed by any shooter, are as rare as a pearl in a bowl of hominy grits.

The language of target shooting contributes to some of the mystery and misunderstanding surrounding the game. For example, in Part IV of this book you will find repeated references to "position" rifles. These are rifles which are used in competitions where the marksman must fire the prone, kneeling, standing, and sometimes sitting positions. Yet, you will also find several references and descriptions to a "prone" rifle. Isn't prone one of the four basic positions? And if so, why isn't a prone rifle also called a position rifle? Well, as it so happens there are a few types of competition which are fired from the prone position only. Thus a highly developed stock form has evolved which is ideally suited for prone shooting, but would be very awkward if fired in other positions. A "position" rifle, on the other hand, is designed so that it fits the shooter in any of the four shooting positions.

There are a host of other seeming contradictions along this line, plus a lot of target terms which have, over the years, made target-shooting lingo sound like the unknown tongue. One of the principal purposes of this book is to unravel some of the confusion. Even if you never expect to fire a rifle at paper, you will learn things that can benefit you in the field—and, too, you may discover that target shooting is more interesting than you thought.

I have also devoted considerable space to custom rifles. If you think these have little to do with the "modern rifle" but are simply quaint toys for wealthy sportsmen—think again. Hardly anything could be more modern, especially in this country.

An innocent bystander might suppose that the final, fragile link to the "good old days" of fine riflemaking exists in the frail forms of a few doddering old souls who represent the end of the great era of craftsmanship. And it is also no doubt widely supposed that custom rifle building is so steeped in tradition that there have been few if any advances in style or craftsmanship which might distinguish today's best work from, say, that of 1920.

Unbelievable as it may seem, however, especially in this age of chrome-plated plastic, fine gun craftsmanship, especially stockmaking, is not just keeping up but actually racing ahead of many areas of rifle development. The biggest misconception of all is that custom gunbuilding is a dying art and when the last of the old-timers lays down his checkering tool fine gunmaking will be seen no more. If one checks back to the era of from 1890 to 1930, a forty-year span which should encompass a full generation of riflesmithing, he will find that no more than a half-dozen American gunsmiths stand out as exceptional craftsmen. But today there are at least two score masters whose work not only equals that of past generations but is so far advanced that often it's not fair to make comparison.

Great craftsmanship in virtually any field is not a mystical happenstance which occurs at random periods in history. Like just about everything else, it obeys the economic laws of demand. Such great gunmakers as the Boutets, who made fabulous guns for Napoleon, and the house of Cominazzo, who fashioned exquisite arms for Italian nobility, flourished because there was someone at hand willing and able to pay for their efforts. Moreover, in response to the same economic law, the number of craftsmen responds with almost mathematical precision to consumer demand. Nowadays there is a considerable demand for nicely built custom guns, and fine gunsmiths are cropping up all over. In other words, great craftsmen in any field don't just die out; they are *allowed* to die out when the demand for their services tapers off—and happily, they also proliferate when the demand intensifies as it has in the past few decades.

Another interesting factor concerning custom gun craftsmanship here in America is that each generation tends to build and improve on concepts laid down by earlier generations. The bad ideas are discarded and the good ones retained and improved upon. I think this is largely due to the fact that we *do not* have a European-type apprenticeship system of masters and students. Instead, in the U.S. a fledgling gunsmith studies everything available, then selects and imitates the features, or combination of features, which he feels best relate to his individual style. Also, the U.S. craftsman can advance as fast as his talent or initiative permits. He has no one to please but himself and his customers. But under the time-honored European system of small shop gunmaking the faults as well as the features tend to be handed from master to pupil, and surprisingly little progress may occur over the generations. This system also tends to discourage innovative thinking. A gunmaker's peers tend to shake their heads and mourn his lost soul if he does it different from the "old ways." This is why American gunmakers have so easily outstripped many of their foreign brethren despite their much older tradition of gunmaking. Stockmaking in particular is an area that is almost wholly dominated by U.S. craftsmen. During my worldwide hunting travels I've visited with several internationally famous hunters and personalities who point to their gun cabinets with pride and count off the rifles made by well-known U.S. riflemakers. The most prestigious bolt-action custom rifles in the world are made in the U.S., make no mistake about it.

Maybe the old .22 single-shot and lever-action .30/30 in your closet are all you ever shoot or plan to shoot. But you wouldn't have read this far if you weren't at least a little interested in finding out if you've been missing anything—literally and figuratively. One thing you've almost certainly been missing is a true understanding of rifles and riflery, and that goes whether you have two guns or two hundred. What this book attempts to do is to trace the relationships between technology, craftsmanship, and the various aspects of the shooting sports and to show how these have determined and will continue to determine rifle design. It is, for me at least, a fascinating area of study, and I hope you will enjoy sharing it with me.

Part I

The Evolution of the Modern Rifle

1

The Action

No matter how you slice it, the heart of the modern rifle is its action—that sometimes simple, sometimes complex, sometimes perplexing, but always remarkable assemblage that locks a cartridge in place, delivers the blow which detonates the primer, then snatches the case out and throws it away.

The influence it exerts over the rest of the rifle, and the purposes for which the rifle may be used, are overwhelming. A target shooter, for example, who contemplates building a super-accurate rifle—be it for bench-rest, smallbore, bigbore, or long-range competition—gives first consideration to a suitable action to build the rifle around. A professional hunter in Africa, choosing a rifle which will be used to protect himself and his clients from attack by dangerous animals, places number one emphasis on a rifle action which will function with absolute reliability. And when you and I go into a gunshop to buy a sporting rifle, we will, nine times out of ten, base our selection on our personal knowledge, or at least on the reputation, of a specific make and model of *action*.

Of course it wasn't always this way. Back in the muzzleloading era the lock, stock, and barrel shared about equal billing. The lock (the action), in fact, was regarded as the least important of the three; as long as it worked reliably nothing more was expected of it. Accuracy—or lack of it—was totally a function of the barrel, with the stock most usually being the rifle's chief identifying feature. Even if both the lock *and* barrel were replaced the character of the rifle remained virtually unchanged. Today, however, the viewpoint is vastly changed. A Model 70 Winchester action, for example, or a Sako or a Remington, can be rebarreled, restocked, and otherwise reworked in a dozen ways but the rifle will still be identified as a Winchester, Sako, or Remington.

In the year 1900 every type of rifle action known and used by today's sportsman had been invented and was in widespread use. Pumps and lever-action rifles were common; beautifully built and accurate single-shots had long been a staple for both hunting and target rifles; both gas and blowback-operated self-feeders had reached a high stage of development; and the turning-bolt mechanisms had evolved from the Dreyse needle-fire design of the 1830s to the sophisticated 1898 Mauser repeater.

If a firearms authority of that time had been challenged to peer into the future and predict what type of rifle would be most popular in three-quarters of a century, there is little likelihood that he could have made a correct guess. Probably he would have predicted overwhelming popularity for some sort of light, fast-handling rifle featuring a multi-shot, self-loading action.

When rifles emerged from the muzzleloading era the main thrust of design and developmental effort, for a long time, was directed toward ever-increasing firepower. As a matter of fact, with few exceptions the worth of a rifle was mainly judged by how many shots per minute it was capable of firing. None other than John Moses Browning, for example, the top-ranking gun designer of the day, directed virtually all of his efforts in the sporting-arms field toward pump, lever, and autoloading rifles and shotguns. His thoughts as to the promise of bolt-action arms for sporting purposes were apparently relegated to simple, inexpensive .22 rimfire plinkers.

But as we now well know, the anticipated ever-increasing popularity of ever-increasing speed of operation did not materialize. Instead, the evolution of the modern rifle took a turn toward cartridge efficiency rather than firepower, action flexibility rather than ease of operation, and, most of all, accuracy rather than speed of operation. Thus the turn-bolt mechanism has become synonymous with the modern rifle. It can be argued, perhaps even demonstrated, that other types of actions equal or even surpass the bolt in terms of strength, ease of operation, repeatability, simplicity of manufacture, and even reliability, but no other mechanism offers such a well-balanced combination of all these features and couples them with the single most distinguishing feature of the modern rifle—unparalleled accuracy!

Virtually every sporting-arms development of the past several decades, be it in the areas of barrels, bullets, primers, powders, stocks, or sights, has been directed primarily toward increased accuracy. Yet, as we consider these factors we run into an apparent contradiction: the modern bolt-action mechanism is made very much in the image of the turn-bolt designs of the last century, and the most widely used bolt-action mechanism is the Mauser design of 1898. In light of this, is the modern rifle truly modern? Or have we progressed not at all since the introduction of the Model 98?

This is the Mauser Model 3000, the latest product of the Mauser bolt-action heritage which began in the 1800s.

Actually, this is perhaps the best example of all to illustrate just how far we *have* progressed both in terms of bolt-action design, manufacture, safety, and accuracy.

First of all, there is a prevailing tendency to view the popular Mauser as if it were virtually the first of its kind and sprang from the genius of its inventor fully developed and totally original. Actually it was the result of many developments and trial-and-error experiments over a period of several decades, and represented ideas and features originated not only by the Mauser brothers and their engineers, but by Von Mannlicher, Bosèle Gras, Nicolas Lebel, Erik Jorgensen, Johannes Krag, James Lee, etc., and literally hundreds of military advisers from all parts of the globe. Thus it is not a landmark development but the logical and inevitable result of many years of rifle evolution.

The point here is that this design evolution did not end with the '98 Mauser, as is apparently widely supposed, but continued on a normal course, resulting in designs as advanced over the Mauser of 1898 as it itself was over previous Mausers and other bolt designs of earlier times. The '98 earned worldwide fame because it was a superb design, of course, but more so because it was manufactured in such prodigious numbers for both military and sporting use. From the standpoints of both design and military effectiveness, however, it was obsolete long before World War II.

In order to fully understand the design features of a modern bolt gun, and the underlying forces which create evolutionary changes, let's compare the new with the old.

The so-called "post-1963" Model 70 Winchester is a good example of recent design features, and the Model 98 Mauser is probably the best, certainly the best-known, example of the most up-to-the-minute thinking of the turn of the century.

One of the most often-voiced features of the '98 is that it has three locking lugs, or a fourth counting the bolt handles turned down for scope use on recent models. This feature was very prominently copied on U.S. Springfield '03 rifles. But why was this feature so prominently displayed in those times but not today? When rifles of that day left the factory, the action was set up

The Winchester Model 70 action.

so that only the two front lugs engaged the locking recesses, just as those of today. The third lug was not in contact with its recess and was intended as a back-up lug in the event of the other lugs failing. Experience with previous Mausers had amply shown the wisdom of this extra safety factor. The steels of that day were not so reliable as those we use today, and far less was known about alloys and especially about heat treating. Also the cartridges of that time were considerably more hazardous. Primers were more likely to blow, the brass cases were weaker and less uniform, and the smokeless powders of that era presented problems too. As a result it was not so uncommon for actions to come unglued. Thus experience told them that an additional lug was pretty much a necessity.

Some time back I bought three beautifully finished 1909 Mausers which had been built for the Argentine army. The rifles had never been issued and were as perfect as the day they left the factory. The only time they had ever been fired was the one time they were test-fired in the German plant. The metal in the receivers was so soft, however, that the single test firing had mashed the front two locking lugs into the receiver so far that the safety lug had come to bear. Without that safety lug additional firing would probably have set the lugs back farther and farther until it became impossible to open the bolt or, much worse, an excessive headspace condition worsened until, at last, a case head blew off and wrecked the rifle and shooter.

Today's two-lug actions, such as the Model 70, do not benefit from additional lugs for the simple reason that the problems which once necessitated a safety lug have been eliminated. The same goes for the big gas-deflecting flange on the '98's bolt sleeve. Ammunition of that time was so likely to produce a blown or pierced primer, or even a ruptured case head, that escaping gases were a very real and ever-present hazard to the shooter. And too, the gas flange was especially necessary on the Mauser, and other actions of its time, because the basic design did not allow for very substantial case-head support. In short, the flange was necessary to compensate for a fundamental design deficiency. The '03 Springfield was even worse in this respect and the error was compounded by the lack of a suitable gas flange. There were gas blowbacks, and shooters were injured. Modern actions seal the cartridge more efficiently and such accidents are all but nonexistent. Mauser fanciers are fond of pointing out that gas leakage is still possible with some of the most modern action designs and that the large flange is a superior protection device. What they fail to take into consideration, however, is that gas flange or no, the Mauser, Springfield, etc. designs are more likely to allow a gas rupture in the first place and in any event the shooter is more likely to be injured than with more up-to-date designs.

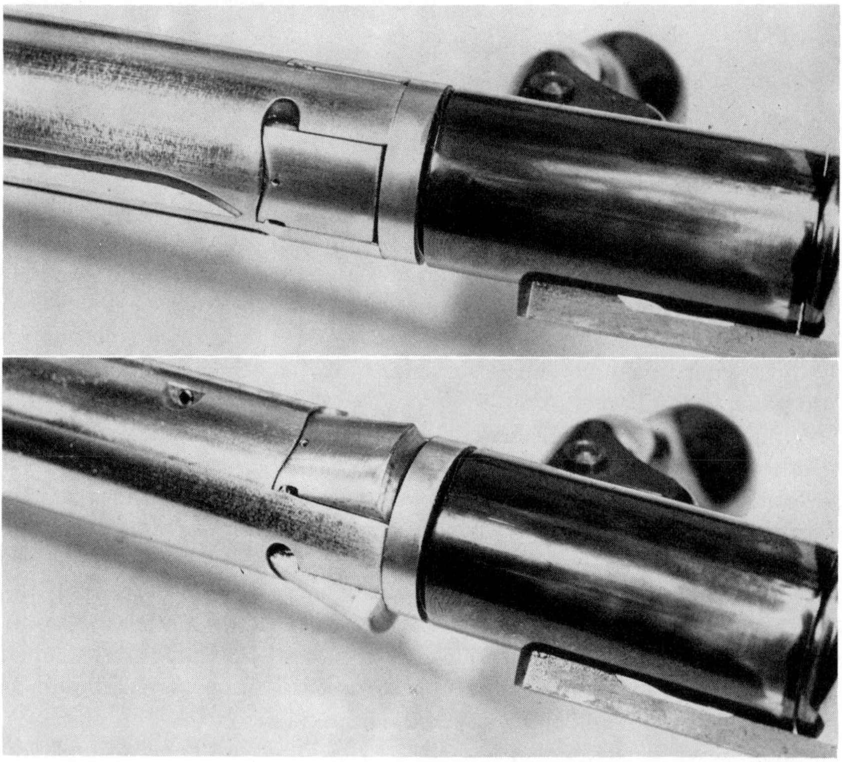

An interesting variation on the basic bolt-action lockup is the recently introduced Colt-Sauer rifle made in West Germany and distributed in this country by Colt Firearms Inc. Rather than locking into battery position by turning the locking lugs into fitted recesses, the Colt-Sauer design features disappearing locking lugs which fold into, and extend out of, the bolt body. With the locking lugs folded out of the way the bolt becomes a simple cylinder sliding within a sleeve and this, of course, makes for extremely slick action operation. It is shown with the locking lugs in both the closed and the extended position.

At this point it no doubt seems that I'm being unduly critical of Springfields, Mausers, and other actions dating to the turn of the century. But criticism is not the purpose here, only to point out, by comparison, that the *modern* bolt-action mechanism represents considerably more improvements and advantages than are apparent to the casual observer. Quite often, in fact, we deliberately ignore or overlook (subconsciously or otherwise) the improvements of modern design and technology. Love, the wise man said, is blind. This is especially evident in our fondness for pet firearms. We tend to be blinded to certain faults altogether, or at least willing to overlook them. In this same vein we often tend to attach misguided importance to the features of our favorite designs.

An example here is the large-leaf spring extractors of Springfields, Mausers, pre-1964 Model 70s, Enfields, etc. I have to admit some prejudice here because this is my favorite type. I like the way they get a good hold on the case rim and jerk the case out of the chamber whether it wants to come or not. And since I prefer the leaf type I'm naturally not so keen on the little hook-type extractors built into the bolt face of more modern actions such as the latest Model 70 Winchester, Remington 700, Swedish FFV, Sako, Savage 110, etc. These don't get such a big bite on the case rim, and somewhere in the back of my mind there lurks a fear that one of these days I might miss a great trophy because one of these little extractors has failed to do its job. I suspect quite a few shooters share this apprehension. The little extractors are also often pointed out as an example of how rifle manufacturing is going to the dogs because of too much emphasis on cheapening manufacture. Obviously hook extractors are less costly to manufacture than the older type, but the real purpose goes beyond cost alone. When we stop to think about it for a moment it suddenly occurs to us that the completely enclosed cartridge head feature of most modern action designs is impossible with the big, external extractors!

With this realization in mind the philosophy of modern action design and manufacture becomes a bit more evident. Faced with a decision between a popular feature and a safety feature, the maker will always go with safety. No rifle manufacturer is liable to get slapped with a lawsuit because an extractor didn't work, but there is the very real possibility that the completely enclosed case head feature might keep an overeager wildcatter from blowing his ears loose.

ACTIONS AND ACCURACY

Up until now we've been talking about fundamental design features which have been developed over the years and make the modern rifle a stronger and safer unit than its predecessors. But as pointed out earlier, one of the most distinguishing features of today's rifle is its *accuracy*. What improvements, if any, has current action design contributed in this area? We all know that the rifles waiting on dealer's shelves offer a remarkable degree of accuracy, tremendously better than that offered by bolt-action rifles of the turn of the century and even significantly better than those of only a few years ago. But is this entirely due to better barrels, sighting equipment, and ammunition?

Again, let's consider a couple of rifles from the first part of this century, the '98 Mauser and the '03 Springfield. At one time the Springfield ruled American rifle ranges, and even as recently as the 1950s the Mauser was a staple in the budding sport of bench-rest shooting. But now both of these types are seldom seen in competition. The most commonly heard explanation for their passing is a relatively slow and sluggish lock time. Lock time—the interval of time between the instant the sear is released and when the firing pin hits the primer—is a vital link in the time span from the moment the brain gives the signal to fire and when the bullet exits from the muzzle. Since a rifle is seldom held motionless, especially when shooting from the standing, etc., positions, it is desirable to reduce this time lapse as much as possible. Otherwise the muzzle direction may wander too far off course before the bullet is on its way.

Generally, lock time is speeded up by using light, fast-accelerating firing pins and by keeping the total striker movement as short as possible. A super-quick action such as the FFV has a striker weight of about 690 grains and a travel of close to 3/10 inch. Mauser and Springfield strikers, in contrast, weigh twice as much and travel twice as far.

However, it must be pointed out that this should not in any way be considered a design fault of Springfields, Mausers, and their class of actions. The advantages of speedy lock time were well known back when they were designed, but other factors were more vital. Remember, these were not target rifles, but military arms, and had to be capable of delivering a solid blow to the primer in spite of a possible wide variety of adverse conditions. This end was achieved by a long, heavy striker thrust. The designers knew what had to be done and they did it.

But there were some things regarding accuracy which they did *not* know about. And it is in these more subtle areas that modern actions take the upper hand when it comes to delivering a high degree of accuracy. It is only in fairly recent years, for instance, that much has been understood about the way the fit of an action into the stock affects a rifle's grouping capability. Accordingly, as more has been learned actions have been designed to take advantage of the knowledge.

For example, it is understood that the action must fit evenly and flatly against the wood with no irregular pressure points. If the pressure is uneven the action will flex somewhat and groups will enlarge. Let me give you an idea of how this happens.

Usually an action is flexed or bent in a more or less downward direction. This is because the action screws pull it downward as they are pulled tight. Seemingly it wouldn't matter all that much even if the receiver was in a somewhat flexed position as long as the screws held it in tight and immovable. But, alas, there's more to it than just being held fast. You see, when the bolt is closed the lugs are in an up-and-down position and if the receiver is bent the lugs do not bear evenly on the receiver's locking surfaces. Usually the receiver is flexed so the center section is bowed upward. This means that the upper locking lug is in contact with the receiver but not the lower.

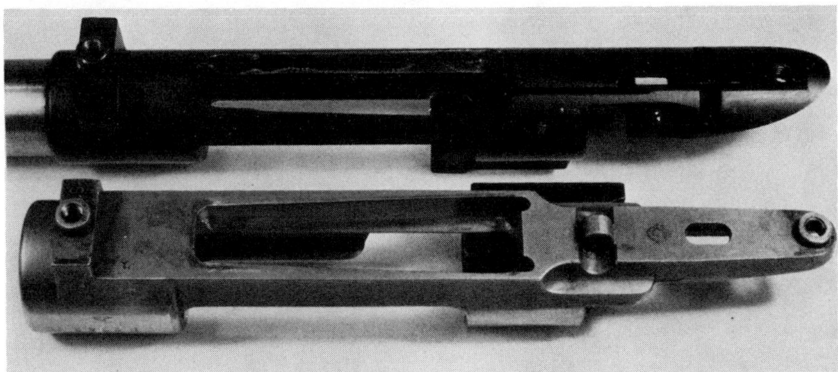

A detailed photograph of the undersides of a Mauser Model 98 receiver, with flat bottom, and a Swedish-made FFV receiver, with a round bottom. To the casual observer the differences in these basic underside configurations would be of little importance but actually they represent a significant divergence of rifle-building philosophies. The differences have far-reaching effects on manufacturing and modern accuracy technology.

When the rifle is fired the powerful rearward thrust of the expanding gases slams the case head against the bolt and, in turn, the locking lug presses terrifically hard against the receiver. Since all this pressure is initially only on one lug, and the top part of the receiver, it tends to bend the receiver back until the bottom lug comes more evenly to bear and equalizes the load. This means the action is in motion while the bullet is still in the barrel. In just what way this affects accuracy is sometimes hard to predict. The barrel, of course, is screwed into the front of the receiver, and it's reasonable to assume that as the locking lugs snap the receiver into a straight position the barrel is given a rather violent twitch. Also, it is not difficult to visualize how that momentarily straightening effect on the receiver causes the stock to bend correspondingly. This could have repercussions in several areas. For one, the alignment and fit of the recoil lug would be altered, and another, in the case of a full-bedded barrel, the stock pressure on the barrel

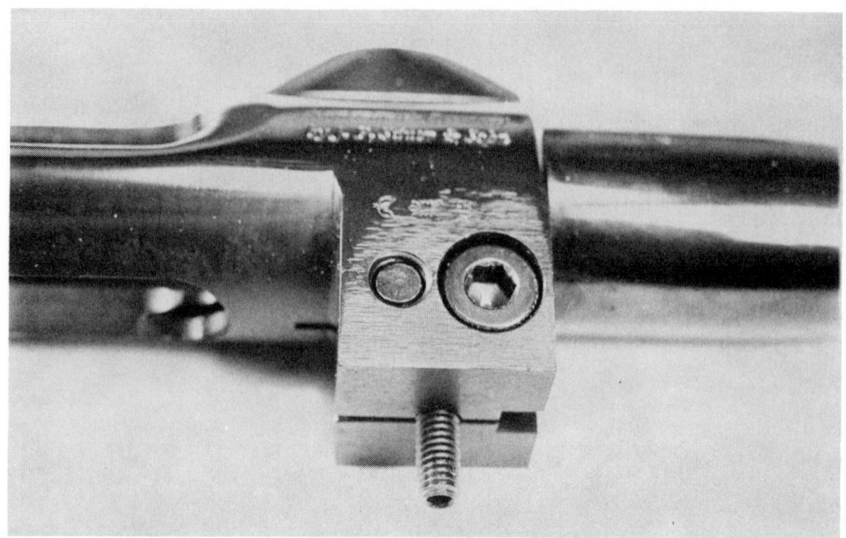

The double problems of recoil absorption and receiver bedding are dealt with at once with this over-size, flat-bottomed recoil lug on the Colt-Sauer receiver.

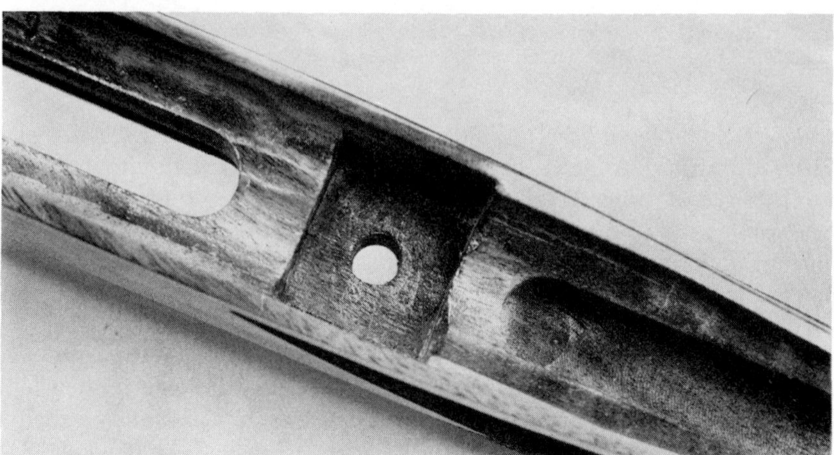

A detail of the Colt-Sauer recoil lug mortise, which also forms the basic action bedding foundation.

would be changing as the bullet traveled up the bore. One way or the other, though, it's not at all hard to see how accuracy is damaged.

In case you're wondering how much of the above information is theory and how much is proved fact, let me describe some experiments that have been made in this area. Supposedly an experimenter would deliberately do a poor bedding job in a rifle and compare the resulting accuracy with a properly bedded rifle. But this is too "iffy" and doesn't allow for precise measurement of the initial problem. Instead, surprisingly perhaps, the experiment is entirely carried out with a perfectly bedded rifle. A highly accurate target-grade rifle is used and its accuracy and point of impact is recorded by firing a string of five to ten five-shot groups either from a machine rest or from a bench rest. The bolt is then removed and a small amount is ground away from the rear of *one* of the locking lugs. This has the same effect, obviously, as flexing the action slightly but for experimental purposes is more precise because it allows more exact control over the variables. The bolt is replaced and another series of groups is fired. The results, both group size and point of impact, are then compared with the original groups. Up to a point both the size of the groups and the place of impact displacement is determined by how much the locking lug is ground out of alignment. After that certain point, however, there is a leveling off. Apparently this is where the misalignment is so great that the ground-off lug never comes to bear on the receiver.

This test can cause a rifle, which originally will have averaged under 1/2 inch for five shots at 100 yards, to open groups to 2 inches. Usually, as a point of interest, the groups tend to be "strung" with the bullet holes more or less in line with one another. Dave Carlson, the former smallbore rifle champion who headed Winchester's custom shop and directed their target-rifle program for many years, once told me that when they tested their finely accurate Model 70 International Army Match and Ultra Match rifles, they could usually trace stringing to uneven locking lug contact. This, as an additional point of interest, is why really savvy gunsmiths, especially accuracy specialists, carefully lap bolt lugs for fully even contact. I'm sometimes amazed when someone pays out good dough for a fancy rebarrel job but won't spring for the extra $10 or so for a lapping job. But by the same token, I'm even more amazed at the "gunsmiths" who don't do it, don't know how to do it, and never even *heard* of doing it.

Now, with this background material firmly in hand let's go back and see how modern bolt-action design meets today's accuracy demands, and where the older designs fail.

If you take a Springfield or Mauser, or any one of several actions of that era, out of the stock you will notice that it is held in place by two action screws on either end of the receiver and that the front screw attaches directly into the recoil lug. Now right there is where the problem begins. When the front screw is drawn up tight, the pressure is not distributed in an even radius but is absorbed only *behind* the screw on the flat bedding table immediately behind the recoil lug. The pressure is greatest closer to the screw, so naturally the wood is most compressed there. You can create a very graphic illustration of this by pressing down on the edge of a mattress. The edge sinks lowest, then curves back toward the center of the bed. On a much smaller scale this is about what happens when the front action screw is pulled tight; the front of the receiver is flexed downward because there is no support in front of the screw. There is, of course, the forward part of the receiver ring, but this is round in shape and cannot under normal circumstances be bedded to the same contact as the flat bedding table behind the screw. This downward flexing is augmented by the rather spindly side rails of the receivers and also by the fact that the only other screw is so far to the rear. As a result we get the uneven-locking-lug problem described earlier. Accuracy suffers.

Now let's consider some modern action designs. Of first interest is the Swedish-made FFV rifle (formerly known as Husqvarna), because the front action screw, like that of older designs, threads into the recoil lug. *But!* In the case of the FFV the receiver extends forward from the lug in exactly the same configuration as to the rear. Thus when the screw is tightened the pressure radiates evenly and is supported to the front the same as to the rear. This keeps the front of the receiver from dipping down at the front and creating a bend. (This is assuming, of course, a proper bedding job to start with. If wood were cut out from under the front of the action it would then bend down as the screw was tightened.) Another interesting example of the action screw attaching directly to the recoil lug is on the new Colt-Sauer rifles made in West Germany. But in this unique design the extra-large, flat-bottomed recoil lug is also what you might call a bedding pedestal. In other words, the bottom of the oversize recoil lug is actually the bedding table, or main receiver-to-stock contact point. The front action screw fits in the center of the "foot" and the pressure is thus perfectly equalized.

One of the best examples of a smart bedding arrangement is the Winchester Model 70. Here again the front screw is not at the forward end of the receiver, but well back into the flat area behind the recoil lug so that the pressure is well distributed. In fact, the screw is kept toward the rear of the action flat directly under the lugs so as to provide as much forward support as possible. This provides the additional good service of giving extra support to heavy barrels which tend to flex the front of actions downward. This is one of the reasons the Model 70 has become the all-time big winner in big-bore target competition.

Another good example is the Remington 700 design, which, though round instead of flat-bottomed, has the front screw directly under the locking lugs, with a lot of stock support forward of the hole. Another example of this same principle is the Savage Model 110. Actually the list of modern designs which utilize this feature is pretty long and constantly growing longer. Also, in an effort to reduce flexing, more and more designs are adopting a third action screw just to the rear of the magazine box. This helps eliminate the tendency of the receiver to bow up in the middle and, obviously, solidifies the entire metal-to-wood union.

A highly original, and successful, bedding system is used in the Ruger

Here I contemplate the action of the Ruger Model 77 bolt-action rifle. The Model 77 is representative of the most up-to-the-minute thinking in action design and manufacturing technology but at the same time returns the best features of bygone days. It is truly a "modern rifle."

Model 77. In tune with the best modern thinking the action has three screws and the bedding table continues forward of the front screw, but the front screw angles to the rear so that as it is drawn tight it accomplishes the additional task of pulling the recoil lug firmly in contact with the matching surface in the stock mortise. To test this out I once completely removed the stock between each shot of a five-shot string. The group measured close to 3/4 inch at 100 yards! In honesty I must point out that I've never tried this stunt with any other rifle. Perhaps any well-bedded, accurate rifle will do as well. But at least I know for a fact the Ruger system doesn't *hurt* anything.

A description of how modern action design has contributed to today's unprecedented accuracy level could go on for many chapters. In fact quite a large book could be written on this subject alone. Therefore it's important to point out that the foregoing brief and simple examples are just that—oversimplified examples. They serve well to illustrate design and accuracy fundamentals but are only part of the total accuracy concept. Attempting to construe such bits of information into a general guideline as to the causes of good or poor accuracy would amount to nothing more than proof that a little knowledge is a dangerous thing.

In the strict sense of design analysis, a design fault exists only when the designers fail to take advantage of the most up-to-the-minute information.

Some of our most modern actions, therefore, exhibit some glaring faults. But often they are purposely committed in a well-considered compromise with competing factors such as cost of production. From this viewpoint some of the older, now obsolete designs such as the Mauser of 1898 may be considered nearly flawless because they utilized the best thinking and experience of their time. Sophisticated features regarding fine accuracy, however, were near meaningless then because accuracy, as we now regard it, was then unknown. Many other factors such as bullet construction and barrelmaking would have to be vastly improved before a minor thing like an action screw in a recoil lug would reveal itself as a specific flaw.

But such examples as these nonetheless well demonstrate how modern the modern rifle really is. Earlier in this section it was pointed out that Mauser actions were commonly used for bench-rest rifles during the decade of the 1950s. Mausers were good, safe, easy to fit, and, best of all, cheap and easily obtainable. And after all, an action was just an action, or so it was commonly believed. It has only been in the past *two decades* that we've learned enough about accuracy to start weeding out the little problems.

One of the most disagreeable things about explaining how modern action design has elevated the level of rifle performance is that it too often involves pointing out, for the sake of illustration and comparison, the design weaknesses of outdated designs. No one likes to hear what amounts to criticism of an old favorite. Remember, those actions represented the best, most up-to-date thinking of their time, just as today's actions represent the fruits of current knowledge and experience. But, hopefully, today's actions will become just as obsolete in a few years. I'd certainly hate to think, for whatever reasons, that we've reached the end of the development road. We're not even halfway there.

MODERN ACTION MANUFACTURING

As the premier position of the turning-bolt action has become more and more established, and the competition among various bolt-action designs has increased, there has been an unending flurry of activity not only toward developing stronger, safer, and more accurate mechanisms but also toward designs that are simpler and less costly to manufacture. As a general rule any attempt to reduce the production costs of a consumer item can be equated with a corresponding drop in performance and reliability. In the case of rifle design, however, there have been remarkable exceptions where just the opposite has happened.

A good example of this is the Remington Model 700, which is the same basic design as the Model 721 and Model 722 developed immediately after World War II. The previous centerfire, bolt-action sporting rifles manufactured by Remington had utilized forged receivers requiring numerous ma-

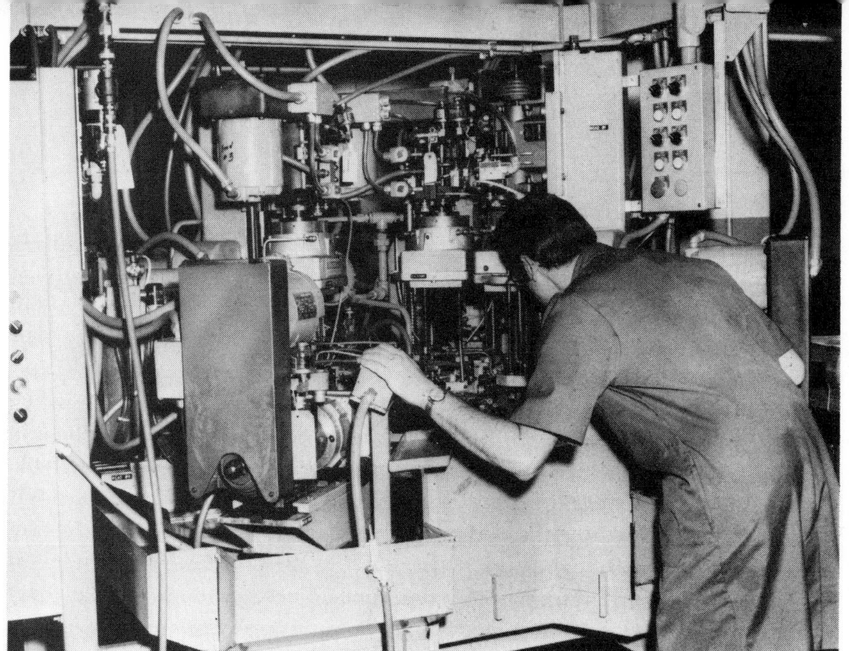

Complex, and expensive, computer- and tape-controlled machinery such as this drilling machine in the Winchester plant permits the machining of complex designs both accurately and speedily. Current labor prices have ruled out most hand operations.

chining operations. The 721 and 722 receivers, however, were simple cylinders, little more than thick-walled tubes in fact, with a pair of boltways broached into the walls and simple cuts made for the magazine, loading port, and trigger. Likewise the Remington bolt, which had previously been a rather complex forged and machined affair, was constructed by simply brazing the bolt head, complete with locking lugs, onto a plain round tube. A bolt handle was brazed on the other end and the bolt was nearly complete.

With the bolt inside the receiver the mechanical unit is little more than a tube within a larger tube. Obviously such an arrangement was, and is, relatively cheap to make, but equally obvious is the fact that the simple combination should be exceedingly strong—which subsequent tests proved to be exactly the case.

But something perhaps not so obvious at first was that the "tube within a tube" arrangement created a highly concentric receiver, bolt, cartridge, and barrel configuration which has a positive effect on accuracy. This is one of the reasons the Model 722 action, and its nearly identical successors, the 600, XP-100, 725, 40-X, and 700, are the number-one favorites for bench-rest rifles. When you consider that today's know-how can produce an action that is cheaper, stronger, *and* more accurate than those of a few decades ago it becomes more than apparent that the bolt action has indeed come a long way.

These up-to-date features, by the way, create a situation which proponents of the "good old days" have a hard time coming to grips with. Every time a newer, simpler, and cheaper action design hits the market there is a great wringing of hands and shedding of tears for the passing of fine riflemaking. But if we establish the end of World War II as the dividing line between the "good old days" and the modern era it must be pointed out that no bolt-action design dating from that earlier period can match the best of our modern products in all of the three most important criteria: safety, economy of manufacture, and accuracy.

Like any lover of finely made rifles I get a sentimental kick out of playing around with one of the smoothly finished '03 Springfields. And I have a deep admiration for the beautifully precise and complex production technique that went into building the magnificent Mauser sporter. But I don't let such sentiments get in the way of my better judgment. If I want to contain a high-pressure magnum cartridge in the safest possible manner, or build a super-accurate target rig, I know that no action design of that long-past era is going to get the job done as well as any one of several more modern actions.

Back in the late 1950s when I was on a military rifle team we were occasionally joined at our practice sessions by a colonel who had been one of the country's top competitive riflemen before World War II. The rifle he used was a finely fitted National Match grade '03 Springfield and, as a matter of fact, probably the most accurate Springfield I've ever seen. But it was nowhere near the equal of our Model 70 Winchester target rifles or, for that matter, even our carefully tuned National Match M-1 Garands. The Colonel was well aware of this, but, as he put it, he only came out to the practice range for a little relaxation and because he got so much sentimental pleasure out of putting the '03 through its paces. After a few weeks of shooting with us, though, during which time his attendance became almost daily, he showed up one day with a sparkling new Model 70 target rifle complete with the latest in sighting equipment. When asked what had become of his cherished Springfield his reply was direct and to the point: "Nostalgia is great but winning is better."

While some rifle manufacturers overcome the expense of complicated and time-consuming machine operations by going to simpler action designs, other manufacturers seek to achieve low-cost production by using highly sophisticated automatic equipment. Basically, these lathes, drills, and milling machines carry out the same operations as when operated by people but rather than being guided by skilled hands they are controlled by program tapes, or even computers. I've seen this type of equipment used on all sorts of gunmaking operations, everything from inletting a stock blank to carving a complex rifle receiver out of a block of steel, and never cease to be amazed at its precision and speed. The advantages, from a production standpoint, are higher output, fewer rejects, and, most important of all, drastically reduced labor costs. One operator, with a few hours training, often turns out more parts in a day than could be machined by hand in a month. And the only skill required is knowing how to feed raw steel into the machine and

The great revolution in modern firearms technology is, and will be, centered around the investment casting or "lost wax" process. The moving assembly line shown here carries a series of "trees," a mold composed of a ceramic slurry formed around a wax core. The "branches" of these trees will become floorplates for Sako rifles. The Sako rifle works was the first and still may be the only investment casting plant in Finland.

punch a few buttons. Sometimes, though, the whole idea of super-automated production backfires completely. One manufacturer I know of had to raise the price of one of his favorite models after installing a big computer-controlled machine for milling the receiver and trigger guard assembly. The fancy piece of equipment, as it turned out, was so expensive that the only way they could offset its cost was by raising the price of their product!

Very possibly the most revolutionary production technique to invade the hallowed halls of firearms production has been the so-called "investment" or "lost wax" casting process. This process, even the mention of its name, tends to cause a rather negative emotional response in many shooters. For that reason some manufacturers have purposely made no mention that they use it in the production of their guns. Others, most notably Sturm-Ruger, not only readily admit that they employ the process but even point with pride to its advantage.

The term "casting" usually evokes visions of rough, brittle, gray-iron foundry items such as sewer-line elbows, engine blocks, pump housings, and myriad other applications where weight and metallic bulk are required but not much strength. In short, *not* the qualities desired in firearms. Opinions against cast gun parts reached a particularly high crest during World War II when some of the Axis powers were forced to resort to roughly cast major rifle components such as receivers, etc. G.I.s picking these up as souvenirs were sternly warned against making any attempt to shoot them because of the distinct possibility that the weak castings might shatter and result in serious injury. And of course this already poor opinion of castings was not helped any by the use of cheap zinc or "pot metal," and aluminum castings commonly used on low-quality pistols, shotguns, and rifles.

But such castings are a far cry from the strong and beautifully precise products of modern *investment* casting technology. Here's how it works. First a wax image is made of the part that is to be reproduced in steel. These wax patterns are usually mass-produced on injection-molding machinery in complicated molds. These molds are sometimes so complex in their shape and operation that they may represent the most expensive and time-consuming part of getting set up to produce an investment-cast product. This is especially true of multilayered molds which turn out the wax likenesses of such complicated forms as revolver frames, rifle receivers, and even jet-engine parts.

The wax image is then coated with several layers of a ceramic slurry. As the ceramic material builds up on the wax model it hardens into a hard shell which looks something like the stuff ceramic pots or chinaware is made of. In fact it *is* about the same stuff. When the ceramic layers have dried and hardened, the "vessel" is put in a high-temperature furnace which melts the wax pattern. The molten wax drains out a spout which was molded onto the pattern just for the purpose, and any remaining wax is burned away by the high temperature. This is where the "lost wax" name for the process originates.

The next step in the process involves pouring molten steel alloy into the empty ceramic vessel. These can be any of the steels used for modern gunmaking, even stainless steel. When the metal cools the ceramic vessel is cracked away like a glass eggshell and a perfect likeness of the original wax pattern remains. Only this time it is tough steel. The casting is so precise that it is often difficult to tell if the product is indeed a casting or has actually been machined from solid steel. This is especially true when the original wax mold was made from a machined part. Even the tool marks from the original machined piece are transmitted to the casting. I know of a European manufacturer who casts an entire action—receiver, bolt, trigger guard, bolt sleeve, firing pin, etc., even *threaded* guard screws—but the "machine" marks are so cleverly left in certain places that very few customers suspect the truth.

The philosophy of Ruger, on the other hand, has been to make a point out of informing the public that the bolts and receivers of its Model 77 bolt gun and the gracefully proportioned mechanism of its Number One and Three single-shots, as well as its revolver frames, are all produced by the investment-casting process. The strength, accuracy, and reliability of these products speak very well indeed for the process. At this writing I know of at least five other popular makes and models of U.S. guns which have investment-cast receivers and other major parts, but I don't think the makers are quite ready to announce the big news.

I get a particularly big charge when I hear someone berate all cast guns as a matter of principle but in the next breath expound on the glowing qualities of a favorite rifle, pistol, or shotgun—little realizing that the pet gun is a mass of beautifully finished castings! Frankly, I suspect that in time such prejudices will be forgotten entirely and that fine investment casting will even become a symbol of high-quality gunmaking. This will become increasingly true as complex machining operations price themselves out of the picture and riflemen are given their druthers between starkly mundane machined products or attractive, gracefully styled investment castings.

2

The Barrel

The single most significant difference between the modern rifle and the rifle of just a generation ago is the spectacular improvement in accuracy. Recent achievements in accuracy have, of course, been due to a great variety of factors, but too much credit is often given—and accepted—in areas that have made only secondary contributions while the principal cause is completely overlooked. As we learn more and more about less and less it seems that many of us are not only missing the forest for the trees but even missing the trees because of too much peering into the underbrush.

Depending on whom you listen to, it might appear that recent developments in bulletmaking or primer design or handloading technique are responsible for the accuracy of today's rifle. What we fail to consider, though, is that all of these advances are totally dependent on a continual improvement of the quality of the rifle barrel. Take the greatest of everything—ammo, sights, action, and stock—and put them in the hands of the finest marksmen, and they still won't be worth a plug of moldy chewing tobacco unless they're used in a great barrel—that mysterious tube with the twisting grooves gouged into its walls.

The modern barrel is, in fact, so good that in order to get a proper appreciation of its quality we must consider the barrel of a few decades ago. Even as recently as the era between the two world wars a really good barrel was considered such a rare prize that it was babied along like a layer of golden eggs. Since I wasn't around in those days I can't claim firsthand knowledge, but I've read hundreds of books and magazine articles dating from that time and have always been struck by the repeated reference to "exceptional" or "irreplaceable" barrels. Writers frequently mentioned their desire to keep sighting and practice shots to a minimum with a pet barrel in order to prolong its life as long as possible. Their reason was that an accurate barrel was hard to come by and that the odds did not favor finding another one as good.

Going back to the turn of the century and thereabouts, Harry Pope stands unique as a maker of accurate barrels. A Pope barrel was, in the eyes of a target shooter, a treasure to be coddled and cherished above all other mortal possessions. The barrelmaking genius of Pope is certainly not to be denied, but the fact that a single individual was able to dominate the accuracy picture stands as proof of how far we've come today.

From my rifle rack I can select, blindfolded, a target, varmint, or even hunting rifle that will, with ease, produce groups thought impossible not many years ago. What's really significant, however, is that I can be totally unconcerned about wearing out the barrels on any of these rifles because I am absolutely certain that they can be replaced with barrels equally good!

In Pope's time the making of an accurate barrel was considered an art. So much so that the great barrelmakers, so I understand, were even given to oc-

Bill Atkinson, the well-known barrelmaker who still uses the tradition cut-rifling process, uses a bore scope to inspect the interior of one of his peerless rifle barrels.

casional fits of artistic temperament. Modern barrelmaking, however, has been blessed with so many technological advances that an hourly wage earner in, say, New Haven or Ilion can punch a few buttons on a control console and in a day's time turn out dozens of wonderfully accurate barrels. Nearly as impressive is that come evening, while he sips a beer and watches television, he is totally unmindful and unimpressed with the fact that he cranked out a truckload of barrels accurate enough to have sent a turn-of-the-century barrelmaker into spasms of ecstasy.

A visitor to a present-day custom barrelmaking shop might have trouble reconciling the equipment he finds there with the accuracy level of the finished product. It is not at all uncommon to find drilling, reaming, and rifling machines which date back to the era of World War I. Why, then, one is bound to ask, are modern barrels so much better than those made on the same machines over a half-century ago?

The answer is the constant experiments and developments in tooling. The best deep-hole drill heads of only a few years ago, for example, could not maintain a sharp and uniform cutting edge and usually had to be resharpened sometime during the course of drilling a barrel blank. As the drill dulled, its cutting character changed, and as a result they were not likely to cut an exceptionally straight hole. Modern-day carbide cutting heads maintain a sharp and uniform cutting edge much longer (up to eight or ten barrels between sharpening) and thus bore a straighter hole. Also, higher boring rpm's are possible with the carbide cutters, and this also contributes to straighter holes.

An interesting sidelight to this and related developments, by the way, is that the straightness of a rifle bore is not so important as it was thought to be. There was a time when barrel quality was judged almost entirely by the straightness of the bore. I suspect the reason so much emphasis was placed on straightness was that it is one of the few features of barrel quality which can be judged by the unaided and relatively untrained eye. Also, of course, there was the prevailing notion that a curved bore was bound to cause a curved bullet path.

Another and even more important factor affecting shooting quality has been refinements in the manner of cutting, or impressing the rifling into the drilled and reamed tube. An example of these improvements is the barrels made by Bill Atkinson of Prescott, Arizona. His barrels are widely considered to be among the most accurate ever made and are eagerly sought by serious competition shooters. Yet, the Atkinson barrels are made on old-fashioned machinery, and the hook-type cutter he employs is basically the same tool used a century, or two centuries, ago. The difference, as he explains it, is the small refinements and innovations which he has added over the years. Some ideas work out, while others don't, but over the long haul the aggregate effect adds up to a more accurate barrel.

The results of these refinements take effect with surprising speed. Atkinson says that at present he is making a more accurate barrel than he was five years ago (even though Atkinson barrels of five years ago are still winning matches and breaking records), and presumably the barrels of five years from now will be better than those of today.

MAKING A RIFLE BARREL

The next time you raise a rifle to your shoulder you might give a little thought to the marvel of engineering which made it possible to drill that small, straight hole through so long a piece of steel. We all tend to take it for granted, but, in fact, deep-hole drilling is so specialized a field that very few otherwise experienced machinists have any idea of how to go about it.

Steel bars being drilled before rifling. This scene is at the Marlin Firearms Works. The drill does not turn; the steel bars turn against the drill bits.

A while back a textile mill in the southern part of the U.S. had need for some special equipment using steel bars with small holes. The chief engineer of the custom machine shop which contracted to build the equipment labored mightily over the problem of drilling the holes and at last designed a twist drill which he said would do the job. His process was slow, there were many rejects, and the cost of each successful hole amounted to a few hundred dollars. This expense was charged to the mill and no doubt was eventually passed along to the consumer—you and me—but as it happened a visitor was watching the painful drilling process one day and getting an earful from the proud chief engineer about how he had singlehandedly conquered the problem of drilling the long holes.

"Why didn't you have a barrelmaker drill the holes for you?" he asked.

"What do you mean?" replied the startled engineer.

"You know, the kind of barrelmaker that makes rifle barrels. That kind of drilling is old-hat to them."

The upshot was that a barrelmaker *was* contacted and an order given to bore the bars at only a few dollars each—at a savings of several thousand dollars—but not without considerable loss of face on the part of the chief engineer. He, like nearly all of us, simply never paused to consider how those long holes in gun barrels get there.

Actually the problem of drilling a rifle barrel is not so much cutting the hole as getting the steel chips, or cuttings, out of the way. As the hole deepens the problem becomes more difficult. A barrel-drilling machine uses a cutting edge mounted on a hollow steel shank. Oil is pumped under high pressure through the drill shank, out a hole in the cutting head, and flushes out the cuttings. Interestingly, the drill itself does not turn; the barrel blank spins against it at speeds of about 4200 revolutions per minute. The hole progresses at about 2 inches a minute, depending on caliber.

Following the drilling operation the hole is rounded out and the uneven areas evened up by reaming. The reamers have a scraping action which brings the bore to a mirror finish, provided, of course, that it is done properly. In truth, the drilling and reaming techniques have not changed much over the years and are briefly described here only for background information. It's what comes next that has made the modern rifle what it is.

Gun barrels, rifle, pistol, or cannon, are usually rifled by one of four different ways. The hook-type cutter was used almost exclusively until a few decades ago, when faster methods came into vogue. Despite the fact that the hook-cut rifling dates into antiquity it still accounts for ultra-precise, finely accurate barrels. This was the method used by such masters as Harry Pope, John Buhlmiller, and now, most notably, Bill Atkinson. It was also the way barrels were rifled in our national armories at Springfield, Massachusetts, and elsewhere from back before the Civil War through World War II. It was also used by all of the world's commercial sporting arms makers up to about the end of the 1950s.

Actually, "hook rifling" is somewhat misleading because the actual cutting edge can be of several shapes and forms. Essentially, though, it is a narrow, knife-edge scraper which slices a thin sliver of metal from the inside of the barrel. The cutting head is attached to a rod which is pulled through the barrel by the rifling machine. As the rod and cutting head are pulled through the bore they are also turned at a fixed rate so that a spiral groove is cut. On each pass of the cutter it slices a chip only about 0.00005 inch—one-twentieth of one-thousandth of an inch—in thickness. If the cutter is set to cut too much at a pass the cutting edge might break off, or might even jam fast and break the rod, or, at best, might leave a rough, uneven cut that looks more like a gouge than a slice.

After each pass of the cutter the barrel "indexes," or revolves, one-fourth, one-sixth, or one-eighth of a turn (depending on whether the barrel is to have four, six, eight, etc., grooves). Then another cut of the same thickness is made. After a cut has been made in each groove the cutting edge is raised slightly, either mechanically or by hand, and each groove is cut slightly deeper. A .30-caliber barrel has a groove depth of about .004 inch. This means that some eighty passes are required for each groove, or a total of nearly 500 passes for a six-groove barrel.

Atkinson says that changes in cutter-head design, sharpening techniques, and cutter materials over the years have had a tremendous impact on the quality of cut-type rifling. If you compare a modern Atkinson barrel to any of the earlier cut-rifling barrels you'll see a startling difference. Some of the very finest pre-World War II barrels look like plowed furrows in comparison with today's best.

Another cut-type rifling is the so-called broaching system. This method uses a series of cutters which cut all of the grooves at the same time as they are pulled through the barrel. The cutter head itself is nonadjustable, and the cutter edges look something like spokes radiating from a central hub. Immediately behind each of the spokelike cutters is another set of cutters which cuts the grooves slightly deeper. The broaching head has enough cutters—usually about ten or so—that only one pass through the bore is required to cut the grooves to full depth.

I've seen the broaching process used for production of military arms from 20mm barrels on up, and it is commonly used for the production of handgun barrels, but almost never in the production of sporting rifles. Obviously it is much faster than the traditional hook-type rifling and might have come into more widespread use if it had not been for the advent of the so-called "button" rifling.

This is a carbide "button" such as used for rifling barrels at the Douglas Barrel plant.

This system, as its name implies, involves pushing or pulling a small plug or "button" through the bore which presses, or irons, the grooves into the barrel. Compared to the hook-cutter technique, button rifling is wonderfully fast and does not involve the removal of metal. After one pass of the button the barrel is completely rifled and ready to be turned and fitted. Also, the button system results in a beautifully finished interior. As might be expected, some of the finest barrels are rifled by this method. Such names as Douglas, Hart, McMillan, and Shilen have become synonymous with finely accurate, match-winning barrels, and all of them use the button process.

This is a machine used to push carbide rifling "buttons" through barrel blanks at the Douglas plant. The button is pushed by the large hydraulic jack shown mounted at right.

Despite the apparent simplicity of the button rifling process a considerable amount of know-how and experience is required on the part of the maker. Also, the button process is not, as has been claimed, a cure-all technique which results in a perfect rifling job every time no matter how rough the drilling and reaming is to start with. I've seen some low-priced, mass-produced button-rifled barrels that were just as rough in the bore as any other low-quality barrel of any other mode of manufacture.

The best button-rifled barrels are first reamed to a dead-smooth finish with internal dimensions held to a very exacting tolerance.

The buttons vary somewhat from one maker to the next, but essentially they are carbide slugs about an inch or so in length and ground to an outside diameter matching the desired barrel groove diameter. Grooves or slots are cut into the button which will form the rifling lands. Naturally the width, depth, and number of lands in the finished barrel is determined by the forming grooves in the button. Likewise, the land-forming slots in the button are cut at an angle which closely matches the desired rate of twist in the finished barrel. All in all, a rifling button is a reverse image of a short section of rifle bore and looks something like a fired bullet.

The button is either pushed or pulled through the bore, and, according to the maker's particular technique, is turned as it traverses the bore or remains fixed while the barrel stock is turned around it. Despite the basic similarity of the button process there is considerable difference from one barrelmaker to the next as to the actual swageing of the metal. One well-known maker, for example, designs his buttons and reams his barrel blanks so that as the grooves are pressed into the wall of the bore the displaced metal flows into the lands. This technique requires that the barrel blank be reamed to a dimension that is not just smaller than the finished groove diameter but is also actually somewhat larger than the final land diameter. Needless to say this technique requires very exacting reaming dimensions and some artful calculations as to what the volume of the displaced metal will be.

Another maker of superb button-rifled barrels reams to a bore diameter which is actually somewhat smaller than even the land diameter. Thus, metal is displaced at all points around the button and is literally ironed into the barrel steel. Of course barrel metal will tolerate very little compression and the outside diameter of the bar stock must expand slightly. Whenever metal is bent or displaced, certain stress factors are created which can ultimately play pure hell with accuracy. Therefore the barrels must be heat-treated to relieve whatever stresses may exist. If this isn't done all sorts of unpleasant things might happen when the barrel is turned down to final shape and fitted to an action. I once had a beautifully rifled target-grade barrel which I'd been saving for a super-special long-range rifle. The bore slugged a perfect .308 across the grooves and there wasn't a tight or loose spot from one end to the other. What I didn't know, however, was that the beautiful barrel had never been stress-relieved, so I had it turned down from a straight cylinder to a medium-taper target-weight configuration. The first time I tried the barrel on the range I was totally amazed. It wouldn't keep three consecutive shots in a beer barrel at 200 yards, much less at the longer bigbore ranges. Back at the shop I went over the rifle from one end to the other, checking bedding, locking-lug fit, sights, and everything else that could conceivably cause such poor accuracy. Everything seemed in perfect order except when I stuck a bullet into the muzzle. For a moment I thought I had mistakenly picked up a 7mm (.284 inch) bullet rather than the intended .308 slug. No such luck—the bullet miked an honest .308. The bore had simply opened up like a funnel when the outside was turned down to usable size.

In addition to stress relieving after button rifling, the barrels by top makers are also heat-treated before rifling. Some makers do the heat treating themselves, while others buy their raw barrel stock already treated. The purpose of preheat treating is to normalize the steel so that the bar will be of uniform structure throughout its length. Otherwise the button would be passing through alternately hard and soft areas and the interior surface would have a bumpy surface with tight and loose places.

Somewhere I once read, or perhaps someone told me, that the button rifling process tends to work-harden the interior surfaces and thus increase barrel life. This is true only in part. While the button undoubtedly *does* have a hardening effect on the bore, the heat-treating eliminates it.

Also, while a button-rifled barrel by one of the top makers will have a beautiful finish, it may be the result of hand lapping rather than the burnishing effect of the button. One of the best-known makers recently told me that the lubricant he uses to help the button slide through the bore actually has a slight etching effect on the barrel steel, and that lapping with a lead slug and fine abrasive may be necessary to get the barrel as smooth as he would like. Especially if the barrel is his top-grade target model. Barrels to be used on .22 rimfire target rifles tend to be especially in need of some extra hand lapping.

As good as it is, button rifling will no doubt get even better in coming years. Competition among the top custom makers is intense, and new techniques are constantly being developed. Very possibly the standard carbide buttons of today will in time be replaced with ultra-slick, super-precise ones made of space-age materials. The ceramics, for example, offer definite possibilities.

The fourth rifling technique in current use is the so-called "hammer-forged" process. The basic method is known by different trade-engineering names such as cold forming, cold forging, roto-forging, etc., and is coming into increasing use in the U.S., Europe, and Japan. When I visited several European military and sporting makers in 1972 I found that the hammer-forge process was used almost exclusively in the more modern plants.

In simplest terms, the process simply presses and molds a steel tube around a "positive" forming die or mandrel which has spiraling ridges around it in the reverse image of rifling lands and grooves. You can get an idea of how this works by squeezing a wad of modeling clay around your finger. Pull your finger out and the clay retains the reverse image of the delicate digit. Exactly the same thing takes place when steel is mashed around the reverse-image mandrel. When the mandrel is pulled out its image is left inside. Only in this case the image is that of a completed rifle barrel—lands, grooves, and all.

The machinery used for this process is awesome in its mass and power. The "hammer" strokes, for example, amount to several thousand pounds of

This giant barrel-swaging, or cold-forming, machine is used to rifle barrels at the Winchester plant.

pressure each and they come so fast that the din is an ear-shattering roar. Not at all the pleasant rat-a-tat of the village blacksmith forge.

Interestingly, the original barrel blank is considerably shorter than the finished length. The drilled steel used by Winchester to make their .22-caliber target barrels is only 22¾ inches long when it goes into the machine but the finished barrel will measure about 29 inches. This is because the kneading action of the forging machinery causes the steel to flow and lengthen as it is reduced in diameter. The original tube is, in fact, reduced in diameter by over 25 percent.

The big question in my mind when I first saw barrels made this way was how tightly the forming die would be stuck in the newly formed barrel. With all those thousands of pounds of pressure squeezing the barrel around the mandrel, they could very well be welded together. Actually, though, as the barrel steel is hammered against the forming die it tends to spring back slightly. This rebound is only a few ten-thousandths of an inch but it leaves enough clearance to allow the barrel to be withdrawn from the mandrel with ease.

One might expect that the smoothness of the finished bore would depend on the smoothness of the forming mandrel. This is important, of course, but the mandrels I've inspected are made of tungsten carbide and ground to a perfectly smooth finish. The smoothness of the finished bore depends mainly on the interior surface of the tube *before* it is forged into a barrel. In the manufacture of their top-grade match barrels, Winchester not only reams but even *laps* the hole to a glass-smooth finish. This results in a beautifully finished bore, and one has only to peer through one of the Winchester International Match grade barrels to see how good hammer-forged rifling can be.

If the barrel tube has reaming marks in it before forging, they will be flattened and "smeared" but not completely obliterated. This results in a "file edge" surface which tends to strip hunks of gilding metal from bullets and create excessive copper fouling. Like everything else, if it isn't done right the finished product is only mediocre at best. Done correctly, however, with a properly prepared blank, the hammer-forged barrel is unquestionably the super-accurate barrel of the future.

From the manufacturing standpoint, hammer forging has a lot to offer; it's fast and efficient, it produces nicely accurate barrels on a high-production basis and, though the machinery is expensive, the per-unit production cost of a rifle barrel is cheaper than by any other method. Winchester produces all of their rifle barrels by this method and other manufacturers are following suit.

Aside from the actual rifling process, hammer forging offers some other features. For instance, a forming mandrel could be used which includes the complete chamber and throat shapes. I don't know of any manufacturer in the U.S. who does this but I've been told that it's not only possible but is actually being done in some plants in Europe. There are hammer-forging machines in use which shape the *outside* of the barrels as well as the inside. The most notable—and obvious—example of this is the barrels seen on the current production of the Austrian-made Mannlicher rifles. They have a curious spiraling pattern on the outer surface which was created as the barrel blank rotated over the mandrel, and the thousands of "hammer" marks can be clearly seen. It is a novel finish for a rifle barrel and not at all unattractive.

As one would expect, the hammer-forging process creates internal stresses in the steel which cause some expansion of the bore as the barrel is turned down to the final contour. For "standard" or production-grade barrels this expansion is acceptable and seldom creates accuracy problems, at least as far as hunting rifle accuracy goes. Barrels to be used on super-accurate target rifles, however, such as Winchester International Match rifles, are heat-treated after rifling and before final turning. This relaxes internal stresses and causes the bore to remain highly uniform. Also, these top-grade match barrels are once again lead-lapped after final crowning and chambering. The bores are already very nearly perfectly smooth but the gunsmiths in Winchester's custom shop (where their top-of-the-line target rifles are made) feel that the final lapping polishes out any burrs left by the chambering and crowning cuts.

From the accuracy standpoint hammer-forged barrels are still largely unproved. This is simply because target-grade hammer-forged barrel blanks have not been made available, in any number, to makers of custom target rifles, especially those who make precision bench-rest rifles. The performance of factory-built target rifles using hammer-forged barrels, however, has been right impressive. In 1970 a Steyr-Mannlicher rifle with hammer-forged barrel was used by an Austrian shooter to establish a world's record in the Military Match category. I use a Winchester Model 52E International-grade barreled action with hammer-forged barrel for smallbore tournament shooting and consider it at least as accurate as any rifle on the line and far more accurate than any rimfire barrel I've used previously.

One of the half-dozen most accurate off-the-shelf sporter rifles I've ever fired had a hammer-forged barrel. It was a Winchester Model 70 with varmint-weight barrel in .225 Winchester chambering. Apparently the barrel blank had not been especially well reamed, because smeared rings could be clearly seen on the top flats of the lands, but it would shoot like crazy anyway. From the bench at 100 yards it would group five shots in ¼ inch on good days and seldom went over ½ inch on its worst days.

In all probability the hammer-forged barrel will reach its most nearly perfect form at the hands of small, independent barrelmakers. They have the time and willingness to devote special attention to fine barrels on a one-at-a-time basis. These makers have produced the finest cut-rifled and button-rifled barrels and they'll no doubt do likewise with hammer forging. The immediate drawback, however, is the expense of hammer-forging equipment, but sooner or later some enterprising soul will get his hands on one of these machines and we'll see some spectacular results.

BARREL STEEL

A discussion of whether modern barrel-manufacturing techniques or modern barrel steels came first is about as productive as arguing over whether chickens or eggs came first. To be certain, the finest efforts of our best barrelmakers would be futile without today's high-grade steels, but, by the same token, constantly improving barrelmaking methods over the years have emphasized the need for better metal.

Back when great-granddad was barking squirrels out of tall hickories with his muzzleloader, shooters weren't especially concerned about barrel steel. Black powder, the propellant of the day, didn't generate enough pressure to create a great need for tough barrel alloys, and the closest thing to wearing out a barrel came about from the abrasive up-and-down rubbing of a hickory ramrod.

With the coming of smokeless powder, however, and high-velocity jacketed bullets, the need for strong, tough barrel metal became acute. Interestingly, the development and improvement of steel and steel alloys have always been closely related to the progress and development of firearms. Such names as Bofors, Krupp, and Whitworth became world-renowned because of their inventiveness in the field of gun metals. A seldom-noted but highly significant historical fact in this respect has to do with the ever popular Winchester Model 94 lever rifle. When it was introduced in 1894 it was not only one of the very first sporting rifles designed especially for smokeless-powder ammo but also one of the very first sporting rifles to be equipped with a barrel of nickel-steel alloy. In fact, it was Winchester's *first* rifle to be so equipped as a standard feature.

The addition of nickel to the barrel metal added strength to withstand the higher pressures of progressive-burning powder and provided additional toughness to resist the wearing effect of high-velocity jacketed bullets. Previously the problem of high chamber pressure had been dealt with simply by making the barrel large enough and thick enough to be safe. With the modern nickel-alloyed steels, however, a barrel could be built light, trim, *and* safe. The Model 94 Winchester was (and is) a perfect example of these metallurgical benefits.

Over the years there were additional improvements in the basic nickel steel such as the addition of carbon, sulfur, and manganese, and up through World War I it continued to be the standard metal for high-quality rifle barrels. It was so good, in fact, that gun manufacturers who used nickel steel for their barrels made quite a thing of it in their advertisements and catalog descriptions. Some guns even had "Nickel Steel" or "Hi-Pressure Steel" stamped on the barrel.

Good things must not always come to an end—sometimes they just get better. In the case of barrel steels it was the introduction of an alloy of carbon and manganese which became known as ordnance steel. The manganese gave a higher degree of machinability, which was especially valuable with the coming of broached rifling. Ordnance steel came into its own during the era between the wars and reached its period of greatest use during World War II. Actually, ordnance steel is not one specific alloy but a general term for a general classification of carbon-manganese barrel alloys. It is still widely used for barrelmaking, especially in Europe.

Even as ordnance steel was on the rise as a barrelmaking material, a new super-steel was being developed, the alloy we now commonly refer to as chrome-moly. Known among steelmakers as the 4140 series, chrome-moly barrels are an alloy of 0.80 to 1.1 percent chromium, 0.15 to 0.25 percent molybdenum, about 0.5 percent carbon, and up to 1 percent manganese. This is a strong, tough alloy which is well suited to high-pressure, high-velocity cartridges. It also machines well and thus can be made into extremely accurate barrels. It is the steel most used by custom barrelmakers and is the best choice for a wide range of different types of rifle barrels. In terms of accuracy it can be beaten only by stainless steel but has the advantage of being blueable. The best in modern hunting rifles have chrome-moly barrels.

The chromium has the effects of increasing wear resistance, a vital factor with modern high-velocity rifles, and of giving added resistance to loss of strength over a long period of use. The molybdenum, as used in rifle-barrel steel, is important because it prevents the steel from becoming soft or weakening at high temperatures. Barrels erode or "wear" as a result of high temperatures in the throat area. As the temperature is increased the metal breaks down and the familiar "shot out" appearance in the barrel of a high-velocity rifle occurs. Molybdenum in a steel alloy helps prevent this from happening, and that's why chrome-moly barrels are popular among high-velocity fans and, especially, wildcatters.

Though the element molybdenum was discovered fairly recently (1790), its use in gun barrels goes back beyond that date. Japanese swords dating back over 600 years were known to be especially tough, so European armsmakers imported tons of Japanese iron ore for the making of high-grade gun barrels. They realized that there was something extraordinary about the Japanese ore but had no idea what it was. Recent analysis of ancient Japanese swords, however, has revealed that the undefined ingredient was molybdenum.

In recent years much has been made of stainless-steel barrels, and there is no questioning that this steel has contributed to significant advances, especially in the areas of competitive shooting. The primary advantage of stainless steel, however, is often completely overlooked by many shooters. This single most vital feature of stainless steel is its uniformity, which, as it turns out, has nothing to do with the fact that the steel is stainless. Uniformity and "stainlessness" just happen to be convenient features brought about by its alloy and manufacturing process. Stainless is an expensive, high-quality steel made to meet rigid specifications for precision engineering and specialty construction such as aircraft building. As such its production and alloying are closely controlled, and this, in turn, results in a high degree of uniformity in both bar texture and lot-to-lot analysis. If, say, ordinary chrome-moly or nickel steels were made to such exacting specs they would probably be as uniform as stainless and result in equally uniform barrels. Still, there is the opinion among some barrelmakers and experienced shooters that stainless steel tends to foul less than other steel, and this contributes to tack-driving accuracy.

The most frequently touted feature of stainless steel is that it wears longer or resists erosion better than other steels. This was well illustrated back in the 1930s when Winchester was faced with the problem of a high rate of barrel wear with their new .220 Swift cartridge. Ordinary steel barrels burned out in a few hundred or, at best, a few thousand rounds, and the cartridge earned a reputation for causing poor barrel life. The problem was solved to large degree when rifles with stainless-steel barrels were introduced. Since that time, stainless has been hailed as the answer to a maiden's prayer when it comes to barrel wear. But why? What is there about stainless that makes it more resistant to the effects of a high-speed bullet squeezing up the bore than other steels?

In order to understand this fully it is necessary to understand what happens in the bore of ordinary steel barrels. If you were to crawl into the throat section of a burned-out carbon-steel barrel you would immediately be struck by the rough, blackened surface of the barrel walls. The surface would have a cracked, veinlike texture which would look a lot like the cracked surface of a dried-out lake bed. In barrel steels this is caused by extreme heat and the burn-out of carbon. When the surface carbon burns out, or evacuates, the "mud bed" surface results. Of course, high-velocity cartridges such as the .220 and various magnums generate enormous temperatures, and this is why barrel burn-out is associated with high-velocity cartridges. (Actually, the bullet velocity has little to do with barrel erosion. There is relatively little barrel wear-out at the muzzle, where the bullet is going the fastest!)

Stainless steel has a very low carbon content, and as a result both the rate and the results of carbon burn-out are far less obvious. The grade of stainless used for barrels usually has a carbon content of not more than fifteen points (0.15 percent), whereas a barrel of 4140 chrome-moly steel will have three times that much.

Some makers of rifle barrels point out that stainless steel is not as resistant to abrasion as chrome-moly steel and that a stainless barrel can even be ruined by the scratching effect of a rough cleaning rod. This is indeed true in some cases but is not necessarily true of all stainless barrels. Some manufacturers prefer to work with milder steels, both stainless and carbon types; and these are naturally more prone to abrasion and marring than would be a harder steel. I've tested the hardness of various stainless barrels and found that the relative hardness may range from 18 on the Rockwell "C" scale up to 32. A stainless-steel barrel with a Rockwell hardness of 32 would be as scratch-resistant as a chrome-moly barrel of the same hardness rating.

Stainless steel gets its name from its resistance to rusting, discoloration, and corrosion. This is not to say that all stainless steel is rustproof, because there are *degrees* of stainlessness based on the chromium or nickel content. Under extreme conditions some stainless-steel alloys, including barrel steel, will rust or corrode. From the gunmakers' standpoint this rust-resistant quality of stainless steel poses a problem, because the ordinary gun blueing process is actually a form of oxidation or rusting. This is why the stainless-steel barrels on fancy target rifles are bright and shiny. Winchester beat the problem on their Model 70 rifle in .220 Swift by giving the barrels a coating of iron. The thin layer of iron could then be nicely blued. This iron plating accounts for the dull, matte barrel surface of Winchester rifles in .220 Swift caliber. More recently, however, a bright unblued finish has become the hallmark of a stainless-steel barrel and even has a certain snob appeal. Remington, for example, leaves the stainless barrels of their Model 40-X centerfire rifles "as is."

In the practical sense, the only real question is how much more accurate a stainless steel barrel is than an otherwise identical one made of another type of steel. A question such as this invites a bit of hedging, because even two seemingly identical barrels made of exactly the same steel may not perform alike. Nonetheless, over the past several years I've owned and used fifteen (that I can recall) centerfire rifles with heavy, target-grade stainless-steel barrels. Each of these has been exceedingly accurate. Not one was incapable of grouping five shots under ½ inch at 100 yards. Some of these were originally equipped with non-stainless barrels of otherwise identical contour, and I can recall a couple that showed a marked accuracy improvement when a stainless barrel was installed. With this much evidence at hand I'm perfectly content to spend the extra money for a stainless barrel when my main goal is getting the most accurate barrels available.

This skilled worker straightens barrels at the Marlin plant. It takes a keen eye and lots of experience to straighten a barrel with a crooked bore.

Aside from our fine barrelmakers and fancy barrel metals, some pretty important tools which have contributed to the accuracy of the modern rifle are our ultra-precise bore-measuring instruments. Without some means of measuring and judging the quality and surface uniformity of rifle barrels it would have been impossible to have taken the tremendous strides in accuracy which we've seen over recent years.

The so-called "star" gauge of Springfield-rifle fame was one of the first precision measuring instruments for rifle barrels and was used to select the choicer barrels and eliminate the really bad ones. The instrument had fingers which rode the grooves and registered any variations in uniformity. Those barrels which varied beyond the allowable tolerances were scrapped, and those which were found to be especially uniform were marked with the "star" stamp.

A more recent barrel-measuring device is the much-discussed but seldom-understood "air gauge." An "air-gauged" barrel is generally understood to have an especially uniform bore, but I feel that the term tends to be somewhat misleading. Actually any rifle bore can be air-gauged, it is only what the gauge tells us that's important. So the next time a shooter brags about his air-gauged barrel ask him what the gauge indicated. Chances are he won't know. Barrel manufacturers, especially the custom makers, use these precision instruments to pick out their most uniform barrels, and they are usually put in a higher-priced "Air Gauge" lot. The gauge operates by means of a constant stream of air which is blown against the barrel wall through a closely fitted plug or button. This plug is so closely fitted to the bore that variations in the groove diameter reduce or increase the volume of air which is escaping through the tiny hole. When the plug passes by a loose spot in the barrel the air escapes more rapidly, and when it passes a tight spot the flow of air slows down. The volume of air lost is read on a vertical scale where a small, lightweight ball "floats" in a glass tube on a column of air. Since the air which supports the indicator ball and the air which escapes from the bore button are from a common source, the ball rises or falls according to the amount of air which escapes in the barrel. A tight spot in the barrel restricts the loss of air and causes the indicator ball to rise; a loose spot allows a more rapid loss of air, lessens the amount of air pressure supporting the ball, and causes it to fall.

Thus by simply passing an air-gauge head through a rifle barrel the operator can quickly read variations in uniformity as small as 0.00005 inch. Without this type of precision measurement, about the only way to find a good barrel would be actual test firing. For some reason or other, barrels which air-gauge very well do not always shoot well, and some barrels which flunk the air-gauge test are ultimately found to be surprisingly accurate. But over the long haul the barrels which do best on the air gauge test are the ones which shoot best as well.

Another instrument which has been invaluable in the development of the modern barrel is the bore scope. These fancy (and expensive) optical gadgets were first developed for the medical profession so that doctors could go peeking about in folks' insides. In time it occurred to some clever soul that this would be a handy tool for peering into rifle barrels, and a special version was developed for this purpose. It works by means of a tiny "wheat grain" light bulb on the tip of a hollow rod which also houses a tiny mirror and magnifying system. The viewer simply looks into the eyepiece on the other end of the tube, and what he sees is a well-lighted and magnified flea's-eye view of the inside of the barrel.

The first and most obvious use of the bore scope is to inspect the interior surface of a barrel for roughness, tool marks, or flaws in the metal itself. They are also handy to check for traces of stubborn powder or copper fouling or for the signs of wear. I once had a fine-looking varmint rifle chambered for the .22/250 Remington cartridge which would shoot about six or seven shots in a nice tight group, then start throwing wild shots all over the target. I checked stock bedding, the scope, and everything else I could think of, but everything looked perfect. The barrel was brand-new and was as bright on the inside as mail-order dentures, but on a hunch I took a closer look with a bore scope. About midway down the tube—too far to see with the unaided eye—there was a sharp-edged gap in one of the lands. This was causing an excessive fouling build-up and, after a few rounds, ruining accuracy. I sent the barrel back to the maker. He took one look at it through *his* bore scope and made me a new barrel. Without a bore scope such inspection and detection would be impossible.

The bore scope and our other sophisticated, modern-day measuring devices are tools which make it possible for barrelmakers to judge their product with a precision that was unthinkable even a generation ago. The effect this has had on accuracy has been incalculable. But look at it this way. Back around the turn of the century, barrel variations were measured or estimated in terms of thousandths of an inch and target groups were measured in inches. Today we measure barrel uniformity in terms of fractions of ten-thousandths of an inch and measure *groups* in thousandths of an inch. . . .

3

The Stock

If you don't think rifle stock design has come a long way in a short while, do this. Compare the illustrations and pictures in gun catalogs from the years 1915, 1935, and 1955 (if you can find them) with those in a 1975 catalog. You'll be impressed right off the bat with two things. First, there was amazingly little change in stock styling, decade after decade, for a half-century. But during the past two decades there has been a sudden and dramatic emphasis on stock design, with some major makes and models undergoing a stock facelift every five years or so. Second, if you read the stock dimensions you'll note that the changes are more than cosmetic. Butt dimensions, for example, have changed considerably, with drop at heel an inch or so higher than before, and a corresponding elevation at the comb. Even that champion of the drooping poopdeck, the Savage Model 99, has had its heel hoisted a few fractions.

These primary dimension changes of the past few years have had an unmistakable impact on the shootability of our rifles. When we compare a stock of recent make to an earlier vintage, the handling qualities are so distinctly better the first question that comes to mind is "Why did it take so long?" An instant analyzer will be sure to point out that today's straighter stocks and plumper combs with cheek pieces are a direct result of increased use of telescopic sights. This of course is true, but it doesn't completely explain the almost revolutionary changes in design concept that produced our current stock configurations. Traditional ideas die hard, often outliving their

These chambers, which look like phone booths, are precision stock shaping machines in the Marlin factory. Keeping the stock turning operation housed inside these chambers controls the accumulation of dust and shavings. The wood turnings are whisked away through the large flexible piping shown beneath the chambers. These stocks, which are not walnut, are for the budget priced Glenfield line. With machinery such as this, cutting several stocks at a time, a stock can be turned to very nearly finished dimension (from a rough block) in only a few minutes.

purpose, and have to be painfully yanked out by the roots like a bad tooth. American gunmakers, by tradition, are notorious cowards when it comes to confrontation with such surgery, preferring to let outdated designs hang about like faded and tattered draperies.

A classic example of this complex was illustrated a couple of years ago when I was visiting a major arms plant and was describing to a department head how I wanted a custom version of one of their most famous rifles made. This model has long had an unsightly mill cut on the receiver bridge, so I explained to the supervisor that I didn't want that cut on my rifle. This threw him into a fit of consternation and caused him to consult his shelf of drawings and manufacturing specs. Finally he advised that he had no authority to make such changes and would have to consult *his* superior. Minutes later the two of them were poring over the drawings again trying to decide what would go wrong if that milling-machine cut were to be left out. I couldn't keep a straight face any longer and gave them the whole story. That particular receiver cut had been instigated decades before to accommodate a make and model of receiver sight popular at the time. In the intervening years the sight lost favor among shooters and eventually production ceased altogether. But the special mill cut on the receiver continued, even after everyone had forgotten why!

Now if you think that's a far-out example, just consider the prevailing stock design which continued right up to modern days. Back in the days of flintlock ignition, shooters preferred to use a more erect and rearward head position because it helped protect the face, especially the eyes, from the ball of fire erupting in the flashpan. (The next time you see an eighteenth- or nineteenth-century print or painting of a shooting scene, pay particular attention to the erectness of the shooters' heads.) Such a shooting stance calls for a stock with a considerable amount of drop at heel, and early stocks were styled accordingly.

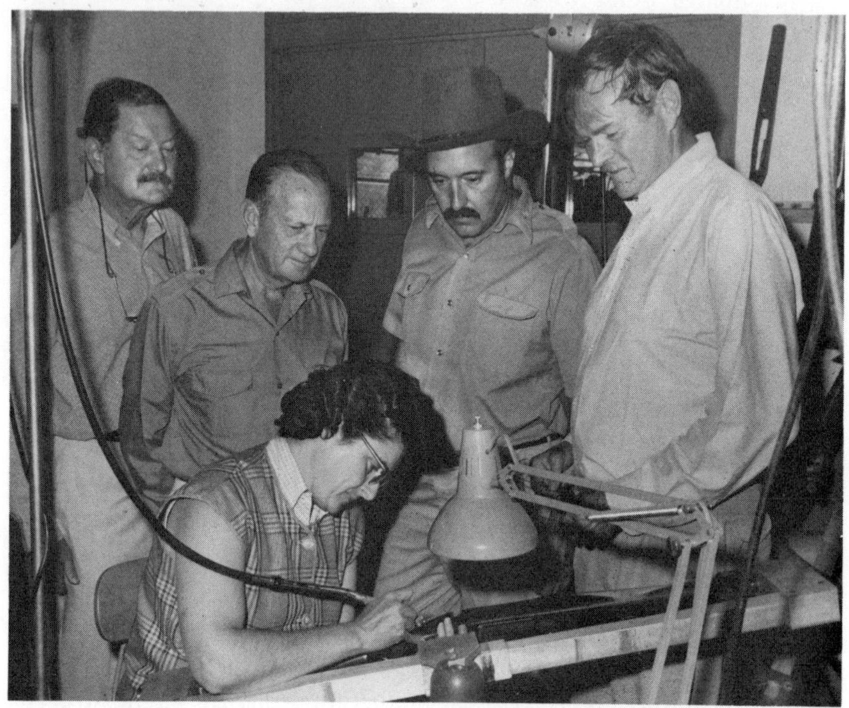

Here, from left, John Amber, Editor of Gun Digest, *Pete Brown, long-time shooting editor of* Sports Afield, *and I, along with Bill Ruger, watch a woman hand-checker a Ruger Model 77 stock. Only a few years ago cut-type checkering was considered too expensive for modern production techniques. Now, thanks to specially trained and highly skilled employees, and/or very sophisticated machinery, the future of cut checkering on mass-produced rifles seems secure.*

The deep stock styling continued through the caplock era but became obsolete with the coming of cartridge-firing rifles and shotguns. Or at least it *should* have become obsolete. But it didn't. There was no longer any danger from flaming flashpans or exploding percussion caps, and a more forward head position would have resulted in better control and thus better marksmanship. But alas, the steeply bent stock design was retained by virtually every manufacturer. About the only exceptions one finds were those guns made in custom shops where either the gunsmiths themselves or their customers recognized the advantages of a straighter stock. The legendary Winchester Model 66 and Model 73 were classic cases of outdated stock design being used on breechloading rifles. The next time you get your hands on a Model 73, or virtually any other make or model of firearm from that era, snap it to your shoulder and notice where your aiming eye is pointing—probably at the backside of the receiver. Only by straightening your head and moving to the rear will you be able to get a good line on the sights. But at the same time you lose both cheek contact and control. Also bear in mind that the shooters of that day averaged several inches less in height than today's shooter, had smaller hands, thinner faces, and shorter necks. This meant that their guns were even more uncomfortable for them than the same guns feel to us!

This stocking style continued for a long time and was perpetuated by some very important manufacturers. The U.S. Krag rifle, for example, was as crooked as a mule's knee, and when the 1903 Springfield was designed there was no improvement. The type "C," or competition, stocks had to be specially made for '03 Springfield match rifles with a higher and fuller comb and less drop at heel because the standard-issue dimension, which dated back to musket days, was such a handicap to precision marksmanship.

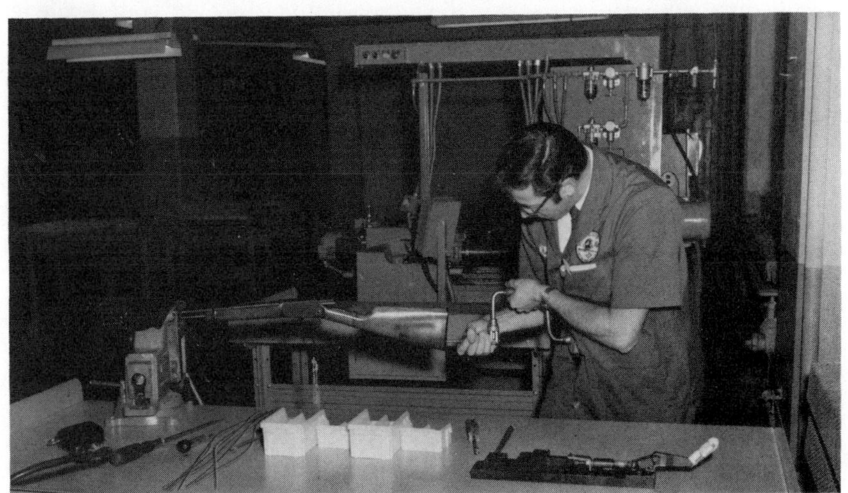

A worker in the Winchester plant puts the final touches on a Winchester Model 9422 rimfire lever-action. Hand operations such as this are becoming more and more rare.

Even though the evolution of stock configuration failed to keep pace with other areas of firearms and ballistic development, one must temper his appraisal of the situation with at least an attempt to understand some of the problems. The biggest problem, of course, was a resistance to change, a refusal to look into the future and establish new trends. But in some quarters there *was* an awareness of the need for more up-to-date stock styling and dimensions. The problem, as it turns out, was trying to discover ways which gracefully met the increasing demand for straight stocks and at the same time retained traditional styling concepts. Examples of this dilemma are best illustrated in the potbellied stocks made for deluxe sporting rifles back around the turn of the century. Another example is the so-called "broken grip" styling which looks as if the butt section was sawed off just behind the grip and reattached at a straighter angle. This, and the pot or "fish" belly, are generally considered by collectors to be only interesting but peculiar aberrations of stock styling, though in fact they were attempts to elevate the heel as much as possible and at the same time retain traditional configurations at the tang and grip. In later years the problem was to be solved by establishing straighter lines at the tang, but such changes, especially so radical a concept, come about slowly. As a matter of fact, some vestiges of the older styling still remain.

Actually, the need for straighter stocks was double-pronged. More convenient eye and sight alignment plus more efficient control were the main motivations for straighter stocks, but recoil management played a big part too. A deeply dropped butt creates a pivotal point around which a recoiling rifle revolves. A straight stock tends to recoil in a straight-to-the-rear direction with little barrel climb or "buck." Deeply dropped stocks, on the other hand, climb as they recoil and are more punishing to the shooter's face. During the last quarter of the nineteenth century, when such hard-recoiling cartridges as the .45/90 Winchester and .50/90 Sharps were used in rifles featuring thin combs and a deep drop at heel, the effect was not unlike getting whacked in the mouth with a dull hatchet. This tragedy reached its bloodied hour during the 1920s when the great English and European dangerous-game cartridges came into full flower and were being chambered for in razor-combed rifles with lots of drop in the butt.

Another feature, a purely stylistic one, which hung around longer than necessary was the deeply curved crescent butt plate. This design style came into prominence early in the nineteenth century (for no good reason that anyone can name) and was a standard feature on nearly all sporting caplock rifles for several decades. Apparently the deeply curved buttplate was intended to conform to the shooter's shoulder, but it did nothing of the sort. Their most dreadful era was late in their stylistic lifespan when they were thought to be especially fashionable when only about an inch across at the widest point. A rifle in .45/70 caliber which sported one of these buttplates, such as did Marlin and Winchester lever rifles, was guaranteed to bring tears to a shooter's eyes every time he pulled the trigger.

The painfully slow development of today's stock is not altogether due to resistance to change on the part of manufacturers. Shooters themselves are a conservative-minded lot who have traditionally taken a dim view of anything representing change. Especially if said change represents a departure from the principles Uncle Mortimer brought down from the mount when he shot a bear back in '98. And too, more than once manufacturers have taken a wrong turn when they bowed to wishes expressed by shooters who thought they wanted one thing when in fact they actually wanted something else. And just as often, stock design takes a wrong turn when manufacturers erroneously anticipate or misread rifle buyers' preferences. By and large the rifle-stock design of today is on just such a detour. This takes some explaining.

Back in the 1950s when it appeared that virtually every firearm manufacturer was bent on continuing a prewar course of rifle-stock design, there occurred an act of almost open rebellion among thousands of gun buyers. These determined riflemen, ex-G.I.s almost to a man, had spent the war years conjuring up visions of the dream rifle they would someday own, complete with scope and all the trimmings. But alas, the postwar market was as dull as sophomore algebra.

But it just so happened that about then a West Coast ballistic buff and riflemaker who also happened to be a supersalesman began getting a lot of publicity for his racy-looking rifles. The stocks were beyond anything most shooters had even dared imagine, with rich inlays, Monte Carlo combs, swept-line forend tips, and white spacers between tip, cap, and butt pad. When the ex-G.I. beheld such a rifle, even a picture in a magazine, it must have seemed like Betty Grable's legs and Lana Turner's sweaters, to be the soul-searing vision of a thousand lonely nights of guard duty. The rifles were called Weatherby Magnums, and compared to the more prosaic Winchesters and Remingtons lined up on dealers' racks, they glittered like King Solomon's treasure. The long-promised postwar miracle come true at last.

But visions have a way of remaining just beyond one's grasp, especially when the price tag runs to three times the price of more earthly goods, and to many it seemed that the dream rifle would remain only a dream. Then another phenomenon arrived on the scene, the semi-finished stock blank. In reality, semi-finished, do-it-yourself stock blanks were nothing new, having been a staple long before Pearl Harbor, but their use had been limited to gunsmiths and devoted gun tinkerers. But beginning around 1950 the stock-it-yourself craze caught on big. Thousands upon thousands of liberated German Mausers and Japanese Arisakas were lying around just waiting to be converted to sporters which, if not the dream rifle visioned in a Pacific foxhole, would be at least something out of the ordinary. And, with Monte Carlo comb, cheek piece, and white spacers, perhaps they could even resemble the pictures of those fabulous looking Weatherbys in the shooting magazines. So thus were sown the seeds of today's commercial stocking trend.

The 1975 catalogs of America's three largest makers of sporting arms—Remington, Savage, and Winchester—feature top-of-the-line bolt-action rifles fully decked out in—wouldn't you know—Monte Carlo stocks complete with white plastic spacers between buttplate, grip caps, and forend tips. Such styling, up to date as it may seem, especially when compared to the look of the 1950s, is not all that advanced. As mentioned earlier, it represents a detour from the logical evolution of rifle-stock design. And too, in the time-honored tradition among gunmakers of making progress with all possible caution, today's rifle-stock design actually represents the consumer demands of two decades ago. At present, shooters are moving away from the splashy spacers and humpbacked combs and calling for more conservatively elegant styling. I think that within a decade or two the rifle stocks by major manufacturers will be quite similar in styling and dimension to those presently being made by our top custom stockers. In fact, this trend has already been started by the Ruger Model 77.

Though it may come as a shock to a few innocent lads, the single most characteristic feature of today's prevailing stock design, the Monte Carlo comb, is little more than a symptom of our ages-old inability to abandon outdated ideas and come to grips with the real problem. In order to fully understand this, let's consider the two most often voiced advantages of the Monte Carlo comb as they apply to rifle stocks. First, it elevates the

At top is a factory stock which achieves a high comb for scope use by means of the Monte Carlo configuration. At bottom is a far more attractive stock which achieves the same effect simply by bringing the drop at the heel up to the same elevation as the nose of the comb. This also results in less recoil.

shooter's face so as to make the use of telescopic sights more convenient. With such a high comb, he has only to snap the rifle to his cheek and he's automatically looking through the glass. The other is that a forend-sloping Monte Carlo comb recoils *away* from the shooter's face and thus reduces the tendency to get smacked in the mouth. These are attractive-sounding claims, but do they really work out as well as they sound?

In truth, a Monte Carlo is not at all needed to get the eye up to scope height. The same results are achieved by simply elevating the nose of the comb and raising the drop at heel. A typical factory-issue Monte Carlo rifle stock will have a drop of around ½ inch at the nose of the comb, ½ inch at the crest of the Monte Carlo, and 1½ inches at heel (measuring from the centerline of the bore). A well-designed *non*-Monte Carlo stock, on the other hand, will have about ½ inch drop at comb *and* at heel! This high, straight stock line gives the same eye/scope alignment advantage of a Monte Carlo but without the humpbacked profile. In other words, to justify a Monte Carlo comb on a *hunting* rifle it is necessary to have more drop at heel than desirable. This in turn causes more recoil punishment than necessary and cancels the much-touted "recoils away from the fore" feature of a Monte Carlo. Remember, the greater the drop at heel the greater the tendency of a rifle to raise or buck upward into the shooter's face as it recoils. A non-Monte Carlo stock with about ½ inch drop at heel recoils more nearly straight to the rear and is less punishing. So, as it turns out, the Monte Carlo comb is only a stylistic venture which adds nothing to a hunting rifle in the way of shootability.

This is not to say that the Monte Carlo comb is worthless—far from it. They serve shotgunners well on trap guns by providing a built-in lead for rising targets. They are often used on target-rifle stocks, where it is necessary for the shooter to position his face high enough to sight comfortably through high-mounted target-type scopes. In such cases the Monte Carlo and cheek piece are usually so high that they block removal of the bolt. This is why the upper "story" of some target stock combs are removable, so as to permit bolt removal.

It's interesting to speculate on where modern stock styling might be today if the Weatherby or "California" trend had not caught on in such a big way and caused the normal course of dimensional evolution in mass-produced rifles to get sidetracked.

Some other offshoots of the great styling revolution of the 1950s are such modernistic features as the rollover cheek piece, thumbhole grips on

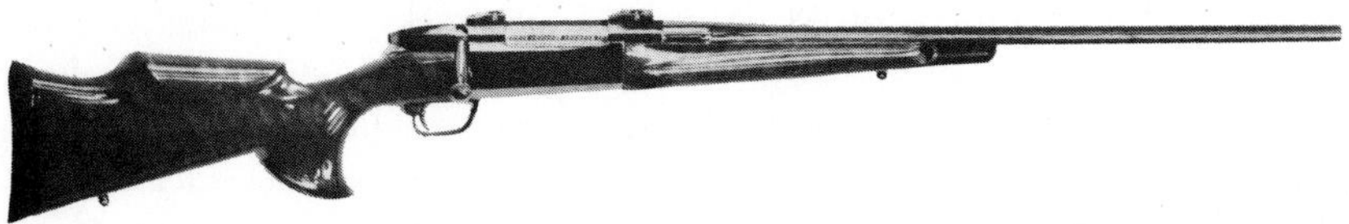

Here is an example of the most far-out in modern stock styling. This radical styling adds nothing in the way of shootability but no doubt is attractive to shooters who want something out of the ordinary in the way of stock design.

sporters, teardrop grip caps, and all sorts of weirdly shaped forends. Perhaps it's unfair to lump these assorted styles and notions together. I'm sure that one stockmaker considers his rollover cheek piece uniquely different from all others, but for that very reason a detailed description will go far beyond the scope of this book. For the most part such dodads do not improve the shootability of a stock, and, as a matter of fact, I can think of several examples where they are even a detriment. But even so, I do not join some of my more hardnosed colleagues in a blanket condemnation. I don't care for offbeat stocks personally and must admit that it's sometimes hard to keep a straight face when confronted by one. But by the same token I can sympathize with the desire of some individuals to break away from the general "sameness" that plagues gun design. And there is nothing morally wrong with expressing one's personal flair and sense of individuality by means of bizarre and even grotesquely configured stocks. Some makers of the new radically contorted designs promote them as the gunstocks of the future. But fortunately such is not the case. They are only a passing phase which, in fact, already appears to be ending.

Another stylistic abomination which bloomed during the 1960s and, fortunately, had all but withered away by the mid-1970s is the "box" forend. Actually, this four-sided forend configuration, which was most notable on the Remington Model 700 and Winchester Model 70, did not reflect any need to update prevailing forend shapes but, rather, a production necessity. This was the sad era, need I remind you, of stamped, or pressed, checkering. This type of decoration is done by means of hot steel plates, or dies, which more or less burn an image into the wood. The technique does not work well on curved surfaces, so it was necessary to redesign rifle forends into relatively flat-sided affairs. Along about 1972, when computer-controlled checkering became operational, pressed checkering was abolished on better-grade rifles. And that was also the end of the box forend. Praise Heaven for small favors.

STOCK DIMENSIONS

Unlike shotguns, proper fitting of the rifle stock to the shooter is not a critical marksmanship factor. Most factory-built stocks have a length of pull (the measurement from the trigger to the center of the buttplate) of about 13½ inches. This stock length provides an adequately shootable fit for shooters ranging in height from about five foot five to a foot taller. Occasionally one runs across or hears about a stock that has been custom-made or altered to a specific length of pull, but frankly such efforts are usually a waste of time. The reason is that rifles, hunting rifles in particular, are fired from a pretty wide variety of positions, each of which, if followed to the letter of perfection, would prescribe a different stock length. For example, a stock that fits perfectly for offhand shooting will, generally speaking, be a bit too short for prone shooting. This is why the best target rifles used in prone, sitting, kneeling, and standing matches are fitted with an extendable butt plate that allows the length of pull to be adjusted from one position to the next. The total change from prone to standing may be an inch or even more, depending of course on the individual.

I once checked my battery of tournament rifles and found that the lengths of pull ranged from 13 inches all the way up to 14½ inches. Such a variation in lengths would be devastating to a shotgunner but is scarcely noticed in rifle stocks.

Far more important, in my opinion, is the drop at heel and comb. But here again, unlike shotguns, a precise fit is not all that vital. A shotgunner will hit above or below the target if the stock is either too straight or too crooked, but the rifleman has a more precise sighting arrangement to guide his aim. Thus he overcomes minor improper stock fit by simply moving his head. The worst this can mean is inconvenience, a certain slowing down of the aiming process. Back when telescopic sights were first coming into widespread use one of the leading objections was that it took too long to align the eye with the scope and get a full, clear field of view. The reason for all this awkwardness was that the stocks of that day had too much drop and when a shooter brought a rifle to his shoulder he tended to look under the scope. Then when he raised his head to look through the scope he lost a measure of head control because of reduced cheek contact with the comb. This resulted in a lot of head dottering just trying to find a clear field of view. No wonder so many first-time scope users gave up in disgust. Scope and scope-mount manufacturers fought the problem by devising ways of mounting telescopic sights as low as possible. Early scope-mount advertisements, you'll recall, made a big thing out of how low their various mounts permitted a scope to be attached. But there is a practical limit to low scope mounting, and shooters weren't presented with a solution to the problem until riflemakers began straightening up their stocks. Nowadays, thanks to much higher combs, scopes can be used faster and more effectively.

If I had my way, centerfire hunting rifles would leave the factory with a ½-inch drop at the nose of the comb and no more than ¾-inch drop at heel. Factory spokesmen have told me that they feel this makes it too difficult to aim a rifle with standard-equipment open sights. Actually this problem is easily overcome by using higher-mounted open sights. In fact, Winchester, Remington, and Ruger are already equipping their top-of-the-line rifles with taller open sights than they furnished a decade or so back. As a point of historical note, some of the stock designs of before World War II and even into the 1960s had too much drop even for efficient open-sight use! Be that as it may, this is the generation of the telescopic sight, and stocks made to compromise between open and scope sights really suit no one. The final proof of the argument, as far as I'm concerned, is the amazement and delight voiced by shooters the first time they snap to shoulder a rifle stocked by a top-rank stockmaker. The instant eye alignment and full cheek control (which contributes to a steady aim) is usually attributed to some sort of wizardry on the part of the stocker, but usually the secret is just a high, straight comb.

The problem with stock dimensions, whether suggested by someone like me or set forth in a manufacturer's specification table, is that they don't tell the whole story, and even if they did very few shooters would be able to relate raw measurements to their personal needs. We can quote dimensions till hell freezes over, but when you get down to the real nitty-gritty it's much more important to be able to recognize when a rifle stock fits you properly and when it doesn't. One might suppose that only a simpleminded yo-yo couldn't tell if his stock fits right, but actually it's a pretty complicated business. In fact, an experienced shooter might have even more difficulty determining if his rifle fits properly than a beginner. This is because there are so many different stock shapes around that we get pretty expert at adapting to different dimensions. The more stocks we use the more unconsciously we adapt, until in time everything we pick up feels about the same. Or, more usually, very *very* few riflemen have ever had the chance to get the feel of a stock that actually fits them correctly. It's a pitiful situation but true.

Hoist almost any scope-equipped rifle, of current or past production, to your shoulder and bring the eye to proper alignment. If you've done it often enough your eye will align with the scope optics almost instantly. It would thus seem that you've got a good-fitting stock. But while the stock is against your shoulder and your eye aligned with the scope, stop and consider how the comb contacts your face. Nine times out of ten the comb will not be comfortably nestled just under your cheekbone but, rather, pressed against your jaw and tooth line. Most often the top of the comb is just about on a level with your molars. You may even discover that you have pressed your jaw against the stock and then opened your teeth slightly in order to elevate the rest of your head enough to see through the scope. This is how we adjust to a poorly fitting stock. With a little experience it becomes so natural we do it without thinking.

Next, disregarding eye and scope alignment, sink your face down on the stock until the comb nestles snugly under the cheekbone. This is how the comb *should* fit when you're looking through the scope. With your head in the lowered position you'll instantly notice that you have a steadier hold and better control over the rifle. When you raise your head to look through the scope again you'll notice that the face/comb relationship becomes less steady, and you'll also notice, possibly for the first time, that it's taking a certain amount of effort, albeit an unconscious effort, to maintain a correct scope alignment. This presents no real marksmanship problems in most shooting situations, especially at a stationary target, but when the target is moving, such as a running deer or elk, it gets pretty hard to keep the cross hairs on the right spot. This is because you are trying to coordinate the cross hairs on the target and, at the same time, keep your eye coordinated with the scope. Even when you think you're being successful you are drawing effort away from a smooth swing, trigger pull, and follow-through.

An effective test of a correctly fitted stock is taking "dry" shots at birds flitting across your backyard. If the stock fits right, your head, shoulders, and the rifle will move as one compact unit. You'll be able to snap the rifle to your shoulder and the flying target will instantly appear in the scope. But if the target tends to jerk in and out of the scope's field of view, or the scope frequently blacks out altogether, you've probably got a stock-fit problem. If you suspect the latter, try wrapping a folded hand towel over the comb. With the towel doubled until you have solid cheek contact *and* good scope/eye alignment, you'll notice that you can also track those darting birds more easily. This is simply because when you move the rifle your head moves too and you don't have to "catch up" with the scope.

The great unlisted and unmentioned stock dimension is *thickness* of comb. Knowing how much drop a stock has at comb is only partially meaningful unless we have a pretty good idea of how plump the top radius is. A comb that is high but thin, for example, may offer no better face support than a lower but fatter one. I've often wondered if a simple measurement system couldn't be used to describe thickness of comb. Perhaps just a radius measurement would do. But probably this statistic, like drop at comb and heel, would be, to many shooters, only another meaningless abstraction.

Another stylistic phenomenon of recent times is the often-discussed but seldom-understood cheek piece. The idea is a very old one. Cheek pieces, or cheek rests, were a prominent feature on stocks dating back to wheel-lock days and are prevalent on nonmilitary rifles of the seventeenth, eighteenth, and early nineteenth centuries. The so-called "Kentucky" rifles of our Colonial days had especially well-styled and decorative cheek rests. With the coming of mass-produced sporting rifles, however, the cheek piece all but disappeared and remained on the wane for nearly a century. Until the early 1960s about the only cheek pieces to be found on anything approaching mass-produced rifles were on Super Grade Model 70 Winchesters and guns of European manufacture.

Today, for better or worse, cheek pieces are standard equipment on most top-of-the-line goods by American manufacturers. The trend, like the Monte Carlo comb, is part and parcel of the California-style craze that infected the industry a while back and will no doubt remain with us for a long time. In my view about the only thing provided by cheek pieces on most rifles is proof positive that an attractive cheek piece cannot be mass-produced.

A cheek piece can do two things. It can provide a comfortable support for the face, which in turn aids aiming. Or it can perform a decorative function—a showcase, so to speak, of a stockmaker's sense of line and proportion and mastery of detail. A cheek piece seldom accomplishes both of these tasks. In fact, very few cheek pieces fulfill either task. A properly made cheek piece is, in effect, a stylistic innovation which subtly performs the job of thickening the comb somewhat and thus providing a stable platform for the shooter's face. In their most elegant usage they compensate for "cast-off" in the butt section and keep the eye in line with the sights.

The problem with most cheek pieces, especially factory jobs, is that they are too thin at top and thus cannot perform their intended function. This poor situation is made worse when the lower line of the rest catches the shooter around the jawbone and actually prevents good cheek contact. Any time you catch yourself having to tilt your head to the side in order to get to the sights this is probably what's happening. A cheek piece that is doing its job will be in even contact with the face from the lower part of the cheek up to the cheekbone.

Good target-rifle stocks, generally the custom jobs, usually have oversize cheek rests which are, in effect, more of a head cradle. Stylistically they are generally pretty awful, but a well-designed one keeps the head both comfortably and positively positioned for each shot. Over a string of twenty or more shots this can be a most valuable asset. Many top-rank target shooters, especially smallbore-prone specialists, check the cheek pieces on their rifles by firing at a target with the rear sight removed. If the cheek piece is properly shaped, and positions the shooter's head as it should, the eye itself becomes the rear sight. Thus by only aiming at the target through the front sight, amazingly small groups can be fired at 50 yards. If the shots are scattered it means that the cheek piece is not uniformly positioning the head shot after shot. In fact, the latest craze among target shooters is to slap a blob of resin putty on the comb of their stocks. Then while in shooting position, they mold the shape of their face into the semi-soft material. When the matrix hardens they have a super-positive head fixture.

RIFLE STOCKS AND ACCURACY

The most intriguing stock-related topic of modern times is the effect proper or improper wood-to-metal fit has on accuracy. This is a relatively new area of study, having come about only in the past couple of generations, and, as any accuracy buff will tell you, there is still a lot to be learned. I think it's interesting that wood-to-metal fit, or bedding, was not seriously looked upon as an accuracy factor before 1900 or thereabouts. Before then the chief ingredients were held to be bullets, loads, and, most of all, barrel quality. I'm sure that accuracy fans of the day appreciated nicely made and

A very neat and clean-cut stock inletting, as done by ace stockmaker Clayton Nelson of Enid, Oklahoma. The flat area around the guard-screw hole shows where the metal has been bearing flat and evenly. This stock is for a Winchester Model 70.

This stock, also for a Winchester Model 70, shows faulty inletting which can result in a twisted receiver and impaired accuracy. The blackened area shows where the receiver has been bearing, but over half of the bedding area does not appear to touch the metal at all.

fitted stocks and were well aware of the importance of at least having the wood snugly fitted to the rest of the mechanism. But even the legendary English gunmaker W. W. Greener, who held forth on virtually every gun-related subject in his book *The Gun and Its Development*, made no mention of stock bedding as an accessory to accuracy. But in that day both stocks and locks were thought as of being attached *to* the barrel—the principal unit. Now the barrel is attached to the receiver and it, in turn, is fastened *in* the stock, a substantial mechanical difference. Another significant difference is that back before powerful smokeless powders came into use the barrel was a more or less inert fixture. It provided a combustion chamber for the propellant and imparted spin to the bullet, but other than being pushed rearward by recoil was not affected in return. Or at least so the thinking went.

But when nitro powders and jacketed bullets arrived on the scene the situation was made vastly more complicated. Sharply rising pressures squeezing a bullet through the bore at high velocity cause a barrel to vibrate like a tuning fork. Just what these vibrations do to a bullet's flight, even if not fully understood, can be, and often is, highly evident. So evident, in fact, that ways and techniques of dealing with vibration have become a topic of major interest in recent years.

Since the barrel is attached to the receiver and the receiver fitted into the stock, the sequence of events, so far as bedding affects accuracy, begins with this basic wood-to-metal fit. The number-one key is that the position of the receiver not shift in relation to the wood, or, if it does, that it move exactly the same way every shot. (This second concept is fairly new and is discussed in the section on bench-rest stocks.) This is why such a premium is placed on close and tight stock inletting. The recoil and torqueing forces of a modern high-powered cartridge will cause the barreled action to move in the stock if the fitting is poor, and each succeeding bullet will take a somewhat different route to the target.

Tightness alone, it has been discovered, is not enough. You can lock an action in a stock so tight that it won't budge till doomsday, but it will still group like a scattergun if the metal-to-wood contact isn't even and free of stress. For various reasons a rifle will shoot poorly if the action is twisted or bent when the screws are pulled tight. Target shooters, especially bench-resters, have found that action flexing of less than a thousandth of an inch will enlarge group sizes. Flat-bottomed actions such as Mausers, Winchester Model 70s, Springfields, etc. must mate against dead-flat stock inletting surfaces with the recoil lug in full and square contact with the recoil shoulder. Round-bottomed actions such as the Savage 100, Remington Model 700, and Swedish FFV must nestle into inletting which prevents lateral movement but at the same time is not so squeeze-tight as to cause binding.

For a graphic illustration of how action bedding affects accuracy, straighten out a bobby pin and tightly wedge one end into a crack in a solid piece of wood. Now imagine that the protruding length of bobby pin is a rifle barrel, the wood is a stock, and the length of bobby pin stuck in the wood is the receiver. As you flip the bobby pin you'll notice that it gives off a certain musical tone or pitch. As long as it remains fast in the wood the pitch will remain the same. Now, pull the pin out of the crack somewhat, or push it in deeper, and vibrate it again. You'll notice that the pitch is somewhat different. Each time you readjust the bobby pin in the wood you'll find that it gives off a somewhat different tone.

Now, with this musical experience in mind, consider a rifle barrel. When the firing pin falls the sharp blow creates a shock wave which sets the barrel to vibrating. The primer explodes and sets off its own set of shock waves, and finally the bullet enters the barrel and creates a specific vibration which also modifies to some extent the vibrations started when the striker fell. With all this activity the barrel is humming like the bobby pin. The muzzle is whipping up and down, or sideways or some other angle, or possibly performing a pattern movement such as a figure-eight or oval. (Go back to the bobby pin and note the patterns described by the vibrating tip.) Obviously, since the muzzle is following a specific motion it "points" in any given direction only once, and for an immeasurable instant of time at that, during each cycle or complete movement. Sometime during that cycle the bullet will fly free of the barrel and speed toward the target. The exact angle of departure will, of course, depend on just which way the vibrating muzzle was pointing the instant the bullet came out. Obviously, if a rifle is to fire tight groups the barrel must be vibrating the same for each shot, and if things are really working right the bullet will tend to leave the barrel at about the same spot, or degree of arc, in the muzzle's cyclic motion. But in order for this to be possible the action must have retained perfectly uniform union with the stock. If the rifle's recoil caused the action to shift there will be a change in barrel vibration just the way the vibrating bobby pin changed tone when its position was shifted.

The so-called fiberglass or resin bedding materials which arrived with such a splash back in the 1950s, and have been very much on the shooting scene ever since, impart a higher degree of accuracy to a rifle than do most metal-to-wood bedding jobs simply because they hold the action firmly in place.

The next problem to be understood is just how much barrel control provides the best accuracy. Skilled stockmakers take great pride in their ability to inlet a barrel and action into wood so close that there is no gap whatever between the two. This means that the barrel is tightly held by the wood and does not vibrate freely. Thus the stockmaker exercises a certain control on the barrel's movement and resulting accuracy. If such inletting is done properly, the result can be even better accuracy than produced by the freely vibrating barrel, especially if it is a slender, hunting-weight barrel. But if it is not done properly, accuracy will go all to hell in a hurry. Control is usually exercised by inletting the barrel so that the tip of the forend pushes up with a few pounds' pressure and damps the tendency to vibrate. Going back to the faithful bobby pin, try vibrating it when you are touching it with a finger tip. The vibration is quickly arrested, you'll note, and the harder you press it with your finger the less it moves. This corresponds pretty closely to the way a barrel is controlled by forend pressure. Winchester used to control

A rather sophisticated means of controlling barrel vibrations is illustrated by this bedding mechanism which controls the exact pressure on the barrel. It can be adjusted to control the barrel vibrations for maximum accuracy and then readjusted as weather and climate conditions change the condition of the stock.

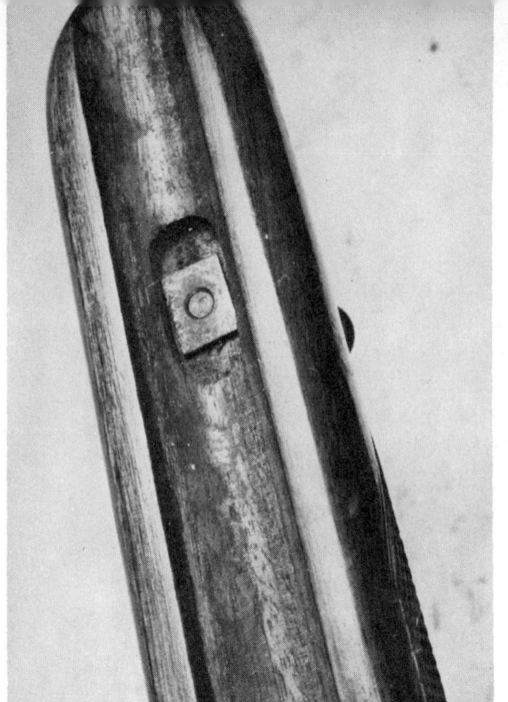

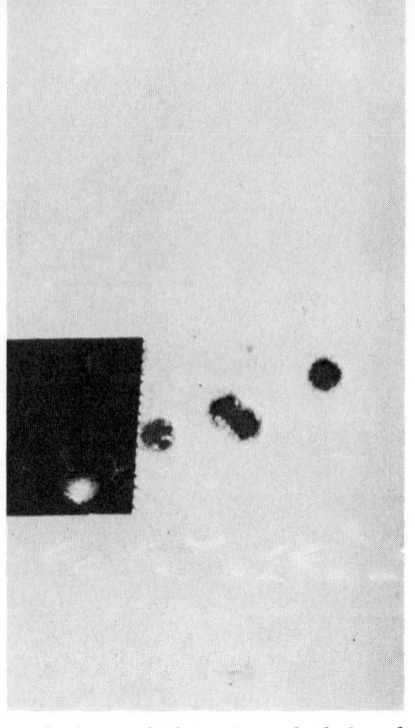

Just along the upper left side of this barrel channel there is a dark band which indicates that the barrel has been pressing hard against the stock. This type of uneven pressure on the barrel will result in horizontal or vertical stringing to the right (shown in the shot group) as the barrel heats up and expands.

the vibrations of their Model 70 barrels in similar fashion by means of a screw which pulled the barrel tightly against the forend. Quite often group sizes could be controlled simply by adjusting the tension of this screw until optimum barrel motion was discovered.

Sometimes barrel pressure gives superb accuracy over a string of several shots, but sometimes it doesn't. As the barrel heats and expands it may press harder against the forend and actually flex itself upward somewhat. This accounts for the familiar vertical shot stringing or "walking" on target when each shot hits a bit higher than the one before. When the stock pressure is not straight up but somewhat from the side, we get angular stringing. Usually, though, walking due to a hot barrel is no problem in a hunting rifle because the first three or four quick shots will go to the same point of impact. When the barrel cools it will, *or should,* return to its normal point of impact. Sometimes hunters make the mistake of shooting a rifle in an overheated condition when sighting in before a big hunt. When the barrel cools the point of impact then becomes lower than the hunter has sighted for.

A worse condition occurs when the rifle has forend pressure and a loose or poorly bedded action. With each shot the action shifts in the stock, never to return, and there is a corresponding alteration of forend pressure. This often accounts for wide target groups with little or no tendency of the bullets to hit anywhere near the same place twice.

This vertical stringing, progressing from bottom to top, is typical of a barrel with too much stock pressure from the underside. As the barrel heats up after a couple of shots, the shots begin to "walk" vertically.

Another problem of the forend-pressure bedding system arises from the nature of wood itself. It can shrink, expand, or warp in different weather conditions and thus significantly affect the rifle's point of impact. This usually accounts for change in zero over a period of time and is one of the best explanations of all of why it is necessary to check your rifle's zero before every hunting trip.

Most target shooters and accuracy buffs avoid the perils of barrel bedding entirely by the so-called "free-floating" technique. As the phrase implies, a free-floating barrel is completely untouched by the stock and is attached to the receiver only, or with only an inch or two of stock support just ahead of the receiver. Though this system doesn't always give best accuracy with

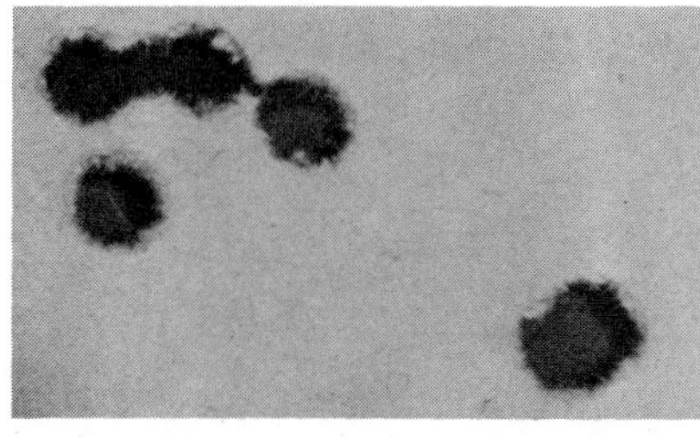

A more insidious type of barrel misbehavior is illustrated by this tight four-shot group with a fifth shot pitched far to the right. This can be caused by uneven locking-lug contact but usually boils down to a basic receiver-bedding problem.

lightweight barrels, which may tend to vibrate erratically, it's great for heavy target barrels and assures a high degree of day-in and day-out accuracy. All of my target rifles are free-floating and so are about half of my varmint rifles, especially those with the heavier barrels. A free-floating barrel doesn't guarantee fine accuracy, not by a long shot, but if a target rifle isn't performing as it should at least you know it isn't the barrel bedding.

As a closely followed rule of thumb I prefer free-floating barrels on target or high-performance varmint barrels and stick to closely inletted barrels on choice hunting rifles. After all, super-close inletting is a skill approaching an art, and when I own a custom rifle by a top stockmaker I want the best possible example of his craftsmanship.

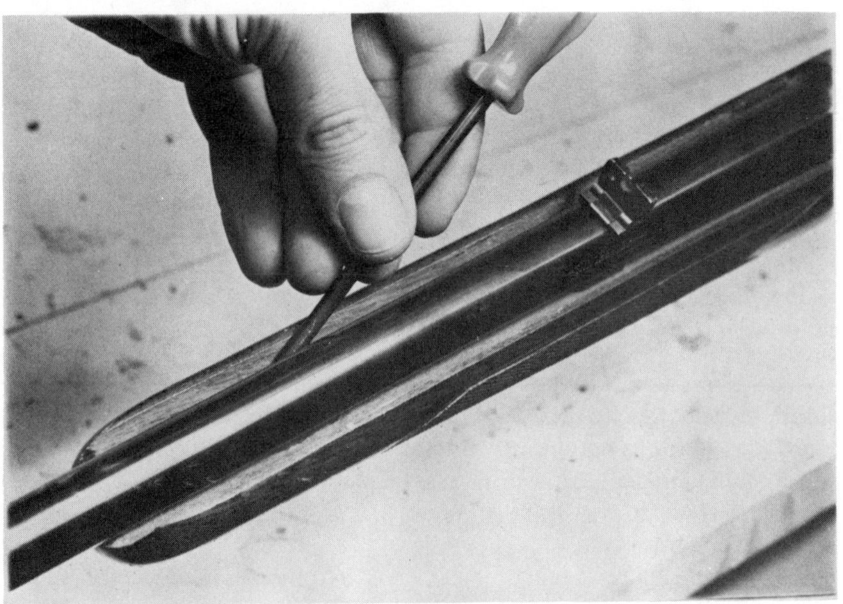

This is carrying the free-floating barrel idea to a ridiculous extreme. This Model 70 Winchester has been hogged out around the barrel until there is about a quarter inch gap all the way around. Nothing was gained by this exercise except ruining the appearance and value of the rifle.

Apparently quite a few riflemen feel the same way I do. Back in 1964 when Winchester introduced their revamped Model 70, one of the most touted features was a "free-floating" barrel. And free-floated it was—with the barrel channel chopped out big enough for a drainage pipe. It may have been an aid to accuracy as they claimed, but aesthetically it was a total flop. The whole idea earned such poor marks among shooters that it was abandoned and Model 70s once again have neatly inletted barrels.

Quite often I get mail from *Outdoor Life* readers indicating that the accuracy of some particular rifle is not what they would like it to be and asking if glass-bedding the action or free-floating the barrel, or both, will help reduce group sizes. This is always a tough question because without watching the rifle perform there isn't much way to judge what, if anything, is causing the trouble. Actually, I'm of the opinion that the benefits of both glass-bedding and floating barrels for *sporter weight* rifles have been somewhat overpraised. They are certainly not a blanket cure for all accuracy ills, and I take a jaundiced view of gunsmiths who habitually recommend one or both "cures" for every sickly rifle that comes their way. A gunsmith who knows something about bedding can, nine times out of ten, pinpoint the trouble area and take corrective action without resorting to glass or gouging out the barrel channel, and usually at less expense to the rifle owner.

Free-floating a barrel is a one-way street, for once a neatly inletted barrel channel is hogged out it can never be as pretty as it once was. Glass-bedding an action, if properly done, doesn't harm the appearance of a rifle but, contrary to common notion, it *can* cause its own accuracy impairment. Any experienced bench-rest shooter will tell you that glass-bedding an action can be a tricky operation. Sometimes the job has to be repeated two or three times before it is right. Also—and this may come as a surprise—some of the resin bedding compounds shrink, or warp in time and destroy accuracy. One brand that is fairly popular with bench shooters lasts only about six months, or less, before the bedding goes sour. The precision shooters are aware of this and take the philosophical view that every few months a rebedding job will be in order whether they like it or not.

So, before rushing into a glass-bedding or free-floating job it's a smart move to first determine, if only for the sake of curiosity, what's causing the poor grouping. I wonder how many rifles have been rebedded when the only problem to begin with was a couple of loose action screws. . . .

The all-time classic dumb move in this direction was the subject of a feature article in a shooting magazine a few years ago. The author, who apparently was, or is, an amateur gunsmith, described how he bought himself a varmint rifle, a Remington Model 700 in .22/250 as I recall, and without so much as a single accuracy test proceeded to glass-bed the action, chop out the barrel channel, and perform similar other "sophisticated" tricks of the trade. He explained that there was no need to test the rifle's accuracy beforehand because he was going to make such improvements that it wouldn't matter anyhow. But how does one make an improvement if he doesn't know what he's improving upon? For all he knows the rifle may have been capable of ¼-inch groups as it came out of the box and his so-called improvements did nothing but decrease accuracy by about 300 percent.

The point, of course, is that it's a good idea to look and think before getting carried away with any grandiose (and expensive) bedding projects. Remember that vibrating bobby pin; just a tiny alteration can completely change its tune.

STOCK WOODS AND OTHER MATERIALS

Century after century the favored wood for gunsmiths has been walnut. There are various types of walnut, from many different places around the world, each with its own characteristic qualities which may make it more or less suitable for stocks. But considered as a whole, no other wood combines the virtues of strength, stability, lightness, workability, and beauty as does walnut. Small wonder that walnut is the standard by which all other stock woods or substitutes are compared.

In recent years the price of good (or even poor) walnut has spiraled, and there may even come a time when the cost makes it impractical for all but the most expensive rifles. Already many manufacturers are marketing guns stocked with various walnut substitutes. Birch, pine, maple, beech, sycamore, and mahogany, for example, are coming into increasingly wider use, and even man-made materials such as the resin plastics are earning acceptance for certain types of stocks. But more about these later.

Occasionally we read articles about the various properties of gunstock woods which list, usually in graphics or comparative ranking, such qualities as hardness, tensile strength, density, machinability, etc. At best these serve as only the roughest sort of evaluation. They may say, for instance, that French walnut is lighter per cubic foot than American black walnut. But French walnut itself varies tremendously in density and hardness. It may be as stringy as ash or as pithy as pine. Some blanks can be as hard as oak while others slice as easily as cheese. The point here is to caution the reader against making any hard-and-fast assumption from the following general descriptions. French walnut may *generally* be better for rifle stocks than American walnut, but I've seen $50 French-walnut blanks that wouldn't make as good a rifle stock as a $5 stick of Missouri bottomland black walnut.

Black Walnut

Good old *Juglans nigra,* black walnut, has been America's number-one stock-making material ever since the first gunsmith to reach these shores sank a chisel in the close-grained, richly colored wood. Though the tight-grained, clean-cutting characteristics of walnut make it one of the best woods for gunstocks, when you get right down to cases it's the warm, rich beauty of the wood that has made it such a favorite.

The variety of color, density, texture, figure, and grain structure within the species *Juglans nigra* all but defies description. A textbook on trees, for example, would describe it as a straight-grained dark-brown hardwood. But sometimes the grain ripples like waves of grain dancing in a breeze or rolls itself into tight curls. And the colors, sometimes within a single tree, may vary all the way from deep chocolate to ivory white with countless hues of brown, tan, and amber reds in between. It can be as soft as pine and as coarse-grained as oak, or so hard as to challenge the sharpest chisel and as fine-grained as bone.

The black walnut usually seen on rifles is pretty straight-grained. This is because the main trunk generally grows quite high before forking or branching and the stump is seldom salvaged. This causes a high yield of straight-grained lumber. And too, a straight, or nearly straight, grain structure has long been held to be the strongest and most warp-resistant. But the crotch or stump cuts of black walnut can display an incredibly varied and beautiful grain structure. This is why some shooters sometimes find it difficult to believe that the nearly black wood on the M-1 Garand they carried in World War II or Korea could have come from the same tree that produced the breathtakingly lovely stock on a $5,000 Model 21 Winchester shotgun.

Likewise, most folks do not have much chance to see the terrific variety of colors of "black" walnut. Most major firearms manufacturers stain their stocks to a more or less uniformly dark shade. Their feeling is that shooters are accustomed to dark-toned stocks and a potential buyer might reject one of a lighter color. Sometime when you happen to have the stock removed from a rifle or shotgun you'll probably notice that the inside is several shades lighter than the outside. Furnituremakers, by the way, do the same thing for the same reasons. "After all," they say, "walnut has to *look* like walnut."

It would be difficult to form even a rough estimate of the number of black-walnut rifle stocks made over the years. The military stocks alone, beginning with the first Harpers Ferry models and continuing through the Springfield Model 1861, the trap door, Krag and '03 Springfields, Garands, and finally the M-14, number in the many millions. Add to these the many millions more sporters and the number becomes incalculable. Sooner or later, it would seem, the supply of this magnificent wood would begin to run low. And it has. Also, as the supplies dwindle there is occurring stiff competition from other areas of consumption. Furnituremakers take a big percentage of the annual cut, and another big chunk is exported to veneer-making firms.

This has resulted in an out-and-out shortage at times and a steady increase in price. When I visited the Remington plant at Ilion, New York, in the fall of 1974 their walnut supply was at such a low ebb that some workers voiced fears that the manufacturing line would be temporarily shut down. Of course walnut can always be found—but invariably at a higher price. In fact, the increased price of walnut has had a lot to do with the spiraling prices of rifles in recent years.

A few generations ago there was a saying among the landed gentry: "Plant a hundred walnut trees when a lad is born and they'll pay for his college education." The day is close at hand when a mere half-dozen of the wonderful trees will pay for a sheepskin.

Much is made of the way black walnut inlets, finishes, and checkers as compared to French walnut. Generally speaking, the black walnut is not so tight-grained as French walnut and will not take fine-lined checkering as well. In fact, most of the black walnut used for commercial-grade rifles is the very cheapest grade with very large and open pores. By and large, about the finest line checkering this grade wood will take without the diamonds chipping is about twenty lines to the inch. BUT! Some of the densest, smallest-grained walnut I've ever seen was black walnut.

A few years ago when master stockmaker Al Biesen was visiting with me for a few days we dropped into a local gun store that carries a fairly large stock of blanks and semi-finished stocks. As is his custom Al poked through the wood while I turned my attention elsewhere. In a few moments he was tugging at my sleeve. "Psst," he whispered, as if he'd just discovered a hidden treasure, "come look at this blank."

It was one of the old-fashioned semi-inletted blanks with only a small amount of undersize inletting and no outside shaping at all other than a roughly rounded profile. The surface was blackened from handling by many sweaty hands but I saw what he meant. In addition to a beautiful crotch feather lacing across the butt section and smoky clouds of reds, purples, and gold gliding across a tawny feathered background, the pores in the wood were so tiny as to be almost invisible. It was not only one of the best sticks of black walnut I'd ever set my eyes on but one of the best of *any* type of wood.

"Are you going to buy it?" I asked Al.

"I'm overstocked on wood already, and besides, I don't use semi-finished stocks like this. But someone who loves beautiful wood *should* buy it."

The stock now reposes in my gun cabinet on a custom .35 Whelen. The checkering pattern is a tiny twenty-eight lines to the inch and is as crisp as cut glass.

French Walnut

The highbrow name for French walnut is *Juglans regia,* which means "royal walnut." In the opinion of most professional stockmakers and other such experts on stock woods this is the more fitting title because it is unquestionably the royalty of stock materials. And, as it just so happens, it didn't originate in France anyway.

The wood we commonly refer to as "French" walnut is a native of the ancient empire of Persia, the land now known as Iran. In the thirteenth century, no less a wanderer than Marco Polo, en route home from a visit to China, became intrigued with the tasty nuts of the Persian trees and brought a crop back to Italy. Later, descendants of these trees were planted in the British Isles. This is why the nuts of "French" walnut trees are called "English" walnuts: The same tasty, easy-to-crack nuts so popular around Christmastime.

According to Joe Oakley, the well-known Sacramento, California, supplier of choice stock blanks and a leading authority on the trees from which they are cut, the walnut trees which were eventually planted over much of Europe were of British stock.

In France there developed the delightful custom of presenting new brides a gift of mature walnut trees. The newlywed couple, in turn, would plant more walnut trees which in time would be gifts at the weddings of their granddaughters. These trees were raised for their wood rather than the nuts. In fact, branching limbs were pollarded (cut off) in order to promote the growth of the trunk. In time France produced so much of the beautiful wood that it became known as French walnut. Sadly, some of France's prime growing area for the walnuts was also the scene of heavy bombardment during the World Wars and many of the groves were destroyed.

The next adventure in the odyssey of the great Persian walnut trees was their immigration to the New World. Northern California proved an espe-

These stock blanks, all from the Pachmayr Gun Works in Los Angeles, California, show the variety of figure, texture, and color contrast of California English walnut. Despite popular impression, California "English" walnut, French walnut, Circassian walnut, etc., are all the same species.

cially happy new home for the trees, and nut-producing groves were planted. Since nuts were the purpose of the California plantings the trees were once again known as *English* walnuts.

Many English-nut groves in California were actually started by grafting English-walnut cuttings into Claro-walnut seedlings. The Claro root system is better adapted to the California soil and promotes more rapid tree growth. Occasionally one sees rifle stocks which exhibit a peculiar color and grain variation where the grafted wood grew together. Generally speaking, though, these trees do not result in especially good stock wood. This is because they were heavily watered and fertilized in an effort to promote growth and nut production. The best California "English" stock blanks come from original nut plantings. These are exactly the same trees variously

This rich, cloudy or "smoky" texture is typical of the best California English walnut. The stock is by Pachmayr.

known the world over as French, Italian, European, Circassian, Turkish Circassian, etc., walnut. However the very best native American "French" stock blanks come from very old trees, and these are becoming increasingly hard to find. Here of late I've seen blanks from some of these choice old trees sell for as high as $500, which is as much as the finest imported French or Circassian walnut will fetch.

Interestingly, despite these spectacular prices the European wood merchants aren't in any rush to supply the gunstock market. In fact, the fine European walnut stocks which elicit admiring oohs and aahs from lovers of fine shootery are most usually second-grade stuff. The really prime blanks are used for veneer. In order to get an idea how breathtaking the best of the best can be you'll have to look at some of the arms made for the European nobility a century or two ago. These are most usually found in museums. I usually get to New York on an average of two or three times a year. On at least one of these sojourns I'll hightail it to the Metropolitan Museum of

Art for a few hours just to admire their collection of magnificent guns. Some of the walnut used in these masterpieces is utterly unbelievable. If such woods were to be offered in stock-blank form today the price might easily run to several thousand dollars. That's why it winds up as veneer.

French walnut, or whatever you want to call it, comes in a fantastic variety of colors and grain patterns. Unlike American black walnut, French walnut is graded more on the basis of coloration than fancy figure. The most expensive blanks are those which have a deeply contrasting smoky or "marblecake" color effect with dark lines and clouds overlying a tawny to reddish background. Some aficionados of fine stock woods prefer a rich coloration in connection with some fiddleback figure, but here of late, I've noticed, some purists look on figure as somewhat vulgar and "overshowy" and pay their top dollars on the basis of color texture only. By and large, in my observation, California English tends to a lighter coloration, running from a medium tan to almost ivory lightness. This gives the dark, sometimes almost black, marblecake clouds more contrast and creates a very striking effect. European-grown wood tends to run darker in color, with the best blanks a glowing reddish hue. Since the marblecake effect of European wood is not usually so richly contrasted, they tend to put more emphasis on figure. But, as I pointed out earlier, these are the most general of guidelines. I've seen California English that glowed with the amber richness of prewar Russian Circassian wood, and I've seen Italian and Yugoslavian walnut with all the "spilled ink on parchment" staining of wood cut in northern California.

If by some slipup of nature *Juglans regia* had not been blessed with its exotic beauty it would still be a favorite of stockmakers. Everything that makes a piece of wood good for stockmaking seems to have come together in the one species. Such a dense, close-grained wood, for example, would be expected to be a chore to cut with a carving chisel. But not so; instead, cutting prime French stock wood has been likened to cutting cheese. That doesn't mean it's as soft as cheese but that a sharp tool slices into the wood with a minimum of grain cracking and splitting. With a spoon gouge, for instance, the stockmaker can bite into the wood at a sharp angle to the grain direction, take a deep cut, and then push the tool up "the other side of the hill" with little risk of the chip splintering or splitting out. Also, the tight grain of good French walnut does not tend to influence the direction of cut as much as other woods. This makes extremely precise inletting possible. Likewise, the dense grain lends strength to vulnerable corners such as sharp edges around the inletting. This reduces the risk of splintering and makes the metal-to-wood fit sharp and clean. Therein, by the way, lies part of the secret of the super-close inletting done by our best stockmakers: they use the best, cleanest-cutting wood.

The next great feature of French walnut becomes apparent when you lay into it with file or rasp. With only moderate pressure of a rasp it seems to dissolve into fine powder. It isn't likely to choke up a rasp or lead a chisel astray. Also, the sanding operation is considerably less onerous than with most other types of wood.

The natural beauty of good French walnut is enhanced by the way it accepts finish. Open-grained woods tend to absorb large amounts of finish, which has a darkening and somewhat dulling effect. French walnut, with its tiny pores, requires fewer applications of finish material to fill the grain. This is why it is often said of French walnut that it has a "glow all its own." In other words, the natural color and clarity of the wood is not obscured by an excessively thick layer of finish. It is one of the very few woods that can be decently finished with linseed oil only.

From the checkerer's standpoint, French walnut is the most agreeable of woods. Its smooth-cutting character makes it possible to bring the diamonds up to sharp, cleanly cut pyramids, and the close grain permits tinier diamonds than do most other woods.

Bastogne Walnut

One of the least known but most interesting of stock woods is the so-called Bastogne or Bastonian hybrid. Years ago the great horticulturist Luther Burbank created an exceptionally fast-growing hybrid tree by crossing the native Claro walnut of California with the English-walnut strain. He called the plant "Paradox Walnut." Nuts from this tree seldom mature and will not grow if planted. Thus the hybrid became known as a bastard tree, or more delicately, Bastogne.

These trees grow so fast that it's not unusual to find growth rings as wide as 2 inches. Joe Oakley, who pioneered the use of Bastogne wood for stocks, once cut one of this species that was over 6 feet in diameter and weighed 28 tons! He also says that every Bastogne he has cut had very thick sap wood, as much as 8 inches, so it's possible to cut a very fine quartersawn blank entirely of sapwood.

Despite its fast growth rate the wood is hard and strong and is becoming especially popular among stockmakers for stocking rifles in the heavy magnum calibers. The recoil of these big bruisers often splits stocks of softer woods and causes all sorts of frustrations. A few years back I stocked a .458 Winchester Magnum with a beautiful piece of Bastogne, the first I'd ever seen. To date the rig has accounted for a mixed bag of about a dozen Cape buffalo, elephant, and lion and still looks brand-new. The hard wood also resists the battering of helpful, but not always gentle, African hands better than any I know of.

The coloration is much like that of its parent Claro and there is usually a considerable amount of fiddleback figuration, but the physical characteristics seem to be largely inherited from the English parentage. Unfortunately, Bastonians are among the rarest of American trees. Since they grow fast but do not produce a nut crop most plantings have been for shade purposes. They make beautiful shade trees and are usually considered too valuable to be felled. Therefore the demand will continue to exceed the supply and prices will strain all but the most affluent pocketbooks. It seems to me that enterprising youths could provide for a very comfortable retirement by setting out a grove of these beautiful hybrids.

I have one more beautiful Bastogne blank, a tawny yellow with ebony streaks running through it and an even fiddleback curl from one end to the other. I bought it from Joe Oakley a few years ago and immediately turned it over to ace stockmaker Al Biesen. One of these days he's going to shape it into one of his peerless masterpieces, probably for one of the big Fred Wells custom magnums chambered for something like a .460 Weatherby Magnum case necked out to .50 caliber.

Claro Walnut

This beautiful wood is an honest native American and was first discovered northeast of Chico, California, around 1840. It is a true species of walnut botanically known as *Juglans hindsii,* and sometimes called Hinds walnut.

The coloration is usually of a notably reddish cast with sharp contrasts of color, running from yellow to black with even a purplish tinting. Quite a few of the more expensive rifles and shotguns imported from Japan and Europe are in fact stocked with Claro wood. Weatherby rifles, for example, are usually stocked with Claro, and so are some Brownings, most notably their new Model 78 single-shot centerfire rifle.

Claro walnut trees tend to fork close to the ground, and this results in a higher percentage of crotch figure than is found in other species of walnut.

The abrupt change in the texture of this stock blank is where an English walnut cutting was drafted into a Claro walnut stump.

Also it tends toward a higher percentage of fiddleback figure. For sheer vibrance and depth of figure, especially the fiddleback curl, probably no other wood can match it.

Early settlers in California planted quite a few Claro trees in the areas of what are now known as Chico, Napa, and Walnut Hill. Interestingly, however, it took Americans a long time to realize the wood's gunstocking possibilities. Long before this occurred, in fact, Europeans were importing vast amounts of the California-grown product to be made into veneers. Between the two wars as much as 2,000 tons of the beautiful wood were being shipped each year. Today the yearly export ranges from 1,500 to 2,500 tons, and suppliers predict that the trees will be all but gone by 1985. Paradoxically, much of the beautiful European veneer is imported back into the U.S. I wonder how many American buyers of these expensive veneers have any inkling that the strikingly colored and figured "European" walnut was grown in the Sacramento Valley of California.

Despite its color and often spectacular figure, most stockmakers have mixed feelings about Claro. It often tends to be brittle and stringy and would rather split than slice. Also, one occasionally hears the charge leveled that Claro tends to loose its color over a period of time and a once richly textured stock might become dull and lifeless. I've seen this happen, but I have my own theory as to the cause. Since Claro tends to be rather coarse-grained it absorbs large amounts of stock finish. As these stock-finishing chemicals dull with time they also dull the wood. A linseed-oil finish, for example, is especially dulling to Claro. The most successful finishes for Claro seem to be the clear space-age varnishes and synthetics, which tend to remain bright for a long time.

Even though the supply of Claro, like all walnut, is diminishing at a heart-rending rate, it is still *relatively* inexpensive in blank form. For a $100 bill you can still get a brilliantly colored and figured piece of Claro and expect some change back too. I can't recall ever seeing a rifle stocked in Claro before 1940, but here of late it's showing up all over the place. Therefore, it can honestly be called the most modern of stock woods.

Maple

Back in Colonial days, maple shared equal billing with walnut as a material for beautiful rifle stocks. Though sundry varieties of maple are found throughout the Northern Hemisphere it is the North American sugar maple and silver maple that first caught on as prize stock wood. European varieties such as the Norway maple tend to be more ornamental shrubbery types than larger lumber-yielding trees suitable for stocks. Thus it is reasonable to suppose that the hard tight-grained wood had never been used for stocks, at least in any quantity, until European immigrants settled on these shores. Maple was abundant in what is now the Northeastern states, and there is no doubt that the early gunsmiths were enchanted with the beautiful grain aberration known as curly or fiddleback. When properly stained the curly grain flashes and flickers like a cozy fire, so much so that it is also known as "flame grain." At any rate the beautiful curl of this rare type is so strikingly distinctive that it has become as much of a symbol of early American rifles as long barrels or fancy brass patchboxes.

Plain, straight-grained maple is occasionally used for stocks, especially on target jobs or magnum-caliber sporters when a high degree of stability or strength is desired and weight is not a factor, but usually it is used in its more ornamental forms. The most common of these are "birdseye," which features a heavy concentration of tiny, speckled knots or curls; "shell" or "quilted" figure, which is caused by an irregular grain pattern; and the popular "fiddleback," also known as "flame grain," "tiger stripe," "curly," etc., which results from a wavy grain. When maple is stained the coloring agent is readily absorbed by the grain fibers which have an exposed cross section. The portion of the curl which lies flat, or lengthwise to the surface, is less absorbent and does not color as well. This creates alternating light and dark bands running at more or less right angles to the direction of the grain. Depending on how the light reflects from the surface, the curl seems to ripple up and down the length of the stock. Another way of finishing figured maple

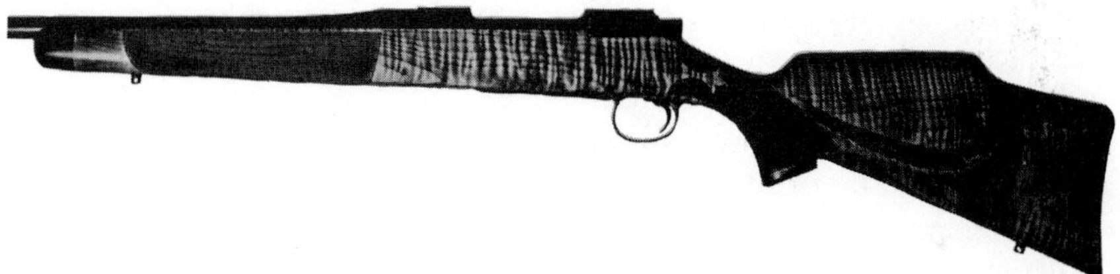

This is an especially fine piece of curly, or fiddleback, maple. The stock is by Hal Hartley of Lenore, North Carolina, a specialist in maple stocks. The rich figure contrast is brought out by lightly scorching the surface of the wood with a blowtorch.

is the so-called *Suigi* technique. A fairly intense flame, such as a blowtorch, is played over the surface just enough to scorch and brown the exposed "end grain" on each side of the curl. The flat part of the curl, being more protected, does not scorch as quickly and the result is a series of dark-brown to black tiger-tail stripes alternating with straw-colored bands. Done properly by such maple specialists as Hal Hartley of Lenore, North Carolina, the effect is very striking indeed.

The exact influence that causes the grain in some maple trees to curl is something of a mystery. I've been told that a tree growing on rocky, shifting soil will develop a curly figure because it is constantly shifting. In truth, though, it is a rare phenomenon which may be genetically linked. A tree in the center of a maple grove may develop a curly grain while all those around it are normally grained. Some experts, I understand, can judge if a maple tree will have a curly grain by inspecting the bark, but mostly the secret is kept until the log reaches the sawmill.

Back when I was making quite a few "Kentucky" rifles I had to scout the surrounding hills and mountains for nicely grained maple. My technique was to peel a small section of bark from a likely-looking tree and take a look at the underlying grain. If the grain was figured enough for good long-rifle stocks I'd look up the landowner and we'd make a deal.

Like walnut, maple is likely to occur in various hardnesses, which affect its checkerability. Though usually close-grained enough to checker nicely, the wood has a fibrous texture which tends to fuzz up in the checkering so that the diamonds do not have a polished, clean-cut look. The old master's trick for handling this problem is to coat the finished checkering with a hard-drying epoxy finish or even model-airplane glue. This freezes the fibers in place and allows them to be cleanly sliced off with a pass of the checkering tool.

Mahogany

Despite its popularity for fine furniture, mahogany has never had much appeal for gunstocks. Its rich, reddish color is nice enough, but by and large both the grain and color are too even and monotonous. Also, the grain is rather coarse for fine checkering and the natural brittleness of the wood makes close inletting difficult.

However, it has been used for gunstocks from time to time and here of late has been getting quite a bit of attention. Being lighter than walnut, and also quite stable, mahogany stocks are showing up at bench-rest tournaments on the Sporter and Light Varmint classes of rifle. The weight limit, with scope, is 10½ pounds for these rifles, and some shooters have discovered that they can save vital ounces by using mahogany. Also, in this same vein, Remington is using mahogany for their special lightweight-grade shotguns. Very likely these uses will create a trend toward wider use of mahogany for rifle stocks, especially as walnut becomes more and more expensive.

Other Hardwoods

Sycamore is another wood that we'll be seeing more and more of in coming years. Like mahogany, birch, beech, etc., it is not as good an all-around stock wood as walnut but is being seriously considered as walnut becomes harder to come by. It is a tough, rather dense wood which is somewhat lighter in weight than walnut. The coloration is a thin lemon brown but the grain can be quite attractive. When properly sawed and laid out the grain has an intricate pattern looking like overlaid ovals. This is where it gets its other name, lacewood. It is also called Am-Wal by some of its promoters.

Cherry is another really fine stock wood but is in generally short supply and will never have much effect on rifle-stocking trends. Like apple and pear, two other surprisingly good stock woods, cherry is sometimes found with a fiddleback figure that rivals the best maple. By the way, some of those curly-maple stocks admired on antique "Kentucky" rifles are not maple at all, but cherry or pear.

Myrtle, a product of the Pacific Northwest, is a gunstock wood that creates all sorts of emotions in stockmakers. If asked if they ever made a myrtle stock many will say, "Yes, once. But never again. . . ." The wood can be strikingly beautiful, with rich coloration and a generous assortment of curl or fiddleback. Also, when properly dried it is quite warp-resistant. But in my experience it is a rather mushy wood that does not cut cleanly or take well to holding sharp, well-detailed edges. Likewise, checkering tends to be fuzzy and extremely delicate. This is why a comparatively high percentage of myrtlewood stocks have carved rather than checkered patterns. Another objectionable characteristic of the wood is that its pithiness makes it highly absorbent. This means that oil-type finishes keep soaking into the wood and making it darker and darker. This is avoided by using surface-hardening finishes such as the modern plastic varnishes. The problem here, though, is that this type of finish has a bright glassy look which many shooters find objectionable. The heyday of the myrtlewood stock occurred during the decade of the 1960s and thereabouts, when wildly radical stock designs featuring extreme rollover cheek pieces, teardrop grip caps, etc. were in vogue. This school of stock design went hand in hand with the striking figure and coloration of good myrtle and glassy finishes. Today's emphasis on more classic, or conservative, stocks will no doubt decrease interest in myrtle. Its chief hope of increased popularity, as I see it, would be a pricing situation which would make it less expensive than walnut.

There are all sorts of other woods of which rifle stocks have, can be, are, and will be made. These include rosewood, mesquite, yama, monkeypod, koa, madrone, sassafras, persimmon, and others. None of these offers any notable rifle-stocking advantages. They are almost always used just for the novelty of it. Therefore, none is really relevant to present or future rifle manufacture.

Laminated Wood

Stocks of laminated woods are very much a product of modern rifle development, especially in the pursuit of accuracy. Since about 1950 various laminations of walnut, maple, cherry, birch, and other woods have become commonplace on the target line and, as a matter of fact, not too uncommon in the field.

The first mass use of laminated stocks that I know of was on some German Mausers used during World War II. The laminations are so thin (about 1/16 inch thick) that the lines where they were glued together look a lot like ordinary wood grain. The next time you look at a Mauser that has a light-colored stock that looks like pine, take a closer look and it will probably turn out to be one of the laminated beech jobs. Though the leading advantage of laminated stocks, in today's viewpoint, is extreme stability, the Germans were mainly trying to keep costs down by laminating a cheap, easily available wood. Also, turning a stock from a slab-sided blank results in a wastage of about 10 percent. But if the laminations are preshaped before glueing together (*not* just turned to shape from a laminated blank) the resulting scrap loss is considerably less.

I doubt if much thought was given to the potential accuracy advantage of these laminated stocks but they proved to be especially strong and resistant to moisture and other weather extremes.

More recently, Remington had a fling with laminated wood in the stocking of their Model 660 Magnum Carbine. This stubby bolt gun, which came in 6.5mm and .350 Remington Magnum chamberings, featured a stock made up of thick laminations of beech and walnut. The rifle didn't catch on and neither did the cartridges, so the model was dropped.

Foremost among the advantages of laminated stocks is their resistance to accuracy-destroying warpage. A single piece of wood may have a characteristic of bending and twisting as moisture leaves or enters the grain structure. In a rifle stock this can have a disastrous effect if the shifting wood alters the bedding contact or creates uneven pressure on the barrel. Laminated wood divides this warping tendency into small portions and pits the warping of one relatively small piece of wood against the strength of several others. Or, in other words, if one of the wood layers in a laminated stock wants to warp it is prevented from doing so by its neighbors. Even if *all* the layers try to warp they are pulling against each other.

Every bigbore target rifle in my battery except one is stocked with laminated walnut. These stocks are hardly what you'd call pretty, but they're pretty to me because they get the job done and don't warp and go sour from one season to the next. Laminated stocks for target, varmint, or even sporter rigs are easy to come by and are offered in a variety of styles and patterns, either finished, semi-finished, or in blanks, by such stock companies as Reinhart Fajen of Warsaw, Missouri, and Bishop Inc., also of Warsaw. Some of the best target stocks available are from Jim Cloward of Seattle, Washington, and most of his stocks are laminated. Such custom and semi-custom firms as Ed Shilen, who makes some of the world's most accurate rifles, and the Ranger Arms Company furnish laminated walnut stocks on their rifles if the customer so orders.

Also, there have been a fair number of laminated stocks made for purely decorative effect. These are most usually thin laminations of alternating light- and dark-colored woods which give a highly unusual color pattern. The more contours a stock has the wilder the effect, so, by and large, the super-radical stock configurations with excessively rolled-over cheek pieces and shovel-shaped teardrop pistol grips are often made of two-tone laminations. The overall results are more or less a psychedelic nightmare. The accuracy qualities of laminated wood used this way are, needless to say, about nil, because as a rule these rifles are made for looking at only and can't hit an outhouse at forty rods.

I'd say there is a fairly good possibility that laminated stocks will become more common on consumer-grade (factory-built) rifles in the not too distant future. Most likely these will first be seen on top-of-the-line target models and perhaps the top-flight varmint rigs. These will, in my opinion, be readily accepted by the buying public because "accuracy is beautiful" is fast becoming an accepted truism in modern rifle merchandising, and the accuracy advantage of laminated wood is widely known.

In time, the use of laminated wood may become fairly common on field-grade hunting rifles. This will depend on how well the idea catches hold on the target lines. But if laminated stocks do make a big splash with the accuracy lines, the promotional advantages for their use on hunting rifles is obvious. Why would a manufacturer want to use laminated wood for a hunting model? The answer is simply that they could be *cheaper*. Already laminated-walnut blanks are made up of either scraps of wood or the softest, grainiest grades. As the price of good solid-walnut blanks continues to go up there will no doubt come a time—soon—when scrap-made laminates are cheaper. Also, the move will be toward fabricated laminates, not just turning the stocks from laminated blanks.

Another type of composition wood stocks occasionally seen is made up of small slices of wood bonded together. Whereas plain laminated wood is made of narrow sheets pressed and glued together, the hardwood chip material is made up of thin slices 1 or 2 inches square pressed together and held fast in a resin bond. Such stocks have virtually no grain characteristic whatever and are extremely stable. The large volume of glue used, however, makes them pretty heavy and so far they've been used almost exclusively on unrestricted bench rifles.

Undoubtedly we'll be seeing other forms of laminates and "composition" woods in the coming years. Most, of course, will prove unacceptable for rifle stocks either because they can't get the job done or because rifle buyers won't cotton to them. But a few will make the grade. There's probably a laminated stock in your future.

Synthetic Stock Materials

Until now we've been talking exclusively about wood as a material for rifle stocks. But what about other materials? Will there ever come a time when walnut and similar woods become so scarce or expensive that man-made synthetics will have to be used? Or could it be possible that synthetics might prove more suitable and thus more desirable than wood? Actually, in some specialized instances this latter possibility is becoming a distinct reality.

During World War II the Germans tried a few plastic stocks for their Mausers, but either they got started too late or the project didn't work out well. The first commercial use of a non-wooden stock that I can recall was on some Stevens guns just after World War II. Their Model 530M double-barrel, Model 124 autoloading shotguns, and .22–.410 combination gun were equipped with stocks of walnut-colored plastic. The plastic wasn't very well received by shooters and tended, as I recall, to break too easily (probably especially in cold weather), so the firm switched back to wood.

The first commercially successful use of a non-wood stock was the Remington Model 66 .22 rimfire autoloader. This stock, made of tough, resilient nylon, was introduced toward the tail end of the 1950s and created quite a

Are plastic or various fiberglass and resin compounds the stock material of the future? They certainly have a lot to offer in the way of accuracy, as bench rest shooters have proved during the past few years. Also, at least one major U.S. manufacturer has expressed interest in turning out a rifle with a fiberglass stock, and already synthetic materials are being used for high-performance rifles for the military and some types of European target rifles. Inletting in this fiberglass stock is for a Winchester Model 70. The stock is made by Chet Brown of San Jose, California.

fuss. Some shooters, embittered by unhappy luck with the Stevens plastic stocks of only a few years earlier, were loud in their condemnation of all stocks that looked or felt like plastic. Remington countered with an effective publicity campaign explaining how the Model 66 would withstand extremes of heat, cold, dust, and mud and continue to function. One test, as I recall, involved running over the stock with an automobile. At any rate the nylon-stocked rifle gradually gained acceptance and now enjoys a deserved reputation as one of the most trouble-free rimfire autoloaders ever made. If I had to survive in the wilderness for a lifetime this is the rifle I'd choose.

The most recent large-quantity use of synthetic materials for stocks is for the M-16 service rifle and its civilian counterpart, the Colt AR-15. These are stocked with a tough but lightweight polycarbonate composition. Another model is the Charter Arms AR-7 Explorer. This rimfire autoloader features a hollow buttstock of Cycloac, which provides flotation for the rifle in the event of its being dumped in water and also is used as a protective storage case for the rest of the mechanism.

Synthetics for centerfire target rifles moved into the big time back around 1971 when a couple of California bench-rest shooters, Chet Brown and Lee Six, came forth with stocks made entirely of fiberglass cloth and an epoxy resin. Their product was developed in response to a need for ultralight yet highly stable stocks for rifles to be used in the restricted-weight bench-rest classes. Both the Sporter and Light Varmint classes, for example, allow a maximum weight, with scope, of 10½ pounds. The rifle design tactic for these classes is to use as stiff a barrel as possible and sacrifice weight everywhere else. Stocks, in particular, were subject to a lot of trimming, but, alas, the trimmer the stock the less stable a platform for the shooting mechanism it becomes. The highly stable qualities of fiberglass are well known, so Brown simply added two and two and came up with a lightweight, foam-filled fiberglass shell in the shape of a gunstock. The success of Chet Brown's stocks was almost instantaneous. Nowadays fiberglass stocks by Chet Brown or Dale MacMillian of Phoenix, Arizona, are a common staple in bench-rest tournaments. Even the most hardnosed holdouts are having to admit the undeniable advantages of fiberglass stocks for highly accurate yet relatively lightweight rifles.

Following up on the success of his bench-rest design, Brown offers a hunting-style stock for most popular actions which makes possible the lightest bolt-action rifles yet. For mountain hunters who want the lightest possible rig these stocks are a smart beginning.

The first completely factory-made target rifle I know of to come furnished with a synthetic stock is a target-shooting version of the Austrian Steyr-Mannlicher. I've had a chance to inspect only one of these and haven't tried one out for accuracy, but from my experience with the three target rifles I own with fiberglass stocks I'd say that the Steyr has a lot going for it. Also, at this writing, I know of at least one major U.S. rifle manufacturer who is seriously considering offering a super-dooper target rig complete with fiberglass stock.

An interesting phenomenon associated with the acceptance of fiberglass stocks is the public taste in colors. Back when Stevens offered shotguns with plastic stocks they were careful to have material blended and colored so it looked as much like natural walnut as possible. Remington followed this basic philosophy with their nylon 66 and XP-100 pistol stocks. But as it turns out, customers for fiberglass stocks want *anything but* a color that resembles wood! Yellows, pinks, baby blues, gold, silver, and a host of garish metal-flake finishes grace the firing line. In short, the brighter the better. The fiberglass stocks for hunting rifles are considerably toned down, of course, and a few I've seen have even been painted in a camouflage pattern. A pretty smart idea. . . .

At present, fiberglass stocks are fairly expensive, running somewhere in the neighborhood of $75 for an unfinished molding. But so far they are products of small one- or two-man operations and are built on a one-at-a-time basis. If mass-produced, however, they could be less expensive than the cheapest walnut. That day is still a long way off, I suspect, but the technology is ready and waiting and the product has already been proved in the white heat of rifle competition.

4

The Sight

The improvement of sighting equipment has been part and parcel of the evolution of the modern rifle. The single most significant characteristic of today's rifles—a high degree of accuracy—would have been unobtainable without the development of sights that make pinpoint aiming possible. Whenever we brag about a rifle that will sock five shots in an inch at 200 yards we are also paying tribute to awesomely efficient sights. In fact, modern sights have reached a state of such high development that we tend to take their precision for granted with little thought of how much they have contributed to shooter efficiency and the development of rifles and ammunition. Needless to say, the modern hunting rifle is a rifle with a telescopic sight.

Since the telescopic rifle sight started coming into its own only in the decade of the 1930s, most shooters consider it a fairly recent invention. Actually scope sights go back a surprising number of years. They were used as far back as the seventeenth century, and I think it's a fair guess that even before then such inventive souls as Leonardo da Vinci (who was a marksman of considerable repute) at least envisioned a magnifying sighting arrangement. By the time of the American Civil War, snipers on both sides were equipped with long-range sniping equipment aimed by means of telescopic sights with as much as 20× magnification, or more! These scopes, however, were long, delicate affairs and not at all well suited for a hunting rifle. Not until after the turn of the century were scopes streamlined to the point where they were really suitable for anything except target shooting—or sniping.

The big holdup in scope advancement was not suitable optics, as one might imagine, but suitable mounts. It wasn't until well after the Civil War that reasonably simple scope adjustment systems were invented. Before then, windage adjustments were made simply by driving the dovetailed scope base back and forth with *a hammer* carried for the purpose.

By the time of World War I, scopes had evolved to a form more or less similar to the hunting scope of today, with sights of about 2× or 2½× magnification being used by both English and German snipers during the conflict. Curiously, the English, who were leaders in developing workable short-profile sniping scopes (which eventually led the way to practical hunting scopes), never developed a peacetime market for hunting optics. This is doubly curious when you consider the fact that during that era they were building the world's finest sporting rifles. Perhaps the notion of using a telescopic sight for hunting game ran against their sense of fair play.

The Germans were bothered by no such ethical considerations, and as soon as possible after the "war to end wars" the great German and Austrian lens grinders such as Zeiss, Hensoldt, etc. were tooling up to make scopes for sporting rifles. Some credit has to be given European scopemakers for pioneering the hunting-scope market. But not too much credit, if you don't mind, because the lensmakers who initiated the rifle-scope industry and the gunmakers apparently never got their heads together. The end product, therefore, was telescopic sights that were great telescopes but terrible rifle sights. They were too fragile, too difficult to mount, had unreliable adjustments and laughable reticules, were overpriced and overweight, and, worst of all, would fog up every time the sun went behind a cloud. Most of the charges of unreliability and fogging, which the scope industry is just now, at last, shaking itself free of, got started with those European scopes sold in the U.S. during the 1920s and '30s. One of the first rifle scopes I ever owned, a 4× Kahles, was fogged up so often that I came to refer to it as my canteen.

Another problem which plagued scope users was the need for a suitable scope mounting system. Despite the Germanic penchant for gadgeteering—or perhaps because of it—the prewar mounts were as complex as a Chinese mouse decapitator, and about as practical. Looking at the rugged simplicity of, say, a modern Weaver base and ring set, one wonders why something similar couldn't have been invented back then. But keep in mind that the quick detachable mounts favored on German rifles were almost a necessity, especially in damp weather. Those complex, oversize contraptions resulted in scopes being mounted so high over the barrel that the rifle was all but unshootable. The shooter could look through the scope or he could put his cheek to the comb, but he couldn't do both at the same time. Some European rifles made during this period even had adjustable "crutch" combs which jacked the shooter's head up so he could peer through the scope.

It wasn't until after World War II that the scopemaking industry became a major part of the hunting picture. Thousands upon thousands of returning G.I.s having been exposed to wartime technology, now viewed a rifle scope as a way of making a rifle better, just as they'd seen bombsights, radar, sonar, and rangefinders increase the efficiency of military weaponry.

At any rate, this demand for scopes, combined with good old yankee know-how and a no-nonsense approach to what a hunting scope ought to be, resulted in the first "working man's" scope. U.S. firms such as Leupold, Bausch & Lomb, Stith, and Lyman proved that rifle scopes could be tough, reliable, finely adjustable, and weatherproof. Best of all, a fellow by the name of Weaver proved they could also be inexpensive. During the immediate postwar years most American scopemakers seemed disposed to retain the prices established by importers of German scopes before the war. (In 1930 a 6× Zeiss retailed for almost $50, equal to a two-week paycheck for a skilled working man.) So in 1950, a 4× Lyman Challenger or a Stith Bear Cub in the same power listed for $85. And a Bausch & Lomb BALvar 2½–4× variable was over $90. But a Weaver K-4, which was to become the biggest seller of all time, only set you back $44. Other makers, faced with this sort of competition, soon realigned their prices.

Since that time two remarkable things have happened. Scopes have gotten better and better, and they have become an increasingly better bargain. The modern scope is probably the best bargain in the shooting industry. Over a period of time that has seen the price of guns, autos, clothes, and labor double, the retail price of top-line optics has remained virtually unchanged. Tell that to your grocery man. And too, the reliability of American-made and American-designed scopes has become so well established that they are the number-one choice of hunters and shooters from Africa to Asia to New Zealand.

Backing up a bit, there is no doubting that the development of some

The popular Redfield JR base and ring. The peep sight can be used when the scope is removed.

good mounting systems, mainly during the late 1940s, had a lot to do with the rapid acceptance of scopes. Simple and reliable rings and mounts such as the Weaver and the old Redfield Jr. overcame in short order the scope-mounting problems of earlier days. Perhaps not so surprising, though, the distrust of scopes which originated in the 1930s continued to manifest itself in scope mounting systems well into the 1950s, by which time solid, dependable scopes were commonly available. There are even some vestiges of this trend visible today. Going back in my files to the five-year period between 1948 and 1952 I checked the brochures of the thirteen popular makes and models of scope mounting systems available and found that only three were committed to a truly solid arrangement which ruled out the use of iron

The popular Ruger Model 77 bolt-action rifle features integral scope ring bases. The grooved receiver ring and bridge, such as shown here, mate with Ruger rings.

sights on anything approaching short notice. The remaining ten made quite a fuss in their brochures and ads that their systems permitted either speedy removal of the scope or instant availability of iron sights.

Unlike the Europeans, however, American makers were fully aware of the fact that in order for a scope to be used efficiently it would have to be mounted quite low on the rifle. Thus, in addition to speedy removal, scope-mount makers strived for a low profile. The almost desperate need for the lowest possible mounting was, for the most part, relieved when the major rifle manufacturers decided that scopes were here to stay and began offering, as an option, straighter, higher-combed stocks such as Remington did with their Model 721 and Model 722 and Winchester's Monte Carlo comb. Nowadays gunmakers assume that almost all of their rifles will be scope-equipped and stock them accordingly. I think one can say the telescopic sight really arrived when riflemakers began offering their various models either with no iron sights at all or at least attached them so they could be easily removed.

Today's variety of makes, models, styles, and magnifications of telescopic rifle sights is far more vast than even the most ambitious of scope promoters would have predicted even a brief two decades ago. Who could have predicted that a firm like Redfield Gunsight Company, a firm that didn't even make scopes until the 1960s, would in so short a time offer a greater variety of optics than all U.S. makers combined in 1950? Or who could have foreseen that the problem of internal lens fogging, that venomous nemesis of telescopes, would have been so completely conquered? Today's scope buyer need scarcely give a second thought to whether or not his purchase will leak. He just naturally assumes it will not, but just in case there's any question, nearly every manufacturer guarantees that its product will not gather moisture and says so in writing. An example of how waterproof today's scopes have become is a Leupold recently dredged up from the bottom of a river. After being submerged for over eight months the scope's interior was as dry as the day it left the factory and in perfect working order. These days about the only scopes that don't come with a waterproof guarantee are the inexpensive, bottom-of-the-line models designed for use on rimfire rifles or a few of the discount-house imports.

The lengths to which some makers go to assure their scopes are leakproof are enough to send a timid soul into a state of shock. Occasionally we read a so-called "torture test" of a new make or model of scope in which the tester commits all sorts of outrageous acts such as dunking a scope in a pot of hot water, the idea being that the heat will expand the scope's internal gases and create a telltale stream of bubbles from any and every point of leakage. Extreme as such "abuse" may sound to some readers, such tests are so amateurish that they don't even make good ad copy any more.

The most recent test devised by Weaver, for example, is filling the scope with a dry gas containing a tracer element which can be detected by sensitive electronic "sniffing" equipment. As the Weaver scopes come off the assembly line they are locked in a cradle which applies a vacuum to the scope's various joints and attachments where leakage could possibly occur. If such a leak *does* exist and the vacuum sucks out even a tiny amount of the scope's internal atmosphere the tracer element will be detected and registered on the testing equipment.

Redfield checks for leaks by increasing the pressure inside their scopes via a port in the scope's tube. If there are any leaks the pressure load will fall off

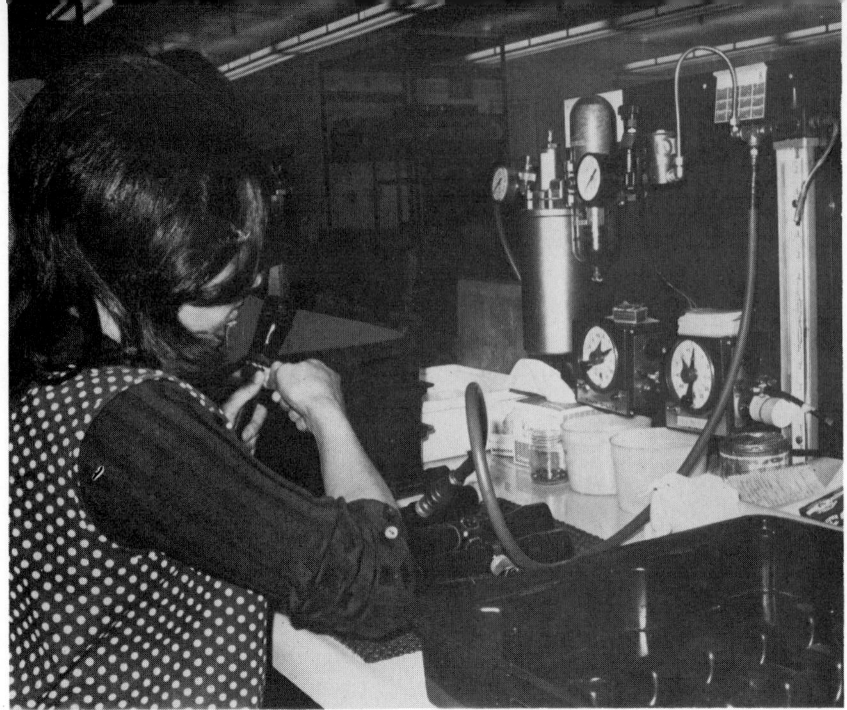

Here, in the Redfield factory, one of the workers applies pressure to a Redfield scope to check for leakage. If the mercury column in the scale falls, there is a leak in the scope which must be corrected.

and register on a mercury scale. Leupold uses the old stick-in-hot-water technique but with an added sophistication: the hot-water "pot" is, in fact, a sealed vacuum chamber in which the air pressure is lowered to well below a normal atmosphere. Thus while the hot water is causing the scope's internal atmosphere to "push" from the inside, another force is "pulling" from the outside. Scopes that flunk these various tests by different manufacturers are held for repair or scrapped. I've watched scope inspectors at work at different plants and I've seen scopes flunk out. So I know for a fact that the tests work.

Here of late there has been a lot of talk about "nitrogen-filled" scopes which has caused considerable misunderstanding. Writers of advertisements, being the breed they are, tend to make aspirin sound like a cure for leprosy, so nitrogen in scopes has been made to sound like the best thing since strawberries and cream. Actually a *dry* gas such as nitrogen is put in scopes simply as a means of replacing the natural atmosphere of a scope assembly plant. A natural atmosphere has a certain amount of moisture, which may, under unusually extreme conditions, condense and form the layer of white droplets inside a scope which usually is referred to as fogging. So the way to head this possibility off at the pass is to fill the inside of the scope with a gas of known composition and dryness. Any number of gases would be fine for this job, but it just so happens that nitrogen is easily available, cheap, and not likely to enter into a chemical reaction with a scope's internal materials, sealants, or lubricants. In time the nitrogen may bleed off but most likely you'll never know the difference. Its purpose is to ensure that the scope is dry when it leaves the factory.

The great problem with scope moisture these days seems to be us shooters. The same curiosity that kills cats is also deadly when it comes to peeking inside scopes. Let's say our old hunting buddy Marvin Misque down in Baton Rouge is tinkering with his variable-power guaranteed fogproof scope one hot, humid afternoon and gets to wondering how it can make a deer look close or closer just by turning a little ring. So he screws the eyepiece off and has a look. Now what happens is that when he gets the eyepiece off the scope is flooded with that sultry Baton Rouge air. Of course when good ol' Marvin screws the eyepiece back on the scope it looks as sharp as ever and before long he forgets the whole scientific adventure.

So three months later Marvin is hunting sheep in Alaska and the first day out the temperature drops down to about 13 degrees above zero. The scope gets cold and all that fine Baton Rouge humidity trapped in the scope does what comes naturally and forms little droplets inside the scope—then freezes. And good ol' Marvin raises hell.

With moistureproofing raised to the current high state, scopemakers are becoming more and more determined to outfox that one last culprit—the scope tinkerer. Weaver, for example, now final-assembles their "K" line of hunting scopes in a one-way process which all but eliminates do-it-yourself disassembly. The eyepiece, the most vulnerable part, now screws out only so far and then locks fast. A bitter disappointment no doubt to some dyed-in-the-wool scope peepers, but a sure way to keep their scopes clear, bright, and fog-free.

A curious but apparently acceptable means of qualifying oneself as an expert on virtually any subject under the sun is to memorize, and be prepared to spout off, long and impressive-sounding streams of statistics. I once knew a chap who memorized the entire 1953 Stoeger's *Shooter's Bible* and could quote the model numbers and prices of hundreds of guns. Statistically, I suppose, he was the world's leading firearms expert. In this same vein, about a generation back, or less, it became very fashionable to memorize the optical qualities of rifle scopes. Those "in the know" could, by simply comparing manufacturers' specs, tell you in a flash which scopes were the good ones and which were to be avoided. This pastime got so popular, in fact, that some manufacturers fell into the trap of even designing scopes, sometimes of outrageous proportions, which yielded impressive optical specifications. Some of the European scopemakers thought this was especially good fun and apparently saw it as a possible way to regain a portion of their lost export market. This foolishness reached full flower in the form of a scope which featured an objective lens over 3 inches across (actually 80mm). Predictably, the scope was designed without a thought as to how it was to be mounted on a rifle.

No existing mounts were tall enough to attach the scope on a rifle without the objective lens resting on the barrel, so custom mounts had to be made. A later version of this same scope was produced with the bottom quarter of the objective bell and lens done away with and looking as though the lower portion had simply been sliced away. Thus the lens looked more or less like a three-quarter moon. If you haven't seen one you've really missed something.

During these days of trial and tribulation such terms as relative brightness, exit pupil, resolution, twilight index, and that all-time favorite—light-gathering power—were tossed about as carelessly as empty beer cans. Back when I was a teenager I recall being enthralled by one particular scope report in which the author held me on the edge of my chair with a hard-hitting digest of specs and measurements. I'm sure an optical engineer would have been utterly captivated but I was left dangling. All I wanted to know was whether or not the scope was reliable and accurate enough to get a bullet on a deer some brisk October morning.

Apparently lots of other hunters felt the same way because I noticed that scopes that had a reputation for getting the job done continued to be the best sellers, while those that didn't, no matter how impressive their vital statistics, fell by the wayside. This was a valuable lesson, and as a result I've followed a policy of quelling any urges to pontificate on my hard-earned but scanty knowledge of the optical sciences. I find it far more rewarding to determine and pass on to the readers of my column in *Outdoor Life* whether a scope whose makers claim has ¼-minute adjustment will actually move the bullet's point of impact 2½ inches at 1,000 yards than to blithely relate that it has an exit pupil of 3 millimeters. Or, even more important, report whether a scope will support the weight of a rifle all day, carried upside down in a saddle scabbard, stand up to the recoil of a .340 Weatherby Magnum, survive the temperature extremes from a subzero night to a horse's sweating flanks, and still get a slug in a bull elk's boiler room from a range of 200 yards. Here of late I notice that the important scopemakers are playing down all the fancy specification tables and emphasizing the more important features they offer shooters. This is good. If I were the boss at a scope plant and a designer handed me a chart of optical specs he'd just worked out I'd fire him for wasting company time.

The great sales phenomenon of recent years is the variable-power scopes. Their appeal is that the magnification can, at the touch of a dial, be turned down when shots at close range or fast-moving game are expected, or turned up when a larger, more finely detailed image is needed for longer-range shooting or pinpoint bullet placement. The list of sales features goes on and on, and, as a matter of fact, the variable-power scope indeed presents some very definite advantages for *some* purposes. I think that by and large shooters tend to be somewhat more mechanically minded than their nonshooting brethren and have a greater appreciation for mechanical doodads. This has had a lot to do with the acceptance of variable-× scopes; twisting a ring and watching a distant object bounce back and forth as if on springs is just too dandy a toy for most of us to resist. But more about this later.

Not too many years ago variable-power scopes were not so hot an item. Back in the early 1950s, for instance, Bausch & Lomb made a scope they called the BALvar (for *Ba*usch & Lomb *var*iable) which had a feeble power variation of 2½ to 4×, and Weaver had a model called the K-5 which went from a 2¾× up to 5×. There were also some imported variable models, but the power ranges were nothing to swoon about. The problem in the design and selling of variable-power rifle sights was that when the image size was increased the cross hairs got bigger too—or at least they appeared to get bigger.

A typical 4× scope has a cross-hair thickness which subtends (covers up or blots out, however you want to phrase it) an area about 1 minute of angle, which is 1 inch at 100 yards, 2 inches at 200 yards, etc. 4× isn't a lot of magnification, so the 1 MOA cross-hair subtention is just about right. It is wide enough to be easily seen, even in poor light, but not so wide as to blot out any detail at 4× resolution. Now a higher-power scope, say in 8, 10, or 12×, will have cross hairs which subtend an area only ¼, or less, MOA. Yet the cross hairs of both the 4× and 10× scopes *appear* to be about the same width when you look at a neutral background such as the sky. If the higher-power scope had a 1 MOA cross-hair subtention it would look as fat as a rail fence and precise aiming would be almost impossible. How could you aim at a ground squirrel at 300 yards, for instance, if the cross hairs were covering up a 3-inch band at that distance and blotting out the target?

Now this leads us to the explanation for why early variable-power scopes were built with only a limited magnification span. The systems used at that time enlarged the reticle as well as the image as the power was turned up. The cross hairs of a 3–9× variable scope would have been so fat at the top power as to be almost useless, just as described above. There would be no actual change in subtention; a 1 MOA cross hair would cover up 1 inch at 100 yards, but it would certainly *appear* to get bigger with an increase in power. This condition was due to the prevailing practice at the time of locating the cross hair, or reticle, ahead of the power changing system. In short, every image, including that of the cross hair, which passed through the magnification changing lens system was amplified or reduced together. There were good reasons for doing it this way, as we shall see later. The problem was dealt with in several ways. Weatherby, for example, imported a beautifully made 2¾–10× variable which had about a ½ MOA cross hair. At the 10× setting it was fine, but with the power reduced the cross hairs faded away until they looked like cornsilk strung across a railway tunnel. The first really effective solution to the problem took place in the form of B&L's 2½–8× BALvar 8 and a target type scope with the absolutely unheard-of range of 6–24×, the

BALvar 24. The crafty technicians at B&L beat the enlarging-cross-hair problem by utilizing an etched-on-glass reticle of thinly tapering cross hairs which diminished to a fine point at the center. Thus, no matter how much the image and reticle were enlarged, each of the cross hairs appeared to taper down to nothingness at the center. It was a great system and they were great scopes, though quite expensive. In the late 1950s, when they were introduced, they were the best available, and though now discontinued are still considered top rate.

The next big step in variable-scope development was to place the reticle *behind* the power-change mechanism. Thus the cross hairs would stay the same size as the target image was enlarged around it. A fine idea, just the sort of inventiveness that makes folks say, "Now why didn't we think of that before. . . ." But it really wasn't all that simple. Here's why. With the reticle in front of the power-changing system the viewed image (the target) and the reticle image remain fixed in precise relationship to each other. If the power-change lenses are out of alignment and bend the image it's no matter because the two images are "bent" together. In other words, as the power-change system "sees" them they are only one image. But this, of course, is why the cross hairs were magnified along with the target image.

But with the reticle *behind* the power-change system there is the possibility of the target image and the reticle not staying in relation to each other as the power is changed. At one particular setting, for example, the target image and the reticle may be perfectly aligned. But when the power-change lenses are shifted the target image may be bent away from the reticle. A shift from alignment as small as a thousandth of an inch can cause an aiming error of as much as 1 inch at 100 yards.

Predictably, this situation caused all sorts of problems, though usually not serious, when manufacturers switched to behind-the-power-change-lens reticle system. But it did bring on lots of talk, and some gun writers got as indignant as all get-out when they found that some scopes would cause a shift in point of impact when the power was changed. One writer I recall got all up in arms because a 3–9× variable he was testing shifted point of impact about 2 inches at 100 yards. His report sounded like an essay on original sin, but I, for one, couldn't figure out what all the fuss was about. Especially since I knew for a fact that in a real-life hunting situation he couldn't hold inside a 12-inch circle at 100 yards anyway.

Nonetheless it came to pass, as we all know, that variable-power scopes moved into the big time. Variables have become such a hot item that most manufacturers offer about as different change-× models as fixed-power. I do not think they are the greatest thing since topless bars. But this is because I have little need for dual-purpose scopes and rifles. While I probably own a rifle or two that could serve for both wintertime big game and summertime varmints, and could thus benefit by the use of a variable, I also happen to own both a big-game rifle *and* a varmint rifle. Each is used for only one type of hunting, and the fixed-power scopes I use are just right for the purpose I put them to.

I've tested a large number of variables, both by shooting and on a grid screen (which gives a more precise measurement of shift of impact with power change), and I know for a fact that some variables *do* cause a shift of impact. Some makes and models are more prone to shift than others, as one would expect, but an individual scope of one certain model will also be more or less prone to error than its production line mates. One scope will cause no error whatsoever while the very next one off the same production line will be a dud. Thus I don't think it's very smart to condemn or endorse any particular brand or model. I also know for a fact that variables are becoming more and more precise. Test models of the past two or three years have shown very little tendency to cause power-change sighting error. So I'm not at all inclined to join any of my fellow gun writers who might wish to put a curse on variable scopes. My attitude toward variables is best summed up as indifference.

Whenever I use a variable-power for hunting I almost always use it at the full-power setting. Since I've also sighted it in at full power the prospect of a power-change sight error doesn't bother me. What *does* bother me, though, is the frequent misapplication of variable-× scopes. My mail indicates that lots of varmint shooters are equipping rifles in such calibers as .22/250 with variable-power scopes such as 3–9× or 4–12×. What possible advantage this might be escapes me, but there *are* some disadvantages. Likewise a 3–9× is poor for a short-range blockbuster that will never be fired at a range of over 60 yards.

All in all I don't think that the variable-power scope is really the sight of the future. However, I think they *are* playing a vital part in scope-sight education which in the long run will result in more effective use of scope-sighted rifles. This takes some explaining. I've long felt that most shooters are not using as much scope power as they can make good use of. Two decades ago, and before, a scope-sight user was handicapped in a number of ways. For one thing, rifle stocks of the day made scopes awkward to use, and for another, shooters were experiencing the pains of transition from irons to glass. In order to compensate for this awkwardness, scope buyers were urged to select lower-power scopes. The increased eye relief, larger field of view, and general ease of use of, say, a 4× compared to a 6× scope made the lower magnification a *safer* choice. And don't forget, the "experts" of a quarter-century ago, and longer, were having their own problems using scopes too and very possibly a 4× sight was all they could manage.

But now the situation is changed in virtually every area. Rifles are stocked for scope use, and the current generation has "grown up" with telescopic sights. Whereas we used to weave our heads around trying to see a full field of view through the eyepiece we now toss a rifle to our shoulder and see the full picture without trouble. In fact, the only thing that has not kept up with the times is advice on how to select and use a scope. For example, writers used to advise a 2½× scope for brush hunting and a 4× for game such as deer, goat, or Western deer and elk hunting. A 6× was advised only for varmints or long-range shots at big game.

But I see it differently. I don't think 4× is the best all-around choice. It's too much power for close-range brush shooting and not enough power for anything else. A 4× was fine for Western hunting back where 100-yard shots at deer and elk were common, but the situation has changed, in my own experience and that of many guides with whom I've talked. As trophy game gets harder and harder to find the ranges at which one must shoot are getting increasingly longer. I use a 6× scope on rifles for elk and Western deer and consider the magnification and definition just right for both open country and timbered areas. In fact, the increased image definition of higher magnification is a definite advantage in poor light conditions or those tricky situations where one has to shoot from cover, across open ground, and into more cover at partially concealed game. The last five head of North American big game I've taken—two elk, a bighorn sheep, and two deer—were all taken with variable-power scopes with the magnification turned up, in my usual fashion, to top power. In these instances the scopes had top ratings of 8× and 9×.

For dense brush shooting I still go with 2½× or 3×, fixed-power only (to keep it simple and ensure the widest possible field of view). And for varmints I don't bother with anything less than 10×. (More on varmint scopes in the section on varmint rifles.)

My observation is that, like me, most shooters tend to keep the power at the max setting when using variable-power scopes. This, in turn, is creating not only an awareness of the advantages of higher magnification but also the ability to use higher-powered scopes fast and efficiently. Thus, the long-term effect will be a general shift toward higher-power scopes of fixed magnification, which are more suitable, I feel, for modern rifles and modern hunting conditions.

RETICLES

Over the years all sorts of strange-looking sighting configurations have been put in scopes. In addition to cross hairs, or more specifically, cross *wires,* there are posts, double posts, triple posts, post with cross wires, dots, double dots, circles, and diamonds. The list goes on and on. Some of these various reticle designs were, of course, originated in a sincere effort to improve a hunter's proficiency; some were designed for one specific purpose, such as running boar target shooting; and some, naturally, were dreamed up simply to attract buyers. But as it turns out the most efficient and accurate reticle of all is none other than the basic cross-hair design of the very earliest scopes. Or at least some form of the cross hair.

No one has seriously questioned the aiming advantage of a simple cross hair. The trick to good aiming is to be able to see as much of the area you want to hit as possible and at the same time precisely pinpoint where the bullet is to hit. A cross hair is perfect for this and the only way it can be improved upon is to use increasingly finer cross hairs. From time to time different scope manufacturers or custom reticle makers have come up with the "ultimate" answer to perfect target visibility with a circular aperture or "ring" reticle which superimposes a circle around the area to be hit but without obscuring it in any way. The idea sounds great in principal but in actual practice it leaves the shooter with an abstraction to deal with. He only sees *about* where the bullet will hit.

Historically, the leading *disadvantage* of cross hair reticles is that they can be hard to see in conditions of poor light or where the brush is so thick that the cross hairs tend to get "lost" or blend in with limbs and saplings. I can recall at least a half-dozen occasions when I was hunting around dawn or dusk and, with a deer or elk in my scope, was unable to see where the cross hairs came together. Many other hunters have suffered the same situation, and this accounted for the development of the so-called post, or tapered post. The idea is simply to use such a bold aiming indicator that it can be seen in the poorest conditions. A hunter who has bungled a late-afternoon shot at an elk because he couldn't see the cross hairs is a pretty sure bet to buy a scope with a post reticle before his next hunt. Thousands have.

But even with the failings of cross hairs I've never had much use for a post. Over the years I've owned and used somewhere between 150 and 200 telescopic sights of all imaginable descriptions, but of all there were no more than three or four equipped with a post. To my notion they cover up too much of the target and do not provide a very exact indicator of where the bullet will go. Of course, in three out of four hunting situations exact bullet placement is pie-in-sky fantasy, but I've spent enough years trying to get a bullet to knock the center out of a bull's-eye that I at least like to think I'm in control of the bullet's flight. Old habits die hard.

About thirty years ago I owned an Austrian-made scope which came with a reticle consisting of four broad arms coming almost together, but giving way to standard cross hairs near the center. The main beams were so wide they'd blot out a 55-gallon oil drum at 100 yards but they were certainly easy enough to see in bad light. Double-width cross-hair design struck me as a practical idea because even in poor light the broad arms led the eye to the finer cross hair at the center. But the rest of the scope was so poor that I soon got rid of it and forgot the dual-width cross hairs for a few years. The next smart move in this direction was the Bausch & Lomb tapered-cross-hair system used with their BALvar 8× and 24× scopes. The wide outer edges tended to lead the eye to center stage. But the etched-on-glass B&L reticle system allowed a certain amount of light transmission which gave it the tendency to look rather grayish in poor light conditions. This made the cross hairs pretty hard to see against a dim background, even with the taper.

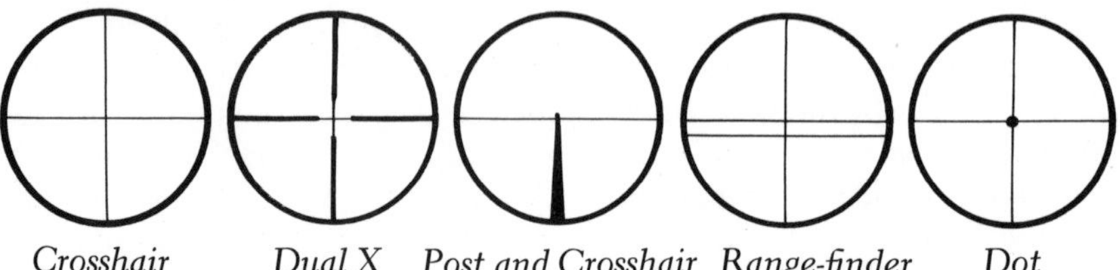

A variety of rifle scope reticles. The dual-X or Duplex type is the biggest seller these days and also, in my opinion, the best choice.

The case of the disappearing cross hair was solved for all time, at least to my satisfaction, in the early 1960s when Leupold introduced their Duplex reticle. Similar to the old Austrian scope I'd once owned, the Duplex has wide outer arms which lead the eye to the center in poor light, but a fine center cross hair which permits precise aiming. This type reticle is now offered by every important scopemaker and outsells all other reticles by a wide margin. It's my number-one choice for *all* types of hunting.

Dot reticles also have some worthwhile, but seldom noted, advantages. Quite a few target shooters use a dot reticle because it fits neatly in the concentric rings of a target. And too, some target shooters share the opinion that looking at a slender cross hair throughout a long day of shooting results in considerable eyestrain and fatigue. A fairly large dot instead of a cross hair reduces any such fatigue. Custom-made reticles with a series of dots on the vertical wire are sometimes used by shooters who want an exact or nearly exact aiming point for different ranges. I've seen these made for ranges out to as far as 1,200 yards with a dot for each 200-yard segment. The idea is interesting, and custom reticle makers claim they can space the dots to very precise minute-of-angle increments. The problem, though, is that rifles tend to behave differently from day to day. Changes in temperature, for example, and even humidity or intensity of light create differences in aiming and bullet placement that tend to ruin the best-laid plans of multiple dots.

Another interesting application of dot reticles is in some of the scopes used for moving-target competition such as International Running Boar. In this match a profile of a wild European pig, with scoring circles in the chest area, runs back and forth on a track. Some scopes used in this type of target shooting have dots mounted on the horizontal wire with the spacing set so as to allow a built-in lead for the moving target. Usually, such scopes have five dots in a row—a center dot for zeroing the rifle and two dots on either side with the spacing set to allow for high- and low-speed target runs. From what I understand the system works out pretty well, but don't get the idea it will work as well on live game. The real thing runs at all sorts of speeds, angles, and ranges, and a scope with a "built-in" lead would only confuse the issue.

Some hunters like dots in hunting scopes, especially in bygone years, but I am told the trend is fading fast. Pretty large dots, often 2 MOA in diameter or more, have, like posts, been used because they supposedly show up right well in poor conditions and because, as some say, they promote quick shooting. I have a Griffin & Howe stocked and customized Model 70 Winchester in .375 H&H that's scoped with one of the old Lyman 2½× Alaskan sights with a dot, which I hunted with on and off for a few years. The dot never caused any problem but I could never see that it was anything special either. The possible problem with a dot in most hunting scopes is that there is nothing to direct your *unconscious concentration* to the dot while your main concentration is on the game animal. The suspending cross hairs of most dot reticles are all but invisible. Just recently Leupold has tried to overcome this problem by mounting a dot in the center of the tapered-arm "CPC" reticle. Thus the eye is more naturally led to center stage. It's a lot handier way, I should think, of finding the bouncing ball.

RANGEFINDERS

How would you like to own a rangefinding scope that emits a pencil-thin radar impulse directly to any object you put the cross hairs on and registers the exact yardage to that object on a small screen at the bottom of the field of view with little illuminated numerals like a pocket calculator? Impossible? No. Expensive? Yes! So expensive probably that the potential market may never encourage the development of such a gadget. But the idea of rangefinders continues to be one of the most intriguing, yet baffling, areas of rifle-scope research. Optical rangefinders themselves are nothing new, and some remarkably accurate units have been manufactured over the years, mainly for the military. But these are split-image rangefinders which work by triangulation and thus must view the distant object from two angles. Generally speaking, the greater the divergence of the two viewing cells, the greater the accuracy of the instrument. Units which offer enough accuracy out beyond 500 yards to be of any use to riflemen may have the cells a yard or so apart. But a cell spacing of only 2 or 3 inches would be too wide to be utilized in a rifle scope, even if it were accurate enough.

Another optical/mechanical distance-indicating technique is the one employed in surveyors' transits. Two stadia, or horizontal cross wires, in the instrument are exactly preset at a specific minute-of-angle separation. Thus, when the calibrated engineer's rod is viewed through the transit the distance computation is made by reading the number of graduations seen between the two horizontal wires. The disadvantage to this system for hunting purposes, obviously, is that no sheep is going to stand still while someone runs over with an engineer's rod so you can take a distance reading. However, if the approximate height of the target is known a reasonably close range estimate can be made. This is the basis on which built-in rangefinders such as Redfield's Accu-Range and the Realist Auto-Range work. These systems are based on the premise that the average deer is about 18 inches deep from backbone to brisket. The Redfield Accu-Range is operated by simply turning the power-adjusting ring of the variable-power mechanism and enlarging or diminishing the image of the deer until he fits between the two stadia wires. The range scale, which assumes an 18-inch chest depth, then indicates the yardage. With this information to work with the hunter then knows how much to hold over the animal for a long shot. The possibility of error is obvious, but even considering the variables which are bound to present themselves in a real-life hunting situation, I'd say that out about 400 yards the system is a more reliable distance estimator than a typical once-a-year hunter trying to "eyeball" the range.

The Realist Auto-Range goes a step further and actually alters the rifle's point of impact, by means of a cam arrangement, so that the hunter, supposedly, can hold dead on target at all ranges. Different cams are fitted for different calibers and bullet weights. This gets pretty iffy, though, because the basic range estimate is, at best, only approximate and the cams are also only approximate and two approximations hardly add up to accuracy.

So it's easy to see that we still have a good way to go toward a really effective combination rangefinder/sight. But who knows, perhaps one of these days someone will develop a little electronic, digital-reading radar gadget that will tell us that the distance to a royal elk is 320 yards, 2 feet, 1⅛ inches. But to tell you the truth, I'm not so sure that it will be such a good thing to have happen.

If I had to name the five most significant advances in telescopic-sight design of the past generation they would be, not necessarily in order of importance, (1) moistureproof sealing, (2) better reticle design (such as the duplex-type cross hair), (3) better mounting systems, (4) nonenlarging reticles in variable-power scopes, and (5) *permanently centered reticles!* Newcomers to the shooting game have no idea what fun we had back in the days when cross hairs could be marched all over the field of view. Damn! What a chore they could be.

Nowadays just about every scope on the market has the constant-center feature, which means that no matter how much the scope is adjusted to line the cross hairs up with the point of impact they still appear in the center of the field of view. Like all modern conveniences, we quickly took this feature for granted and all but forgot what it was like in the good old days. Today when we bring the reticle to alignment with the bullet holes in the target the sighting-in job is over and done with. But only two decades ago it was often only the first step. The next step involved bushing, shimming, and sometimes even redrilling and tapping just to get the cross hairs somewhere close to center field.

The importance of such improvements, considered either singly or together, to the present state of the modern rifle cannot be overstated. In fact, stated simply but accurately, without a scope the modern rifle is not so modern after all

IRON SIGHTS

So what is the fate of the old-fashioned "open" sight? Is it only a holdover from another generation of shooters? Or will the bead front and notched rear continue to hold a viable position in the scheme of sport shooting?

Back when I was a farm lad I recall being regaled from time to time by older and wiser heads about the various merits of different sorts of sights. Back then a notched rear and post front were not referred to as "open" or "iron" sights. When a man said sights, that was the only kind he was referring to. All others were specified as "peeps" or "scopes" or whatever. So a discussion of different kinds of "sights" meant only gold beads as opposed to ivory beads or V-notches as opposed to U-notches. Every old-timer has his

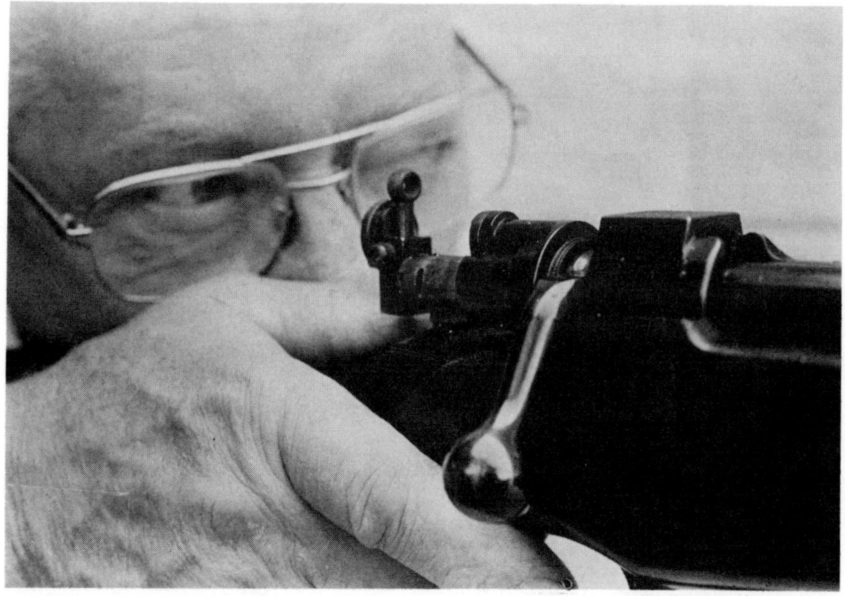

A specimen of the cocking piece peep sight such as was fairly popular before World War II.

special ideas about what combinations of beads and notches best made a bullet "fly true."

But alas, such scholarly discussions are all but a thing of the past. No one seems to care much any more. Even the most determined holdouts have had to admit that the day of the scope has long since arrived. Some riflemakers don't even bother to put "sights" on their wares, especially the high-performance models, and those who do make sure that they are easily removed lest someone's delicate sensibilities be offended. The front-sight base on a Model 70 Winchester, for instance, used to be integral with the barrel and the rear sight firmly dovetailed into a specially turned flange. But now they can be easily swept out of sight with a screwdriver. The recent Winchester catalog even points out that they are easily detachable. The same goes for most other makes and models.

Even so, the open sight is a long way from a dead issue. For short-range shooting in brush or timber a simple bead-and-notch arrangement is tough to beat. The Winchester Model 94 lever gun, the all-time best-selling hunting rifle, is still a hot item, and the overwhelming majority are used with the original open sights. Also, there are thousands upon thousands of .22 rimfire rifles bought every year that will never be aimed and fired any way except by means of the simple sights put on at the factory.

The day of the open sight is far from over. For example, there is a recent renewal of interest in quality folding-leaf rear sights such as the custom-made model shown here. After this sight unit is fitted the notches will be filed and adjusted for different ranges.

And believe it or not, open sights are even experiencing a comeback of sorts on cream-and-caviar rifles. Back in the days of flappers and raccoon coats the best rifles made here and abroad sported elaborate multi-leaf sights for ranges out to as much as 500 yards. These were especially common on the better British and Continental rifles and those made by such domestic carriage-trade specialists as Griffin & Howe. In truth, all those folding sights weren't much help, but they did look impressive and added a certain appeal.

Here of late there seems to have occurred a revival of interest in some of the classical features of that generation of riflemaking with such niceties as trapdoor butt plates, quarter ribs, and, especially, folding-leaf open sights. Of course many of these are bound for collectors' cabinets and may never be fired, much less hunted with.

The most serious thought I've given to open sights was on a 1973 safari to the Republic of Botswana. I spent several tedious days tracking lions in spotty bush and waist-high grass where the big cats can hide until you almost step on their tails. With every thicket a death trap that could launch a lion like a maneating express train, I did some serious thinking about what sort of sight would be best for a charging blur of teeth and claws. My conclusions were, first of all, that both front and rear sight should be totally simple and attached by the sturdiest means available—preferably dovetailed, pinned, screwed, and finally *welded* for good measure. Nothing fancy, not even adjustable. Certainly none of the folding-leaf variety. Just a big, bright, unhooded front bead about 1/8 inch wide and a low, shallow V-notch at the rear. In the event of an eyeball-to-eyeball-encounter with an elephant, lion, Cape buffalo, or ugly-tempered bear, such a set of sights would be downright comforting.

Peep or aperture sights are all but a forgotten issue on the hunting scene. Back in their heyday they offered a considerable accuracy advantage over ordinary open sights at the longer ranges. But in this respect they've lost out to scopes almost entirely. It hasn't been a painless death, either, because there are any number of diehards like myself who have fond memories of great rifles equipped with peeps. I once attended a turkey shoot back in the hills of eastern Tennessee which had been billed as a "no scopes allowed" affair. I had a pretty nice peep-sighted rifle which I could shoot fair to middlin', and I assumed it would be a legal entry. But some of the local boys took one look at the rig, held a brief conference among themselves, and allowed that I couldn't "shoot no rifle with peep sights." This seemed like a "fair" decision, seeing as how there were several of them and only one of me, so I accepted the ruling without comment.

But the next Saturday I took the same rifle back to the turkey shoot—along with some pals of mine who had decided they wanted to shoot it too. To make a long story short, there was a considerable exchange of opinion, several oaths spoken, and more than a few threats of violence. Fortunately, "reason" prevailed and my rifle was allowed, whereupon it won all but one of the turkeys shot off that autumn afternoon. I've had an especially warm feeling toward peep sights ever since.

Probably the great era of peep sights occurred back in the last half of the 1800s when adjustable tang sights were used on the great long-range hunting rifles. Many buffalo hunters equipped themselves with peep-sighted Winchesters, Sharpses, Remingtons, etc. Being finely adjustable and allowing considerably more precise bullet placement than ordinary open sights, peep or aperture sights were to hunters of that time what scopes are to today's shooters.

To someone who has encountered peep-type receiver sights only on target rifles they no doubt seem rather slow and unwieldy to use. Hunting peeps, however, can be amazingly fast. The trick of using them efficiently is learning to look *through* the rear aperture and not at it. This, of course, requires a considerably larger rear aperture than is normally used for target shooting. Also the closer the eye is to the peep the easier it is to see *through* it. The speed of a peep arrangement comes from the fact that the shooter doesn't have to consciously align the front and rear sights with the target. Just putting the front sight on target brings the rifle to bear because simply looking through the rear aperture automatically takes care of this part of the sight alignment picture.

Back between the two world wars there were a few aperture-type sights marketed, or custom-made, which mounted directly on the rear of the striker of Mausers, '03 Springfields, etc. This sounds like a pretty precarious place to attach a sight but the reason, as noted above, was to get the sight closer to the shooter's aiming eye. When the striker fell the sight moved away from the eye, of course, and gave him a bit more eye relief just at the moment of recoil. Needless to point out, though, strikers can be pretty wobbly, so in many cases a striker-mounted rear sight was not all that precise. To

This detail photograph shows the V-shaped sear which fits into a notch in the trigger sear. This holds the cocking piece in rigid shot-to-shot alignment, thus making the cocking piece peep sight more reliable. This was a custom feature found only on better guns.

overcome this problem a few savvy gunsmiths cut a V-slot into the striker sear and milled a mating crested shape into the trigger sear. Thus when the opposing sear surfaces came together they were held in a rigid alignment which eliminated most of the striker wobble. Very clever.

I've always felt a good bit of admiration for shooters and, especially, hunters who had enough on the ball to use an aperture receiver sight in preference to open sights. And I will always feel, scopes notwithstanding, that learning to be a good rifleman includes becoming proficient in their use. That's why I outfitted Eric, my oldest son, with a peep-sighted .218 Bee Model 43 Winchester for his first varmint hunts. You learn a lot about marksmanship with peeps that you miss with any other aiming system.

These days about the only widespread use of "peep" or receiver sights is in the area of target shooting, where their use is specified by tournament regulations. (More details on target-type peep sights are in Part IV of this book.)

Many makes and models of peeps that were popular two decades ago or before have either been discontinued altogether or will cease to be cataloged when current stocks run out. When that not too distant day arrives, peep sights on hunting rifles will be a thing of the past. The Lyman firm, once the leading maker of peep sights, cataloged their great Model 48 sight for the last time in 1974, Redfield has trimmed their selection of target models only, and even the popular Williams "Five Dollar" sight costs a lot more these days.

5

The Cartridge

Reflective souls who delight in arguing over how many angels can waltz on the head of a pin might also find a measure of excitement in debating whether modern cartridges followed rifle design or if today's rifles came about because of the need to keep pace with ballistic developments.

This is an interesting question, and the more one sinks into it the more involved the issues become. After a moment's thought on the matter one realizes that during the past three-quarters of a century astonishingly few original basic rifle mechanisms and cartridges have been developed for each other. Instead, rifles and cartridges tend to develop independently of each other but with a peculiar back-and-forth cooperative overlapping.

For example, say a ballistics engineer for a sporting-arms and ammunition company is given the word to develop a hot new 7mm hunting cartridge. His very first consideration will be what *existing* rifle actions he has to work with. Once this is established he goes ahead and designs a cartridge which will function safely in one or more of these actions.

But now let's take the other view and say that a rifle manufacturer wants to turn out something really new and different in the way of an action with which to titillate rifle buyers. When the chief engineer gets the word from upstairs to get on the ball and come up with something really ingenious his first thought is what *existing* cartridges the action must be designed to handle.

This condition smacks very stoutly of a stalemated situation, and to a cer-

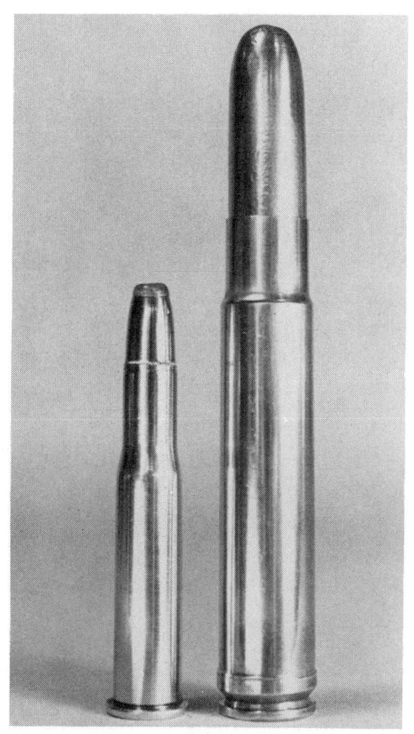

Here is the large and small of it. Compared to a standard .30/30 round, at left, is the huge .475 A&M cartridge. The big .475 fires a 500-grain bullet at nearly 3,000 fps. Naturally it's only for rear-end shots at elephants, assorted dinosaurs, etc.

tain degree that's exactly the case. But ever so slowly the above-mentioned overlapping pattern slowly grinds along and, over the years, produces new rifles *and* new cartridges. Even so there are lovers of red-hot cartridges, mostly wildcatters, who claim that they would have long since "developed" rounds that would shove a 180-grain .30-caliber bullet over the 5,000 fps mark if only someone would design an action strong enough to hold the pressure. Of course what they are overlooking is that designing an action to hold these pressures would be one of the most easily overcome steps in achieving such velocities. The real problem would be in finding barrels, bullets, cases, etc. equal to the task.

Actually much, if not most, research and development in the area of modern sporting ammo is not in turning out new cartridges but in modernizing old ones. A perfect example of this is the ageless .30/06. After seven decades of existence it supposedly should be on its last legs, but we all know that such is not the case. What keeps it on the front row of popularity? First of all, it is *not* the same cartridge of 1906, or for that matter 1920, or even 1950. The round of 1906 and the next few decades utilized a corrosive primer that would cause heavy rusting if the bore was not carefully cleaned within a short while after firing. The bullet-jacket material often caused such heavy barrel fouling that accuracy was destroyed after a few rounds, and the hot-burning powders then used created a notably higher rate of barrel erosion than we need worry about today. Velocity was lower, bullet expansion far less reliable and effective, and, perhaps most important of all, accuracy was nowhere near what we get today.

The upgrading of existing calibers is a far greater service to sportsmen than simply offering an endless stream of new cartridge designs.

Another blessing bestowed on modern shooters by arms and ammunition makers is a shift away from the proprietary trends of a half century ago and before. Around the turn of the century the habit of gunmakers was to chamber their rifles for a more or less specific line of cartridges made or distributed only by themselves. The intent, clearly, was to monopolize, to whatever degree possible, the sales of certain calibers. When Winchester offered its .25/35 in 1895, which was chambered for use in the Model 94 lever gun, Marlin countered with an almost identical, but not quite, round for its lever rifle, called the .25/36 Marlin. The same year Stevens introduced its .25/25, and nine years later Remington introduced its version of a quarterbore, the .25 Remington. This kind of competition meant that there had to be a lot of cartridges that would soon fail and be discontinued. The real

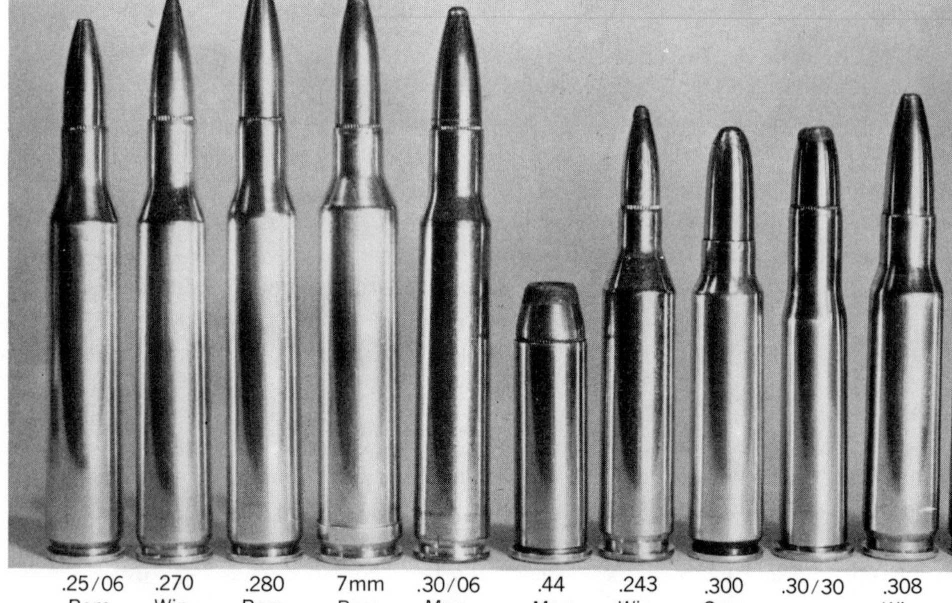

This is a comparative line-up of the difference between long-range high-energy cartridge thinking and short-range "brush-type" rounds. The five cartridges at left, identified on the picture, are typical of the high-intensity cartridges such as might be favored for Western deer, sheep, elk, etc. The half-dozen cartridges at right would be more favored for eastern-type hunting in conditions where heavy cover or brush prevail.

losers, needless to say, were rifle buyers who made the wrong selection and eventually found that ammo for their rifle was discontinued.

From the standpoint of raw ballistics the single most overwhelming characteristic of the modern cartridge is an ever-increasing emphasis on velocity. With extremely few exceptions, every cartridge introduced since the close of World War II has featured higher velocity than previously existing cartridges either in terms of bullet diameters and weights (the .300 Weatherby Magnum, for instance, which uses the same bullets as a .30/06 but at a notably higher velocity) or getting more velocity out of cartridges of essentially the same length and thus offering more energy per cartridge volume. (An example here is the .308 Winchester, which yields significantly more velocity than the .30/30 or .300 Savage rounds but can be used in similarly short-action rifles such as the Savage Model 99.)

Up until about 1930 or so when such relatively smallbore but high-velocity rounds as the .270 Winchester, .300 H&H, .280 Ross, .257 Roberts, and .250 Savage had conclusively demonstrated their advantages in the game fields, the traditional guideline for selecting a hunting cartridge was to use bigger and bigger bullets for bigger and bigger game. This habit dated back to black-powder days when muzzle velocities were limited to the 1,300–1,800 fps muzzle velocity range regardless of the volume of powder used. Faced with this limitation, cartridge makers could increase the energy and killing power of their product only by using bigger, heavier bullets. Though there are literally scores of black-powder cartridges which could be used to illustrate this situation, a fine example is the familiar .45/70 Government cartridge which developed 1,640 foot-pounds of energy with a 405-grain bullet at 1,350 fps. When someone wanted to market a more powerful round than the .45/70 they had to do so by manufacturing a cartridge which utilized a heavier bullet. Muzzle velocities could be increased marginally, but by and large energy was achieved by *size*. This trend no doubt reached its apex around the 1890s with the mysterious Winchester .70-150, a shortened 12-gauge brass shotshell necked down to .70 caliber and said to fire a 900-grain bullet at about 1,300 fps.

With the coming of nitro "smokeless" powders the velocity lid was knocked off, and in short order rifle and ammo makers were able to demonstrate what physicists had been saying all along—that velocity was a far more efficient way of generating energy than simply increasing the mass. Nonetheless, a trend in popular thinking had been established which was to have long-term effects. Even today there are traces of big-bore sentiment. In fact, in case you haven't noticed, it has been somewhat fashionable of recent times for outdoor writers, especially gun editors, to cross swords over the relative killing power of light high-velocity bullets as opposed to heavy slower-moving projectiles. I've read any number of these spite-fence accounts and can conclude their only possible purpose is to sell a few extra magazines.

The only thing a reader can hope to obtain from them is either a passing titillation or, more usually, being bored to cerebral numbness. Anyone who expects me to join in or take sides in any of these discussions is doomed to disappointment.

Back when I was a callow youth of twenty-five I had hunted just enough deer, bear, and boar with enough different rifles and calibers to figure I had unraveled all the secrets of killing power and had them securely pocketed away. Some deer, I'd observed, went down as if they'd been struck by lightning when hit by some calibers, but others, which were surely well hit with another caliber, scrampered away as if hardly hurt at all. With six or eight whitetail bucks, a couple of black bears, and a boar or two to my credit I was willing and eager to argue killing power at the drop of an empty case.

But now, after quite a few experiences on the world's deserts, mountains, snowfields, swamps, and savanna grasslands, I have become absolutely positive about only one thing, that being that the quickest and surest way a hunter can exhibit his ignorance and inexperience on the subject of cartridge performance on game is to pontificate on conclusions drawn from isolated experiences in the game fields. Even sillier is to equate these observations with personally held convictions concerning the relative killing power of different cartridges.

These three 6mm cartridges, from left .243 Winchester, 6mm Remington, and .240 Weatherby Magnum, are typical of the modern-day emphasis on high-velocity smallbore ammunition. They have proved particularly effective for medium game such as deer and antelope because the low recoil promotes more precise bullet placement.

In the accounts of the effectiveness of bigbore vs. smallbore I've read I've always been impressed how each proponent unfailingly had great success with whatever cartridge class he advocated and equally uniform failure with rifles representing the opposing viewpoint. But alas I have never been so blessed. Every time I have amassed enough experience with a particular cartridge on some particular species of game to feel that I can confidently deliver a learned opinion something throws my observations out of kilter.

When I was on safari in Botswana in June of 1973 I shot a zebra at about 80 yards with a 7mm Remington Magnum loaded with some hot 160-grain loads. It was a broadside shot and I had a solid hold when I settled the cross hairs just behind his shoulder and pressed the trigger. I thoroughly expected him to drop in his tracks or take only a couple steps at most. Instead he kicked up his heels and galloped off at full speed. Judging by his getaway I would have declared the shot a clean miss if my trackers had not spotted traces of blood. After tracking the wounded animal some distance through heavy cover we found him standing in a clearing with his head down but still steady on his feet. This time I crept to within 40 yards and let him have another round behind the shoulder—the opposite shoulder, by the way, from where I'd hit him the first time. He jerked his head up and charged off at full tilt again but went down before we lost sight of him.

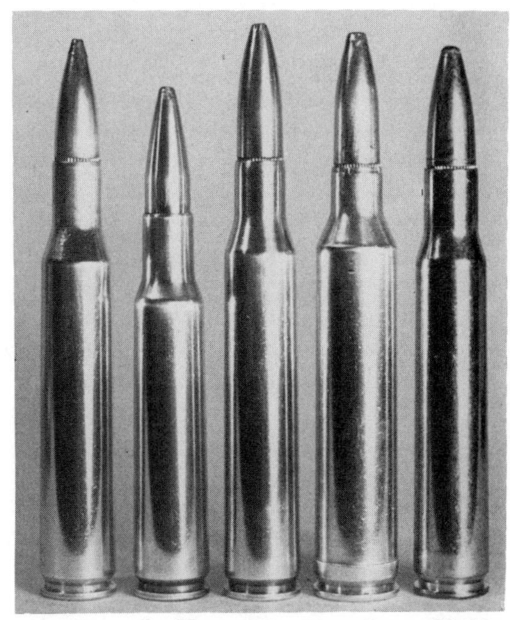

.270 Win. | 7 × 57 | .280 Rem. | 7mm Rem. Magnum | .30/06

These five cartridges, identified in the print, fairly well typify modern high intensity cartridges such as favored by big game hunters.

The experience was hardly a textbook case for the high-velocity crowd—not at all typical of the "smack 'em dead" claims made for the 7mm Remington Magnum and other high-velocity members of its class. In fact I could have come home and picked up a nice piece of change for myself by writing a story about how the 7mm is poor fare for zebra.

A year later to the week, I was once again in Africa and only about 40 miles from where I'd had the zebra experience the previous June. I was carrying the same 7mm Remington Magnum rifle, a Ruger Model 77, and ammo from the same batch I'd used the previous year. We were looking for camp meat for our crew when I spotted a zebra in some tall grass about 200 yards off. Taking a solid rest against a tree, I settled the cross hairs as near to the exact spot where I'd aimed on the other zebra as I could and pressed the trigger. At the instant the rifle barked the big zebra stallion dropped out of sight in the grass. When we arrived on the spot we found him exactly where he'd been standing when the bullet hit. Apparently he was stone dead even before he hit the ground.

Again, if I'd been of a mind to, I could have picked up a nice check for a zebra-hunting story, only this time about how the 7mm Remington Magnum is the surest medicine for zebra this side of a 155mm field piece. So how does one score these two isolated experiences? In favor of or against the killing power of high-velocity smallbore cartridges?

But just for the record let's take another example. During my African wandering I have bagged one lion, six elephants, and an assortment of Cape buffalo with the .458 Winchester Magnum. Each of these hit the dust within an instant or two of my pulling the trigger. Naturally, based on this multiple experience I could state with reasonable confidence that the .458 is an awesome killer. Yet only a few months ago I was circling an African waterhole with a shotgun hoping to flush a few francolin or guinea fowl for the mess tent. For safety's sake my hunting companion was carrying my .458 just in case we met up with anything bigger and meaner than a covey of the tasty birds. As luck would have it we happened onto a nearly grown wart hog, just the right size for the pot and one of my favorite game dishes. It was a simple head-on shot of only a few paces and the bullet from the .458 hit it square in the chest; I was close enough to even see the hole. The pig sank back on its haunches and kicked a couple of times just as I would have expected it to, but then it did something I didn't expect. It got up and ran off!

Five of us, including three keen-eyed African trackers, scoured the area for over an hour but never found a trace of the porker, not even so much as a blood spoor. There was a fair amount of blood where the wart hog had been hit but after that not a sign. Which, by the way, does away with the often heard tale about bigbore rifles causing greater blood loss. If this had been my only hunting experience with a .458 I could very easily have deduced that it wouldn't even kill an 80-pound pig.

But this is exactly the point. Time and time again we hunters tend to form and hold hard judgments on the basis of isolated experiences. This is compounded by the fact that the vast majority of big-game hunters manage only one big-game hunt, usually for deer, per year. Also, taking into account the average hunter success ratio of all game-hunting states, we know that the average hunter will bag less than one head of game every five years. This ratio does not permit many hunters to accumulate very many firsthand experiences with cartridge performance on game, but, by the same token, it causes those few experiences to be intently regarded.

Let's say that our pal Marvin Misque buys himself a handsome scope-sighted rig in .308 Winchester caliber. The first day of the new season is only an hour old when Marvin spies a fine buck and shakily levels the cross hairs on what he figures is the heart area. The gun goes boom and the deer is out of sight in three bounds.

"Shot him right in the heart I did," Marvin tells us, "hit dead center in the heart but yet he got away. Take it from somebody who knows, that .308 ain't no good for deer."

We've all heard variations on this tune a dozen times over, but the simple question we're all too polite to ask is: "Marvin, if he got away how do you know you hit him in the heart? In fact, how do you know you hit him *at all*?"

I once thought I had the only reasonable and logical answer to the killing-power question. If big bullets *and* high velocity were both efficient killers, then a bigbore, heavyweight bullet traveling at high velocity would be most effective of all. This of course is obviously true, but paradoxically, more so in theory than actual practice.

A few years back I equipped myself with a fine-looking custom-built .338 Winchester Magnum for a Wyoming elk hunt. Though the cartridge is a hard kicker (since it performs the above-described feat of driving a heavy, large-diameter bullet at high velocity), it has a flat trajectory and plenty of punch out at the longer ranges. I'd taken a couple of elk with a .338 before and had been impressed with the way it could anchor a big bull.

One late afternoon as my guide and I were riding into camp we came across an especially fine mule deer buck, and as I had a deer license I decided to take him. When we worked to within good shooting position the range was no more than 200 yards and the big buck was peacefully feeding, totally unaware of our presence.

The deer was on a steep hillside standing well above and left-quartering toward me. At that angle, I figured, the bullet would enter low in the brisket and angle up and diagonally across the chest cavity. A more devastating bullet path is hard to imagine. But when the rifle cracked the buck just raised his head as if to see where the noise was coming from and trotted toward the crest of the hill.

All I could figure was that I had missed clean. No deer could take a hit from a .338 and act like that. In fact I recall thinking to myself that I was lucky to discover my rifle was off zero before finding a trophy elk. But just as the deer neared the crest of the hill it turned and started walking back down more or less toward me. Again the deer was quartering toward me, but this time to the right. I fired again but the deer seemed to pay no notice. But five steps later he collapsed and rolled down the hill. Both shots had been perfectly placed. They had hit low on the brisket, angled up through the heart, and completely destroyed the lungs. Also, as one might expect from a .338-shot deer, both shoulders were all but ruined where the bullets had crisscrossed.

Since then I've tallied a couple more elk with that same rifle and load, and both fell where they were hit. So why did that deer stay on his feet after being so hard hit? If he had crossed over the crest of the hill instead of turning and coming back both my guide and I would have certainly argued that he had been missed clean. And think how easy it would be to conclude that the .338 isn't ample power for deer and that something bigger is needed. Unfortunately, all too often loudly voiced (and published) opinions are based on just such extraordinary one-of-a-kind circumstances.

Recently a Colorado big-game guide showed me a .30-caliber 180-grain Silvertip bullet he'd found under an elk's hide. It was the most nearly perfect recovered bullet I've seen. Aside from the rifling imprint on its sides it appeared to have just come out of the box. The guide who found it is a savvy shooter who immediately recognized what had happened. The elk had been fired at from extremely long range and the spent bullet had arrived on target with just enough energy to lodge under the animal's skin. But what if the bullet had been spotted by a less knowledgeable guide or hunter? Most likely he'd have made a career of denouncing Silvertip bullets, complete with evidence in hand.

After spending many hours considering these and dozens more similar experiences, and weighing the factors as fairly as possible, I've reached a conclusion or two. The hunter will always have to take into account that there are certain factors over which he has no control and very little understanding. If I were to hunt deer with a .338 Magnum for the rest of my life (which I have no intention of doing) probably every one I hit would go down as if he had been poleaxed. But this would not alter the fact that one buck in my hunting experience, for whatever reason, did *not* go down after being hard hit with a .338.

My number two conclusion is that while there is nothing the hunter can do to overcome such one-in-a-hundred unexplainable circumstances he can at least lower the percentage of those trophies that "run away with their heart shot out" by using more *hittable* cartridges. Over the long haul the best "dropped 'em where they stood" ratio will go to the hunters who tally the best shot placement. This is not just opinion but fact. Far too often a shooter who blows his chance for a fine buck by using, say, a .30/06, shows up in the woods the next year armed with a .300 Magnum or something even bigger. What he hasn't realized is that the reason the .30/06 didn't drop the deer in its tracks is that the bullet missed altogether or was poorly placed in a nonvital area. And the reason the shot was poorly placed was that for *him* the .30/06 is not a very *hittable* round. The noise and recoil cause him to jerk the trigger and flinch—and miss. So the following year, convinced a .30/06 won't kill a deer, he shows up with a rifle that bellows louder, kicks harder, and, naturally, causes him to miss even worse. Of course what he needed was a more *hittable* rifle—perhaps a .250 Savage or a .243. He would find these pleasant to shoot and soon discover that he could put the bullet right where it counts. But sometimes it's hard to convince people that the correct remedy will work.

In this respect I'm reminded of victims of hyperventilation. When this happens the victim's system is oversaturated with oxygen but the symptoms are similar to those of suffocation. Thus, even though the individual is suffering from too much air he feels that he must breathe deeply in order to overcome his suffocation. So the condition gets worse and worse. The most effective way to combat a condition of hyperventilation is for the sufferer to put his head in a bag and cut down his supply of air. But it's sometimes damn hard to get someone who's convinced he's suffocating to put his head in a paper bag.

This is exactly the problem with shooters who use cartridges they can't kill game with. If they're convinced their rifle isn't powerful enough to kill a deer they will be mighty hard to convince they'll be better off with a less powerful cartridge.

Fortunately, though, it is in exactly this direction that modern cartridge development tends to be going. Even in the face of widespread misuse of the word "magnum," the truly modern cartridge is a considerably more *hittable* round than those of the past. To illustrate this point let's take two seemingly quite different cartridge developments of recent years, the .243 Winchester and the 7mm Remington Magnum, and see how they both fit the hittability profile of the truly modern cartridge.

The .243 fires a relatively light bullet at quite high velocity. It offers a flat trajectory, very mild recoil, and, in most rifles, beautiful accuracy. Since it has a small-diameter, lightweight bullet it does not fit the mold of *traditional* deer cartridges such as the .30/30, .32 Special, or .35 Remington. In fact, though, the .243 is a better deer cartridge than any of these for a variety of reasons. First of all it is a more accurate cartridge which in addition is available in more accurate rifles. This factor, which pure and simple is a result of modern technology and development, means that even if all other factors are equal the hunter will be better able to hit the game animal where he wants to. At a range of 200 yards this alone may reduce his placement error by as much as 3 inches.

Next, since the .243 is more pleasant to shoot, especially so far as recoil is concerned, it allows the hunter to be a better marksman. He will jerk and flinch less and is thus better able to give a good *personal* shooting performance. This varies greatly from one shooter to the next, but what may be an improvement of a fraction of an inch with some individuals may be—and often is—the difference between a hit and a miss with others.

If you doubt this for a moment just show up at a pre-deer-season sighting-in session at your local rifle range. Some shooters grit their teeth, squeeze their eyes shut, and even try to turn their heads away just at the moment they pull the trigger on their deer rifles. If a hunter, even a beginner, is equipped with a really *shootable* rifle such as a .243, after a few rounds he discovers he isn't being punished and settles down to do some pretty decent shooting.

If the range is beyond 150 yards or so the flat trajectory of the .243 makes up for errors in range estimating and thus ensures more precise bullet placement. At the longer ranges, where the rainbow trajectories of the older rounds make a hit altogether unlikely, the .243 still offers the prospect of a well-placed hit.

Even at short range in brush-shooting conditions the flat trajectory of the .243 offers a significant advantage. In fact this may be the overwhelming reason why the .243 is one of the very finest "brush" cartridges. It must be understood that there are no good brush rounds in the sense of a bullet that plows its way through saplings and limbs and bulldozes to the target. Instead, a good brush cartridge is one that makes it possible to avoid the brush. But how is that done? First of all the hunter selects an open path to the deer. There are several such openings or else he would not be able to see

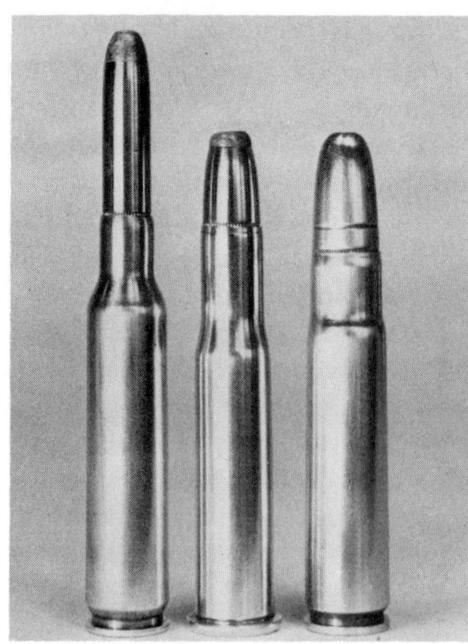

The small-caliber cartridge at left, which is a 6.5 Mannlicher, is actually a better "brush buster" than the popular brush rounds at right—the .30/30 and .35 Remington. The long 6.5mm bullet with its much greater sectional density and rotational stability does a better job in brush.

the animal. He is aiming *straight* at the spot he wants to hit but it must be remembered that the bullet will follow a *curved* path. Thus the more curved the bullet's trajectory the more liable it is to hit an obstacle above or below the line of aim. A .243, however, with its flat trajectory, remains quite close to the line of sight over a considerable bit of yardage.

Thus even without considering the superior energy of a .243 over the three other cartridges listed above, especially at longer ranges, its advantages are abundantly clear.

Essentially the same goes for the 7mm Remington Magnum. To be sure it is louder, kicks harder, and is harder to hit with than the .243. But with the 7mm Magnum you are moving into a larger, tougher class of game, such as elk. So here again, the 7mm offers milder recoil, a flatter trajectory, better accuracy, longer range, and greater energy than other cartridges traditionally used for game of that class. In short, just like the .243, it is a more *hittable* round, and that, above all else, is the hallmark of the modern cartridge.

HANDLOADING

There is absolutely no way to overstate the effect handloading has had on the quality of modern factory ammunition. Probably the single most valuable service it has performed in this direction has been to raise the level of accuracy *consciousness* of both shooters and manufacturers. Back before the beginning of what this book refers to as the era of the modern rifle, most shooters had no really well-defined idea of accuracy. If a rifle just happened to hit the target better than another rifle it was judged accurate. The other

Here I charge a batch of .243 Winchester cases with an RCBS powder measure.

was judged inaccurate. Likewise, a brand of ammunition that hit the target better than another brand was considered accurate and provided a rough basis of comparison by which a consumer made his selection when buying a box of shells. But beyond this he had little control. He naturally assumed that the manufacturer was doing his best and made few demands and offered no complaints unless the cartridges failed to go off altogether.

The manufacturer was happy too. He was satisfied that he was making ammo the best way he knew how and regularly upgrading his product by the addition of such modern developments as noncorrosive priming, nonfouling bullet jackets, and a variety of bullet-expansion gimmicks.

But then the handloader arrived on the scene and suddenly all such formerly peaceful relationships were torn asunder. The breed of handloaders which sprang up like weeds around the early 1950s were a loudmouthed lot. I know, I was one of them. Never did a reloaded cartridge spring from a tool without its creator loudly proclaiming that it was finer, faster, flatter, and more accurate than any factory-loaded round known to man. When I was about fifteen or so I ran an ad in the local paper advising that I was in the reloading business and could supply, at one dime each, .30/06, .270, 8mm Mauser, 6.5, and 7.7 Jap handloads *guaranteed better* than the finest factory stuff.

This was pretty strong talk, but as it just so happened I, and increasing hundreds and then thousands like myself, could, more often than not, back up our claims. The upshot was that performance that had previously been considered good, or at least acceptable, was no longer considered so hot. A shooter who for twenty years had bragged that his rifle would keep five shots in a 3-inch circle at 100 yards was all at once informed by a hotshot hand-

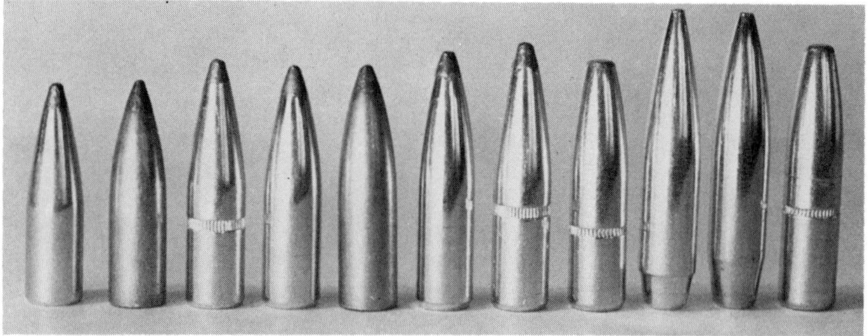

Here is one of the reasons handloading has become so popular. These eleven bullets, all a different weight, are 7mm caliber. With such an enormous selection of bullets in this and other calibers the handloader can select the combination of bullet, powder, etc. that gives the best possible accuracy and performance.

loader, even a fresh kid (like me), that some carefully tailored handloads for his rifle would make it possible to keep five shots inside 2 inches! And then he would proceed to do just that. And thus were sown the seeds of discontent.

But there were other factors at work which contributed to the cause. In truth, handloaders were really nothing all that new. They had been around as long as cartridge-firing rifles had been in existence, and as a matter of fact their numbers, in proportion to the total number of shooters, had even been on the decline between about 1920 and 1940. Their sources of supply had been either lead-alloy bullets which they cast themselves or jacketed bullets made by commercial ammo manufacturers. Thus, no matter how else he might struggle to improve the quality of his loads the handloader was ultimately limited by whatever degree of quality the bullet manufacturer chose, or was able, to bestow on his product. Accuracy was frequently improved by carefully working up a load to match a particular rifle, but by and large the main attraction was economy or, just as often, the pleasure of handloading.

During the great gun boom after World War II the ranks of handloaders swelled prodigiously and there appeared on the scene three or four new bulletmakers. A significant thing about these new bullets was that they were made in small shops, usually garages or basements, by men who were dedi-

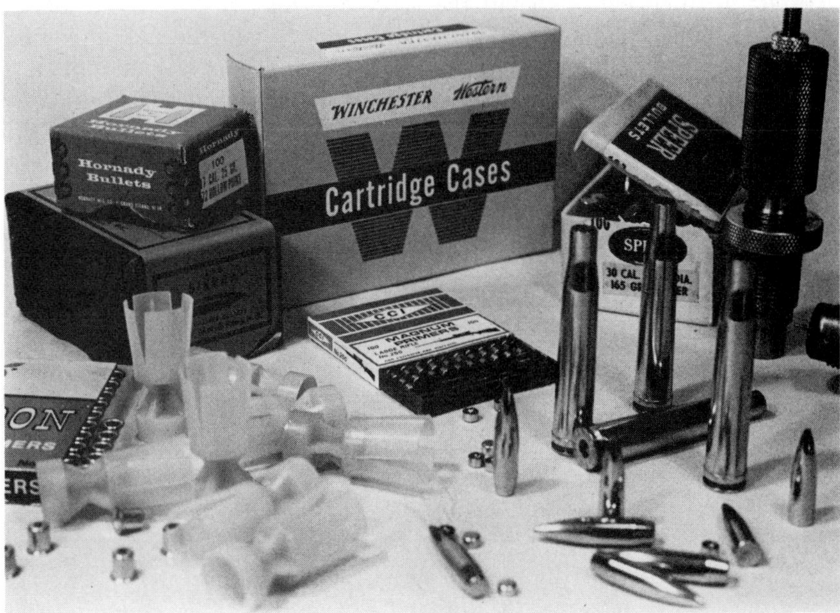

This photo gives an idea of the terrific assortment of reloading components available to handloaders.

cated shooters and had some very definite ideas about how precision bullet construction affects accuracy. One thing they realized for sure was that the only way they could win a share of the market and successfully compete with the major ammo makers would be to turn out a demonstrably more accurate bullet. And they did. This is why shooters will forever be in the debt of such gentlemen as Joyce Hornady, John Nosler, Vernon Speer, whose names graced their products, and the trio of Frank Snow, Loran Harbour, and Jim Spivey, who started an outfit called Sierra Bullets.

All of these new makers supplied reloaders with bullets which materially increased accuracy over most factory loads. The evidence was overwhelming. At first the attitude of the major manufacturers was simply to ignore the increased rumblings, but soon it became a definite annoyance and, at last, a tidal wave that swept them out of their traditional complacency. Even non-reloaders were well aware of the remarkable accuracy handloaders were getting and clamored for similar performance in storebought ammo. In other words, they had been educated as to what the word "accuracy" really meant. Never again in history would an American ammo maker be able to say to his customer, "If it's good enough for us it's good enough for you."

Nowadays the results of this kick in the seat are abundantly clear. Perhaps it's difficult to tell much difference in the accuracy of rounds like the .30/30, but cartridges that fall in the high-performance category frequently are so accurate as to challenge all but the very finest reloads. I've tested lots of .222, .225, 6mm Remington, .30/06, and 7mm Remington Magnum that would group five shots well under a minute of angle. And of special interest and encouragement to both handloaders and factory-ammo users is the way the big commercial ammo makers have adopted the philosophy of the smaller companies and try to earn a piece of the pie by producing bullets as accurate as modern technology allows for. Remington, for example, now turns out a premium-grade .22-caliber target bullet that many bench-rest shooters claim is as accurate as even the bullets made on custom swaging dies. And Winchester is going hard out with bench-rest-quality .22- and .24-caliber bullets and a long-range .30-caliber match bullet that may prove to be the best yet.

6

The Trigger

A distinguishing characteristic of modern rifle design is the thought and effort that have been invested in *shootable* triggers. Ever since man first figured out how to make a gun go off by means of a mechanism that could be activated by finger pressure, riflemen have been trying to make better triggers, but only recently have we come close to succeeding.

Over the centuries of rifle history the development of suitable triggers has been seriously handicapped by a general failure to understand the problem. Ask an average, experienced rifleman what kind of trigger will give the best performance and ninety-nine times out of a hundred you'll get an incorrect answer. His answer will seem fair enough, and even appear to be couched in sufficient reason, but nonetheless will reflect the prevailing misunderstanding of the problem. In order to fully appreciate the whole situation let's discuss how triggers affect rifle and shooter performance and how shooters themselves *think* they are affected.

If you try to fire a rifle with a creepy, gritty, 10-pound trigger pull the bad effect it has on your performance is obvious. The finger pressure required to overcome the trigger's resistance tends to shake the whole rifle, and maintaining an accurate sight alignment is difficult. This experience tells us that we will shoot better if the trigger is easier to pull. This, in principle, is correct, but this is also where shooters, generation after generation, have headed in the wrong direction to find a solution.

The tendency has been to develop mechanisms which fire at a very slight touch. I call this the hair-trigger syndrome. It usually fails on at least two counts, one physical and the other mechanical. First of all, few shooters are able to deal effectively with a light trigger pull. In my gun rack is a target rifle with a trigger release set to release at a pressure of 1 pound. Occasionally I hand the rifle to a visitor with an invitation to test the trigger. I always warn him that the trigger is very light and that he must be careful not to set it off before he is ready. But almost without fail he "blunders" into the trigger and it releases before he intended. When the rule requiring a minimum 3-pound trigger pull on smallbore target rifles was abolished there was a general rush among smallbore competitors to set their triggers to the merest

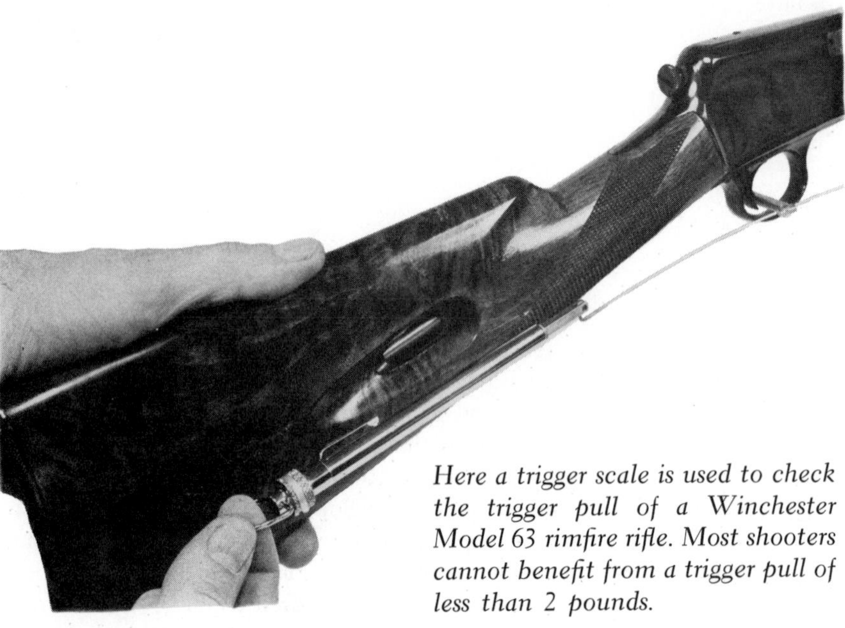

Here a trigger scale is used to check the trigger pull of a Winchester Model 63 rimfire rifle. Most shooters cannot benefit from a trigger pull of less than 2 pounds.

ounces. The result was a rash of wide hits on target because of premature discharges. After a few months of this many shooters had to increase their trigger pull weight because they found that even with considerable practice they could not adapt to an extra-light pull. You see, trigger pull is actually trigger *control,* and this control is best exercised when a specific degree of resistance is felt by the trigger finger. There is no one best amount of trigger resistance, as this varies from individual to individual, but a 2½- to 3-pound pull is, in my judgment, about as light a pull as most shooters can benefit by. Below that they begin getting in trouble, as will be discussed more thoroughly later in this chapter.

The second problem, the mechanical one, of the hair-trigger syndrome is caused by trigger devices which allow extra-light letoff. The most common form of "hair trigger" is the double set mechanisms which were popular on nineteenth-century muzzleloading "squirrel" rifles and, more recently, cartridge-firing rifles of predominantly European manufacture. Basically, the double set trigger works by means of a spring-activated mechanism which is cocked by pulling or pushing one of the triggers (usually the rear one but sometimes the front). Then, when the firing trigger is touched or pulled, the cocked mechanism releases and slams against another sear mechanism in the rifle and thus causes the hammer or firing pin to fall. For a long, long time this was considered to be the ultimate trigger, but here of late it has fallen into ill repute because it does two bad things. First of all, it takes too much *time.* A generation ago when neither rifles nor shooters were so precisely accurate as now, this time lag went unnoticed. But now it is recognized as an undesirable link in the time chain between the instant the brain gives the command to fire and when the bullet leaves the muzzle. The offending time lag occurs because the double set mechanism actually places *two* firing mechanisms in the rifle. The set unit has its own sear arrangement which must be released before the signal is passed along to another sear arrangement which then must also be released.

The other fault of a set-trigger mechanism is considerably more complex and has been understood only recently: barrel vibration, which I have discussed at length in Chapter 2. The very nature of the set trigger increases vibration and makes it difficult to control. The spring-loaded set mechanism strikes a solid blow against the barrel and action unit and thereby creates a fairly severe motion impulse even before the round is fired. If you study the brochures and publicity blurbs of various target rifles you'll notice that they usually tend to make a big thing out of having a "vibration-free" trigger mechanism. Now you know why. Also, back in the early 1950s when bench-rest shooting was just getting started, set triggers were used almost universally. But now they are seldom seen in competition.

This is not to say that set triggers are necessarily evil and have always been so. There have been times when the alternative was much worse. Back about 1953 or so I had a heavy-barreled .220 Swift built up on a surplus '98 Mauser action. The complete outfit with scope weighed over 15 pounds and my goal was to have the best long-range crow-getter in the community. The original Mauser trigger was so terrible that accurate shooting was impossible, so I fitted an old set of German-made double set triggers I'd salvaged out of a wrecked Mauser sporter. With these triggers set to fire at a feather's touch all I had to do was get the cross hairs on ol' bre'r crow and gently caress the front trigger. What rapture.

Double set triggers were almost a staple on rifles of German and Austrian make up until just the last few years. This was because the original Mauser trigger was miserable for sporter use and also because of the Germanic love of gadgetry. A double set trigger, like a cuckoo clock, is an intriguing gadget and hence all but irresistible.

The day of the double set trigger is on the wane. They are still widely used on muzzleloading rifles and probably always will be, but we'll see fewer and fewer of them on cartridge-firing guns. Some updated versions, such as are available for Anschutz target rifles, are available, and the old-fashioned German type is still around. But this latter will be seen less and less. Even in Europe, their final stronghold, they are losing ground to more modern adjustable single-trigger designs.

This is a German-made double-set trigger mechanism. The unit is "set" by pulling the back trigger, which cocks the mechanism, and then touching the front "hair" trigger. Such a trigger mechanism as this fires the rifle at the touch of a feather but does not promote as good accuracy as once thought.

A variation of the double-set mechanism is the so-called single-set. The single-set design made by M. H. Canjar Company of Denver, Colorado, is the best known, but the concept goes back many years. Single-set designs are found on American rifles dating to the Colonial era as well as English and American cartridge rifles dating back to the last half of the 1800s. Some Winchester rifles were so equipped on special order.

Almost every single-set mechanism ever made is activated by pushing the trigger forward with the thumb. This cocks the spring which will supply the

This is the Canjar single-set mechanism. The trigger shoe is pushed forward with the thumb, as shown here, and a small firing tab extends from the face of the trigger. The rifle fires when the tab is lightly touched. Otherwise the trigger will operate as a normal single stage unit.

energy to disengage the primary sear when the trigger is pulled. Like most double-set triggers, the better single-set designs have an adjustment screw which permits the weight of pull to be regulated from several ounces right down to fractions of an ounce. Also like most double-trigger designs, most single-sets give a heavy, creepy letoff if you want to fire the rifle without engaging the set mechanism. The most notable exception to this is the Canjar design, which, when not set, operates like a crisp, high-quality adjustable trigger, which in fact it is. When set, a small tab extends from the front of the trigger shoe. When this tab is touched it causes the spring-loaded shoe to kick the trigger stem and fire the rifle. This design creates less motion and commotion than most set-type mechanisms and also consumes less time, thus minimizing the previously described objection to spring-loaded mechanisms.

The purpose of the foregoing coverage of different set- or hair-trigger mechanisms is to provide background information into the various ways the trigger-pull problem has been dealt with over the years and to give a keener insight into the complexity of the situation. With this in mind let's consider what we're looking for in a truly modern trigger. Obviously, for maximum shooter and rifle performance a spring-loaded set design is out. Since shooters differ considerably as to just what release weight is most satisfactory, the trigger unit must be adjustable as to weight of pull. Also, the trigger should have as little movement as possible both before and after the sear is released. Trigger movement before the release is usually termed "creep," and after-motion is called "backlash." Excessive creep has a confusing effect on the shooter because it tends to obscure the exact instant when the rifle will fire. You no doubt recall, or at least have heard of, military marksmanship instructors exhorting the trainees to "squeeze" the trigger so that they will be "surprised" when the rifle fires. Actually this is only a training technique—in fact a ruse—to help overcome the tendency of new shooters to flinch in anticipation of a rifle's recoil. In truth, being "surprised" when the rifle fires is a poor way to get a bullet to go where you want it. Experienced target shooters want to determine the exact instant when they fire a round. This is possible only with a crisp, clean-breaking trigger without appreciable creep. When a certain amount of pressure is applied the sear should release like the proverbial glass rod breaking.

Do not confuse "creep" with the two-stage trigger mechanisms of military rifles and some target models. The two distinct movements of a military trigger are a built-in safety factor. Two-stage triggers are also used on some target rifles, especially by shooters who want additional sensitivity and control for position shooting. After the first stage is taken up only a slight pressure is required to "break" the second stage. You can be sure there is no "creep" in the second stage.

Backlash, or backslap, trigger movement after the sear release presents another sort of problem. This motion of the trigger finger interferes with a steady aim and hold, just as does creep, and can cause aim-destroying twitch or jerk when the motion is arrested. With triggers that have excessively bad backlash the trigger finger accelerates a bit just after the sear release. This movement usually does not slowly come to a halt but is blocked when the trigger hits a positive block or stoppage. Thus the effect is something like a light blow to the rifle. This disturbs the aim *while the bullet is still in the barrel.* The results are never good.

These three criteria—adjustability, freedom from creep, and freedom from backlash—seem modest enough, but in fact they cause riflemakers all sorts of frustrations. In order for the sear to release, some movement is necessary. By taking advantage of leverage and precision-ground sear points, such as in the custom-made Kenyon trigger, trigger movement is all but imperceptible. But unless the sear contact points are carefully ground and hardened—an expensive proposition—the release weight will vary from pull to pull and, if set

Detail of the Winchester Model 52 target rifle trigger. The small screw just ahead of the trigger-guard bow adjusts the weight of pull. This is one of the most finely precise triggers ever offered on a factory-made rifle.

too fine, may cause an accidental discharge when the bolt is closed. This factor in particular causes sleepless nights among riflemakers who put adjustable triggers on their rifles. All too often an overzealous tinkerer, convinced the sure way to fine accuracy is a hair trigger, will adjust his trigger so that it isn't at all safe. When I adjust a trigger I set it only to the point where no amount of violent bolt slamming will cause it to release.

A trigger mechanism with a series of levers reduces the tendency of accidental discharge when the unit is adjusted to minimum trigger pull and travel, but additional levers increase mechanical reaction time. So as it turns out we tend to lose something every time we gain something. The problem is far from solved, but the modern adjustable triggers on the Remington Model 700 and 40-X, Winchester Model 70 and 52, Weatherby Mark V, Ruger, Sako, and Anschutz are a giant step in the right direction.

I've long favored the Model 70 design because it is simple and terrifically

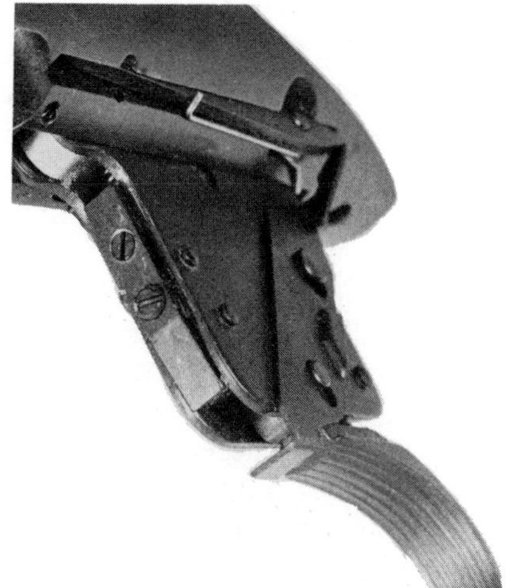

The trigger mechanism in the Remington Model 700. The two adjusting screws in the front adjust the weight of pull and the amount of travel or "backlash."

tough. The rapid-fire strings fired in bigbore competition are notoriously hard on triggers, but the Model 70 stands the punishment with few failures and very reliable shot-to-shot uniformity of pull. This is one of the reasons the Model 70 is the all-time favorite with bigbore competitors. It has only a limited adjustment range, however, and should not be set for a light pull.

Unfortunately, do-it-yourself tinkerers occasionally get to messing with M70 triggers and end up with an unsafe rifle. I've seen the engagement shoulder *filed* down so that a hard look would set it off. Though it looks simple enough it should be adjusted only by an expert. An expert, by the way, is the chap who realizes that attempts to get the pull much below 3 pounds are courting disaster. If for some reason it is considered imperative to have a Model 70 with a super-light pull, the only smart thing to do is to remove the original mechanism entirely and install a Canjar, Timney, or similar unit.

The Remington Model 700 or 40-X design is considerably more flexible in that it has simple screw adjustments for pull, creep, and backlash. Like the

This Winchester Model 70 target rifle is fitted with a Timney adjustable trigger. Weight of pull is set by turning the screw shown extending through the upper side of the trigger-guard bow. Finely adjustable but relatively low-cost trigger units such as this have played an important role in upgrading the "shootability" of rifles built on actions from surplus Mausers, Springfields, Enfields, etc.

Model 70, the M700 trigger is frequently done wrong by clubfisted tinkerers, but, unlike the Winchester, the Remington can be easily corrected once a wrong adjustment is made. For super-light trigger buffs, especially bench shooters, Remington offers a special-order trigger which can be set to 2 ounces. Most of the higher quality rifles being made in the U.S. and elsewhere at present feature trigger mechanisms more or less similar to the Remington, with at least an adjustment for weight of pull and usually another adjustment for creep and sear engagement.

Likewise, older rifle designs such as the Mausers, Springfields, Enfields, etc. have been updated by a half-century by the addition of custom triggers made by Canjar, Jaeger, Timney, and others. Getting rid of the original military triggers or outdated commercial designs will make a rifle about half again more shootable. Probably the finest triggers ever made are a few limited editions by a Southeastern gunsmith by the name of Jack Lane. But the Lane triggers have never been commercially available, and very few competitive shooters have had a chance to even see one. The best triggers offered for sale are made by the Ely, Nevada, gunsmith Karl Kenyon. The Kenyon triggers are as close to a work of art as milled steel can get, and top-flight smallbore shooters swear by them. Winchester offers Kenyon triggers on their top-of-the-line smallbore match rifles as a premium-priced special-order accessory.

The trigger of the future, especially on target rifles, may very well be electrically operated. I've tested a couple of electric designs, one on a rifle and the other a pistol, and there are some distinct possibilities. First of all, the trigger itself can operate totally independent from the sear mechanism. Since the pull of the trigger does nothing but establish electrical contact between two points the range of "pull" weight can be set down to a small fraction of an ounce. This also means that the shot-to-shot uniformity of pull can be very nearly absolute.

Energy for the electric trigger is supplied by batteries held in the pistol grip or, for that matter, almost anywhere else. There is still a good bit of development to be done with the electric-trigger concept. For one thing, every effort must be made to make the solenoid or magnetic unit which releases the sear lightning fast. Sluggishness has been the chief complaint with existing electric mechanisms. But this should be no problem for an electronics wizard.

But, whenever I get to talking about electric triggers, someone always says, "Why bother with an electronically activated sear at all? Why not eliminate sear, striker, firing pin, and all, and go directly to electrically fired cartridge?" This would eliminate the problems of lock time entirely, wouldn't it? And this may very well be the direction in which we're headed.

Part II
Hunting Rifles

7

Lever-Actions

The lever-action rifle is as all-American as Mom's home-baked apple pie, Tom Sawyer, and the Saturday-night bath. It's the rifle that won the West, hastened the demise of countless movie and television ruffians (and even a few of the real thing), and also won a place for itself, for all time, in the hearts of American sportsmen. Yet, strangely, despite the enormous popularity of lever-loaders in many parts of the world, until recently they remained an almost exclusively American product. A little-known fact, outside of collectors' circles, is that lever-action military rifles were used by such diverse countries as Spain, Russia, Turkey, France, Canada, several of the South American banana republics, and the U.S. But virtually all of these were made by Winchester. An even more interesting fact is that the early management at Winchester envisioned the lever-action repeater as primarily a military weapon and pinned their hopes of commercial success on its acceptance in martial circles. Oliver F. Winchester himself, the president of what was then the New Haven Arms Company, predicted: "Probably it will modify the art of war; possibly it may revolutionize the whole science of war. Where is the military genius that is to grasp this whole subject, and so modify the science of war as to best develop the capacities of this terrible engine—the exclusive control of which would enable any government to rule the world?"

Of course what good old Oliver had in mind was earning for himself a princely fortune such as then being amassed by a few of the European arms-

The Winchester Model 94 is one of the all-time great brush rifles—not so much because of the calibers in which it was offered, as commonly supposed, but because it is such a handy and quick-pointing rifle for brush shooting where fleeting targets are the rule.

making moguls. But alas, no "military genius" bent on conquering the world with that "terrible engine," the lever-action rifle, came forth, so Winchester turned toward the civilian market. The chief benefit of the military contracts was that they provided cash, sometimes at critical moments, and in the long run provided some interesting specimens for modern-day Winchester collectors.

The great European armsmakers argued that their bolt-action designs, which were just taking hold, were a far more reliable and efficient instrument of war. The lever-action, they pointed out, did indeed have a high rate of fire, but when the magazine ran dry they were too slow and cumbersome to reload. A soldier with a clip-fed bolt gun had greater firepower over a lengthy span of battle, and, besides, lever rifles were too complicated and costly for ordinary soldiers. By the time Winchester got around to a clip-fed lever rifle (a modification of the Model 1895 rifle), a far more terrible engine—the machine gun—was in production here and in Europe.

During the last half of the 1800s several U.S. designers and manufacturers tried their hands at marketing lever-action rifles, but of these only Marlin and Winchester survive. These two firms have, over the years, presented sportsmen with a fascinating array of models and calibers of lever guns. So many, in fact, that a comprehensive description would amount to a nice, fat book. Therefore, we'll concern ourselves here with current makes and models and touch only lightly on past models.

MARLIN

Perhaps the most distinctive feature of the Marlin approach to lever-action design, as opposed to Winchester, is side port ejection. Winchester's eject out the top. Early claims were that this arrangement better protected the mechanism from dirt, dust, water, and other pollutants. I doubt that the designers had any inkling that the solid receiver top would pay off handsomely generations later as a very convenient place to mount a scope.

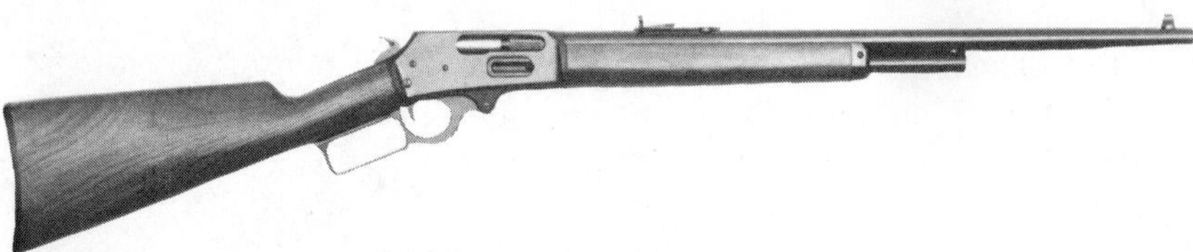

The Model 95 Marlin, which comes in .45/70 chambering. The .45/70 cartridge is a fun proposition for handloaders.

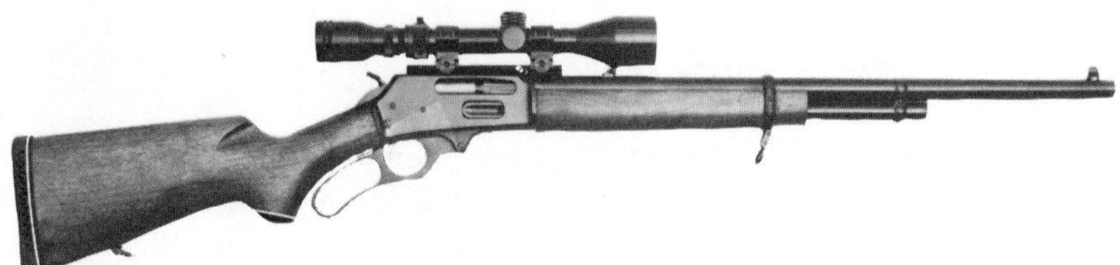

The Marlin Model 444 lever gun, which is available in Marlin .444 caliber.

The popular Model 336 Marlin, shown here with Marlin scope. This rifle, which was introduced in the late 1880s, has sold over two million copies and is currently offered in .30/30 and .35 Remington calibers.

The four basic Marlin centerfire lever designs in current production are the Models 336, 444, 1894, and 1895. Of these the Model 336 is by far the best seller, coming in popular .30/30 or .35 Remington chambering and two or three different stock stylings and barrel lengths. Introduced in 1893, the Model 336 is one of the all-time big sellers; over two and a half million have been sold. Over the years there have been a few changes, of course, such as Marlin's adoption of Micro-Groove rifling, and a host of chamberings have been tried and in time abandoned. Basically, though, it is still the solid, dependable rifle of over three-quarters of a century ago, just made better by better materials and modern technology.

A few years ago a Marlin public relations man called me and, sounding as if the world was about to end, tearfully advised that the retail price of the 336 was at last forced over the one-hundred-dollar mark.

"Well, if I were you," I said, "I'd buy one before the price increase becomes effective."

"But I already own one," was his confused reply.

"Then what are you so worried about?"

At this writing the price is well over a hundred dollars, but as always the buyer gets a lot of rifle building for his money. Most of the action parts are machined out of forgings, and the rich walnut stocks are among the few in the whole industry that are individually fitted to each receiver. A few years back a book entitled *The Compleat Just Jim,* a collection of not-so-serious shooting tales I wrote for *The Rifle* magazine, rolled 'em in the aisles with my account of the gunsmithing Bowman brothers and their "secret" stock-inletting process of heating a barreled action until it was red hot and then letting it burn its way into a stock blank. But as it so happens the people at Marlin actually use a similar technique. The tang extensions are heated in an induction coil, then pressed into the almost but not quite finished butt-section inletting. This results in a very uniform seating of metal against wood, and since the fit is so uniform it is very uncommon for Marlin stocks to split as a result of recoil butting away at an unevenly fitted area. Even though the stock has to be removed for final finishing (while the receiver goes on for barrel fitting and blueing), the two are rematched at the end of the assembly line.

A cut-rate version of the 336 is the Glenfield Model 30A, which cuts such cost corners as not using real walnut for stocking, but basically it's the same rifle.

When Marlin announced their Model 444 and its companion round the .444 Marlin cartridge in 1964, there was a considerable murmur among the "hit 'em with something big" crowd. Actually the .444 Marlin is only a stretched-out .44 Magnum, and Remington even uses the same 240-grain .44 bullet used in their souped-up .44 Mag. rifle loads. The long .444 Marlin case jacks the velocity up to around 2400 fps at the muzzle compared to 1850 fps for .44 Magnum rifle loads. This means it has more punch than, say, the Model 336 in .30/30 or .35 Remington caliber, but it still isn't anything to go into a swoon over. With its big, fat, blunt nose it has the classic appearance of a mighty brushbuster—but in fact it ain't.

If the current nostalgic craze, featuring such stars from the past as the .22

Hornet, .30/40 Krag, and especially the venerable .45/70, had been in full flower back in 1964, I doubt if Marlin would have bothered with the .444. Their more recent Model 1895 in .45/70 chambering is a lot more fun to play with, especially if you're a handloader. Factory-loaded .45/70 ammo boxes carry a stern warning against being fired in old trapdoor Springfields and other such fragile stuff and recommends that it be used only in 1886 Winchester rifles and rifles of similar strength. Even so, they are loaded down to a meek milksop of their potential. A handloader who owns a modern rifle such as the Ruger Single Shot or the Marlin 1895 can load up to some really bonecrushing power. There must be upwards of a dozen rifles chambered for the .45/70 on today's market, but the Marlin is far and away the best choice if you're interested in some serious hunting. It's the only repeater available, and it also happens to be one of the most accurate.

The little Model 1894 is offered purely and simply for lever-action fans who are keen on the .44 Magnum cartridge. It's a trim, good-looking rifle, but the cartridge hasn't a whole lot of range, and to my mind is at best an under-100 yard affair for whitetail, boar, and similar game. Still, it makes pretty good sense for hikers and campers who like the idea of a matched-caliber rifle and handgun set.

WINCHESTER

After over a century of unquestioned leadership in the field of lever-action rifle production, Winchester, as of 1975, is down to a single centerfire

The all-time favorite and number 1 seller, the Winchester Model 94. The production record now hovers around the three million mark. Over the years it has been offered in a variety of styles and calibers but at present the only chambering is the venerable .30/30.

model: the Model 94 in .30/30 caliber only. The handsome Model 88, which probably represents the high point of lever-action technology, was dropped in 1974. I always felt that the M88 was an extremely good-looking rifle, and the samples I tested and hunted with were fast-pointing, slick-operating, and accurate enough to get the job done. Most important, though, it combined lever-action operation with a locking system strong enough to use with modern high-intensity cartridges such as the .308, .243, and .284. Presumably it had everything—tradition, ease of operation, and power. If I were inclined to hunt with a lever-action rifle this would have been my number one choice. Very likely, in a few years the Model 88, especially the scarcer carbine version, will be grist for the collector's mill.

The Winchester Model 88 was a thoroughly modern lever action rifle designed for use with modern high-intensity cartridges such as the .243, .308, .284 Winchester, etc. It was discontinued in 1974.

Also, just a few years back Winchester had a stab at reintroducing the Model 64, a dolled up and sportier version of the basic M94. After a brief run the project was dropped. By and large the passing of the Model 88 and the fizzled reoffering of the M64 point up the simple fact that the lever-action is becoming less and less the darling of the American hunter. Of course, dropping the M88 can be attributed to a number of factors—increased production cost, being priced too high for the market, having to compete with too many other lever models, diverting too much of the plant's efforts away from more important projects, etc. But all of these reasons are just another way of saying that consumer demand wasn't sufficient to continue production.

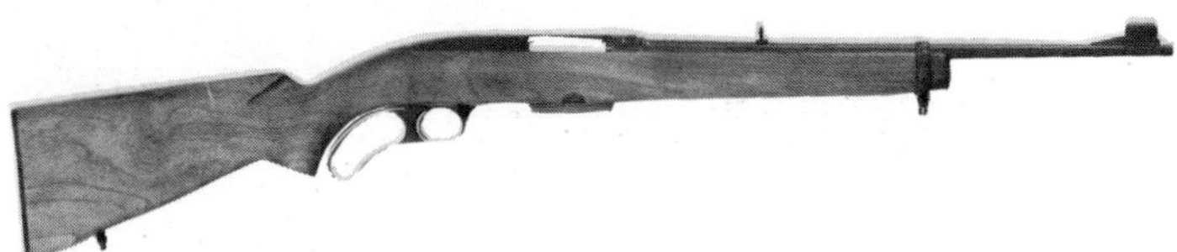

The carbine version of the Winchester Model 88. In .243, .284 or .308 Winchester caliber it was a superb brush rifle.

Thus the venerable Model 94, with sales now around three million, carries the flag. Needless to say it is probably the all-time favorite lever-action rifle. It is light, fast-handling, and reliable. Should the day ever arrive when it passes from the scene we'll lose the symbol of a vibrant chapter in the American saga.

SAVAGE

Back in 1899 when the Savage Arms works introduced their new lever-action rifle they undoubtedly knew they had a fine rifle, but I doubt that they realized that the action's inherent strength and flexibility would ensure its survival for what, most likely, will be a century or more. Like other rifles of that early time the Savage 99 was chambered for such rounds as the .30/30, .25/35, .32/40, .38/55. etc., but *unlike* other rifles of the day it proved

The Savage Model 99, one of the most flexible lever-action designs ever developed. This is the Model 99A version, which has recently been resurrected in .250/3000 caliber.

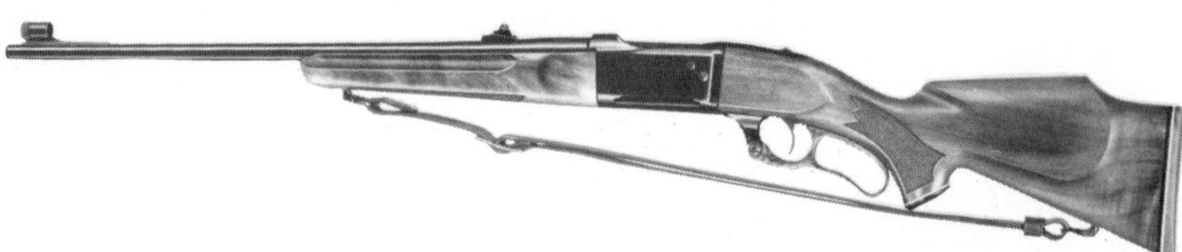

This is the recently introduced Model 99 CD with clip magazine and deluxe Monte Carlo cheek-piece stock.

adaptable to new cartridge developments over the years. The first evidence of this occurred in 1915 with the introduction of the .250/3000 cartridge. More recently it has proved a fit companion for such high-pressure rounds as the .243, .308 and .284 Winchester. No other currently produced lever model dating from that era has proved so adaptable.

A strongly contributing factor to the functional reliability and ease of operation of the Model 99 is the rotary or "spool" magazine. Recently, a "C" type or clip-fed version was introduced. The clip version is not, I feel, as desirable as the rotary feed, but I understand it is popular among road-driving meat gathers who obey the letter of the law by keeping their rifle unloaded in the vehicle but quickly jam a loaded clip into the rifle when game is sighted.

Interestingly, both the .250 Savage chambering and the prewar straight-stock "A" model styling seemed a dead and forgotten issue only a few years ago, but just to satisfy some remote clammerings, the Savage people made a limited run of 99s in this combination. The item proved such a big seller that it's now a standard Savage catalog item. I'm not surprised at this success, because the .250 Savage is one of the best possible choices for deer-size game in all sorts of hunting conditions. I wouldn't consider it a very good choice for elk, but I have to point out that the "quickest deadest" I ever saw a bull elk dropped was with none other than a Model 99 in .250/3000 caliber.

BROWNING

Since the Browning line of sporting guns has tended to center around quality-built, prestige items with emphasis on autoloaders, shooters thought it somewhat incongruous when the firm introduced a lever-action centerfire a while back. But did you know that none other than John M. Browning was the designer of such lever-action Winchester rifle favorites as the Models 1886, 1892, 1884, and 1895, and the Model 1887 lever shotgun? Thus the only thing really incongruous about the BLR (Browning Lever Rifle) is that after such a history of designing successful lever rifles the model finally produced by the company bearing his name is *not* an original John M. design.

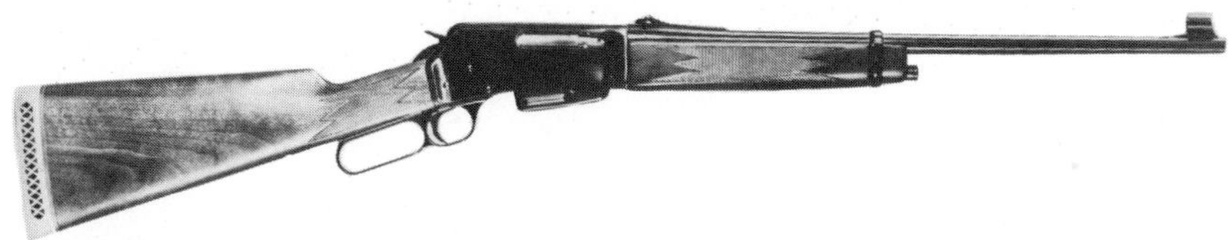

The Browning BLR lever rifle is a combination of traditional styling and a thoroughly up-to-date clip-fed action with rotary locking lugs.

The BLR is especially interesting because of the three lever designs of late years (Browning, Winchester 88 and Sako Finnwolf) it is the only one with which such advanced concepts as rotary locking lugs have been combined with more or less "traditional" lever-action styling. This of course adds nothing to the shootability or usefulness of a hunting rifle but might be a smart idea in light of today's merchandising techniques. The BLR has, in the few years of its existence, proved itself a solid, dependable performer and capable of surprisingly good accuracy for its type. Much of this good accuracy is no doubt due to the .243 and .308 cartridge for which it is chambered. Nonetheless I can't help but wonder if the BLR might not have been a better rifle if some of the "traditional Western" styling had been omitted.

SAKO

The Finnish-made Sako Finnwolf is one of the very, *very* few lever-action rifles designed and built outside the U.S. The Browning BAR is another example, though I understand it was designed in the U.S., and prior to World War II some Spaniards tried their hand at making copies of Winchesters. Other current imports such as the Navy Arms "1873" and Model 66 are only

The Finnish-made Sako Finnwolf rifle is a thoroughly up-to-date design and one of the slickest-looking lever-actions ever marketed.

replicas of Winchesters. Likewise, the Rossi Saddle Ring carbine is a look-alike of the Winchester Model 92. But the Finnwolf is the first truly non-American effort of any stature.

Like all members of the Sako line it is beautifully built and finished, and it also sports a price tag of over two hundred and fifty clams.

The mechanism features an interesting gear-and-lever linkage system for operating the bolt. Actually, like the Winchester Model 88 and Browning BLR it can be honestly classified as a turning-lug bolt-action which just happens to be lever-operated. The locking-lug arrangement gives strength on the order of a modern bolt-action rifle and allows the use of the .243 and .308. Naturally, the reason these two rounds are so popular for modern lever-action rifles is that they are short and thus suitable for the short-throw lever mechanism. (About five years ago a Sako representative showed me a stretched-out Finnwolf chambered for the .300 Winchester Magnum. Production plans at that time were indefinite, and since I've heard nothing more on the matter I assume the project has been set on the back burner or dropped altogether. If and when they get it on the market it will be the first long-throw lever job in quite a few years.)

With a 23-inch barrel and a weight of 6¾ pounds the clip-fed Finnwolf hardly qualifies as a featherweight carbine. It tends to handle and feel more like a modern bolt rig. This impression is emphasized even more by the Monte Carlo comb and cheek piece (which, by the way, is available right- or left-handed).

Though the Finnwolf is one of the most accurate and certainly one of the slickest-looking lever rifles ever marketed, I have my doubts about its future. Due to the regal price tag very few of them are seen on dealers' racks. And, come to think of it, I've never run across a hunter in the field carrying one.

MOSSBERG

Though the gunmaking firm of Mossberg just recently presented a line of centerfire lever-action rifles, it is not really their maiden effort with levers. Back before World War II, as I recall, they made a lever-actuated, falling-block rimfire rig called the Model "L," and there have been other lever-stroked Mossberg rimfire actions since. The new centerfires, which were first

The Mossberg Model 472 lever gun is quite similar to the Marlin Model 336.

unveiled at the 1973 National Sporting Goods Association show in Houston, Texas, are from three paces almost dead ringers for the Marlin Model 336. I've never had a chance to test-fire the new Mossberg Model 472 lever guns, so I can't really offer much in the way of a positive statement as to their accuracy. But I would expect that the grouping ability is very much on the order of the Marlin 336 or Winchester Model 94. Like the Marlin, the Mossbergs have a solid top, which makes use of a low-mounted scope much easier. Also like the Marlin, the Mossbergs come in .30/30 and .35 Remington calibers and are offered in different barrel lengths and stock styles. In this respect my advice to the prospective buyer is the same I give for the Marlin: buy the shortest barrel length available. Great "brush" guns are great because they are easy to carry and handle in brush; the shorter the better.

OTHER LEVER-ACTIONS

For the most part the balance of the centerfire lever-action designs currently available fall into the plinking or collecting category. Two rifles imported by Navy Arms Co., the Model "1873" and Model 66, are replicas of early Winchesters, and while handsomely finished hardly qualify as serious hunters. The Model "1873" comes in .357 Magnum or .44/40 chambering, and the Model 66 comes in .22 RF, .38 Special or .44/40. If I were buying one I think I'd go for the .44/40 just for old times' sake.

A somewhat more serious hunting rifle is the Rossi, which is available in .44 Magnum. This qualifies it as a pretty serious piece for short-range shots at deer-sized game.

A few years ago I met a fascinating gun designer by the name of L. W. Seecamp who showed me a prototype of a lever-action rifle which could be used for magnum-class cartridges right up through the .458 Winchester Magnum. The prototype he showed me was a masterpiece of simplicity and design ingenuity, and I urged him to get the rifle made on a production basis. We've kept in touch since then and he assures me that he is still working on the project. In the meantime, though, he has busied himself manufacturing such clever little items as a short-throw lever mechanism for Marlin rifles. Whether or not Seecamp gets his lever rifle on the market remains to be seen, but it could very well herald the dawn of a new lever-action era. There are lots of shooters, I suspect, who would like to get their hands on a lever-action rifle in, say, 7mm Remington Magnum caliber.

The prototype of the Louis Seecamp lever-action rifle, which is designed for use with magnum calibers.

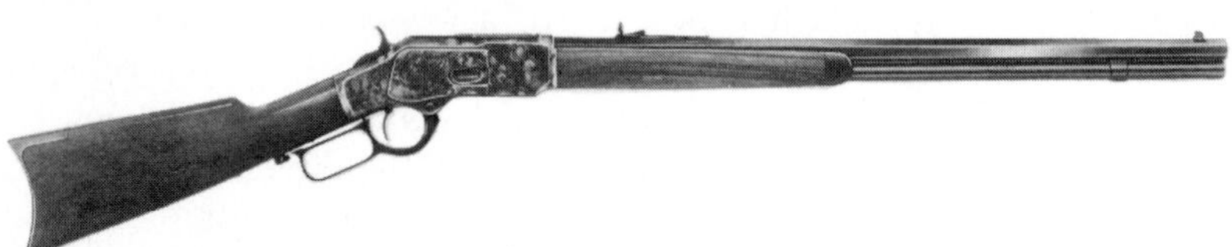

This replica of the famed Winchester Model 1873 is imported by Navy Arms Co. Chamberings are a choice of .357 Magnum or .44/40.

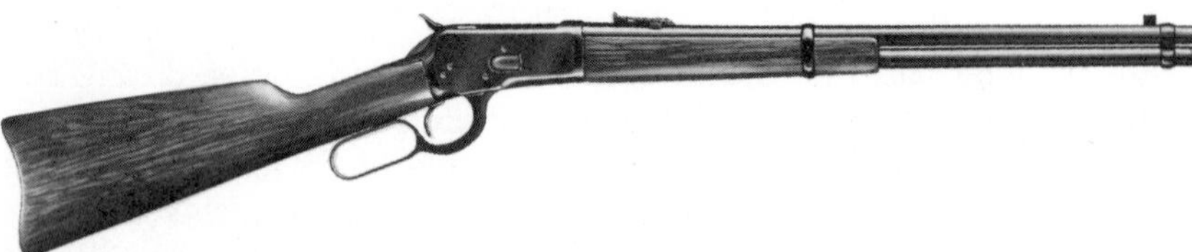

The imported Rossi saddle-ring carbine is a close look-alike of the Winchester Model 92 lever gun and comes in .44 Magnum chambering.

8

Autoloaders and Pumps

Ever since the idea of a repeating rifle entered men's heads, the foremost goal of gun designers has been ever-increasing firepower. The landmarks in firearms design, from the Hall breechloader through the early repeating Winchesters and the designs of John Browning, have invariably centered around means of making guns fire and reload themselves in the shortest possible time. If speed of operation is the great criterion by which firearms development is gauged, then it would logically follow that the various semiautomatic sporting rifles (since both law and good sportsmanship prohibit full automatic fire for hunting rifles) most truly represent the modern rifle. No doubt if a last-century buffalo hunter or Indian scout could be resurrected from his moldy surroundings and offered a choice of today's riflery he would select something that fired—and fired again—at the touch of a trigger.

But as it just so happened, by a queer turn of circumstance, the evolution of the modern *sporting* rifle took a turn away from sheer rapidity of operation just about the time the modern autoloader reached its current form. Instead of operational speed, the hallmarks of the modern rifle have become accuracy, advanced ballistics, and aesthetic appeal. The ability to shoot rapidly got shunted off on a side road that may eventually turn out to be a dead end. Functional reliability may also be claimed as a criterion of a truly modern rifle, but even if so, no more demerits could be scored against autoloaders than any other basic system. You see, the occasional tales we hear about the unreliability of autoloaders is mostly just talk. Stoppages do occur with autoloaders, but not so often as we hear. No more often, in fact, than most other types, except for single-shots, and even then the jam is usually caused by some external circumstance such as bum reloads.

Be that as it may, the attitude of many shooters and hunters toward centerfire autoloading rifles is that at best they are capable of only so-so accuracy and are only in their element at short range or where dense cover and fleeting targets prevail. The reasoning is, in other words, that autoloaders do their thing where *quantity*, not *quality*, of shooting is required. This attitude has proliferated to the point, I feel, where some hunters eye a fellow hunter equipped with a self-loader and categorize him as a poor slob who knows he's a bum shot and tries to make up for it by blowing the woods down.

I don't happen to buy either of these theories, especially the one about autoloaders being inaccurate. Some autoloaders, to be sure, were woefully prone to scatter shots all over the target. The Remington Model 8, which was introduced back in 1906, is one that comes to mind. And so was its successor, the Model 81. These rifles functioned on the old long-recoil system, with the barrel inside a jacket and the sights attached to the jacket, so accuracy never had much of a chance from the beginning. Another set of unimpressive performers were the Winchester autoloading models of 1905, 1907, and 1910. They were as heavy as target rifles, but the two-piece stocks and simple blowback mechanism hardly contributed to target accuracy. Like the Remingtons, their principal contribution to the lore of riflery was that autoloaders, if given half a chance, can prove outstandingly inaccurate. This curse has fallen, like a wet blanket, on all autoloaders since.

But, just to keep our opinions in balance, how accurate *can* a self-feeder be? And how accurate are *modern* autoloaders?

I'll start off with the *most* accurate autoloader I've ever tested. It is the so-called M-14 (A1), which is a commercial (non-full-automatic) version of the military M-14. There are, I understand, two or three outfits making similar rifles, but this one was made by the Springfield Armory, of Geneseo, Illinois. Actually, with the exception of the receiver, the complete rifle is built up of surplus parts. It comes in standard and National Match grades. Ordinarily, as a matter of principle, I shy away from surplus military junk and military look-alikes, especially the autoloaders, because they have very limited sporting application. But as it so happens the Springfield Armory M-14 (A1) Model rifle fulfills a demand in the area of target shooting. Some bigbore matches are limited to service rifles only—meaning either the M-1 Garand or the M-14 or the M-16. In its present state and under the existing course of fire, the M-16 is all but worthless, the M-1 is good, and the M-14 is better. The problem, though, is that M-14s are not readily available to civilians. Thus most civilian competitors have to toe the line with M-1s while their military brethren go at it with the superior M-14. The commercial M-14

(A1) has changed all that and made it possible for non-military shooters to compete with less rifle handicap. So I took the rifle pretty seriously.

To see how accurate the Geneseo, Illinois, "Springfield Armory" M-14 is, I fitted one with a 12× scope and bench-tested it just like any other target rifle. At 100 yards the best five-shot group I fired measured an amazingly tight .600 inch and the largest groups ran 1.250. The average was about an

The Browning automatic rifle. My tests indicate this is the most accurate of the self-loading sporting rifle designs available. It is also the only one available in magnum-class chambering.

inch or slightly under. Now this is fine accuracy for *any* rifle, much less an autoloader. The ammo was my standard .308 (7.62 NATO) target load of 39 grains of 3031 behind a 168-grain match bullet.

An autoloader which has far greater appeal to the average sportsman, and can also be remarkably accurate, is Browning's BAR, which at present comes in .243, .270, .308, .30/06, 7mm Remington Magnum, .300 Winchester Magnum, and .338 Winchester Magnum. In addition to being the only commercially available autoloader in magnum chambering it is also, in my experience, the most accurate of its class. The three or four I've tested will group five shots inside 2 inches at 100 yards most of the time with good ammo, and I hear of similar results from other shooters. In truth, I feel that a fair degree of this accuracy is based on the BAR's *shootability*. They are pretty heavy, which aids holding; they have a well-designed stock, a rigid forend, and a surprising crisp trigger. (Most autoloaders have terrible triggers.)

The BAR, in fact, is accurate enough to rate serious consideration for hunting conditions where long, open-country shots at such game as prong-

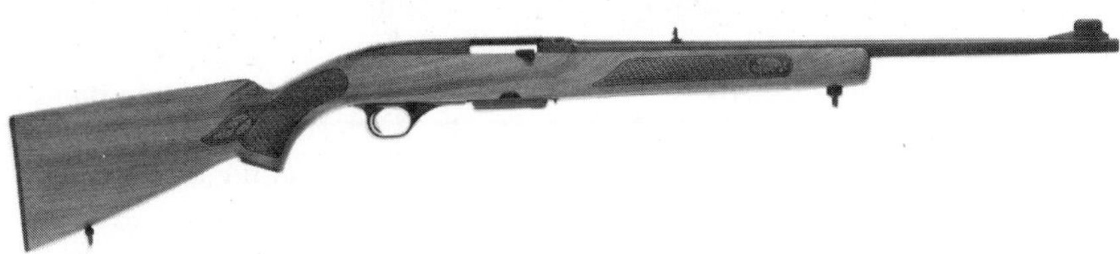

One of the trimmest and best-looking autoloaders was the discontinued Model 100 Winchester.

horns are the rule. Also, the thought has occurred to me that one in .338 Winchester Magnum would be great stuff for our big, mean bears or in Africa for "walking up" such dangerous game as lion. A BAR in .458 Magnum chambering would have great possibilities for African game, and, as a matter of fact, some Browning autos have already been custom-converted to this caliber for just such purposes.

A disappointment in the accuracy department was Winchester's Model 100. Introduced in 1960, this rifle always impressed me as the trimmest of the autoloading lineup, and the little carbine version was a fine little friend in heavy brush. But despite the M100's one-piece stock, which should have aided accuracy, the rifle could never perform well because of the U.S. M-1 carbine-type receiver attachment at the rear and the simple front-end tie-down. The anchoring system was sometimes improved by freezing the recoil block in place with fiberglass bedding compound, but by and large the M100 pretty much lived up to the unfortunate stereotype of autoloading rifles—fine for brush hunting but not much in the way of accuracy. For one reason or another the Model 100 was axed from the Winchester tree in 1974 and will in time, I suppose, become fuel for Winchester collectors' boundless enthusiasm.

One of the most popular autoloading rifles of all time is the Remington Model 742, shown here in deluxe grade with Monte Carlo comb and cheek piece.

The Remington Model 742 autoloader, which like the Browning and Winchester self-stuffers is gas-operated, is by all counts the big seller in the class. In my view it's also a rifle of considerable puzzlement. I've tested rifles in this model which would group as well as a good bolt gun, but I've also tried some which wouldn't group in a 30-day chamberpot. Actually, I'm not being quite fair, because I'm lumping the older Model 740, a direct ancestor of 1955 vintage, in with the revised version. The 740 had a stock as crooked as a barley scythe and was almost impossible to aim well. The erratic grouping is said to be caused in part by the barrel heating up and changing point of impact as the expanding metal alters the tension between the barrel stud and forearm screw. The lads at Williams Gun Sight Company even offer an "accuracy block" which fits in front of the barrel stand and is claimed to stop some of the shifting of bullet direction.

The later versions of the Model 742 come with more shootable stocks, even a Monte Carlo for scope users, and some of the working parts are coated with Teflon. This no doubt slickens up the operation. Also, to the everlasting credit of the Remington folks, the 742 is available in .243 and 6mm Remington calibers. Despite the popular concept of the "ideal" brush cartridge as a hulking bruiser that blunders through dense cover smashing everything in its path, the .243 and 6mm Remington are among the very best choices for brush-country deer hunting. And too, their relatively light recoil contributes to faster shooter recovery between shots. This can speed up the *effective* firepower of an autoloader considerably.

The raciest-looking of the current crop of autoloaders has to be Harrington & Richardson's Model 360 "Ultra Auto." Gas-operated and clip-fed, this

The Model 360 Harrington & Richardson autoloader, which comes in .243 or .308 Winchester caliber.

slickly finished dude comes with such stuff as a rollover cheek piece and teardrop grip cap, and, naturally, white spacers. Despite all this fluff, the 360 has a trimly engineered mechanism and some pretty sound, no-nonsense features. The only two calibers for which it is chambered, the .243 and .308, make good sense for an autoloader. My only experience with this rifle is a north woods whitetail hunt, and my only testing was the half-dozen or so rounds of 180-grain .308 loads it took to check the zero. The function was OK, but you'll have to check with someone else about the Ultra Auto's accuracy, because I haven't shot one enough to know.

The only other autoloading centerfire worth mentioning is Ruger's Model 44. As its model description implies, the little lightweight comes in .44 Magnum caliber only. Gas-operated, of course, and a tube-feeder. In the charac-

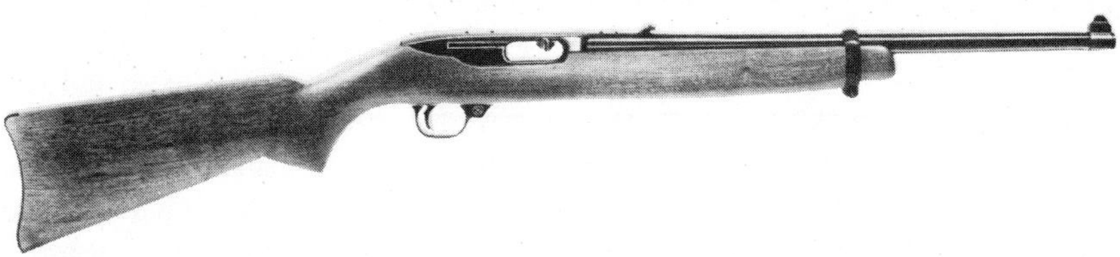

An extremely light and fast-handling autoloader for short to medium range shots at deer-sized game is the Ruger Model 44 in .44 Magnum caliber.

teristic manner of Ruger designs the Model 44 was engineered with a specific purpose in mind—deer-sized game inside of 100 yards in heavy cover. For this purpose it is hard to beat. Its light weight (5¾ pounds) makes it lightning-fast, and the short overall length (36¾ inches) makes it ideal for carrying in tough country. The thumb-sized .44 Magnum bullet looks like what many good souls think a brush buster should look like, but in fact it offers nothing special in the way of bush ballistics. The jewel in the crown in this instance is the rifle. It is a great brush *rifle.*

There are a dozen or so other autoloading centerfire rifles on the market, but they are of no real interest to the hunter. What might be considered worthwhile designs, such as the Ruger Mini-14, are for police and military purposes only and as such are beyond the scope of this book. Others, such as various contraptions that look like machine guns but aren't, or copies of the worthless .30 carbine, aren't to be taken seriously.

PUMPS

Any discussion of pump-action centerfire rifles is bound to be short and sweet—there just aren't that many of them. The topic opens with Remington's Model 760 "Gamemaster" and closes with the Model 170 Savage. Despite the historical popularity of slide-action shotguns among American shooters, rifles of similar operation have never caught on big. (Nor, of course, have bolt-action shotguns.) Back around the last fifteen years of the nineteenth century the Colt works had a pretty serious go at pump-action rifles when they produced various forms of their "Lightning" rifles. These were

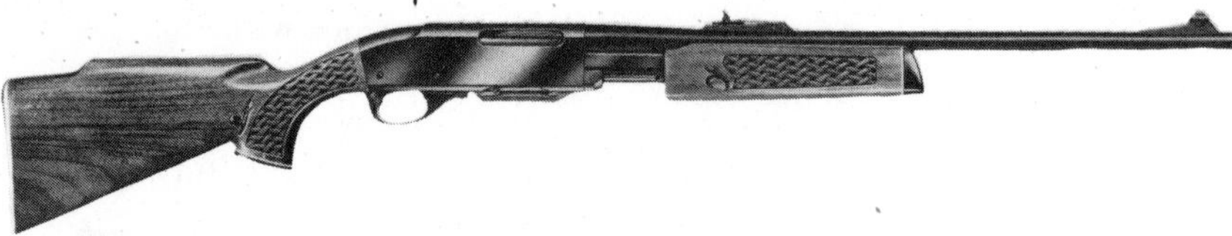

The Remington Model 760 pump-action big-game rifle.

nicely finished guns and came in a fair variety of calibers, but they lost out to the lever-action designs then so much in vogue.

Back in 1912, Remington entered the pump-action rifle field with their Model 14A, one of the first centerfire pumps designed for smokeless powder. This was followed by the 14½ and 141A, the 25, and eventually the 760. I've heard it said that the earlier Remington pump designs didn't cut a wide swath saleswise because they were available only for cartridges of limited popularity. Personally, I can't swallow this reasoning without gulping. True enough, the .25, .30, .32, and .35 were never barn burners, but they could have been if the rifles had earned wider acceptance. (For example, never, *never* make the mistake of thinking the Winchester Model 94 became so popular because it was chambered for the .30/30.)

These were beautifully made rifles, and I think this, plus their relative complexity, was a source of their limited acceptance. They were too expensive. In 1950, when the M141 was on its last legs, the retail price was $104.95. By comparison, Remington's top-of-the-line bolt gun sold for only $79.95 and the popular Winchester Model 94 lever gun cost only $62 and change. So when the Model 760 was introduced in 1952 the relative price was revised downward and it was made available in popular calibers such as .30/06 and .270. It has been a steady seller ever since.

Even by looking at the catalog picture it's plain enough that the Model 760 Remington is just a muscle-powered version of the self-powered Model 742. In the autoloading version the action is driven open by a gas-powered operating rod; the pump just has the forend attached to the operating rod. It's a strong system, with lugs that lock up with the barrel and form an interlocking compartment which completely encloses the cartridge. The few of these I've seen that blew up, for whatever reason, split or shattered the barrel but didn't dislodge the bolt. Most functional problems I've run across with the M760 (and 742) have to do with poor extraction. But as it usually turns out this is due to faulty ammo. Unlike a bolt action, pumps, levers, and autoloaders do not have a powerful camming action on the closing and opening strokes. An oversize case therefore is not easily forced into the chamber of a pump. Instead, it wedges tight in the chamber and blocks the final travel of the closing motion. Then, with the case wedged in the chamber, and the bolt holding onto the rim by means of the extractor, the action is also difficult to open.

Some factory loads can cause this problem, especially if they are dirty or bent, but usually the blame can be placed on reloads. The solution is special

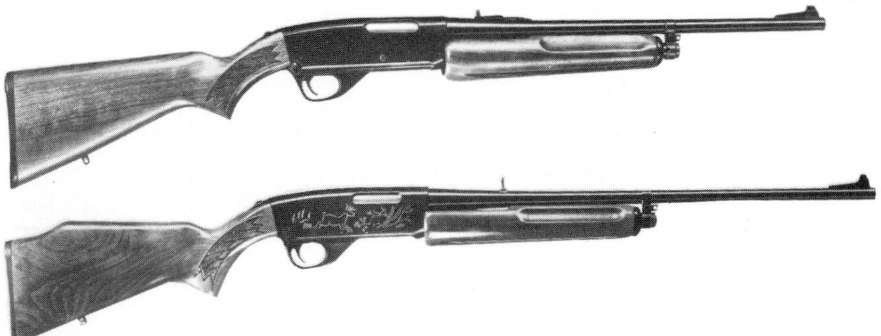

Two versions, carbine and standard-length, of the Savage Model 170 pump-action rifle, which comes in .30/30 caliber.

sizing dies which reduce the head diameter to minimum dimensions. This cures the difficulty nine times out of ten.

In terms of accuracy, the Remington 760 Gamemaster seems to fall into the same category as the 742; some will and some won't, but the extreme is not so great in either direction. I once sat down at the test bench with three apparently identical 760s in .30/06 caliber. After trying a dozen different brands and bullet weights of factory-loaded ammo in each, I decided that while none of the three was going to shoot so poorly as to cause a miss on a buck out to about 200 yards, none was going to wad the bullets up in a tight little group either. But nobody's claiming that anyway.

The Savage Model 170 pump was introduced a couple of years ago, mainly, I suppose, as a lower-priced alternate to the Remington. The action design was less sophisticated, though, and, lacking a high-pressure locking arrangement, is limited to such cartridges as the .30/30, which is the M170's only chambering at this writing.

Frankly, pump-action rifles don't turn me on, so I've never been seized with a burning need to test-fire the Savage. And too, I've never received a letter from an owner offering either praise or criticism. Which means, as I take it, the Savage pump does what it's supposed to do, but like any .30/30, not in spectacular fashion.

As I see it, pumps don't fit very well into the scheme of today's or tomorrow's rifle movement. Hunting conditions will, more and more, call for increased range and accuracy or, in the case of the dense brush hunting, increased firepower. In any event, the pump is going to be left behind. Its only "redeeming" appeal, as in the case of the Remington Model 760, is in offering a quick shooter in high-intensity cartridge chambering as an alternate to an autoloader. Or, as in the case of the Savage 170, a competitively priced alternative to the lever guns. But of course there are plenty of sporting souls who just happen, either by upbringing or fancy, to be partial to slide-action guns.

9

Bolt-Actions

Hunting rifles, like the people who use them, come in all shapes, sizes, weights, and styles. Over the years, however, the predominant style has become the bolt gun. Just why this has happened cannot be explained simply. But foremost among the causes is that as attention has been focused more and more intently on cartridge performance and rifle accuracy the bolt action has inevitably gained more of the spotlight. At the same time, manufacturers the world over have increasingly directed their attention toward turn-bolt design and manufacture. In short, the bolt is where the action is. (Forgive me.)

Because the world's marketplace offers so many bolt-action rifles the following survey is far from complete. Those makes and models discussed here are included because they have had a major impact on the shooting scene or because they represent what I consider a worthwhile contribution to rifle-building technology. Or perhaps I just included them because they embody some pet like or dislike I want to talk about.

CHAMPLIN

The Champlin rifles are largely a hand-built proposition. This means that they are very expensive, and it also means that very few of them will ever find their way into the Maine woods or the Georgia swamps. Nonetheless, they are worthy of more than passing comment for a variety of reasons.

First of all, they represent the first serious attempt in a long while by a U.S. manufacturer to produce a truly elegant, high-style hunting rifle. In the main, such rifles have been turned out by such renowned purveyors of excellence as the British firm of Holland & Holland or, here in the U.S., by top-flight custom gunsmithing firms—such as Griffin & Howe and the now defunct Hoffman Arms Co.—or individuals. But Champlin is unique in modern times because they use an action of their own manufacture. There are other small firms, such as Texas Magnum and Omega, that build rifles on actions of their own design and manufacture, but these firms are not so committed to the classical concept of custom riflemaking as is Champlin.

The firm got going a few years back when design wizard Jerry Haskins teamed up with Doug Champlin, a well-heeled lover of fine rifleware. The firm was first known as Champlin-Haskins, but when the young designer went on to conquer other worlds his name was dropped from the logo.

The Champlin action is a good one, in fact one of the best. It is super-strong, smooth-operating, and beautifully finished, and probably has the most attractive exterior configuration of any bolt action ever made. The partners got off to a good start when they hired ace stockmaker Clayton Nelson to take charge of the Champlin stocking department. His superb craftsmanship and style, aided by really choice walnut, was just the needed touch to set off the distinctive action profile and help achieve an air of true elegance. Since then Nelson has also gone his way, but the stocks are still meticulously crafted in fine woods and beautifully checkered.

One of the favorite pastimes of rifle lovers is to speculate on how wonderful and smart it would have been to have invested in some of the stylish Griffin & Howe custom rifles back before they became such valued collector's pieces and the prices for choice specimens went through the roof. So, a word to the wise. The Champlin is another great American classic which just may be the last of its kind.

COLT-SAUER

In the fall of 1972 the Colt people invited a gaggle of gun writers to the wilds of northern New Mexico for the purpose of bagging a few deer with a brand-new offering from the old-world firm of J. P. Sauer & Son. Colt has steadfastly maintained a tradition of getting in over their eyebrows nearly

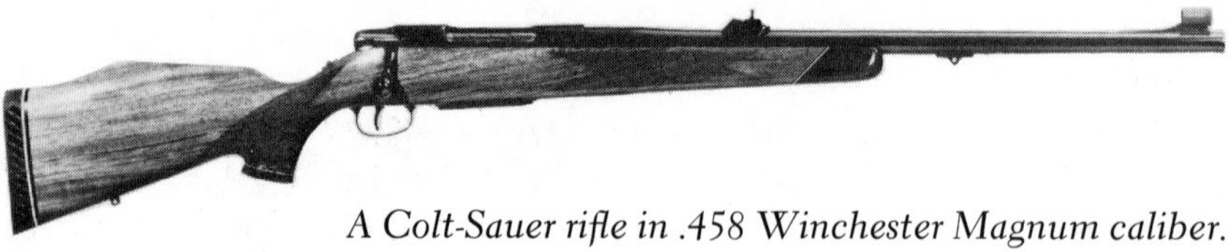

A Colt-Sauer rifle in .458 Winchester Magnum caliber.

every time they stray too far from their pistolmaking bailiwick, and I, for one, predicted no exception this go-around. But I've been wrong about such things before and apparently I was wrong this time.

As the Colt executive explained it to the assortment of deaf and semi-deaf gun writers present, they felt there was a good potential market for a prestige rifle in the Weatherby, or thereabouts, price range. As it turned out they must have known what they were talking about, because the rifle has

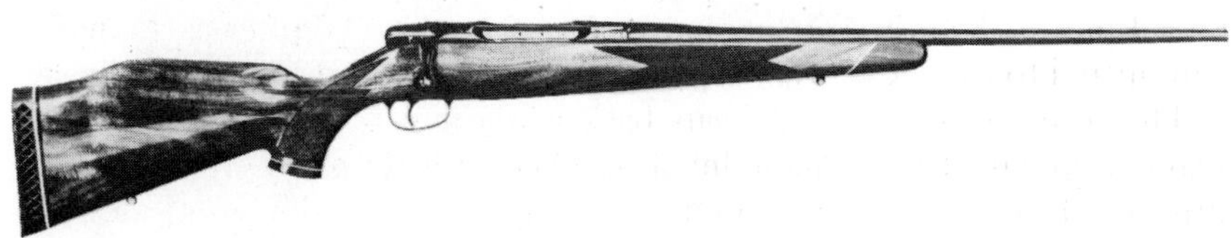

Here is the short-action version of the Colt-Sauer design, which is used for the shorter cartridges such as the .22/250 Remington, .308 Winchester, and .243 Winchester.

done well ever since, even at around $500 per copy. But then, it also happens to be a handsome rig which features a unique locking arrangement and a bolt that works as slick as a toad's tongue.

Fundamentally, the action could be described as a rear-locking model in the same general class with the Shultz & Larsen or even the Remington 788. But this is hardly an apt or fair description. The most striking feature of the Colt-Sauer design is the three locking lugs which actually fold down into the bolt body when the handle is lifted. It sounds like a pretty complicated apparatus, but actually it isn't. The lugs, which are actually struts, are operated by a simple cam. When the bolt handle is in the closed position the lugs are extended out of the bolt body and mesh into locking recesses in the receiver bridge wall. Naturally, with the lugs folded out of the way the bolt becomes little more than a sleeve sliding within a larger sleeve, so the operating movement is one of the slickest in the business.

The mechanism features clip feeding, a tang safety, an indicator which tells if a cartridge is in the chamber, and even a button at the root of the bolt handle which permits the action to be opened with the safety in the ON position. Everything is neatly built and well thought out except the trigger mechanism. It looks like the last creation of the mad mousetrap maker before they shipped him off to the funny farm.

The stocks, as befitting a rifle in this price range, are of handsome wood with uncommonly good checkering, but the styling and finish, for better or worse, are pure California.

Here my hunting partner levels on a mule deer in northern New Mexico while I keep an eye on the action with binoculars. We are both equipped with Colt-Sauer rifles in .30/06 caliber.

FFV-HUSQVARNA

When the famous riflemaking firm of Husqvarna got shuffled around a few years back, one of the terms of the deal was that the renowned name was to be phased out. The Husqvarna people, who are closely watched by the Swedish government (like everything else in Sweden), are in the business of making chainsaws, sewing machines, motorcycles, and the like, and wanted their name out of the gun business. This is too bad, because the Husqvarna-made Mausers were among the best ever and had given the name a fine reputation.

Searching around for a new name, the riflemakers had a go at Viking, which bombed. Then they tried Carl Gustaf. Carl Gustaf was the great warrior-king of Eskilstuna, and quite a hero with the Swedish people. Since the city of Eskilstuna, where the FFV-Husqvarna rifles are made, is also the site of Gustaf's great armory, Carl Gustaf seemed like another good name

Here I run an accuracy check on the Swedish-made FFV rifle in .30/06 caliber.

possibility for the rifle. But not too many people outside Sweden, especially Americans, have much recollection of Carl's exploits, so the royal name hasn't made much of an impression either. So the new rifles have simply become known as FFV, an abbreviation of the firm that makes them, Forenade Fabriksverken.

There is a lot to like about the new FFV and a few things not to like. The worst feature is a rather ungainly stock design. When I visited the FFV plant in 1972 the management expressed some concern over their stock shape and indicated that they would like to add a bit more style. I suggested that they hire a good American stockmaker to come up with a fresh design,

A detail of the Swedish FFV action. The three-shot group, which measures under an inch, was fired at 100 yards with this rifle in .30/06 caliber. The FFV is one of the smoothest-working and most streamlined actions currently available.

but so far their stocks are no different. Another stylistic problem is the overly large and rather roughly cast and finished aluminum trigger-guard assembly. It's an unsightly thing to behold, especially on a premium-priced rifle.

The action, however, is just about the most thoroughly up-to-date design on the market. It is slick, simple, strong, and, at this writing, on the threshold of proving itself the most accurate design available on a mass-produced rifle. In this respect it combines a highly concentric bolt and receiver configuration with a striker-assembly weight of slightly under 700 grains and a super-short firing-pin movement. Its lock time, in other words, is ultra-fast. In the 1974 Varmint class bench-rest championships a bench rifle built on an FFV action placed near the very top, and as a result quite a few precision accuracy buffs are giving the FFV–Carl Gustaf action a try. To help them on their way the Swedes are now manufacturing an extra-rigid single-shot (no magazine cut) target version of their action and also have begun making a version for .222-size cartridges.

All in all, the FFV–Carl Gustaf is probably the most advanced action design around, and if they ever find a stock design and perhaps a better trigger, it will become a classic.

MAUSER

So many brands and models of rifles have been built on the basic '98 Mauser action design that any attempt to get them all cataloged would reduce the researcher to a gibbering idiot. At least once a month the mailman presents me with a smoothly written news release proclaiming the introduction of yet another "dramatically styled" bit of fluff built on some make of Mauser action.

Since the 1950s the huge Belgian firm of Fabrique Nationale, to name but one, has turned out a trainload of these basically '98-style actions which, in addition to their finished rifles, have served as the foundation for rifles bearing the trademarks of Browning, Colt, Harrington & Richardson, Sears Roebuck, Weatherby, Hi-Standard, Kodiak, and literally scores of others.

The FN Mauser rifles, such as shown here, are built in the giant Fabrique Nationale factory in Belgium. It is the same plant that turns out most of the Browning shotgun line. The FN actions are basically the same as the tried and proven Model 1898 Mauser.

For quite a few years the availability of the well-built F. N. actions presented a fast, cheap, and easy way to get in the gun business. The action design is one of the soundest and best known of all time and, thanks to a favorable pricing schedule, could be bought so cheap as to make in-house designing and manufacturing impractical, especially here in the U.S.

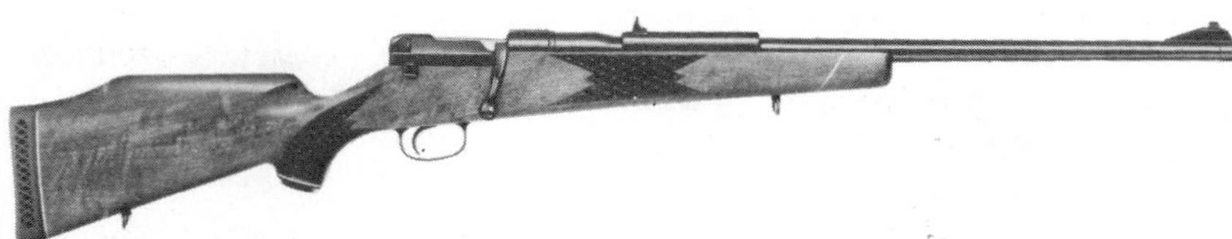

This is the recently introduced Mauser Model 660, made in the West German town of Orberndorf, the original home of the Mauser firm. The Model 660 is a radically different design featuring an interchangeable barrel system that has not proved at all popular in North America.

The Mauser Model 3000, immediate successor to the famed Mauser line.

But those happy days of bargain-basement rifle merchandising are all but over. Runaway inflation, rampant labor union demands, and a no longer favorable dollar exchange rate have just about priced the F. N. Mauser, probably the last of the great '98 makers, out of the market.

At present there are firms in such diverse places as Yugoslavia and Spain turning out facsimiles of the popular Mauser action, and no doubt they offer good prices, but the quality is not so good. About the last bargain-priced

This racy-looking bolt-action with teardrop pistol grip and rollover cheek piece is the Harrington & Richardson Model 300. It is built on a basic Mauser action.

Mausers around are actual military-surplus rifles from the armies of the world or sporting rifles built on surplus actions.

The original home of the Mauser rifle, in the village of Oberndorf, West Germany, not far from the Swiss border, is still in the business of making sporting rifles under the Mauser banner, but they long ago gave up on the

This is the Harrington & Richardson Model 333 bolt-action rifle, also built on a Mauser action.

'98 design. Their current products are the Model 3000, a considerably updated and more streamlined version of the basic Mauser concept featuring a "California-styled" stock, and their radically different Model 660.

German gunbuilders have traditionally exhibited a passion for all sorts of gadgetry, and I expect whoever thought the 660 up must have been from the old, *old* school. The principal feature is a removable barrel system which

The Mauser Sporter is at home in the field.

allows the hunter a selection of several calibers in one complex but expensive unit.

When the rifle, which can more accurately be referred to as a system, was introduced a few years back its makers expected to take the world, especially the U.S., by storm. But if they had done a bit of snooping around beforehand they would have learned that Americans have always managed to keep even their wildest urges for swap-barrel rifles well under control. In honesty, the Model 660 is a beautifully made piece of equipment, possibly one of the last great examples of German craftsmanship we shall see, but it's a clumsy-looking thing that only a mother could love.

Early in 1975 I had a long and very serious conversation with Rolf Gminder, managing director of the Oberndorf Mauser works, about the possibility of his firm making finely finished rifles in the style and pattern of those wonderful sporters made up until World War II. Two decades ago such a project would have flopped, but today with shooter's tastes in rifles taking a noticeable turn toward the conservative, there exists a lucrative market for just such a rifle bearing the original Mauser banner.

REMINGTON

Back in 1948 when Remington unveiled their two new centerfire bolt guns, the 721 and the 722, I doubt if many gun experts would have voted either of them the rifle most likely to succeed. The stocks were as plain as a picked chicken, the trigger guards looked like crooked strap iron, and the actions looked as if they had been designed in the cost accountant's office. Which, to a certain extent, is not far from the exact case.

But, as it has come to pass, the direct descendant of those ugly ducklings is currently billed as the largest-selling rifle in the world. Remington's top

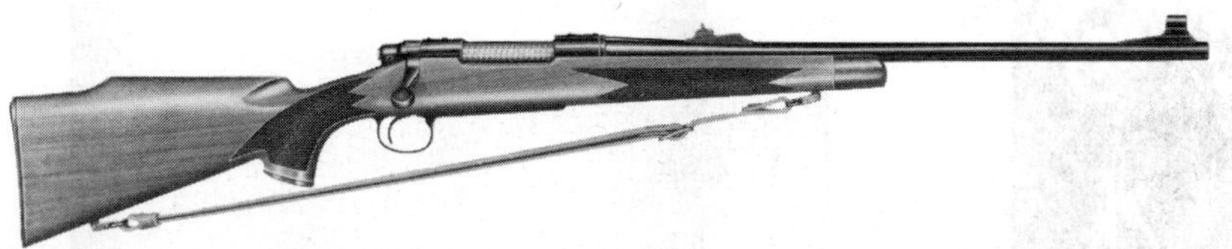

The Remington Model 700 in BDL grade. The Remington Model 700 is one of the strongest and most accurate actions ever designed.

rifle of today, the Model 700, is actually too closely related to the 721 and 722 of 1948 to be described as a descendant. In fact, it is nothing more than exactly the same design but with a different bolt-handle shape, another trigger-guard assembly, and a dolled-up stock. Nothing else has changed two cents' worth. The 721 and 722 action designs, in case you weren't around then, were basically the same except that the 721 was a stretched-out version for longer rounds such as the .270, .30/06, etc. The 722 was for the .300 Savage, .257 Roberts, and similar rounds. Both forms still exist in their original lengths, but each is now known as the Model 700.

During World War I, Remington was one of the armsmakers who tooled up and produced the Pattern 14 and Model 17 Enfields. At the close of hostilities, finding themselves with all that tooling on hand plus a lot of parts already made up, they saw they could get in the sporter bolt-rifle business in a hurry just by making a few cosmetic changes in the Enfield design. That quick changeover resulted in the Remington Model 30 of 1921. This Enfield look-alike was offered in three or four modifications over the years and was produced in a goodly assortment of chamberings. By the late 1930s, however, the new Winchester Model 70 was cutting a wide swath in rifle circles, so Remington sought to beat the competition with a new rifle, the Model 720. It was introduced—and discontinued—in 1941. Very few were made, and they are seldom seen these days. By chance the National Guard unit in my home town bought a rackful of 720s in 1941—I don't know why, unless they were short on equipment and needed rifles any way they could get them. After the war they sold the rifles to local folks, and I eventually ended up with two. In fact, I used one of these to nail my first Smokey Mountain black bear. The Model 720 Remingtons were beautifully made rifles and would probably have made substantial inroads into sales of the Model 70 if the war hadn't come along. They were no doubt very costly to manufacture, however, and when Remington regrouped after the war to predict what the coming generations of rifle buyers would be looking for, they apparently decided to hit the economy trail.

The 721–722 actions were the vanguard of modern design trends. The in-head extractor and plunger ejector permitted an unbroken ring around the bolt face, which, in turn, is partially encased in a recess in the breech of the barrel. This arrangement completely encloses the cartridge head and makes the 700 one of the strongest and safest actions ever built.

And too, the design, with its fast lock time and stiff, easy-to-bed receiver, has proved the darling of accuracy buffs. At any given bench-rest competition it's a sure bet that at least half, usually considerably more, of the tack-driving rigs will be built up on a Remington action.

One of the most accurate factory-produced rifles ever offered is the Remington 40-X. The action is exactly the same as the Model 700 except the magazine cut is omitted to make the receiver a bit stiffer. The repeater version of the 40-X is just a 700 action with a target stock and a better barrel. This is certainly not to imply that you don't get your money's worth with the 40-X, but only to emphasize that the inherent accuracy of the 700 can't be improved on even for Remington's highest-priced target rifle. In this same vein, the basic 700 design has proved so hard to improve upon in so many ways that other Remington bolt models such as the 600, 660, and even the XP-100 pistol are only slight modifications.

Over the years as the reputations of the 721, 722, 725, 700, etc., have waxed fat there has been a gradual movement away from the original economy concept and toward the richer market. Thus, along about the tail end of the 1960s Remington found itself looking for another model to plug the

The Remington Model 788, shown here, has been something of an embarrassment for its manufacturer. Though intended as a budget-priced centerfire it has proven itself to be exceptionally accurate. As a matter of fact some super performing bench rest rifles have been built up on the basic Model 788 action.

bottom-of-the-line price gap. This took place in the form of the Model 788. To be sure it's a plain little thing, but, true to the tradition of the 722, it has proved more accurate than its price indicates it should be. The most radical feature of the clip-fed 788 is its multi-lug rear-locking system. I don't think this contributes as much to the accuracy of the rig as the lightning-fast lock time and the extra-thick walled receiver. Happily there is indeed such a thing as an *accurate*, economy-priced rifle, and this is it.

SAKO

The Sako rifles are a sterling example of how a good design and good workmanship can still go a long, long way. A hundred years from now when today's designs are obsolete and in the hands of collectors, I predict that the epitaph bestowed on the trim little Finnish-made rifles will be "No one ever said anything bad about a Sako."

Back in the early 1950s when the first Sakos reached the shores of the New World, someone described the little actions as a miniature Mauser, and the name, unfortunately, stuck. I'm sure the Sako people weren't too happy with the sobriquet because the design is highly original and anything but a Mauser. They were indeed miniatures, though, and this has added immeasurably to their charm. The little Vixen is perfectly scaled to the .222 class of cartridges, and the Forrester, the next size up, is just right for .22/

250s, .308s, etc. Thus the rifles are beautifully balanced for the cartridge and the hunter doesn't feel he's carrying around excess baggage.

One of the special charms of these rifles, in addition to their obviously sound design and unfailingly good workmanship, is their almost paradoxical ability to combine light weight with a most satisfying degree of accuracy. This is especially mystifying in light of the emphasis we tend to put on heavy barrels and stiff, heavy actions for rifles intended for top accuracy.

The standard-grade Sako Finnbear sporter comes in .25/06, .270, .30/06, .338 Winchester Magnum, 7mm Remington Magnum, and .375 H&H Magnum.

This is the deluxe model Sako Vixen, the shortest action in the Sako line. This is a beautifully made and trim little sporter which comes in .222 and .223 Remington chamberings.

The delightfully trim Sako Vixen carbine also comes in .222 and .223 Remington chamberings. Though a compact little lightweight it is amazingly accurate.

The Sako secret, for one thing, can be traced to a remarkably stiff receiver. Despite their apparent trimness, the Vixen and Forrester receivers have a lot of steel in them, especially in the rail-like structure on the bottom side. And too, of course, the fact that they are minimum length adds to their stiffness. Another reason is the super-smooth finish of the Sako bores. For a while in the 1960s, in fact, Sako was doing a fairly brisk business selling barrel blanks to bench-rest shooters.

Despite the *comparatively* good accuracy of the Sako rifles, they do not improve much by conversion to competitive form. Even though a single-shot bench-rest version of the Vixen action is made, it has never met with any success with the pinpoint-accuracy crowd. The design is at its best, evidently, in trim, lightweight rifles, and that, after all, is what it was intended for.

The largest of the Sako actions, the Finnbear, is not as appealing as the shorter versions, because, except for fine workmanship, it offers no particular advantages over any number of other actions in its size class. As with kittens and puppies, the grown-up version is never quite so appealing.

SAVAGE

The success of the Savage Model 110, and its progeny the Models 111, 112, etc., has if nothing else been an object lesson to anyone wanting to get in the gunmaking business: find a hole in the market and fill it. In this case the hole was all those left-handed shooters who had been struggling with right-hand bolts. Also, just to prove that they had more than one bright idea, they offered plain actions for sale. Up until then it was considered

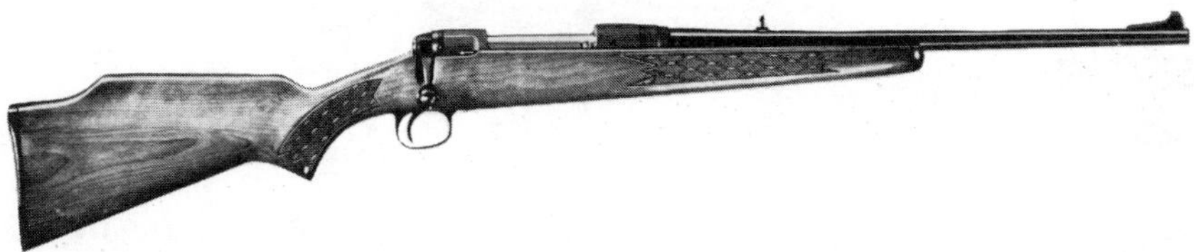

The Savage Model 110.

The recent Savage Model 111 Chieftain, which, with Monte Carlo comb, cheek piece, and white spacers, is a dolled-up version of the basic Model 110.

heresy for a major American manufacturer to sell actions or barreled actions only.

In truth, aside from the immeasurable joy the lefty version brought to thousands of southpaws, the 110 rifle's intended purpose, as far as its manufacturers view it, is to be simply a strong, safe, reliable bolt-action rig that can be marketed at an attractive price. In that respect they have succeeded overwhelmingly. Occasionally they are taken with a fit of social climbing, as in the case of the Model 111 Chieftain, but hanging a premium price tag on a rifle with the basic 110 action tends to draw sideways glances.

The most ambitious application yet of the 110 action is a solid-bottomed single-shot heavy-barreled job called the 112-V. This target-varmint rig comes in .222, .22/250, .243, .25/06, and most notably .220 Swift. With its comfortable, high-combed semi-target stock, the 112-V is pleasant to shoot from a bench or at varmints, and the grouping tends to indicate that the inherent accuracy of the old 110 action may have been somewhat underrated all these years. The Savage trigger, however, is a major stumbling block to really fine performance.

STURM-RUGER

The first time I set eyes on the Ruger Model 77 bolt gun I wasn't exactly sure what to think. I'd known its creator, Bill Ruger, for some time and had enormous respect for both his design genius and his unerring good taste.

The popular Ruger Model 77. The Model 77, which combines traditional classic styling with modern manufacturing techniques, is one of the most up-to-date rifle designs available. It is an outstanding dollar value.

That's what made it so hard to accept a bolt handle shaped like a dog's hind leg. But, as it has turned out, like a husband who quickly learns to live with a cross-eyed wife if she sets a great meal and warms his back on chilly nights, the funny bolt handle is soon forgotten in light of the rifle's other qualities.

In the manner characteristic of Ruger guns, the Model 77 combines function and clean styling. The stock is by all odds the best-looking piece of timber ever offered on a mass-produced rifle. In fact, few custom houses can match either its fit, finish, handling qualities, inletting, checkering, or style. Leonard Brownell, one of the finest stockmakers ever to pick up a chisel, was hired by Ruger and made head of the stock department for the sole purpose of designing the stock and teaching others how to make them. The ladies who do the checkering were trained by Brownell to hand-cut the checkering with little electric tools just like the ones used by most of the top custom craftsmen. They are proof that a stock can be hand-checkered neatly, quickly, *and* economically.

Here I practice some offhand shooting with a Ruger Model 77 in 7mm Remington Magnum caliber. I used this rifle with great success in Africa on several types of game.

Another prize feature of the 77 is the integral scope bases and matching ring sets. The popularity of this feature was well summed up when, in response to dealers' demands, Ruger introduced a plain, round-topped receiver which uses ordinary scope bases. Quite a few dealers, it seems, were complaining because when they sold M77s they couldn't make a few more bucks on a separate ring and base set. But rifle buyers didn't take to the idea at all. Not only did the Ruger ring system save money, spoke the majority, but it also happened to be a very *good* system.

All in all, the Ruger combines modern thinking with some of the most popular features from the past. A Mauser-type extractor, for example, is used in conjunction with a spring-loaded plunger-type ejector. The tang safety, formerly a deluxe feature on the best custom rigs, was neatly included, and so was an adjustable trigger, hinged floorplate, and guard bow floorplate release. One of the most novel features is the use of an angled front action screw which is said to ensure more positive contact of the recoil lug with the stock mortice. This, plus the large, flat bottom surface of the receiver and its built-in stiffness, makes the rifle one of the most accurate off-the-shelf propositions available.

As a matter of fact, the single most accurate factory-made rifle I've ever seen, target, varmint, or otherwise, is a M77, in .220 Swift. With no alterations whatsoever—no rebedding, no free-floating of the barrel, just some good handloads—the rifle will hammer in five shots not much wider than 3⁄10 inch at 100 yards. The *average* is less than ½ inch. Out of pure contrariness I entered it in a state championship bench-rest tournament a couple of years ago just to give the lads a turn. Ordinarily the bench-resters giggle up their sleeves when an out-of-the-box rifle shows up at the range, but these guys figured I was up to something, especially because the wind was howling like mad. To make a long story short, I didn't win anything but I took a second in one match, and a third in another, and finished well up in the top ten.

WEATHERBY

Back when I was a teen-age farm lad, one of the most boresome duties to fall within my sphere of responsibilities was hoeing, worming, and suckering the family's government-allotted 9/10 acre of burley tobacco. It was an onerous chore at best, with the Southeastern sun toasting one's scalp and offering nothing more substantial in the way of mental stimulation than contemplating the geography of a mule's rear end. I passed the hours in

A Weatherby Mark V, left-hand version, flawlessly stocked by Winston Churchill.

tolerable contentment, however, by daydreaming of the day I would own a genuine Weatherby rifle in .257 Weatherby Magnum caliber.

I'd never seen one, and it's a fair guess that none existed within a 200-mile radius of our tobacco patch, but the gorgeous pictures I'd seen in the hunting magazines convinced me that heaven must be a place where everyone owned a Weatherby. Back then crow and groundhogs were about my limit when it came to big game, and according to the ballistic charts the wondrous .257 Weatherby would allow me to hit a clover rover farther out than had any varmint shooter since time began. But alas, at four bits an hour for hard labor that Weatherby remained only a daydream.

Back then the creations of Roy Weatherby's shop were built up on just about any action at hand—Mausers, Enfields, Schultz & Larsons, and Model 70s. Regardless of the action, the rifles were made distinctive by Weatherby's rakish Monte Carlo combs, white spacers, and fancy inlaid stocks.

In the late 1950s, Weatherby moved into the really big time with an action design all his own and—like everything else in his line—quite different from anything else, the Mark V.

Among other things it was big. It needed to be in order to house the big Weatherby cartridges. But it was streamlined, very nicely finished, and slick-operating, and was billed as the strongest action in the world. I've never been sure if this last claim is true or not, but it really doesn't matter because it is certainly one of the strongest and plenty stout enough to handle the job for which it was intended. The most novel feature of the Mark V action is its locking system of an interrupted-thread arrangement which amounts to nine locking lugs rather than the more usual two. The principal problem of a multiple-lug system such as this is getting all the lugs to bear evenly. The most common complaint against this type arrangement is that if the lugs don't bear evenly the system can't be as strong as supposed, and that it is very difficult to manufacture such an action to the exacting tolerances required. This is true, but I suspect that even if the lugs do not seat uniformly to begin with they will after the rifle has been fired a few times. A certain amount of setback is normal with most all types of lug arrangements, and since the Weatherby lugs are each fairly small they probably equalize themselves pretty fast.

Much of the smoothness of the Mark V comes from the fact that the outer diameter of the lugs is no greater than the bolt body. In the more usual lug arrangement the lugs extend and rub on the action walls and rails as the mechanism is operated. This increases friction. But the Weatherby operation is, in principle, a cylinder within a sleeve, and a polished one at that. The safety, to Weatherby's everlasting credit, is the honest striker-blocking type.

From the standpoint of safety the Mark V Weatherby is one of the very best. The face of the bolt fits *into* a recess in the breech and completely surrounds the cartridge head. If I had an uncontrollable urge to build up a super-pressure cartridge to break the world bullet velocity record this is probably the action I'd use.

During the last couple of years I've received a fair amount of mail from *Outdoor Life* readers commenting on the fact that the Weatherby rifles are marked "made in Japan" and asking my opinion on this. Formerly the mechanism was made in the prestigious West German plant of J. P. Sauer and apparently this made everyone happy. But when, for various reasons, the operation was moved to Japan there was some apprehension. But there is no difference whatever in quality that I can see. I do understand that the Japanese version has a somewhat improved trigger mechanism. If this is true I would personally prefer the Nippon model because I never had much luck getting the German trigger to adjust the way I wanted it.

Since Weatherby rifles have, until recently, been promoted and priced as prestige items there has formed a sort of reverse snob attitude in some quarters of the shooting masses. Sneering remarks are sometimes heard about Weatherby rifles appealing only to pantywaist playboys planning their first safari, and that they aren't much in the way of reliability or accuracy. There is, as a matter of fact, a grain of truth to the former charge, and this has encouraged the latter charge. Weatherby has indeed courted the carriage trade and this has resulted in some of its rifles winding up in some conspicuous predicaments. When I was hunting in Africa in 1973 I crossed trails with a Weatherby-outfitted hunter who had lost the rear action screw out of his .378 Magnum. Obviously he wasn't too swift when it comes to rifles or he would have checked the screws beforehand. To correct the situation his guide had bound the rear of the receiver down with black electrician's tape. An ignominious way to wander around in the bush, to be sure, and I'm sure Roy Weatherby would have cringed at the vision.

Likewise, big-game guides the world over are especially fond of relating the antics of their Weatherby-equipped clients. I think, however, that their antics and eccentricities would have been the same regardless of their choice in hunting rifles.

In plain truth, though, it's a mistake to underrate either the accuracy of the Weatherby rifles or the performance of the cartridges. The rifles are relatively light and the big cartridges generate a lot of recoil, a combination that makes them tough to shoot. (Being cut around the eye by the scope on a hard-recoiling Weatherby rifle, for instance, is so common that the term "Weatherby eye" has become part of our shooting idiom.) But a competent marksman who isn't too recoil-conscious can sit down at the bench and slug out some surprisingly small groups. Each rifle comes with a test group attesting to its accuracy, and, as a point of some interest, I've yet to test a Weatherby rifle that didn't produce better accuracy than indicated by the original factory-fired test group. Also, don't make the mistake of believing the big Weatherby Magnum rounds won't shoot either. The .300 W.M. is even occasionally used in 1,000-yard target competition.

WINCHESTER

Few rifles in shooting history stand in less need of introduction than the Winchester Model 70. I don't know who first called it the "rifleman's

A super-grade version of the Model 70 Winchester. The Model 70, which is offered in a variety of calibers and grades, has earned for itself a reputation for accuracy and dependability which is without peer in the shooting world.

The Model 670 Winchester is basically the Model 70 action and barrel but with some of the more expensive features such as hinged floorplate cover left out.

I used this custom rifle built around a Model 70 action for my first African safari. Here I am shown with a trophy greater Kudu. The Model 70 is a favorite with big-game hunters the world over.

rifle"—probably some New York press agent who never ventured beyond the wilds of Nassau County—but it's an honest slogan nonetheless.

From the standpoint of pure accuracy, the Model 70, or rifles built up on Model 70 actions, has won more bigbore target championships than all others put together. Most notable of these, no doubt, are the ultra-demanding 1,000-yard Wimbledon matches. Its toughness and reliability have made it a favorite of big-game hunters the world over, and the trim style and graceful proportion of the Model 70 action made it the number one choice among custom riflebuilders who want to make rifles that perform well *and* look good. In short, it has become both a legend and a collector's item in its own time.

Like most enduring designs, the Model 70, when it was introduced in 1936, was the result of a trial-and-error period. This was in the form of the Model 54 which had been introduced ten years earlier. After a decade of evaluating the Model 54 the Winchester brass knew they had a winning action design but that it needed some improvements. The simple bent-steel trigger guard and floorplate were replaced with a milled-steel guard and hinged floorplate. The trigger mechanism, which had also served as a bolt stop, was redesigned and an independent bolt stop installed. Since scope sights were on their way in, the safety was redesigned to permit easier operation with a scope and the stock was completely redesigned. The forearm was given a more hand-filling contour and the butt section straightened out. Though it is seldom mentioned, there were actually fewer fundamental design changes between the Model 54 and 70 changeover than there were during the traumatic Model 70 revamping of 1964. This date, by the way, is the subject of much discussion among Model 70 lovers because it is widely regarded as Winchester's darkest hour. By and large I would tend to go along with this if it were not for a couple of factors which have come to light since then. But this takes some explaining.

When Winchester introduced their reworked Model 70 in 1964 it was clearly an effort to reduce manufacturing costs. In fact, this process had been under way for a number of years. The lovely curved-steel butt plate had been replaced with a plastic job around 1960 or so, the wood had been increasingly cheaper-looking, and both the quality and the amount of checkering had been in arrears for a few years. These had been considered bad enough, but the changes of 1964 were too horrible to contemplate. The beloved Mauser-type extractor was gone, replaced by the flimsiest-looking of gadgets; the receiver and bolt had the frosted look of castings; the familiar barrel contour had been changed; the magazine follower was a cheap stamping; the stock was terrible.

For a while the publicity people made a big thing out of the stock's "free-floating" barrel channel, but in the face of public indignation this was soon to go. But just as bad, possibly even worse, was the insipid pressed checkering.

Dollars and pennies are always a good way to make a point, so I'll use it here. Today, on a gun dealer's used-gun rack a Model 70 made in 1964, '65, etc., will be priced somewhere in the neighborhood of a hundred dollars. You'll be lucky to find one made in 1963 or before at twice that amount!

But, there's more to the saga of the "new" M70 than just ill will. In my experience the new action design is *inherently more accurate* than the so-called pre-'64 version! Altogether I estimate I've owned around sixty-five to seventy-five Model 70s. About a dozen of these have been target grades, and perhaps ten more have been the heavy-barreled varmint models. Some have been delightfully accurate. Of all of these, only four have been made since 1964. Of these four, one is at this very writing being made into a custom target job and so far untested. But of the other three, two are the most accurate Model 70s I've ever owned *or seen!* One, a varmint-weight .225, gave the best accuracy I've ever known from a Model 70 on an out-of-the-box basis. The other, a .308 target job, has won more bigbore competition awards than any rifle I've ever used. In bench-rest tests it has grouped *under* 1/4 inch for five shots at 100 yards. The third rifle, by the way, is an experimental 1,000-yard 7mm wildcat which hasn't been tested enough to say one way or the other. Of course it could be pure coincidence, but I think it's highly significant that those two "new" models should outperform all those dozens of pre-'64s I've owned.

At any rate, the Model 70 has been considerably upgraded since those bleak days in the mid-1960s. The stock has been completely restyled and features cut checkering. The action is nicely polished and blued, the stamped follower has long since been discarded, and the horrible cast-aluminum trigger guard and floorplate are now of good steel.

This isn't to say that the Model 70 is better than ever, only that it has regained a large measure of its respectability. When I go to the expense of having a custom rifle built I definitely still prefer the old style. The older-model receiver is shorter, and this makes a trimmer, more compact-looking job. I also prefer the big, old-fashioned extractor and slimmer trigger guard of the pre-'64s. But when all I want is accuracy, I'm convinced the new model will win the marbles.

10

Single-Shots

A phenomenon among modern centerfire hunting rifles is the return of the single-shot. It seems ironic that after over a century of intense firearms research and development, carried out primarily to overcome the one-shot handicap, single-shot rifles should all at once make a popular comeback. Only a few years ago the only factory-made single-shots were inexpensive .22 rimfires. But now Sturm Ruger offers their superb Number One and Number Three centerfire single-shots; Browning markets an updated version of the famous external-hammer one-shot rifle designed by John Browning before the turn of the century; and Colt makes a redesigned facsimile of the legendary Sharps rifle. Despite the fact that each of these is strictly a one-round-at-a-time affair, don't get the idea that they are for the bottom-of-the-

The Ruger Number One with the stylish Alex Henry forend. Most single-shot rifles, far from being an inexpensive bottom-of-the-line item, are in fact prestige rifles with the very finest in workmanship and materials. Note the quality of wood used in this Ruger.

line market. Quite the contrary! Each is a prestige item manufactured for the carriage trade.

Before getting into the peculiar quirks of the shooter's psyche and addressing ourselves to the puzzlement of why we and our fellow riflemen will pay $300 (or even much more) for a single-shot when a high-performance autoloader can be bought for half that amount, let's define a true single-shot rifle. First of all, it is a rifle that was designed as a single-shot with no intention or provision for a magazine. Each cartridge is hand-fed into the chamber. A rifle that just happens to hold one round at a time but is really only a modification of a basically repeater design does not qualify as a single-shot in the correct sense. An example of this type is the Remington Model 40-X, which is only a Model 700 without the magazine box. In fact, no bolt-action design will pass muster, even if a magazine version is not nor ever has been made.

The charm of the single-shot rifle has been explained in a variety of ways, but the most often heard reason, that they are more sporting than repeaters, is actually the poorest. The "more sporting" notion is based on the fact that the hunter gets fewer shots, possibly only one, at game before it disappears, and thus the quarry has a better chance to get away. I don't buy this attitude because I feel that a hunter should always assume his first shot is a hit whether the animal goes down or not. Once the hunter has committed himself to killing a game animal he should make every effort by every means to follow up on that commitment. A hunter who lets a possibly wounded game animal get away because he is incapable of a fast follow-up shot is hardly being sporting. Now, on the other hand, if a hunter wants to face charging lions or elephants with a single-shot I agree that that *would* be pretty sporty.

All in all, I relegate the only modern-day practical hunting application of single-shots to the kind of shooting one usually gets at plains-type game such as pronghorn and the longish shots one generally gets at sheep, goat, caribou, and some Western deer. The best application of all, of course, is varmints, where the shooter most usually gets only one long carefully aimed shot. Back before Bill Ruger introduced his Number One single-shot the great demand for Winchester High Wall actions centered around their popularity for rebarreling to varmint calibers. In truth, it's not that single-shots make all that great varmint rifles (very few single-shots will compare in accuracy with an average off-the-shelf Winchester, Remington, or Sako bolt-action varmint rifle), but they are a lot of fun to shoot. And too, a good modern single-shot reflects the tradition of such great single-shots as the Sharps and Remington Creedmoor long-range target rifles, the magnificent British-made Farquharson, the Ballard rifles, and the great Winchester High Wall of 1885.

All of these were finely made rifles, representing the top craftsmanship and accuracy of their day. This explains, in large measure, the current boom in single-shot popularity. We are living in an era of mass-produced gadgetry that has made permanence obsolete. Like old movies and antique autos, a single-shot rifle is a window in time through which we can glimpse, and even fleetingly partake, of a time when the shooting sports were a more elegant and leisurely recreation and the tomorrows held no dread surprises. This is why the Ruger Number One, the Browning Model 78, and the Colt Sharps are top-ticket items representing the best in materials and workmanship their makers have to offer. This is also why the Browning is available in an octagonal barrel and why the Ruger Number Three is available only in .45/70, .30/40 Krag, and .22 Hornet chambering at present, and the stocking reminiscent of the last century. They are all tokens of another, pleasantly remembered era.

Up until the first decade of this century the single-shot action was considered the most basically accurate. It featured a simplicity and solidarity not yet available in repeating rifles and was almost universally used for both short-range and long-range target rifles.

International-style target rifles built on single-shot Martini centerfire actions were used by some shooters in Olympic competition until after World War II, but the bolt-action has long since left these in the dust. At present the only honest single-shot action used in serious competition is that on the English-made BSA .22 rimfire rifles. These are especially appealing to left-handed shooters because they come in a mirror-image left-hand version.

Their passing from the target-shooting scene notwithstanding, a good single-shot centerfire rifle can turn in pretty fair accuracy. My shooting and hunting pal Jack Slack, who is one of the chief honchos at Leupold Scopes and Nosler bullets, has a Ruger action beautifully stocked by Earl Milliron and rebarreled to a .223 Remington with a Shilen tube that has grouped around a quarter MOA at 100 yards. I own another custom-stocked Ruger Number One, this one in .243 Winchester chambering with original Ruger barrel, that will usually poke five shots somewhere between 3/4 inch and 1 inch but has gone as small as .6 inch. But on the other hand I've got a Number One with varmint-weight barrel in .22/250 that isn't much good. The first five shots out of a well-scrubbed barrel go pretty tight, but from there on flyers open groups to 2 inches or more. The problem is a miserably rough

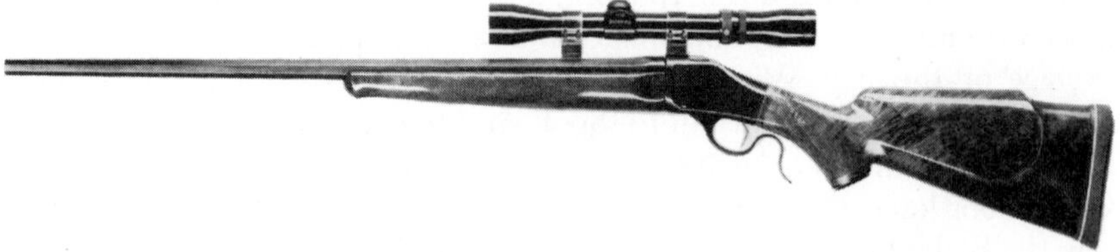

This is the Browning Model 78 single-shot rifle. The action is similar to the High Wall Winchester introduced in 1885 and designed by John M. Browning. This rifle has the stylish octagonal barrel.

bore that fouls excessively. One of these days I'm going to have it rebarreled to .220 Swift with a premium-grade stainless tube and my problems will be over. And I'll also have one sweet single-shot varmint rig.

At this writing the Browning Model 78 has been out for only a year or so and my testing has been limited to one specimen, a .30/06. With factory loads, groups have run around 1¼ inches, which, I must add, is about as well as that ammo has done in any rifle. However, the rifle is one of those jewels that tends to shoot different loads and weights of bullets into the same point of impact. I'll lay anyone three to one that with some neatly built handloads, or even a select batch of factory stuff, the Browning single-shot will crack the MOA barrier three groups out of five.

The fate of the Colt Sharps rifles seems somewhat confusing as of this moment. Some dealers are demanding collector's prices for the few modern Sharps actually delivered, apparently under the impression that production has been dropped. However, the last time I asked a Colt official about the status of their prestige single-shot I was told that the project was still very much alive but had only been shunted to a back burner while the factory tried to keep up with the demand for their standard production items.

My only exposure to the fancy Colt Sharps came about some five years ago when I tried one in .22/250 caliber. It was a pretty thing with fancy stocking, jeweled innards, and a single-set Canjar trigger. I ran a couple boxes of factory loads through it and wound up with five or six groups that

Here I bench test a Colt Sharps single-shot rifle in .22/250 chambering.

averaged about 1¼ inches for five shots at 100 yards. The shape of the group, as I recall, indicated a tendency toward stringing the shots. With whatever was causing this eliminated (probably forend bedding), I suspect accuracy would have been much more impressive. But I never had time to find out. The Colt Sharps is a massive action that should prove capable, with a little gunsmithing, of very impressive grouping. Perhaps one of these days I'll get a chance to really find out what they can do.

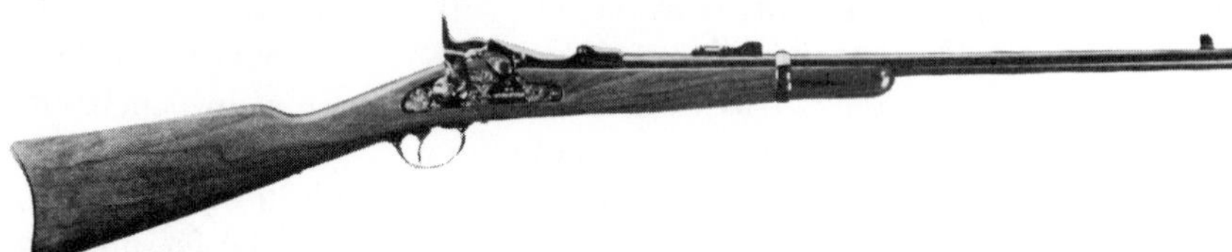

Harrington & Richardson's replica of the Springfield trapdoor 1873 service rifle in .45/70 caliber has proved very popular. These guns come in several different grades and price ranges, and in addition to being great decorators and conversation pieces are a lot of fun to shoot.

The next group of single-shot rifles fall more or less into the replica category. Typical of these are the rifles being built by Harrington & Richardson which are close look-alikes of the 1838 Springfield "trapdoor" .45/70 service rifle. These replicas, which come in grades and prices ranging from about $150 up to $1,000, are very well finished and a whole lot of fun to shoot. The .45/70 round is especially adaptable to cast lead bullets, so handloaders can plink to their heart's content at little more than the price of .22s. Other replicas include assorted imports based on the early Remington "Rolling Block" design, and I know of at least one that is in the image of the English Martini. This one is imported by Navy Arms Corporation and comes in .45/70 or .444 Marlin chambering and features an attractive half-octagon-half-round barrel pleasantly reminiscent of Creedmoor days. By and large, though, these replica actions are meant to be "lookers" and "plinkers." They

This replica of the famed Remington Rolling Block action of the 1800's is imported by the Navy Arms Company and is available in .45/70 or .444 Marlin chamberings.

do not have the fine triggers or speedy striker fall required for a super tack driver.

For hard-shell conservatives who insist that the only reasonable excuse for a one-shooter is budget pricing, H&R offers a couple of honest-to-goodness "poor boy" breakdown centerfires. One, the Model 155, comes in .44 Magnum and .45/70, and the other, called the Model 158 Topper, is available in .30/30 or .22 Hornet. Both of these are external-hammer breakdown jobs built on simple single-barrel shotgun frames. The Model 155 has a ramrod fitted under the barrel and a straight-grip stock styled with a frontier flair. The plainer and cheaper Model 158 is just styled for what it's supposed to be—a budget-priced hunter for the chap who wants to lay in his winter supply of venison with the least possible cash outlay.

Part III

Varmint Rifles

11

The Evolution of Varmint Rifles and Varmint Cartridges

Not since the legendary "Kentucky" long rifle of Colonial days has any gun been so thoroughly an American development as the modern varmint rifle. Virtually every varmint cartridge is also an all-American effort, and until just recently even the varmint rifles built in Europe and elsewhere were made almost exclusively for the U.S. market and chambered for American varmint cartridges. But then where else but in the U.S. and Canada would a shooter lay out $300 or more for a rig to shoot nonedible animals or birds whose only sporting value is that they are small and tough to hit?

Anyone who thinks that varmint shooting is only an informal little game for kids with .22s or, at best, good only for off-season rifle practice had better think again. There is no other member of the hunting fraternity who lays out more dough for his rifles, scopes, and reloading equipment than the real dyed-in-the-wool varmint shooter, or is as expert in their use. Whereas a real gung-ho deer hunter will have only one or, at most, two rifles for his sport, a true varmint buff is more likely to own at least three snappy rigs for busting crows, foxes, groundhogs, or prairie dogs.

Here, for the sake of students of hunter psychology, is the key to the psyche of the varmint shooter: To deer hunters, or any other hunters, for that matter, the hunt is the thing and the rifle only a tool. In the varmint-shooting league the order is reversed. The rifle is the focal point, and something to shoot at is secondary. All the varmint shooter wants is just *something* to shoot his rifle at. Since varmints can be shot in any numbers year-

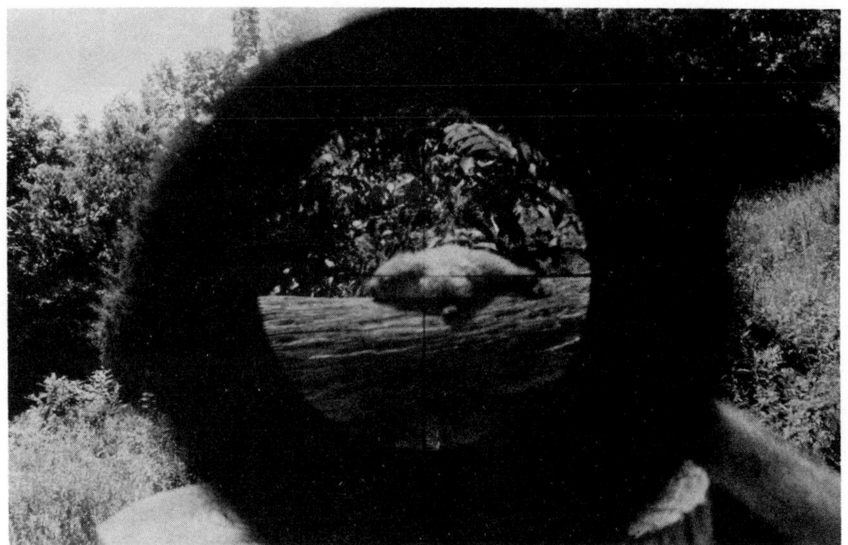

Here's the guy that got it all started. This snoozing woodchuck doesn't know it, but he's being looked at through a BALvar 24× scope mounted on a .220 Swift.

round and since their destruction is actually a kind service to landowners, what could be a more suitable target for an accuracy-oriented rifleman?

If all big-game hunting were to be stopped tomorrow the sale of big-game rifles would come to a total halt. But if the shooting of varmints were to be prohibited there would still be plenty of takers for varmint-type rifles. It's just because there are lots of shooters who enjoy owning and tinkering with finely accurate rifles.

The age of the varmint rifle is generally considered to have begun with the .22 Hornet back about 1930. Actually, the sport goes back much further than that. Our pioneer forefathers no doubt showed off their marksmanship by dusting off an occasional woodchuck with their long rifles, but it wasn't until nearly the turn of this century that "pest" rifles, as they were then known, became a recognizable class of firearms. The pest cartridges of that era weren't very impressive by today's hotshot standards, but such rounds as the .22 WCF, .22/15/60 Stevens, .25/20 or .25/21 Stevens, with their small, light bullets and relatively large cases, would look vaguely familiar to today's varmint shooter. About 1600 feet per second was the maximum for these black-powder whizzers, but this gave a range of upward of 200 yards, with, say, an 85-grain .25-caliber bullet.

Then as now, however, the cartridges were mated with the most accurate rifles of the day. Most popular of these were the single-shot designs by Winchester, Ballard, and especially Stevens. The Stevens "schuetzen" rifles were favorites among target shooters—who, as it just so happens, were also the first dedicated varmint shooters. Rifles and cartridges which proved them-

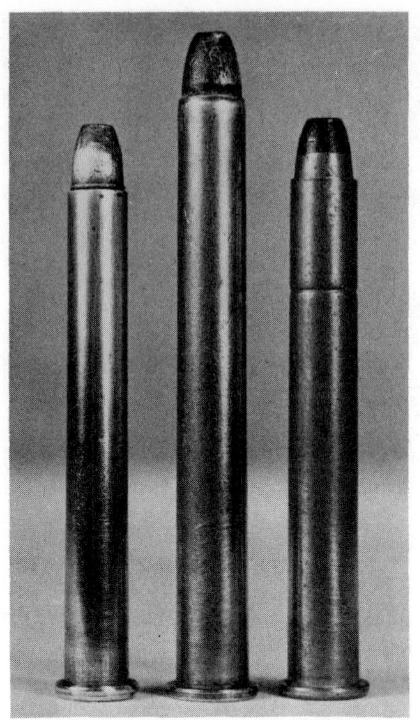

These target and "test" cartridges, with their relatively large cases and small bullets, should look vaguely familiar to a modern varmint shooter even though they date back to the turn of the century. From left to right, they are the Stevens .22/15/60, .25/25, and .25/21.

selves on the target range were naturally carried afield after chucks and crows.

Back around the turn of the century and even earlier, the northeastern part of the U.S., especially New Jersey and New York, was the center of formalized target shooting. Thus it was only natural that varmint shooting on anything like a popular scale also began in the Northeast. Also, then as now, a good target/varmint rig was the most expensive sort of rifle one could buy. At a time when a Winchester Model 1873 lever rifle retailed for $5, a good-grade single-shot target or "pest" rifle would set you back three times as much. I get a chuckle every time my mind's eye conjures up a vision of a skinflint Vermont farmer being asked by a nattily dressed big-city target shooter for permission to shoot woodchucks.

Interestingly, the varmint shooters of that time were not at all preoccupied with high velocity or flat trajectory. Their accounts of pest shooting seemed to revolve entirely around target rifles and target cartridges. Apparently, accuracy was the limiting factor. Bear in mind that the 6mm Lee Navy cartridge, which had a muzzle velocity of over 2500 feet per second with a 112-grain bullet, dates back to the 1890s, and the .22 Savage High Power round, which sent a 70-grain bullet on its way at 2800 fps, was introduced around 1912. These would more nearly meet the modern criteria of a varmint round, but not so back then. From the ballistic standpoint they offered more range than the prevailing "pest" rounds, but I suspect the problem was a matter of accuracy. These two rounds, like some others of their high-velocity, smokeless-powder class, simply weren't available in suitably accurate rifles. Another problem may have been the general reluctance to reload smokeless-powder cartridges in those days. Target shooters felt more at ease with the more familiar black-powder cartridges. Looking through old firearms catalogs dating up to about 1916, I've noticed that while much is made of the "smashing velocity" of such rounds as the .22 Savage, .250/300, etc., they are never described as varmint or pest rifles. Instead, they are suggested for deer and even moose. It just hadn't occurred to anybody that a gun buff might lay out greenbacks for a rifle to plaster pasture poodles.

Varmint shooting as we know it today didn't really get rolling until the early 1930s, when the .22 Hornet hit the scene. Quite a few Springfield Model 1922 .22 rimfire rifles were converted to Hornet chambering by such custom firms as Griffin & Howe, but the cartridge mainly got around in the form of Savage's Model 23D, and the Winchester Model 54. Keep in mind that a rifle purely for varmint shooting was a near-revolutionary concept and manufacturers didn't work themselves into a high fever to win the lion's share of the market. No one was really sure that any such market even existed, and some of the more traditional-minded sales representatives didn't take kindly to jibes about peddling "rat rifles." Winchester adopted a wait-and-see attitude and actually produced .22 Hornet ammo before they offered a rifle in the chambering. In truth it was the writing and promotional efforts of such experimenters as Townsend Whelen that created an interest in varmint shooting. Manufacturers themselves did little at first to support the budding sport.

The mild little Hornet was a delight to shoot, and many rifles, especially the Winchester Model 54, proved amazingly accurate. This in itself revealed a remarkable phenomenon that has since been the most profitable appeal of varmint equipment: rifle buffs simply like to sit down at a shooting bench and fire an accurate rifle. Seldom is a varmint rifle burned out in the woodchuck fields; they get that way being fired at targets.

Even as the Hornet was being introduced, some experimenters across the country were already working on bigger and better things. Grosvenor Wotkyns and Jerry Gebby, to name only a couple, were thinking the unthinkable—velocities of 4000 feet per second or better. Their experiments led directly to Winchester's introduction of the great .220 Swift in the mid-1930s. Though a few Model 54s were made in .220 Swift chambering, the happiest marriage for the new round was with the equally new Model 70. This was a combination that sent the shooting fraternity into lightheaded raptures. Gun scribes of the day, unable to relate the Swift to anything in their previous experience, wrote all sorts of conflicting reports which even today make fascinating reading, provided you suitably fortify yourself with strong drink beforehand. Winchester salesmen, I'm told, referred to the Swift as the postage-stamp rifle because they could demonstrate that the trajectory was so flat that they could hit a postage stamp at 50 or 100 yards with the same sight setting.

Surprising as it may seem to a varmint shooter of a more recent generation, the Swift, for all its wonderful ballistics, did not sweep the barrel clean. For one thing it arrived during the tail end of the depression era, and everyone on the block didn't rush out to buy every new gun that came along. And too, some fuzzy-headed writers were pretty effective at discouraging sales. One chap, to cite one example among many, wrote in an important shooting journal that for an amateur to attempt reloading the Swift case was to court disaster. Either he had a poor opinion of his fellow reloaders or, more likely, was a lightweight in the reloading department himself. At any rate, sales of the Swift were held to a level which discouraged Winchester competitors from marketing another rifle in .220 chambering.

There is a vague notion among some shooters that the .218 Bee cartridge was introduced somewhere between the Hornet and the Swift. This is a logical presumption, perhaps, seeing as how the Bee is hotter than the Hornet but not up to the style of the Swift. But as a matter of fact, the .218 didn't see light until 1939, when Winchester offered it in their Model 65 lever-action rifle. A year earlier, Winchester had introduced yet another varmint round, the .219 Zipper, and offered it in the Model 64 lever rifle.

Both of these efforts were ill-fated. The rifles were good ones, among the most finely finished of Winchester's long list of lever-action rifles, and there was really nothing wrong with .218 or .219 cartridges. But the fact that they were offered in lever rifles discloses, to today's observer, that the powers that dwelt in New Haven still had not fathomed the varmint-shooting psyche. The company was founded in the lever-action tradition, and at the time it no doubt seemed that a cute lever-action rifle would have enormous appeal to that mysterious new breed of hunter who "plinked" at crows and gophers. But this is where they made their mistake. The new breed of varmint shooter was not a "plinker" in any sense of the word. He was dead serious about his sport, and to offer him a semi-accurate rifle that couldn't even be well mated with a scope bordered on the insulting. So few Model 64s and 65s were sold in the varmint calibers that today they are considered prize acquisitions by Winchester collectors. Years later, the Marlin Company, still unconvinced that lever rifles and varmint shooters wouldn't mesh, cataloged their Model 336 for the Zipper and did thereby create a few—very few—collectors' items themselves.

Despite these occasional mistakes, Winchester, which was carrying the varmint-shooting ball almost singlehandedly, made some brilliant moves. The most spectacular move in the varmint direction was to make the target version of the Model 70 available in .220 caliber. This combination has yet to be beaten by any factory-produced rig regardless of make, model, or caliber.

During this same era, there was quite a bit of well-ballyhooed ballistic development going on in Europe, and if you believe everything you read, it appeared that they were getting some pretty spectacular velocities. But absolutely nothing was accomplished in the way of turning out a good varmint round. There were some rounds developed which were *potentially* good var-

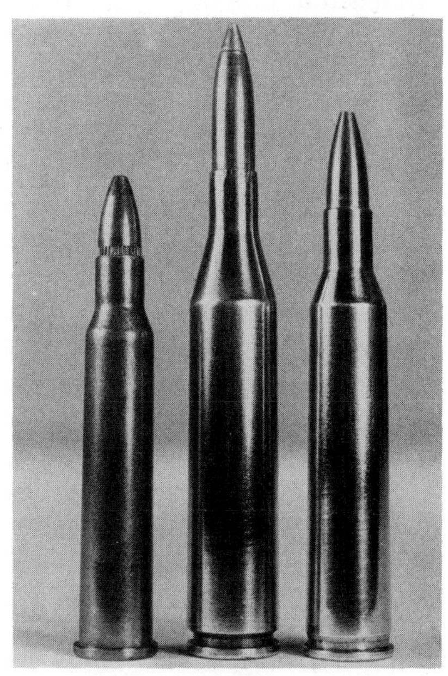

Though some European manufacturers designed and produced some cartridges that had potential as varmint rounds they never really got off the ground. A couple of these are shown at left. At far left is the 5.56×50 rimmed Magnum and in the center is the 5.6 Vom Hofe Super Express. At right, for comparison, is the American .220 Swift. The Vom Hofe Super Express was introduced in 1937 but was looked on by Europeans strictly as a big game hunting cartridge for deer-sized animals. The muzzle velocity with a 77-grain bullet is nearly 3,500 fps.

mint calibers, most significantly the 5.6×61 Vom Hofe Super Express, which had a muzzle velocity of 3700 feet per second with a 77-grain bullet, but the Europeans never looked at these as varmint cartridges in our sense of the word. There are few animals in Europe which would qualify for what we'd call varmints, and even fewer hunters who would be interested in such a sport, especially in the era before World War II. A cartridge similar to the .22 Hornet, the 5.6×35R Vierling, was a popular round in Europe then, but was mainly chambered in drillings or other forms of multiple-barrel guns and was used only for large fowl or small game animals. Similarly, the .22 Savage High Power, known in Europe as the 5.6×52R, was popular, but only for medium-sized game such as roebuck or chamois. In short, the sport of varmint hunting did not exist in Europe.

As far back as the early 1920s, the British firm of Holland & Holland had introduced a hot 6mm varmint-like round they called the .240 Apex or .240 Nitro Express. It gave a muzzle velocity of 3000 feet per second with a 100-

grain bullet. But like the Continental gunmakers the English were not in the least aware of any such thing called varmint shooting and could not have cared less. As a result their speedy littlebore cartridges, like those dreamed up by the Germans, were doomed to teeter forever on the brink of extinction. It's fascinating to speculate on what effect the English and German gunmakers might have had on the U.S. varmint-shooting picture if they had been more aware of what was happening in the world. Today European manufacturers cater very graciously to the demands of American varmint shooters, but only to the extent of courting American whims with rifles chambered for purely American calibers. They lost the chance to promote their own cartridges four decades ago. Nowadays even the European rifle buyer demands U.S. calibers such as the .222 Remington, .243 Winchester, and 6mm Remington. Perhaps the Europeans would have seen the light in time, or perhaps they were already figuring out how to get in on the American varmint-shooting action, but the coming of war stopped any such plans.

To my mind it has always been a matter of some puzzlement that Remington, Winchester's traditional rival, stirred not at all as Winchester moved boldly with varmint-shooting developments during the prewar era. Their beautifully built Model 720 would have been fine for the Swift or a similar design, but the .257 Roberts was the closest thing they offered to a varmint cartridge, and little effort was made to court the market even with that one.

The immediate postwar years brought about a completely different attitude at Remington. First came new rifle designs, the Models 721 and 722, and then in 1950 a brand-new varmint cartridge all their own, the .222 Remington. And thus was born what may be the all-time most popular varmint cartridge.

When the folk at Remington designed the accurate little .222 they were doing themselves a far greater service than they realized. A valuable by-product of its wonderful accuracy was a demonstration of the inherent accuracy of the basic 722 rifle design. No matter what cosmetic changes were made in following years, be they called the Model 725, 700, 600, 660, or 40-X, the basic 722 action remains unimproved-upon and serves as the basis for some wonderfully accurate varmint rifles not only in .222 but .223, .222 Magnum, .22/250 Remington, .243 Winchester, 6mm Remington (.244 Remington), and the diminutive .17 Remington. A source of disappointment to me, however, is that they have not offered .220 Swift chambering. Now that Winchester no longer offers the Swift in their Target Model 70 (or any other model for that matter), a single-shot 40-X Remington with heavy stainless-steel barrel could be the finest long-range varmint-getter offered by any arms manufacturer.

When Johnny came marching home at the end of World War II, one of the things he had on his mind was hunting. Apparently five years of war had only whetted his appetite for guns and shooting, because the postwar demand for guns, any kind of guns, was unprecedented. Apparently also, the G.I. marksmanship training had aroused considerable interest in pinpoint bullet placement, because varmint shooting came on stronger than ever.

I personally consider 1950 the year varmint shooting officially came into its own as a major branch of the rifle sports. Before then it had been more or less a one-company (Winchester) show and was not taken very seriously by the majority of the hunting public. In the early 1950s, several forces united to change the picture dramatically. First of all, of course, the war was well over; the G.I.s had returned home and reestablished their domestic lives and lots of them were looking for shooting-related sports. Many of them who would never have considered wasting their time hunting woodchucks in prewar days now saw varmint shooting as a pleasant, relaxing, and inexpensive way of passing a summer's day, and it also gave them an extra chance to try out the rifle they'd promised to buy themselves when the war ended.

Domestic armsmakers had tooled up for sporting-gun production again, and some completely overhauled their lines. Remington now offered their 722 in .222, Winchester introduced the inexpensive bolt-action Model 43 in .22 Hornet or .218 Bee, Savage soon offered their Model 340 in .222 Remington, and the popular Model 70 was available in Hornet and Swift. The big influence, though, was a-building in Europe. Armsmakers all over the continent had to sell guns in order to survive, and the only sportsmen of that time who had money to spend on guns were Americans. So, casting a shrewd eye to the West, European gunmakers studied the market, and one of the things they recognized was that varmint shooting was the shooting sport of *their* future. Thus, even before the 1950s were half over, varmint shooters were treated to a host of beautifully made and finished, reasonably priced, and, best of all, accurate varmint rifles.

The Belgian firm of F.N. started turning out the second factory-made .220 Swift rifle ever. A trim little German rifle called the Tyrol was being chambered for the .222 Remington, and in Finland a company no one had even guessed existed, and bearing the unlikely name of Svojeluskuntain Aseja Konepaja Osakeyhtio, watered the mouths of gun lovers with a delightfully trim but wonderfully accurate little sporter which could be had in .222 Remington, .22 Hornet, or .218 Bee. The tonguetwisting name meant "The Arms and Engineering Workshop of the Civil Guards Company Ltd.," but for varmint shooters the simple initials SAKO sufficed.

I bought my first Sako, a .222 with Mannlicher stock, back about 1952. The retail price then was about $125, which in those days was pretty steep, more even than a Model 70. In my neck of the woods no sporting-goods dealer would consider stocking such high-priced merchandise, so I ordered one sight-unseen through a mail-order house. Outfitted with a Lyman 10× Wolverine scope, the trim little rifle would put *ten* rounds inside an inch on any occasion and was light enough to carry over the hills from dawn to dusk.

I have no idea how many crows and chucks I did asunder with that first Sako, but their numbers were legion. By then I was a hopelessly lost varmint-shooting addict. When I was no older than seventeen I owned, and reloaded for, rifles in .22 Hornet, .222 Remington (2), and .220 Swift (2) caliber.

The next, and last, step toward putting varmint shooting in the big time was the introduction by Winchester and Remington, in 1955, of their .243 and .244 cartridges. These two really capped the stack. Not only because they were fast, flat-shooting varmint rounds but also because they served double service as excellent cartridges for medium game such as deer and antelope. A fellow who had been torn between shelling out his hard-earned dough for a deer rifle or a varmint rig could now have both in one rifle. Even sports who had never given much thought to varmint shooting felt compelled to give it a try once they had a deer rifle in one of the new 6mm calibers in hand.

These two cartridges also opened the door for even more U.S. and foreign rifles in varmint configuration. Sako, for instance, introduced a medium-length action, and such old-line firms as Steyr (Mannlicher-Schoenaur) offered rifles in .243 caliber. In other words, the "varmint movement" had come on so effectively that one could buy his favorite make and model of rifle in at least one varmint chambering. A far cry from the situation of only fifteen years earlier when buying a varmint rig was virtually a choice of one rifle in one caliber.

The growth of varmint shooting had some side effects which had a major impact on the whole shooting industry. First of all, it raised the awareness and understanding of guns and ammunition tremendously. In prewar days the typical gun buyer was satisfied if his rifle could hit a moose. That's what he bought the rifle for and that's all he cared about. But when a member of the fast-growing varmint-shooting clan discovered that his new rifle wasn't accurate enough to hit a crow at 300 yards, he started looking for reasons why. This brought about an unprecedented consumer-level awareness of everything that has anything to do with gun performance. Stocks, barrels, actions, triggers, scopes, mounts, and especially ammunition components came under scrutiny.

The far-reaching effects this was ultimately to have can best be illustrated by an experience a target-shooting pal of mine had back in the 1950s. He had bought what was supposed to be one of the finest target-type centerfire rifles available, and naturally, for the kind of money he had to lay out, he expected good accuracy. At 200 yards, however, the gun wouldn't keep ten shots inside of 6 inches. He and I went over the rifle from front sight to butt plate looking for the problem, but everything was tight and as it should be. Then we ran a lead plug through the bore and found that the groove diameter was about .003 inch oversize. Obviously this was the cause of the problem, so the rifle was returned to the factory with a description of the rifle's performance and our opinion of what was causing the trouble. To our astonishment the rifle was returned with a note stating that they too found the bore to be somewhat oversize but even so it still fell within their "normal manufacturing tolerances." What they were saying, in other words, was that the tolerances under which they made barrels meant that some rifles might be accurate and some others obviously wouldn't, but they weren't especially concerned one way or the other even though the rifle in question was an expensive target model.

Today, thanks to varmint shooters, the situation is vastly changed. A rifle that won't shoot well, especially if it is a bolt-action model in varmint chambering and configuration, is just cause for complaint, and what's more, the manufacturer is very much inclined to do something about it. There are rifles on today's market which are *guaranteed* to deliver a given level of accuracy. Two decades ago such a claim would have been unthinkable. Varmint shooters have led the way in reversing the "Don't tell us, we'll tell you" attitude of prewar gun manufacturers.

Varmint shooting was also a major factor in the growth of the handloading industry. Here again, if factory ammo wasn't good enough the varmint fan wasted little time learning how to load some that was. The long-

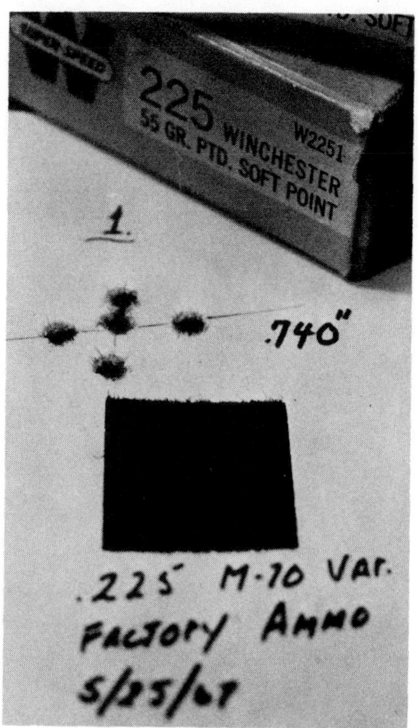

Varmint shooters had a lot to do with the accuracy of today's rifles and ammunition. This group, which measures less than ¾ inch, was fired with standard factory .225 Winchester loads in a Winchester Model 70 varmint-weight rifle. The group was fired in 1967; a generation earlier such accuracy from factory ammunition would have been unheard-of.

This stack of varmint loads gives you an idea of the various calibers and brands available today. Before World War II there were only three or four varmint loads altogether.

term effect of this has been to considerably upgrade the accuracy of factory-loaded ammo. It's not at all uncommon to find factory-loaded .22/250, .222, .243, or 6mm Remington that will group five shots under an inch at 100 yards. In 1966 I tried a lot of Winchester-Western-loaded .225 Winchester loads that grouped under a half-inch with a varmint-weight Model 70. Ten years earlier such accuracy would have been all but unthinkable with factory loads.

Another interesting firearm-industry development which is largely traceable to the demands of varmint shooters is the widespread availability of actions and barreled actions. During the 1950s, when varmint shooters began to get fussier about their equipment and started getting some pretty inde-

Most of today's manufacturers of rifles supply barreled actions such as this Winchester Model 70 varmint-weight rig. Before about 1950 most manufacturers would not supply anything but finished rifles, but the trend was changed by varmint shooters who insisted on making their own specialized stocks for long-range accuracy.

pendent notions about what a varmint rifle should look like, there was a wholesale movement in the do-it-yourself direction. Domestic makers had long held a hard line against selling components such as barreled actions, but the Europeans didn't even give it a second thought. If plain actions or barreled actions were what the Americans wanted, then that's what they'd

The new Savage Model 112-V Varminter. It features a varmint-configuration stock with nice checkering, a heavyweight barrel, and single-shot action. The rifle comes in .222, .22/250, .220 Swift, .25/06, and .243 calibers.

get. I have no idea how many Sako, F.N., or Husqvarna actions were sold, but they must number in the hundreds of thousands. Finally the U.S. manufacturers were forced to give up and offer barreled actions as well. But as it turned out they had already lost a big chunk of the market. Today, the do-it-yourself craze isn't what it was, but if you'll take a look at the stocks on modern factory-made varmint rifles you'll find wide, wide, flat forends and straight butts with high combs and cheek pieces—exactly the same features varmint shooters were having to build for themselves not too many years ago.

These reasons, and many more, are why today's varmint rig has become the symbol of precision accuracy. If it had not been for that four-footed alfalfa addict known as the woodchuck, and the determination of a few hard-core riflemen to hit him at ever-increasing ranges, there wouldn't be any such thing as the modern rifle as we know it.

12

Varmint Cartridges

The first widely accepted purely varmint round, the .22 Hornet, was placed on the market not as a competitive enterprise but mainly just to take care of a demand. Decision-makers in high places recognized that there existed a certain demand for a varmint cartridge, and the Hornet was produced simply to fill that demand. I doubt if any thought was given at the time to the possibility that there would come a day when varmint cartridges would compete in the marketplace. But now we know that competition for a share of the varmint market is one of the most important in the sporting-arms business.

I expect most companies first learned that supplying the varmint market was truly a sophisticated business when it was discovered (sometimes too late) that demands for certain types of rifles and special calibers varied from one region to the next. This was a well-known factor in selling shotguns and big-game rifles, but who would have guessed that varmint shooters' likes and dislikes could be broken down on a regional basis and that these preferences, as unpredictable as they might sometimes be, would make or break a rifle/cartridge combo? So, with the fickle pleasures of the rifle-buying public uppermost in mind, let's consider some varmint cartridges one by one and see what they have to offer that would tempt a prospective buyer.

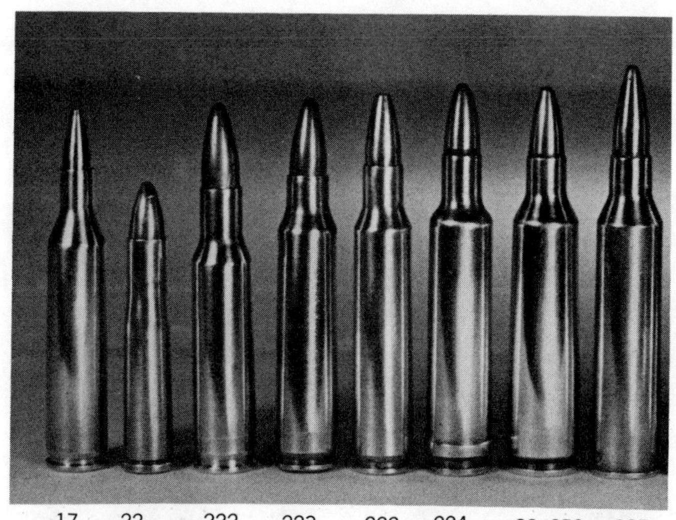

.17 Rem. | .22 Hornet | .222 Rem. | .223 Rem. | .222 Mag. | .224 Weath. Mag. | .22/250 Rem. | .225 Win.

.220 Swift | .243 Win. | 6mm Rem. | .240 Weath. Mag. | .250/3000 Savage | .257 Roberts | .25/06 Rem. | .257 Weath. Mag.

A line-up of the standard factory varmint rounds.

My wife, Clarice, took this woodchuck with a Model 70 Winchester in .22 Hornet caliber topped with a 10× Lyman Super Targetspot scope.

.22 HORNET

When the Hornet was introduced in 1930 it was actually the third time around for a cartridge which started out as the .22 WCF way back in 1885. The second phase was in a European form known as the 5.6X35R Vierling. Cartridge historians love to point out the differences between the .22 WCF, the Vierling, and the Hornet, but there is no getting around the fact that both the Hornet and the Vierling were jazzed-up versions of the older case. Actually, whatever "development" took place was little more than replacing the black powder of the .22 WCF with smokeless and watching the velocity increase. And in rather haphazard fashion at that. For instance, the original .22 WCF fired a lead bullet of about .226 inch diameter. But the Hornet, when introduced, had a .223-inch slug. Did this represent a dynamic ballistic achievement? Not on your life. The first Hornet experimenter just happened to be using some .22 rimfire barrels with a .223 bore size, so the .22 WCF cases they used were slightly reduced at the neck and smaller bullets used. Thus when Winchester first marketed Hornet ammo the .223 bullet diameter was used so as to fit the rimfire barrels then generally used for Hornet rifles. Later, when factory-made rifles in the chambering were produced, the bore size had to match the existing ammo specs. Scarcely a ballistic breakthrough, but matters of expediency have had even stranger and wider-reaching effects in the gun world.

The Hornet's muzzle velocity of 2690 feet per second isn't very impressive by today's varmint velocity standards, but for its time it was pretty hot (though the much older .250 Savage topped 3000 fps) and accuracy was reasonably good. Some pretty high-sounding claims were made for the accuracy of the Hornet, but the *average* accuracy of early Hornets would cause a varmint shooter of today to giggle up his sleeve. But the Hornet was, at best, a 200-yard gun, and for that range a rifle need only be capable of grouping inside a 2-inch circle at 100 yards. It was—and is—one of the most pleasant of cartridges to shoot; a day spent afield with the Hornet was a very pleasant occasion indeed. This perhaps is the chief reason why it has become such a sentimental favorite.

The coming of the Swift had little to do with the decline of the Hornet. They were simply too different for one to have much effect on the sales of the other. It wasn't until after the war and the acceptance of Remington's .222 that the Hornet became a dead issue. The new Remington cartridge offered an improvement of about 100 yards of range over the Hornet and was still mild of report, and as shooters quickly learned, it was far more accurate.

Over the years I've owned perhaps six or eight rifles in Hornet chambering, but must admit the round's early publicized accuracy has largely escaped me. A couple of Model 70s would occasionally put five shots close to an inch at the 100-yard range, but the overall average for both factory and handloaded ammo has been closer to an inch and a half. The best accuracy has been with a 1974 vintage Anschutz Model 1432, which groups between ⅞ inch and 1¼ inches, the average being slightly under an inch. Gun writers of the 1920s and 1930s loved to report on the accuracy of their devel-

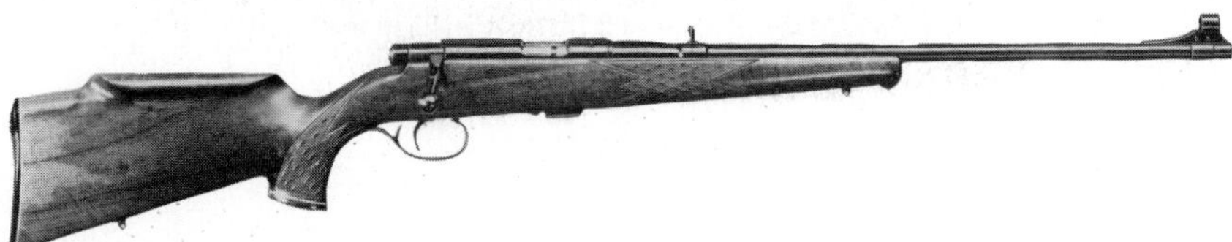

For lovers of the .22 Hornet the Anschutz Model 1432 is about the best thing going.

opments, but I've long suspected that they usually described their *best* groups rather than *average* groups. I also suspect that if one of the early Hornet rhapsodizers had had a Hornet as accurate as the Anschutz mentioned above he would have expressed his adoration in sizzling stanzas of poetic reverence.

Here of late the vintage cartridge has made a comeback of sorts, but not for any reason that represents a ballistic "gap" in need of plugging. With the nostalgia craze in full bloom, the Hornet has an undeniable appeal because it is straight out of the era of Duesenberg limousines, Bonnie and Clyde and nickel beer. The Ruger Number Three single-shot, which is chambered for the Hornet, has a rich appeal of its own, and for the fellow who wants to own one the Hornet chambering is no significant drawback. The Anschutz 1432 is a high-priced trinket but a nice item for the gun buyer who has

This is Ruger's Number Three single-shot carbine, which is available in .22 Hornet among other chamberings. Both the ancient .22 Hornet chambering and the late-nineteenth-century styling should appeal to nostalgia buffs.

everything. Similarly, the Czech-made Brno is available in this caliber and has special charm for fans of Old World gunmakers. And if there is still such a thing as a barefoot farm lad, Harrington & Richardson has for him an economy-priced, break-down, single-shot, hammer rifle in Hornet caliber based on their Topper shotgun frame.

The Model 70 Winchester Hornet has long since been abolished, but for those lucky enough to own one they still represent the Hornet's finest hour. Mostly, though, they are in the hands of collectors who willingly pay up to three times what the rifles originally sold for. Even the Model 43 is becoming a collector's piece.

I am very much of the opinion that the recent rebirth of the Hornet is the result of a sort of cultural backlash among varmint shooters. Having discovered how far away they can nail a chuck, they become interested in what can be done with a cartridge dating back a half-century. I frequently take a Hornet along on prairie-dog shoots and glory in a 200-yard hit as much as one at twice the range with one of my more modern hotshots. It's fun. And fun, come to think of it, is what the .22 Hornet has always had to offer.

.218 BEE

The little Bee is presented here mostly for historical comparison. Like the Hornet it became a dead issue with the advent of the .222, but unlike its older cousins it isn't likely to be raised from the grave. Most descriptions of the .218 say that with a muzzle velocity of some 2860 fps it has greater punch and somewhat more range than the Hornet. What these descriptions

My son Eric strains mightily to hoist a woodchuck he knocked off with a peep-sighted Model 43 Winchester in .218 Bee chambering. I started him out on peep sights for varmint shooting, but he soon expressed a desire to move up to scopes.

fail to take into account, however, is that until Sako made a few Bees in the early 1950s there had never been a really accurate rifle in the chambering. It was introduced by Winchester as a caliber for their lever-action Model 65, but this was a disaster from the accuracy standpoint. Not that the rifle itself was woefully inadequate, but it just wasn't *shootable*—too much drop in the stock, hard trigger pull, and not much way to get a scope mounted low over the barrel. Thus even with its 170 fps velocity edge over the Hornet it didn't have the range of a good Model 70 or 54 in the lesser caliber. The few really accurate rifles in .218 chambering I've seen have been custom affairs built on BSA single-shot actions with accurate barrels, crisp triggers, and good scopes.

The Bee was also offered for a while in Winchester's Model 43 bolt gun but unfortunately didn't make much of a hit. This seemed to me like a pretty lively little low-priced combination for the budget-bound shooter. When my oldest son was still in short pants I outfitted him with a peep-sighted Model 43 .218 and felt that it was just about the perfect outfit for a

The best rifles in .218 Bee chambering have been built up on trim little BSA Martini single-shot actions such as this custom rig stocked by Don Allen of Northfield, Minnesota. Scope is a 10× Weaver.

beginning hunter. But pretty soon he let me know that my .220 Swift was more like what he had in mind.

Not too long ago I got a letter from an experimenter telling me that he'd decided that the .218 Bee case necked out to .25 caliber would make a nice little cartridge for plinking squirrels and other such smallish game. I wrote back and told him that he had a fine idea but was about seventy-five years late. The .218 Bee was first made simply by necking the old-favorite .25/20 WCF *down* to .22 caliber!

.219 ZIPPER

Students of the evolution of the modern rifle will find the saga of the .219 Zipper especially instructive because it is a classic example of what happens when arms manufacturers miscalculate the direction of rifle buyers' habits.

First of all, keep in mind that it is reasonably difficult for a varmint cartridge to be a commercial failure. This is because of the buying habits of varmint shooters themselves. Unlike, say, the average bear hunter who feels he needs only one rifle, the varmint specialist enjoys owning and using two or even several rifles of different styles and calibers. Thus, he delights in trying every new varmint cartridge that comes down the pike.

First made by necking a .25/35 Winchester case down to .22 caliber, the design is about as accurate as any other hotshot .22 centerfire. I've seen any number of wonderfully accurate rifles in this chambering. The rimmed case is particularly appealing to single-shot rifle fans, and anytime you run across a High Wall Winchester action that has been custom-built into a varmint rig the chances are that it is a Zipper, or at least a close cousin. With 50- to 55-grain bullets the round can be handloaded to upwards of 3600 feet per second, a velocity range which has proved quite popular with the majority of varmint shooters.

If, when it was introduced back in 1937, it had been made available in an accurate rifle and loaded from about 3300 to 3500 fps with a 50- or 55-grain bullet, it would undoubtedly have met with high success. At that time most varmint shooters wanted more velocity than the Hornet offered but, at the same time, many were hesitant to move up to the terrifying Swift, especially in view of the bad press the .220 was getting. The proof of this thesis is the enormous success of the .222 Remington a few years later, which fitted right into this niche.

Yet, the .219 was factory-loaded with a 56-grain bullet, loaded to only 3050 fps, and, even worse, available only in the Winchester Model 65 lever gun. One thing a varmint shooter won't stand for is having his sophistication insulted, and any varminter who had advanced beyond the Stevens Favorite stage knew that one doesn't hit groundhogs at 300 yards very often with a lever-action rifle. So the whole project fizzled and the .219 Zipper never got off the ground. Approached differently it could have become the all-time favorite.

.222 REMINGTON

Everything Winchester had done wrong with the .219 Zipper, Remington did right with their offspring of 1950. It was a cute little round to start with, looking like a scaled-down .30/06, and was factory-loaded to 3200 fps with a 50-grain bullet. Of first importance, though, it was made available as a chambering for the plain-looking but inexpensive and amazingly accurate Remington Model 722 bolt-action rifle. (Retail price in 1951 was $74.95.)

Compared to the sizzling ballistics of some .22 centerfires the muzzle speed of the .222 is rather demure, but in actual practice it's about all many shooters can take advantage of—or even want. Sighted in to hit dead on at 200 yards the .222's point of impact is 1½ inches high at 100 yards and a little less than 8 inches low at 300 yards. With a little estimating for bullet drop this gives the round an effective range of upwards of 300 yards, and this is about as far as most of us can hope to hit a chuck-sized target anyway.

My first .222 was the economy-priced, clip-fed Savage Model 340, which I fitted with a $9 6× scope. It wasn't exactly a bench-rest outfit but served very nicely to bust crows farther than I had any reason to expect. Since then I've owned six or eight .222s of various persuasions and have never owned one that wouldn't put five shots inside a 1-inch circle at 100 yards. I've handloaded so many different calibers in so many bullet weights for so many rifles that I make it a rule never to try to memorize any of my loads. There is too much room for confusion and error. Yet, the one load that is indelibly impressed on my memory is the .222 load of 21 grains of IMR 4198 powder behind a 50-grain bullet. For many years this was my "standard" .222 load. It must have accounted for a wagonload of chucks, crows, gophers, and sundry other vermin.

The accuracy of the .222 is reaffirmed every time bench-rest shooters hold a tournament. At least half of the precision shooters will be using this design, and matches *not* won by the .222 are an exception to the rule. The shape of the case, plus its moderate capacity, gives extremely uniform ignition and combustion, both prime factors in achieving top accuracy. Combined with this fine accuracy is a relatively mild muzzle report which isn't all that likely to get landowners upset when you venture out to pot a few varmints. The moderate velocity of the .222 ensures a pleasantly long barrel life of somewhere between 5,000 and 8,000 rounds of varmint accuracy. Actually I can't say how long a .222 barrel will last because I've never worn one to the point where accuracy failed altogether. But when you think about it, even 5,000 shots means many years of use for most varmint hunters. A bench-rest shooter might easily consider his .222 barrel worn out, or at least its accuracy life at an end, after as few as perhaps 3,000 rounds, but that kind of "worn out" is the difference between groups measuring 2/10 and 3/10 inch.

Come to think of it, one of the factors which has helped the .222's accuracy reputation is that its unique rim size has protected it from ragtail gunsmiths. The "standard" rim size of the .22/250, .220 Swift, and other such cases has permitted a motley collection of rifles in these calibers to be built up on surplus Jap, Mauser, Springfield, Enfield, and other actions. Some of these do-it-yourself contraptions are about as accurate as a dowager duchess tossing horse apples at her cut-glass punch bowl. The .222 case, on the other hand, requires a much smaller bolt face, and as a result even the do-it-yourself efforts are most usually built around a fundamentally accurate action such as a Sako or Remington.

Sako "Vixen" heavy-barreled varmint rifle in .222 caliber. These little Finnish rifles set the varminting world on its ear in the early 1950s.

Back when the .222 was first introduced, quite a few owners of Winchester Model 70s in .22 Hornet had their rifles rechambered for the newer round. This was a relatively simple operation for a good gunsmith, and Griffin & Howe, in particular, for a while did a land-office business chambering out the conversions. The chief drawback to top accuracy with this rechambering job was that the Hornet barrels had groove diameters somewhere around .223, while factory-loaded .222 bullets were .224. Factory loads would work, but odd flyers would show up in most groups. Handloaders beat the problem easily enough by simply using the smaller-diameter bullets. The rub came along years later, however, when Winchester had discontinued the Model 70 Hornet and it became a much-desired—and expensive—collector's item. A rechambered one is worth $100 or so *less* than one in original condition!

.222 REMINGTON MAGNUM

I'm sure there were a number of factors which contributed to the introduction of the .222 Magnum by Remington in 1958. The .222 had been one of the hottest-selling cartridges in history, but seeing as how hunters, especially varmint shooters, are always on the prowl for something to stretch their yardage, a souped-up version no doubt seemed like a good idea. And too, let us not forget that the era of the late 1950s was the time of the great magnum mania. It makes my head hurt to think of all the magnums introduced in those days, but there's no getting around the fact that the word "Magnum" had a magic ring to it that meant money in the cash drawer. Remington contributed their share of magnums, of course, and apparently nothing would suit them but to give the moniker to their stretched-out .222. Even if it's no more a magnum than I'm a dead ringer for Clark Gable.

In truth, the new muzzle velocity of 3240 fps stretched one's effective yardage by about 50 paces or so (with a little imagination), and the heavier 55-grain bullet of factory loads offered better performance in the wind as well as a flatter trajectory. Despite the additional velocity and the catchy name I resisted falling in love with the round and even to this day can claim with a clear conscience that I've never owned one. It would have been a best choice for a shooter buying a one and only varmint rig but wasn't worth ditching a faithful standard .222 for. Neither was it the logical step up for varmint hunters who had been weaned on the .222 and were ready for better things. At that time the only real step up was to a .220 Swift or a wildcat such as the .22/250.

The accuracy of the .222 Magnum is virtually equal to its smaller kin, and, as a matter of fact, several bench rifles in this caliber have done well in competition. The Model 700 bolt rifles made by Remington were fully as accu-

I look over a woodchuck just bagged with a Remington Model 700. The .222 Remington was a good round in the M700, though I never saw much reason to own a rifle in that chambering. This one is a .22/250, with 10×Weaver scope.

rate as an off-the-shelf .222. But even so, if fate had not dealt a crooked hand the .222 Magnum would never have achieved the success of its predecessor. There just isn't that much difference. The intervention of fate came in the form of a round which was to be known as the .223 Remington, a round actually somewhat inferior to the .222 Magnum but with a lot of other things going for it.

Shortly after the .223 hit the scene the .222 Magnum was relegated to the rear burner and allowed to die a fairly painless death. Today, it isn't even chambered for in the Remington Model 700 and the only way its parent company will sell you one at all is in the form of their custom-shop 40-X. I'd say that it is one of the least ordered calibers in that model. Two or three European firms still offer rifles in the chambering, but I expect even these will give it up before many moons. Ironically, it appears that the greatest long-term success of the .222 Remington Magnum will be in the form of the so-called 6X47. This wildcat cartridge, made by simply opening the neck of a .222 Magnum case to 6mm, gets its name from its metric caliber and length and is the most popular cartridge for the Sporter Class rifles used in bench-rest competition. Thus, even if no rifles and little .222 Magnum ammo is sold there will be a continuing demand for the cases for years to come.

.223 REMINGTON

When Remington "introduced" the .223 Remington in the early 1960s their catalog began to look pretty confusing. Sporting souls who delight in poring over ballistic charts were acutely distraught by the similarity of the newcomer to the just recently ballyhooed .222 Magnum, and gun salesmen were at their wit's end trying to explain to customers the difference between the .222, .223, and .222 Magnum.

The .223 had actually gotten started some years before when it was developed as the companion cartridge for the Armalite military rifle. When the powers at Remington saw that the little .22-caliber cartridge was headed for the big time, they figured it would have commercial possibilities and got in on the ground floor by lending their name to what was to become the civilian version. Winchester had done the same thing a decade earlier when they glommed onto the 7.62 NATO cartridge and called it the .308 Winchester.

In military terms the .223 is the 5.56mm, exactly the same round that gathered so much publicity in Vietnam when some overeager journalist wrote home about its "buzz saw" effect.

The commercial success of official service cartridges is virtually unavoidable. (Consider the four previous service rounds—the .45/70, .30/40, .30/06, and 7.62 NATO.) So Remington made a smart move when they adopted the 5.56mm. If they hadn't, someone else would have, and either way the .222 Magnum, which hadn't had time to become established, would be a dream turned sour. Nowadays when you see a rifle marked .223 Remington you're looking at a gun that probably would otherwise have been a .222 Magnum.

Ballistically there isn't much difference between the two; Remington loads them to identical velocities with identical-weight bullets, but the handloader can squeeze a bit more zip out of the Magnum. The Magnum case is about 1/10 inch longer than the .223 and has about 5 percent greater capacity. The rim diameters are exactly the same.

Like the .222 before it, the .223 is an exceedingly accurate design and has even made some notable inroads among the bench clan. I own a varmint-weight Model 700 Remington which grouped five shots only slightly over ½ inch the first time I tried it and hasn't done worse since. This is a straight out-of-the-store rifle, and other than adjusting the trigger it hasn't been tampered with or "tuned" in any way. My fighting half, Clarice, totes a little .223 H&H Ultra Wildcat after prairie dogs, and despite the rifle's total weight, with scope, of only 6½ pounds, she can hit a golf ball at 200 yards ten times out of ten.

Some talk has been made of the fact that the .223 has a shorter neck than the .222 or the .222 Magnum and for this reason isn't as good for handloading. Why such tales as this get started I'll never understand, but apparently they're made up by a swamp-dwelling ogre with one eye and pimply green skin who only comes out at night. On the other hand, I'm still not all that enthused by the suitability of surplus G.I. ammo. One of the most

My wife took this orchard-dwelling woodchuck with her H&R Model 317 Ultra Wildcat in .223 Remington caliber. The scope is a Redfield variable-power.

often voiced advantages of the .223 is that low-cost G.I. "salvage" ammo can be used. The few lots I've tried have all given pretty poor accuracy—at least poor compared to good handloads or commercial stuff. Most surplus military loads group no better than 1½ MOA. Also, of course, the nonexpanding military bullets are a bit more ricochet-prone than expanding types and at the longer ranges will only penetrate a chuck-sized animal but not stop him in his tracks. Out to about 200 yards, though, the sheer velocity of the speedy little bullet, soft tips or not, has an explosive effect on animal tissue.

Since the .223, not counting the .222 Magnum, is most similar to the .222, buyer comparison between the two is inevitable. What the choice really boils down to is the superior velocity of the .223 weighed against the wonderful performance history of the .222. If I were about to buy a varmint rifle and had to select one of the two I'd take the .223 and run.

.225 WINCHESTER

The star-crossed .225 Winchester is worthy of mention here if for no other reason than that in a few short years it will be utterly forgotten. Someone had better write something about it now so there will at least be some sort of testimony to intrigue cartridge historians a hundred years hence.

Despite its two- or three-year journey from womb to grave the .225 is a dandy varmint cartridge. The two rifles I've owned in this caliber, one a standard-weight and the other a varmint model, were both beautifully accurate. Winchester-Western factory-loaded ammunition in this caliber was also remarkably accurate. Some groups measured under ½ inch for five shots at 100 yards out of a standard off-the-shelf varmint-weight Model 70. Rarely, if ever, have shooters been treated to such outstanding accuracy with strictly factory goods. But alas, the poor .225 had too many crosses to bear.

The first of these was the 1964 version of Winchester's Model 70, the first rifle available in .225 chambering. When the famous design was revamped in 1964 many of the changes didn't sit at all well with the legions of M70 fans. These changes are discussed elsewhere in this book, but one of the side-effects was that many, many varmint shooters who would otherwise have gone for the .225 simply wouldn't buy the redesigned rifle. I was plagued with misgiving along this vein for a short while, but more upsetting from my standpoint was that Winchester had dropped the .220 Swift. Dropping a round with a top velocity of 3650 fps to go to one of over 4100 might make pretty good sense, but to do it the other way around was cause for more than a little head-shaking. Of course I'm being simplistic in this respect. It's no secret that the Swift had been maligned by a bad press for nearly thirty years, and Winchester-Western no doubt wanted to wash its hands of the affair and start off with a clean slate.

But why a rimmed case like the .225? Perhaps it was hoped that the distinctive rimmed profile would be held as attractive by some shooters. I think I recall some writers describing the .225 as being based on the .219 Zipper round or at least being a close look-alike. Actually there is little similarity. The one and only effect of the rimmed .225 case (which headspaces on the shoulder rather than the rim, incidentally) was to create feeding problems in bolt-action magazines.

It would be a great case for single-shot actions, and I even had a vision that it would be a worthwhile chambering for the Ruger Number One single-shot. But when I mentioned this to company officials they said that my suggestion was the one and only time the possibility had ever been mentioned. I suppose it was then that I realized that the .225 was a lost cause. Still, if I were going to have a nice varmint rifle built up on a single-shot action I think my first choice would be none other than a .225 Winchester.

Despite its minor mechanical faults the .225 would have succeeded if Remington had not introduced a legitimized version of a tried-and-true wildcat cartridge, the .22/250. With three decades of advance publicity the .22/250 "Remington" was an overnight sensation and the .225, alas, was lost in the shuffle.

Aside from Winchester's Model 70 the only other manufacturer of wide repute to chamber for the .225 was Savage, with their Model 340V bolt gun. Neither of these is any longer available, and they were sold in such meager numbers that they will soon be collector's items.

.224 WEATHERBY MAGNUM

The .224 "Magnum" comes about as close to being a magnum as grape-flavored Kool-Aid is champagne. But since Weatherby wouldn't sound right without Magnum tacked on I suppose the hyperbole is forgivable. (At least as much as the .222 Remington "Magnum.") Some self-styled varmint experts who get giddy at the sight of all sorts of goofy-looking wildcats like to act sophisticated by turning their noses up at this smallest of the Weatherby line. But they're only kidding themselves. The .224 W.M. is a fast (3750 fps with 50-grain bullet), flat-shooting little number that holds its own in any company. It will never be a big seller for the simple reason that it's chambered only in the premium-priced Weatherby Varmintmaster rifle, a scaled-down Weatherby Mark V. But then there will be enough steady Weatherby customers to keep the .224 W.M. alive and healthy for many years to come.

It's a handsome little cartridge and though the belt around the case head contributes nothing worthwhile it is unmistakably Weatherby. I've tried only a couple of rifles in this caliber; both were nicely accurate, and other shooters have reported fine accuracy in their rifles. The miniature Mark V action is stiff, locks up well, has a good trigger, and is properly bedded. This accounts, in large measure, for the fine accuracy reports.

The Weatherby Varmintmaster is available in a 26-inch varmint-weight barrel as well as the trim 24-inch standard-weight. The heavier tube should have special appeal to the more serious-minded varmint fan. Also, in order to give the Varmintmaster a somewhat wider sales appeal, it is available in .22/250 Remington caliber. Frankly, the .22/250 has only a slight ballistic edge on the Weatherby round and, in identical rifles, no accuracy edge whatever. If I were buying a Weatherby varmint rifle I would be inclined to choose the .224 W.M. if for no other reason than that Weatherby cartridges and rifles go together.

.22/250 REMINGTON

Even before the Remington folks gave this cartridge an honest name it had become the most famous wildcat in rifle history. Reports of a speedy and wonderfully accurate varmint round made simply by necking a .250 Savage case down to .22 caliber date back before 1930. In fact this is the cartridge that might have become the .220 Swift had not Winchester changed their plans, so it is said, at the eleventh hour. G. O. Wotkyns, who gained a measure of fame for his work with the .22 Hornet, did a good bit of experimenting with the necked-down Savage case in his search for the 4000 fps cartridge and is recognized as one of the .22/250's founding fathers. Another is J. E. Gebby, who called it the .22 Varminter and copyrighted the name. There were, no doubt, many other experimenters who worked with a necked-down .250 case, probably even before it occurred to Wotkyns or Gebby, but didn't have the flair for publicizing their efforts or were not interested in publicity.

There was a good bit of bitter acrimony when Winchester's .220 Swift didn't turn out to be based on the Savage case. The reason, I suspect, that it was necessary to change the design was that the announced objective was a velocity of 4000 fps or over. This is not impossible with a 50-grain bullet in a .22/250 but the pressures go well above what any manufacturer would consider prudent. Thus, if a 4000 fps velocity level was the criterion of Winchester's new varmint round they had no choice but to drop the Savage case.

Nonetheless, the .22/250 flourished as a wildcat round and even became the bread-and-butter chambering specialty of scores of gunsmiths across the country. It is impossible to calculate the numbers of Mausers, Enfields, '03 Springfields, and other bolt-actions rebarreled to .22/250 over the years but there were thousands upon thousands. Sometime around the mid-1950s I had a couple of custom-made .22/250s, one a heavy-barreled job built on an Oberndorf Mauser action and stocked by Monty Kennedy. The other was a

Model 70 action and stock fitted with a standard-weight barrel. The heavy rig was the first rifle I'd ever owned capable of drilling five shots under ½ inch on a regular basis, and the number of crows my pals and I shot with it became legend in our small farming community. Anytime we settled the 12-X cross hairs on a crow out to 300 yards it was safe money that his corn-robbing days were over. The lighter rifle was carried in the mountains after groundhogs for a couple of years but wasn't the equal to some other rifles I owned at the time so I passed it along to an itinerant gun trader.

No wildcat cartridge has ever been able to live up to the claims made for it by its inventors and disciples, but the .22/250 probably came closer than any other. It combined accuracy with velocity, the two most important ingredients of any varmint cartridge, and didn't seem to suffer too much at the hands of club-fisted gunsmiths and handloaders. During the decade of the 1950s its accuracy reputation soared when it became the darling of many shooters in the new sport of bench-rest shooting. Also it benefited from a peculiar phenomenon of human nature—the tendency of many shooters, and gun writers in particular, to feel that they cannot favor or praise one cartridge without maligning another to equal degree, and vice versa. For many years it was exeedingly fashionable to take a swipe at the .220 Swift, and almost every time a writer said something bad about the Swift he would toss in a few good words for the .22/250. In fact I've read some articles on the .22/250 which were, in reality, nothing more than thinly disguised attempts to heap more abuse on the Swift. At any rate the publicity had such an ef-

Remington Model 700 with varmint-weight barrel chambered for the popular .22/250 cartridge. The scope is the superb 12× Unertl Varmint.

Ruger Model 77 varmint-weight rifle in .22/250 Remington chambering topped with 10× Leupold in Ruger mounts.

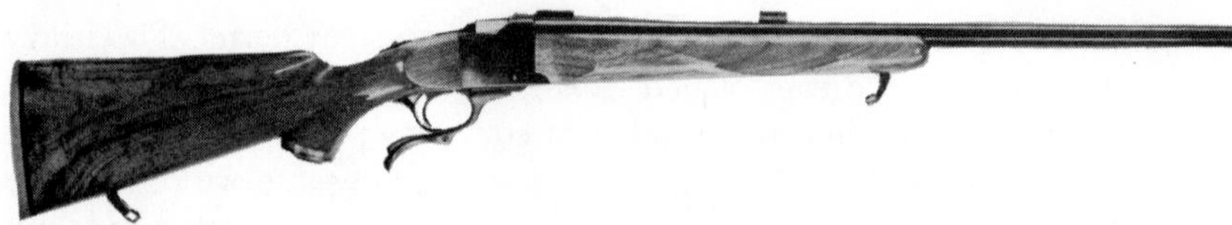

For single-shot aficionados, Ruger offers a varmint-barreled version in .22/250 and .25/06 calibers. Note that the rifle comes with standard scope bases for target-type varmint scopes.

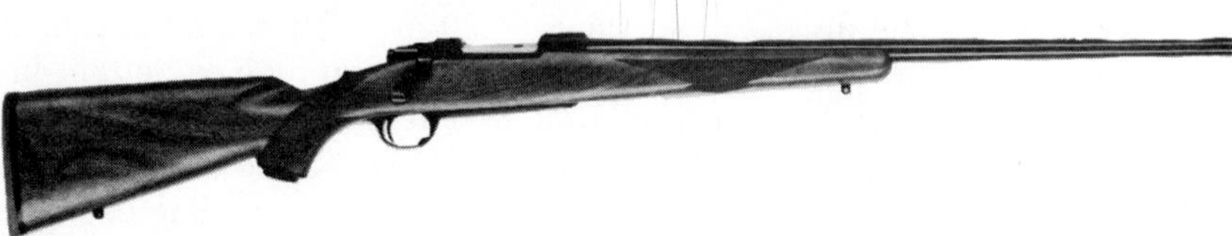

Ruger Model 77 varmint-weight rifle in .22/250 caliber.

fect on varmint shooters that when the cartridge was introduced as a factory round in 1965 there was an army of eager varmint shooters waiting, cash in hand.

Interestingly, even though it was Remington that took the .22/250 under its corporate wing and offered standardized factory-loaded ammo, it was staid Browning that first offered it as a factory chambering. For a concern as traditionally conservative as Browning Arms to market a rifle chambered for a handloadable-only cartridge was bold indeed, but plenty smart. The Browning rifle was built around the medium-length Sako "Forester" action and beautifully finished in the Browning manner. They even offered a varmint-weight barrel, which made it one of the most sophisticated and best-looking varmint rifles available. I bought the first one I saw, a pretty thing stocked with beautifully fiddlebacked walnut which still resides in my rack. After tinkering with the bedding it would shoot five rounds inside an inch but has never been a tack driver.

Shortly after announcing their plans for the .22/250's future, Remington sent me a Model 700 BDL and several boxes of ammo to play with. What with my experience with super-accurate .22/250s and unfailingly accurate Model 700 rifles I expected the new combination to be a real barn burner. But, fate of fates, that rifle couldn't keep five consecutive shots in a frying pan at 100 yards from a dead rest. I sent the rifle back along with a bit of gentle kidding about having achieved the unheard-of—an inaccurate .22/250. Its replacement rifle, you can be sure, would keep *ten* shots under ½ inch all day.

It is not the most accurate cartridge ever to come down the pike, nor is it the fastest, but comes close enough to both to be one of the best choices in a varmint caliber ever. It ran so roughshod over Winchester's .225 that Winchester dropped that chambering in the Model 70 and replaced it with the .22/250 Remington. At present it is available in such a wide variety of makes, weights, models, and styles of rifles that the varmint shooter who can't find a rifle that suits him just isn't trying.

Another blessing of the .22/250 Remington is that factory-loaded ammo

My varmint-shooting buddy Carroll Dale, former star split end for the Green Bay Packers, and the groundhogs he took with his Model 700 in .22/250 chambering with Weaver scope.

by both Remington and Winchester comes with a 55-grain bullet. This weight bullet, at 3730 fps muzzle velocity, is better on a windy day than would be, say, a 50-grain bullet even at the higher permissible velocity level. My favorite handload is one of the 52- or 53-grain bench-rest-grade bullets such as made by Hornady, Speer, Sierra, Nosler, etc., backed by 38 grains of IMR 4320. This goes close to 3800 fps in a 26-inch barrel and will usually squeeze out the last dollop of accuracy any rifle has to offer. Sighted in an inch above point of aim at 100 yards, this load is still a fraction high at 200 yards and only about 4 inches low at 300 yards. Thus despite all the claims and gossip we read and hear, the .22/250 is one of the few cartridges that has the *hitability* to qualify as an honest-to-goodness 300-plus-yard varmint cartridge.

.220 SWIFT

When it comes right down to the business of busting a chuck at 400 yards or over this cartridge is the king. At 4110 fps it is the speediest factory round ever produced and an ever-constant thorn in the side of wildcatters who, blow their hands off as they may, can't better it. Yet it is the most thoroughly bad-mouthed cartridge in history!

The chronic ups and downs of the Swift are hard to explain in the cold light of ballistic analysis. It is super-fast, has the flattest trajectory this side of a banjo string, and has been factory-offered only in well-built, accurate rifles. So why all the criticism? Well, let's go back to the beginning.

My wife draws a bead on a crow with a Model 70 Winchester in .220 Swift caliber topped with a 10× Unertl Vulture scope. The superb .220 and such optics as this allow pinpoint bullet placement.

If the Swift were a brand-new development, being offered for the first time this year, any savvy salesman would promote it for just what it is—a fast, flat *varmint* round. But back in 1935, when Winchester first offered it in their Model 54 bolt gun, most factory reps and gun salesmen had not accepted the idea of a purely varmint rifle. To many, varmint shooting was a playboy's folly and would never be anything more. Thus, in a misguided effort to boost sales they felt constrained to present it as sudden death on deer-sized game. Stories about how the little bullet would blast a moose as if he had been zapped by double forked lightning were widely circulated. Such claims, some of them honestly reported, no doubt had a short-term effect on helping sales but nonetheless served mainly to set the stage for Act I of the Swift's decline.

Act II was the result of Winchester's own lack of research and development. The first Swift barrels had a rifling twist of one turn in 16 inches, the same as the .22 Hornet and most .22 rimfires. Also, the barrels were of Winchester's standard centerfire steel, a form of so-called "ordnance steel" that was popular at the time. As it turned out the relatively slow rate of twist didn't give best accuracy, and the mild barrels burned out at a rate unlike anything seen before. Now commenced Act III, the culmination of the tragedy the Swift had to endure.

To the gun editors of that day the .220 Swift was a completely new proposition—so radically different, in fact, that there was nothing in their experience to which it could be related. Whereas they had been struggling to snipe a woodchuck at 200 yards they suddenly had thrust into their hands the means to do it at twice that distance. It was like taking a motorist out of the seat of a Model T Ford and plunking him into the cockpit of a Grand Prix Ferrari. He's bound to make some mistakes.

Some writers were so unequal to the task that they just sat back for a while to see what their peers thought about Winchester's new offering. Of course there were knowledgeable shooting experts who were able and did give fair and comprehensive reports on the Swift, but there were also some well-followed writers who had an ax to grind. Remember, the necked-down .250 Savage case had been an early choice to become the .220 Swift. This route had been advocated by a few writers and experimenters of the day, and when Winchester took an unexpected turn they took it as a direct insult to their good services and sound advice. Thus scorned, they took the only available redress, the press. Some of the early published comments on the Swift read like low comedy. It was said to be inaccurate, impossible and unsafe to handload, and, that dearest gem of all, "inflexible in its range of loading." One bantam-sized but loud-crowing author whom I well remember even went so far as to publish the bullet diameters and land widths which, in his opinion, were "critical" to Swift accuracy. (He was wrong on both counts.)

So, now that the ice had been broken, our retiring lilies picked up the drift and wrote their own, albeit secondhand, reviews of the Swift. Along about this time reports began filtering in from the field about big game that hadn't fallen, as promised, when hit by the speeding bullet. Also, some shooters began peeking into their barrels and wondering why the throats were black and scarred. Needless to say, all of this was grist for the mill of the anti-Swift faction, and a second round of "reports" were in order.

Now let's jump the war years and move into the early 1950s. The editor of a shooting and hunting publication gets a fair amount of reader mail requesting dope on the .220 Swift, so he judges that a fullblown feature story will be well received. He figures the story will be right down the groove for good ol' Col. V. P. Foghorn, U.S. Army (Ret.), and hands him the assignment. Now it just so happens that Col. Foghorn never owned a Swift in his life, never fired one, and wouldn't know a woodchuck from a Jersey cow, but that's no bother. He just gets out his collection of circa-1936 magazines and learns all he needs to know about the Swift. So it comes to pass that all the bum dope on the Swift is rephrased and passed along to a new generation. It doesn't matter a bit that the rifles made by Winchester are far more accurate than ever, that they now have erosion-resistant stainless-steel barrels, or that factory ammo is much better than in prewar days.

It just so happened that I was raised in an area where there were plenty of groundhogs to shoot at in the summer and millions of crows in the winter. Big-game hunting was all but nonexistent for hundreds of miles around, so if a fellow wanted to hunt with a rifle he hunted varmints. And too, as it just so happened, there was hardly a varmint shooter in the area who didn't figure he was just about the best shot ever to squint through a scope. Whenever two varmint shooters went out for a pleasant day of shooting the affair quickly turned into a hard-fought contest of who could make the longest shots. In an atmosphere such as this the .220 Swift ruled supreme. Anyone who didn't use one was waging a losing battle. During that time the cartridge was so popular in our part of the world that one of the local gunsmiths owned only one set of chambering reamers—.220 Swift.

When I was a youngster I had a hard time reconciling those long, beautifully placed .220 Swift shots on crows I'd seen with the articles I read about how the Swift was only a spotty performer. Later when I owned my own .220 rifle my standard load was 36 grains of a cheap surplus powder called "3031 Data," which became known as 4895, behind a 50-grain bullet. This mild load developed only about 3600 fps but was wonderfully accurate. Hardly an example of the "inflexible" loading I'd read about or the need to load the Swift to top levels to get good accuracy. But by then too much damage had been done to the Swift's reputation, and it was on the decline.

Over the years I've owned more Swifts than I can definitely remember but I specifically recall eleven. One of these was worn out when I got it and didn't group well. *It was the only Swift I've ever owned that wouldn't group at least inside 1 MOA with a wide variety of handloads.*

The only Swift I've managed to visibly wear out was the Belgian-made F.N. offered a few years back. The four lands were quite wide, and apparently the barrel steel was on the mild side, because after about 4,000 rounds the lands in the throat area appeared to have been flattened out. I countered this by seating the bullets farther and farther out in the throat and finally went to 63-grain bullets. In those days I always fired ten-round test groups and the day never arrived when that rifle wouldn't put them all in an inch at 100 yards.

The charge most often leveled against the Swift is excessive barrel wear. This was no doubt a problem when the Swift was first introduced back in 1935 because of the barrel steel used. Also, I suspect the hot-burning double-base powders often used in Swift loads contributed to the erosion problem. Hercules' HiVel Number 2 powder, for example, an erosive nitroglycerine-base powder, was the most popular powder for handloading the Swift. More recently, many of the so-called "burnt-out" Swift barrels have been found only in need of a good cleaning. I've bought a couple of supposedly "washed-out" Swifts which were restored to pristine accuracy with no more effort than a thorough brushing. The late Harvey Donaldson, a well-known shooter and experimenter, fired upwards of 10,000 rounds through one of the *early* Swifts and reported the bore still looked good. His "secret" was regular bore cleaning. On a prairie-dog shoot I may run as many as a hundred rounds through a barrel without cleaning, but otherwise I give it the brush-and-solvent treatment every twenty to thirty rounds. This is a definite aid to accuracy, *regardless of caliber.*

In my mail from *Outdoor Life* readers I frequently am asked about the barrel life expectancy of different calibers. My stock answer is that a shooter only needs to hope that he will be so *lucky* as to wear a barrel out. With proper care a .220 Swift barrel will last long enough to shoot a groundhog every day for nearly fifteen years!

When the Swift was dropped in 1963 it looked as if it had breathed its last. Varmint shooters, preparing for the worst, bought up every available Model 70 in .220 caliber and hoarded them like gold. Prices on rifles in the caliber went up so fast that by 1966 a good Swift would bring twice its retail price of only a few years before. Orders for custom rifles in .220 chambering

I inspect the very first Ruger Model 77 in .220 Swift caliber. The scope is a Leupold 12×.

began to increase, and today many gunsmiths tell me that it is one of the most often requested calibers for custom rifles and caliber conversions.

In the fall of 1972 my shooting pal John Amber, who edits *Gun Digest*, and I were hunting with firearms manufacturer Bill Ruger near his New Hampshire plant. As might be expected, much of our conversation centered around the topic of guns. Some time before, Ruger had made a limited run of Model 77 bolt guns chambered for the 7×57 Mauser, .257 Roberts, and .250 Savage. These had sold like hotcakes and he was picking our brains about other "obsolete" calibers that might sell a limited run of rifles. Without hesitation both John and I named the Swift as our first choice.

Back at Ruger's Newport plant we discussed the details further. I pointed out that the short version of the Model 77 action would be ideal, and also suggested that the barrel contour should be exactly the same as their existing varmint-weight barrel but 2 inches longer.

Some of the Ruger people balked at the whole Swift idea and pointed out that only stainless-steel barrels would give satisfactory resistance to erosion. I knew from experience, though, that a chrome-moly alloy steel such as they used for their other calibers would do fine and successfully argued my point. (Later, when the Ruger Swift became an overwhelming success, a few of Ruger's skeptics admitted to me that their initial objection had been based on various articles they'd read!)

John and I were both eager to try the Ruger rifle in Swift chambering, but since there were no .220 chambering reamers in the plant there would be some lost time while tooling was ordered. To save time, two *unchambered* rifles were forwarded to me. After having them chambered locally I sent one to John and began testing the other.

And thus was reborn the .220 Swift. When Ruger officially announced their new chambering a few months later the rush of orders was so overwhelming that plans for a limited run were changed and the .220 was made a standard production item. Sales continued at such an impressive pace that when Savage introduced their new stiff-barreled Model 112V varmint rifle early in 1975 it was announced that it would be available in Swift chambering.

With two standard production rifles now being chambered for Swifts the future of the cartridge is fairly secure. But the nonavailability of factory-loaded ammo by Remington or Winchester presents a squeeze. Winchester still makes cases, however, as does Norma, which also continues to offer loaded ammunition. Norma's tables list a speed of 4111 with a 50-grain bullet. If and when a U.S. firm offers loaded shells I think a 50- or 55-grain bullet would be better than the 48-grain pills which were last available. As a matter of fact, Winchester recently introduced a super-accurate hollow-point boattail match bullet which would be ideal for Swift loads.

From time to time I bring up the subject of once again offering the

Model 70 in Swift chambering, but the Winchester chiefs with whom I've discussed it are only lukewarm to the idea. The so-called "post-1963" Model 70s, whatever else they may be, are more accurate than the earlier version and would make superb Swifts. One Winchester executive suggested that they might make some special-order Model 70 Swifts in their custom shop where their best target rifles are made. This, in my opinion, would result in the finest factory-made varmint rifle ever offered, but I fear that the one-at-a-time custom-shop rifles, even at upwards of $400 a copy, would never meet the demand.

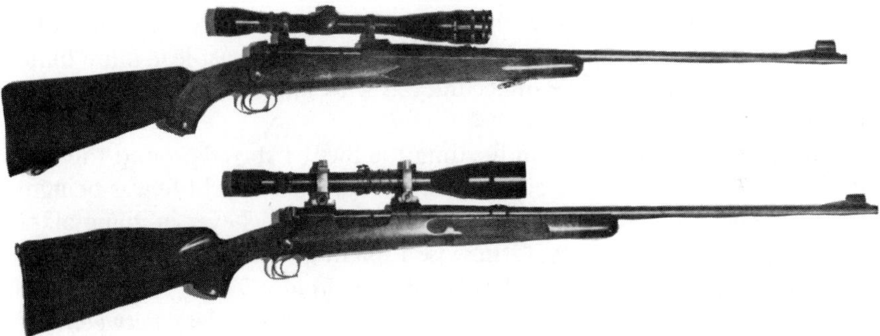

Here are two superb long-range varmint rifles. Both are pre-1964 Model 70 Winchesters chambered for the .220 Swift. At top is a rare Super Grade version topped with a 10× Lyman scope, and below it is a magnificent custom rifle beautifully stocked by Al Biesen and topped with a Unertl 10× Vulture scope.

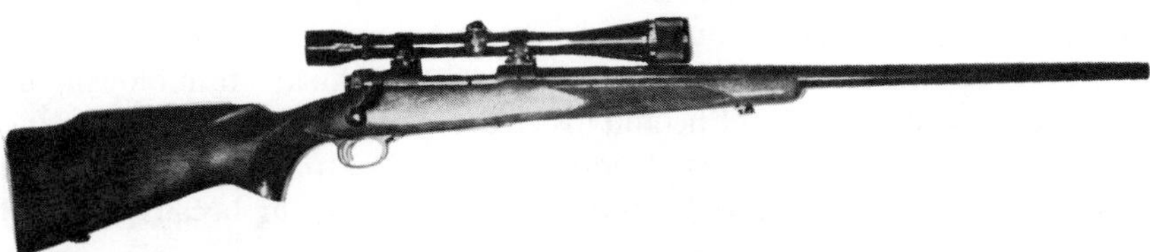

Another pre-1964 Model 70 rifle in .220 Swift caliber, this one varmint-weight and topped with a 12× Weaver.

Another great rifle for the Swift would be Remington's 40-X centerfire with single-shot action and heavy stainless-steel barrel. Still another good choice would be the Swedish-made FFV, which is smooth, stiff, and has a quick firing pin fall. And perhaps the best of all present rifles would be the newly announced (at this writing) Shilen sporter and varmint rifles. These have basically the same action as the super-accurate Shilen bench rifles but have a full magazine and sportier stocks. In Swift chambering it would be a worldbeater. Of course, there are all sorts of rifles and action types which could be used for the Swift, but many are too outdated or comparatively inaccurate to be suitable. It wouldn't make much sense to hitch a racehorse to a plow.

Handloading the Swift is as easy as handloading any other caliber. The problem of neck stretching, often reported as a chronic fault, is no more serious than with any other cartridge. When the necks get too long, pressures become erratic and accuracy suffers—exactly the same as with any other cartridge. You can load right up to maximum velocities or back off as much as you like with no more loss of accuracy than you'd expect with any other caliber. I've dropped velocities down to the 3000 fps level with no loss of accuracy whatever, and even at the 1800 fps range with cast-lead-alloy bullets I've gotten the same degree of accuracy as with identical bullets in .22 Hornet or .222 Remington.

During my early days of handloading the Swift I stayed around the 3600-fps level. This gave me fine accuracy and I felt that barrel life was being extended somewhat. Nowadays, however, I'm a firm believer in going all the way and getting top velocity. Otherwise I might as well use a lesser cartridge. My favorite load is 39 grains of IMR 4064 behind a 52- or 53-grain bench-rest-grade hollow-point bullet. This gives a muzzle velocity between 3900 and 4000 fps, depending on the rifle. One rifle in my rack will digest 41 grains of 4064 without undue pressure signs for a reading of nearly 4100. With the rifle sighted in to hit an inch above point of aim at 100 yards, it is still high at 200 yards and only a fraction low at 300. Even at 400 yards I can aim ear-high at a standing prairie dog and get him in the breadbasket.

A few years back I published an article on the facts and fantasies surrounding the .220 which created considerable response. One irate letter (written under a fake name but sent by an old-time outdoor writer) claimed that I left out information on how to keep .220 handloads from blowing up rifles. He went on to say that he and his pals had blown up lots of Swifts and if I didn't know why he wasn't going to tell me. In my return letter I pointed out that I must have been doing something wrong because none of my Swifts ever blew up. . . .

.243 WINCHESTER

Back in 1955, when Winchester announced their spanking-new .243, but before rifles of that caliber reached dealers' shelves, I sent a 1917 Enfield action to Bob Wallack, a well-known New England gunsmith, for rebarreling to the new cartridge. The Enfield was hardly the best choice for the .243, but with speed-lock unit and Mashburn trigger installed it wasn't such a bad outfit. Besides, it was all I had.

When the rig arrived, replete with a 26-inch heavy straight-tapered

Douglas (as I recall) barrel, I got in such a high heat to give it a whirl that I couldn't wait to fit some sort of decent stock. Instead, I just hogged out the barrel channel of the original military stock so as to accommodate the heavy tube. With a high-mounted Unertl Ultra-Varmint 10× scope and low En-

Custom-stocked Ruger Number One single-shot in .243 Winchester chambering with Leupold 7.5× scope.

field comb, a more ungainly outfit is hard to imagine. A rifleman would have needed a head shaped like that of a jackass in order to rest a cheek on the stock and peer through the scope at the same time. Nonetheless, it was shootable after a fashion. My first shot at game with that rifle was at a crow which had deposited itself on the skinny uppermost twig of a locust tree and was overseeing a late-afternoon ravaging of a stand of corn by a host of its fellows. When the bullet took hold of him, from a range of about 200 yards, he simply disintegrated. The upper parts catapulted straight up for 20 feet and the wings whirligigged down like autumn leaves. That told me all I wanted to know about Winchester's new cartridge, so I took it home and began work on a more respectable stock.

Since that afternoon I've busted enough crows, woodchucks, and prairie dogs with .243 Winchester rifles to sink an Erie Canal barge, and also have collected enough whitetail and mule deer, plus pronghorn, to be convinced that it's one of the all-time best varmint/big-game combination cartridges. Notice that I do not say *compromise* cartridge. In fact, the .243, along with its close kin and chief competitor, the 6mm Remington, is one of the best possible choices for varmint *and* an equally good choice for medium game.

The .243 came into existence by simply necking a .308 Winchester case (7.62 NATO) down to 6mm (.243 inch) with no other changes. Even the 20-degree shoulder angle is retained. Warren Page, then the shooting editor of *Field & Stream,* had previously done the same thing and come up with a wildcat he called the .240 Page Pooper. The Pooper, however, has a somewhat sharper shoulder and greater neck length. Though the Pooper did not become Winchester's final version of a 6mm round, Page must be credited with instigating its development.

When the .243 hit the scene it caused more than normal stir among the shooting public, because it, and the .244 Remington, represented an intriguing new bore size about midway between the .22 and .25 calibers. Actually, the 6mm was not new, but only forgotten. Back before the turn of the century, Winchester had made a straight-pull bolt-action rifle for the U.S. Navy chambered for a hot little number (for those days) known as the 6mm Lee Navy. Over the years some sporting rifles were chambered for this round, but by the time of World War II it was all but forgotten. Also, in England and on the Continent the 6mm bore was fairly well known in the form of such cartridges as the 6×57 Mauser, .244 Halger Magnum, .240 Apex, and a half-dozen or so others.

When introduced, the .243 was viewed by many as a strictly varmint-shooting proposition. With a velocity of 3500 fps with an 80-grain bullet, how else? But Winchester wisely offered a 100-grain bullet load, which soon

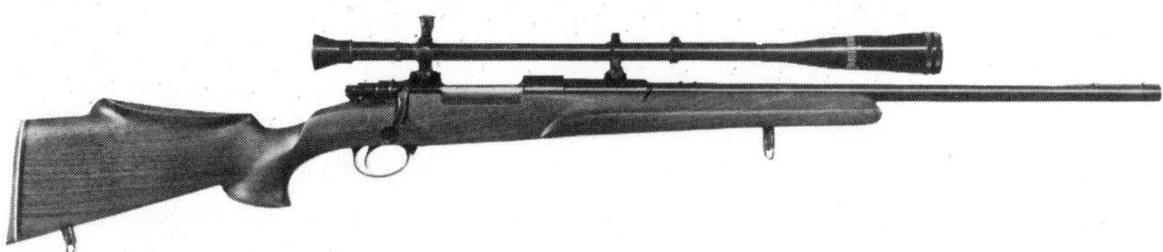

H&R's Model 370 Ultra Medalist varmint rifle. These long-range rifles, built on Mauser actions, come in .243 Winchester and such other varmint calibers as .22/250 Remington and 6mm Remington. This rifle is topped with a Lyman Super Targetspot scope. The all-out varmint design of this stock is fairly typical of the way manufacturers now court the varmint-shooting market. A brief two decades ago such attention was not paid to varmint shooters' needs.

Winchester Model 70 varmint-weight in .243 topped with a 10× Weaver.

caught on with deer hunters as the best thing since spray deodorant. Western deer hunters, in particular, took to the little cartridge because of its ability to cover the longer ranges neatly and accurately and still pack a wallop when it got where it was going. Though it was to be a few years until I tried it on bigger game, I couldn't help but be impressed by the way it anchored the big Appalachian groundhogs I hunted. I'd seen chucks make their way to a den after seemingly being well hit with some high-velocity .22 centerfires, but the .243 always dropped them in their tracks. During the spring hunts when a stiff breeze whistled through the mountain passes, the .243

again offered a noticeable advantage. Then, as now, my favorite varmint load was 45 grains of IMR 4350 propellant behind a 75-grain bullet for a muzzle start of about 3350 fps. A 10-mile-per-hour crosswind will blow this bullet off course about 3½ inches. By comparison, a 50-grain .22 caliber Spitzer at the same velocity is blown off course by an inch more. At the longer ranges the difference is more considerable.

Another factor which contributed to the fast rise in the .243's popularity was the variety of superb 6mm bullets which were quickly marketed by various custom bullet makers. Within months of the .243's appearance, handloaders were treated to all sorts of shapes, weights, and styles of delightfully accurate bullets. I tried them all and recall only one which was really inaccurate. This was the second run of a 60-grain discount-priced bullet by a notorious Midwestern mail-order outfit. Their first run was unusually long for a 60-grain bullet, hollow-pointed with almost the entire front half of the jacket empty. They were wonderfully accurate, though, and ideal for crows. I was so impressed by their performance, in fact, that my shooting pals and I ordered several thousand. But when the shipment arrived it turned out that the bullet had been redesigned and wouldn't group in a chamberpot at 100 yards.

The mild nudge of the .243 has been a terrific boon for recoil-shy hunters. I especially recommend it as a "starting-out" caliber for youngsters and ladies who might develop a serious case of flinching with harder-kicking rifles. My wife, who weighs in at a svelte 100 pounds with her safari jacket pocket full of shells, carries a trim little featherweight Winchester Model 70 in .243 with 22-inch tube for everything from prairie dogs to pronghorn. After hundreds of rounds she hasn't developed the slightest hint of a flinch and presses the trigger as gently as a French chef turning a batch of *crêpes Suzettes.* During the spring and summer I keep her .243 cases loaded with 75-grain hollow-points for varmints, and come fall, I switch the load to 100-grain Noslers over 42 grains of IMR 4350 and she's ready for bigger game. After a summer of busting varmints a 400-yard shot at a pronghorn presents little problem.

This is why I often ask "Why?" when a deer hunter writes me that he's thinking about buying a new deer rifle and wants to know if he'd be better off to buy, say, a .270 or a .30/06 or a 7mm Magnum. The .243, I tell him, will kill a deer just as dead, will probably allow him to place his shot better, and offers four-season shooting.

6MM REMINGTON

The 6mm Remington and the .243 Winchester left the starting gate almost neck and neck and have been in a hot race ever since. Actually, from the ballistic standpoint there is scant difference between the two. But what little difference that may exist has triggered discussions, arguments and all sorts of written opinions vastly out of proportion to any real importance.

The cartridge now promoted as the 6mm Remington (thank heaven it escaped the "Magnum" entitlement) was initially announced as the .244. Bales of copy have been produced explaining why the .244 became the 6mm Remington but no single reason stands alone and all explanations suffer from oversimplification.

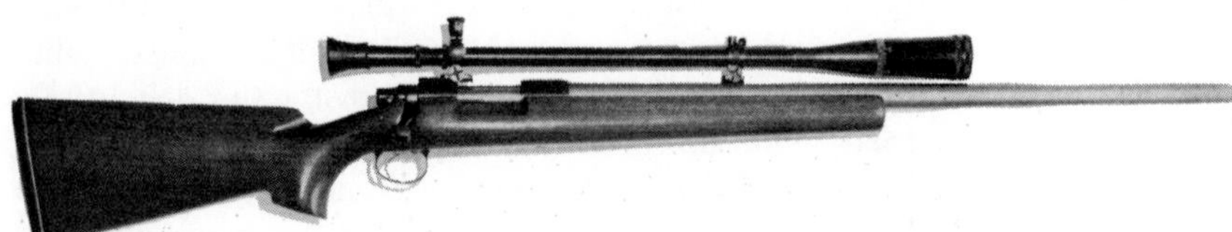

Remington Model 40-X with heavy stainless-steel barrel chambered for the 6mm Remington. These super-accurate single-shot rifles make superb long-range varminters. This one has a 15× Lyman Super Targetspot scope.

A little-known fact about 6mm is that in fact it *did not* begin its days in 1955 as the .244 Remington but way back before the turn of the century when it was known as the 6×57 Mauser! In those days the velocity, with a 120-grain bullet, was reported as 2750 fps. It was developed by necking the popular 7×57 Mauser case down a millimeter, which, as it turned out, was the same way the .244 came about. Back during the late 1940s and early 1950s there was a good bit of fooling around with 6mm (.243-inch) bullets. One of the most popular wildcats was the .243 Rockchucker, designed by Fred Huntington of RCBS reloading tool fame. Fred's .243 Rockchucker was a .257 Roberts case (the .257 Roberts in turn having first been made by necking the 7×57 Mauser case to .25 caliber), necked down to 6mm and with the shoulder angle increased to 32 degrees. (The standard .257 shoulder is about 20 degrees.) The Rockchucker case proved to be ideal for a goodly range of 6mm bullet weights, and there was very little that could be done to improve the design. Thus the finalized Remington version differed only in a slightly less steep shoulder. But about here is where legend, fact, and speculation begin to get somewhat snarled.

It has been charged that the folks at Remington got off on the wrong foot by envisioning their new round only as a varmint-getter, while Winchester touched all bases and claimed its .243 was great for both big game and varmints. The source of this charge is that the early Remington rifles had a rate of twist of one in 12 inches, ostensibly for varmint-weight bullets only, while Winchester barrels packed a one-in-10-inch twist in order to stabilize longer, heavier hunting bullets. Now this sounds like a clever piece of supposition, but doesn't explain why Remington offered both 75- and 90-grain bullets. Obviously, if Remington had seen its round as a varmint cartridge only, it wouldn't have bothered with the heavier bullet loading. Winchester, at the same time, offered both 80- and 100-grain bullet loadings. Anyone who thinks that the .243 load with a 100-grain slug is a big-game load (muzzle energy 2090 foot-pounds) while the 90-grain .244 isn't (at 2050 foot-pounds) has been reading too many comic books.

In time such arguments *did* come into vogue and no doubt impressed a good many people. But this was after the fact. At the time of the first encounter between the two cartridges the vote went to the .243 *mainly* because it was available in a far more attractive rifle! Remember, the Model 722 Remington, for which the .244 was chambered, was a decidedly plain-Jane affair; no checkering on the stock, a finish that looked like clear fingernail polish, and the rattiest-looking tin-can floorplate and trigger-guard unit yet devised. The .243, on the other hand, was available in the great Model 70, one of the most stylish and beautifully made bolt-action rifles ever placed on a dealer's shelf. Its reputation was without peer. Keep in mind that during this time period shooters were actually buying Model 70 .22 Hornets and having them rechambered to .222 rather than face the ignominy of buying a M722 in .222.

Also, don't be led down the primrose path and fall for that yarn about the 12-inch twist not stabilizing the heavier bullets. It sounds great in unschooled theory, but in actual practice there's no way to tell the difference. For example, I get great accuracy with 60-grain bullets in a 10-inch-twist barrel. And I also get terrific results with a 105-grain bullet out of a 12-inch-twist barrel. The point here is that no other firearms-related topic is more guaranteed to make someone sound like an expert and make a fool of him at the same time.

Finally, when their Model 725 was announced Remington began to capitulate by offering it in .243 chambering as well as their own .244. With the writing on the wall, the .244 was dropped altogether, or at least the name. Obviously the .244 case configuration was too good to change. Thus in a deft move, they shucked the .244's loser image by simply changing the name. Also, just to block any protests, their rifles in the "new" caliber had a one-turn-in-9 twist (though my Remington 40-X in 6mm has a one-in-10 twist), and loads in 80-, 90-, and 100-grain bullet weights were offered. The faster twist offers no improvement whatever over the slower turn—possibly it's not even as good—but was undoubtedly considered necessary to pacify the hordes of ballistic experts overrunning the country. (In fact, I think the 9-inch twist was specified with some malice of heart.)

In reality, the foregoing gossip makes nice conversation, but that's about all. The only important stuff worth knowing is how good is today's 6mm Remington, née .244? Well, just for openers I've about come around to the conclusion that it's better than the .243. Especially if you can get ahold of one of the older rifles with a one-in-12-inch twist. But, as always, there are other weighty considerations. For instance, if you get to hankering for, say, a Sako in 6mm Remington caliber you're out of luck. But you *can* get a Sako .243. So, what choice do you make? Probably a Sako in .243 because there really isn't that much difference.

The 6mm Remington case capacity is just about perfect for the 6mm bore size. Even when slightly enlarged, as with the 6mm Improved wildcat, the law of diminishing returns becomes evident. And when capacity is reduced a bit, to that of .243 for example, you lose upwards of 150-200 feet per second with heavier bullets. (Factory charts for a .243 with 100-grain bullet read 2960 compared to 3130 for the 6mm Remington. This difference remains about the same for handloads.)

The accuracy of a good 6mm Remington rifle is beyond reproach. My Remington Model 40-X with heavy stainless-steel barrel in this chambering will poke five shots inside an inch at 200 yards and is about the best possible choice on breezy days. With a 75-grain bullet loaded up to about 3500 fps I simply sight it dead on at 400 yards for prairie-dog shooting. At all ranges less than 400 yards I just hold on the ground line. This will put the bullet close enough to get the job done and I don't need to bother with range estimating.

The principal disadvantage of the 6mm Remington as compared to the .243 Winchester is that it is not available in such a wide variety of makes and models of rifles. It is not available in the always popular Winchester Model 70 or the Savage 110, and this no doubt limits its popularity. But it is available in Remington's Models 700, 40-X, and 788, of course, and also in the Model 77 Ruger. Though I think of the 6mm as primarily a bolt-action proposition, Remington offers it in their M742 Autoloader and 760 pump models. To my notion the best union of the 6mm with a quick shooter would be with Browning's BAR autoloader. But alas, this most accurate of autos comes in .243 but not 6mm—a considerably less effective combination, especially when you consider that the Browning rifle is primarily a hunting arm.

The 6mm is a smart choice for anyone considering a custom bolt-action rig in one of the 6mm calibers. It adapts perfectly to most actions of the '98 Mauser, Springfield, and Enfield varieties as well as to most commercial actions one might barter for. A custom rifle built up on a pre-1964 Winchester Model 70 receiver would be mighty stylish indeed.

.240 WEATHERBY MAGNUM

When the .240 made its debut in the late 1960s, there was the usual shooting-press hoopla, but since this died down little more has been heard. As all Weatherby cartridges, it has the distinctive belt around the case head. The belt isn't needed, as you might have guessed, but I've always considered this Weatherby round especially interesting because the rim diameter is the "standard" .30/06 size. This opens the door for several possibilities which will be discussed later.

The .240's fps ballistics of 3850, 3500, and 3395 with the 70-, 87-, and 100-grain-bullet factory loadings are certainly impressive, and I think the three bullet weight choices are good ones. My initial tests with the .240 W.M. were not very satisfying, however, because of only so-so accuracy. The 70-grain loading, I feel, is purely a varmint-popping proposition, but groups with this load were not tight enough to make it trustworthy for pinpoint bullet placement at long range. After shooting up a few boxes of factory

I bench-test a .240 Weatherby Magnum rifle with Redfield 6–18× scope. The .240 Weatherby is a fine cartridge for long cross-country shots at varmints.

loads I reloaded the empties, but accuracy was only moderately improved. I assumed therefore that the fault lay with the rifle and suspended testing.

Later, just to see how hard it was to swage a belt on a .30/06, I ran a few surplus G.I. cases into the .240 sizing die. The operation was easy enough and resulted in a few cases with a belt neatly squeezed in place. So, with these cases on hand and nothing else to do, I loaded them up and gave the rifle another bench test. Groups for three five-shot strings were under an inch, by far the best accuracy so far. The experiment was repeated and again groups were small. This doesn't at all mean that the only way to get top accuracy out of the .240 Magnum is to convert surplus G.I. '06 cases, but nonetheless is an object lesson in the need to explore the causes of poor accuracy. In this instance, performance could have been plagued by unusually irregular factory cases, a condition which no doubt has long since been removed. Perhaps they would have performed better in another chamber.

At nearly 3400 fps with a 100-grain bullet, the .240 Weatherby is obviously a fine long-range cartridge for medium-class game such as deer and pronghorn. Since the Weatherby Mark V rifle in .240 chambering comes only in standard-weight hunting configuration, at this writing, I favor it more for bigger game than varmints. Yet the cartridge itself should have special appeal for varmint shooters who prefer the 6mm caliber and want every available foot per second. Velocitywise it ranks in the class with some of the "wilder" wildcats (such as a .30/06 necked down for a .243 bullet). I always prefer a standard factory cartridge to a wildcat for a multitude of good reasons. Also, since the .240 W.M. rim is the same as the .30/06 groups, there are all sorts of actions that readily adapt to a rebarreling to this caliber. A '98 Mauser, for example, works fine with no needed alterations to bolt face or magazine. Have a barrel fitted and you're in business. Barrel life won't match that of the .243 Winchester or 6mm Remington, but a 12-pound affair with some hot loads for the Sierra 85-grain hollow-point boattail bullet would be mighty impressive for those extra-long cross-canyon shots.

OTHER VARMINT CARTRIDGES

The term "varmint cartridge" is subject to a fairly broad definition. If someone feels that nothing less than a .378 Weatherby is acceptable for Columbian ground squirrels, there's little point in arguing the definition. Many hunters, including myself, frequently use, and may even prefer, such rounds as the .250 Savage, .257 Roberts, .25/06 Remington, .257 Weatherby Magnum, or .264 Winchester Magnum for an assortment of varmints. The .25/06 is especially used for this purpose, and Remington even offers their varmint-weight Model 700 in the chambering as well as the 40-X.

Arguments in favor of these larger-bore rounds for varmint shooting invariably include mention of their flatness of trajectory at longer ranges and the greater wind-bucking ability of the heavier projectiles. But these are armchair arguments, conceived in a ballistic daze without considering that most important feature of a really good varmint round: *shootability*. Precision long-range shooting requires delicate aiming, holding, trigger pulling, and follow-through. As recoil and muzzle blast are increased, all of these delicate techniques become more difficult to perform well. In short, regardless of what you may tell yourself, you can't hit as well when you have to absorb recoil and be rocked by muzzle blast. It takes its toll. Interestingly also, one does not, as is commonly supposed, get accustomed to it. Just the reverse is true; even if you aren't affected at first you will be in time. This was effectively proved a few years ago when the .308 Winchester cartridge case came on so strongly in bench-rest circles. Rifles in .308 were wonderfully accurate and even established several world records. But in time many of the competitive bench-resters found that their scores were falling off. The cumulative effect of absorbing the recoil from the 10½- and 13½-pound varmint-class bench rifles in .308 caliber was resulting in sloppy shooter performance.

Back when Winchester announced their .264 Magnum, some varmint shooters hailed it as the final solution to long-range accuracy, but, despite its spectacular ballistics, it didn't turn out to be *shootable* enough. This is why I draw the line for honest varmint calibers at 6mm and below. Above that, 99 percent of us will be biting off more than may prove healthy in the long run.

But this is certainly not to say that the larger calibers should be entirely avoided for varmint shooting. A hunter who wants a big-game rifle first and a varmint rig second can't beat such cartridges as the .25/06, .264, etc. These will take game up to the elk class and still permit some real show-off shooting at varmints. Likewise, light-bulleted loads for the .30/06, .308, 7mm Remington Magnum, .270, .280, and several others permit an acceptable *compromise* for off-season varmint shooting. But never, never make the mistake of believing that a big-game cartridge is "just as good" for tiny targets as the true varmint rounds.

THE VARMINT-CLASS WILDCATS

Roughly 20 percent of the cartridges currently cataloged by U.S. ammo makers fall into the varmint classification. But at least half of the wildcats dreamed up over the past half-century were done by wildcatters with pure varmint shooting in mind. But, after all, accuracy and velocity are the measures of a varmint cartridge, and these same two requirements, with very few exceptions, are the inspiration for most practicing wildcatters. There are few experiences as satisfying as knocking off a 500-yard woodchuck with a cartridge you developed yourself, and indeed, many of our most popular factory cartridges, most notably the .22/250 and .25/06, are "legalized" forms of successful wildcats.

Other wildcats which never earned an honest factory name but did enjoy a flash of glory include such familiar names as the "K" Hornet, .219 Donaldson Wasp, .220 Arrow, R-2 Lovell, .17 Javelina, and 6mm/284. Of these the "K" Hornet, Wasp, and Lovell have been the most widely used. The "K" Hornet was designed by Lysle Kilbourn and simply involved opening up the chamber in a Hornet rifle so that a factory-size case would expand and form a more generous shoulder when fired. The somewhat enlarged case could then be reloaded to upwards of 200 fps more velocity than possible with the standard version. This was an extremely popular conversion just before and just after WW II but nowadays is almost forgotten. There are a lot of riflemen who had fine Model 70 Winchester Hornets "K"ed back then and now are suffering severe regrets. A converted Hornet is worth $100 less among Winchester collectors than is one that escaped such tampering.

The .219 Donaldson Wasp, made famous by such expert shooters as its originator Harvey Donaldson, is made by shortening and fire-forming .219 Zipper or .30/30 cases. With a 50-grain bullet, top velocities are in the 3400–3500 fps class. The rimmed case made it popular for custom rifles built on single-shot actions such as the Winchester Hi-Wall, and for a while it was popular among accuracy buffs.

The 2-R Lovell, sometimes called the R-2, is in fact a wildcat based on another wildcat. The first version, called the .22/3000, was the .25/20 case necked down to .22 caliber. This made possible a velocity of 3000 fps. Next, an "improved" version was made by enlarging the chamber and fire-forming the case to greater capacity. With a 45-grain Hornet bullet velocities of close to 3400 fps were possible. The renowned New York gunsmithing firm of Griffin & Howe made quite a few rifles in this chambering and converted many others. With the disappearance of .25/20 cases to work with they had new 2-R Lovell cases made, which are so head-stamped. Thus it became a sort of semi-legitimate cartridge. The 2-R name, as you're no doubt wondering, comes from the second chambering reamer made by a gunsmith named Risley when an updated .22/3000 was being tinkered with. This second reamer cut the shape they were looking for, and the code name stuck. Yet, despite the self-styled sophistication of the average garden-variety wildcatters, most wildcat designs are not nearly as good as their inventors claim and seldom equal standard factory loads.

The basic premise under which most wildcat designs have originated is that the more powder you can get behind a bullet the faster it will go. This line of reasoning has resulted in such spectacular-looking creations as the .378 Weatherby Magnum case necked down to .22 caliber and the .348 Winchester reduced to .17. Back when I was a tender youth of seventeen, and brimming with more notions about guns and bullets than an Alabama 'possum hound has fleas, I concocted a design which I allowed would push a 120-grain hand-swaged .243 bullet out the barrel at 3800 fps. The cartridge, which I modestly named the .240 Carmichel Express, was to be a front ignitor with a *triplex* load of 4831, Ball-C, and 4895. Fortunately, I was perpetually short on funds during that period and thus was unable to have such a rifle built, and no doubt was saved from blowing my head and other parts off.

There is not nearly so much wildcatting these days as there was back in the 1950s. I have a pet theory which explains this. Back then, chronographs were almost totally unavailable except in prohibitively expensive forms.

Therefore velocities of various wildcats were rough estimates at best, and invariably on the wildly optimistic side. When good, low-priced chronographs became available, wildcatters rushed to buy them in order to confirm the velocities they suspected their creations of generating. What was most usually proved, however, was that velocities were only ordinary and all that extra powder served only to cause excess pressures, and about the only thing significantly accelerated was barrel wear. The wildcatting game hasn't been the same since.

Also—and this may come as a shock—the bulk of wildcatters are not what one would fairly describe as rifle and ballistics experts but are merely passing through an adolescent phase which, with luck, will be outgrown. The usual manifestation of this condition is the chap who shows us a cartridge of unique configuration and announces, "This baby is at least 200 feet per second faster than the fastest factory round in the books."

The purpose of the foregoing negative comments is only to separate the honest wheat of wildcat development from the chaff. There are in fact some wildcat designs which accomplish tasks that no factory round is equal to. A

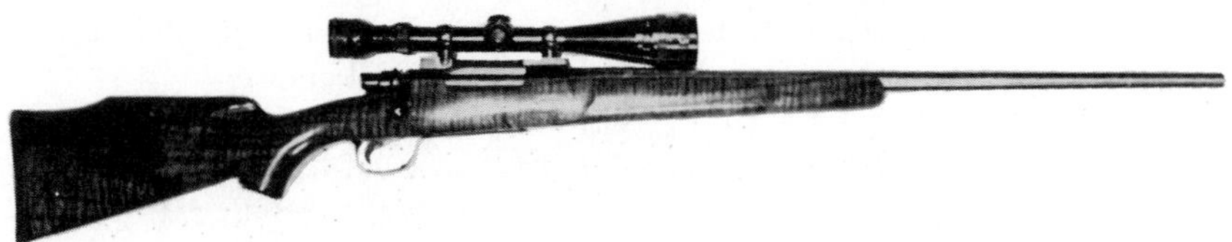

A super-long-range varmint rig chambered for the .224 Clark wildcat, which is the .257 Roberts case necked down and blown out, using an 80-grain .22 caliber bullet. This rig, which has a Hart stainless-steel barrel, is built up on a Mauser action with Canjar trigger and 6–18× Redfield scope. The stock, which is a beautiful piece of fiddleback Claro walnut, was made from a Pachmayr semi-finished stock.

notably successful case in point is the .224 Clark, designed by gunsmith Ken Clark of Madera, California. Clark correctly analyzed the problem of long-range varmint performance not as high initial velocity but as *retained* velocity. Since retained velocity is a function of a high ballistic coefficient and sectional density, he began manufacturing super-streamlined .22-caliber bullets weighing 80 grains. At the longer ranges, especially out around 500 yards, these special bullets arrive on target with more zap and less drop than lighter bullets which start out 300 or 400 feet per second faster. It's one of the finest ultra-long-range varmint cartridges ever developed, but, like fast horses and high-stepping women, isn't for the average chap.

Such wildcat cartridges as a blown-out .243 puzzle me no end, because if the experimenter simply wants about 200 feet more than a standard .243 is safely capable of with a given bullet weight, why doesn't he just buy himself a 6mm Remington to start with? The same goes for a .222 Improved when a .222 Magnum is available. But of course I'm deliberately ignoring the undeniable sense of pride which comes with owning a rifle that is different from anything that can be bought in a gun shop.

Another worthwhile and interesting area of wildcatting is the between-caliber calibers such as .20, .23 etc., and the sub-calibers such as .14 and even .12. Someday one just might hit on a combination that will lead to a place in the ballistic hall of fame. Remember, until the 1950s the 6mm bore size was pretty much an unknown area and thus wide-open for development by such experimenters as Fred Huntington and Warren Page. Remington has ventured into the .20-caliber area with their 5mm Remington Magnum rimfire round, but a centerfire is still waiting. A 40-grain bullet on, say, a necked-down .222 case might be just what the doctor ordered for low-key varmint-popping in some of the more thickly populated Eastern rural areas. I'm not sure what a .12 or .14 bore rifle would be good for, except possibly sniping at sparrows or boll weevils, but at least you'd be the only lad on the block to own one. And, after all, isn't that what wildcatting's all about?

THE SWEET SEVENTEENS

Though the one and only factory version of a .17-caliber cartridge appeared in 1971, the history of the semi-bore goes back much further. Even back in the 1930s there was a fair amount of experimenting with such rounds as the .22 Hornet and the R-2 Lovell necked down to .17. The idea then, as now, was an interesting one but seriously hampered by the state of the barrelmaking art of that time. The problem of drilling and rifling a hole so tiny resulted in a high ratio of rejects, and even those which passed in-

A .17-caliber bullet alongside an ordinary .22 rimfire cartridge.

spection were usually only mediocre. After the war that inveterate wildcatter P.C. Ackley did a good bit of experimenting with the .17s and produced such designs as the .17 Ackley Bee. Ackley is also a barrelmaker, so he was aided by a limitless supply of barrels during the period when he was testing the various minibore case configurations. When the .222 Remington was introduced the case was seized upon by .17 wildcatters and developments went ahead more rapidly than before.

The first really successful .17-caliber cartridge was the .17 Javelina, designed by Bill Atkinson and Paul Marquart of what was then the A&M

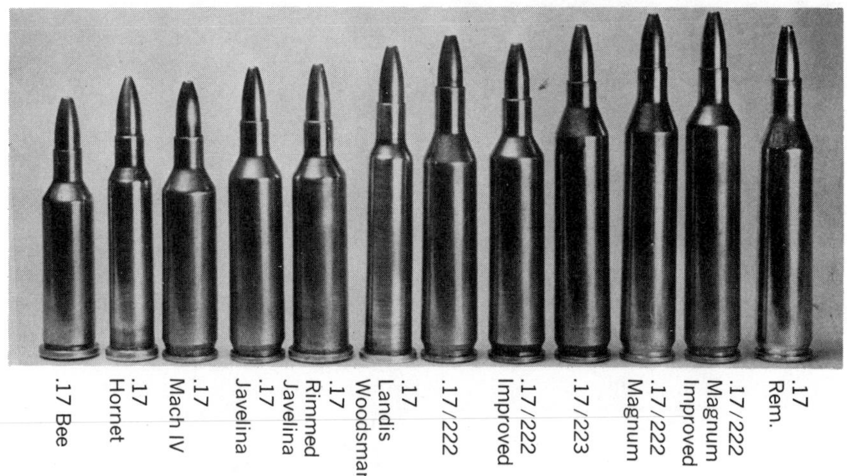

A line-up of the various .17-caliber wildcats tried over the years. The only factory standard cartridge in the bunch is the .17 Remington at far right.

Gunshop of Prescott, Arizona. The A&M shop conquered the problem of producing a truly high-quality barrel in the .17-bore size and for several years led the way in producing both barrels and finished rifles in the caliber. Their .17 Javelina was based on a shortened, blown-out .222 case and proved to be a remarkably deadly killer on varmints and small game up to the size of the small wild peccary of the Southwest. With a 25-grain bullet, velocities could be pushed past the 3800 fps mark.

After A&M beat the barrel problem, there still remained, for a time, the problem of satisfactory bullets. Three or four small custom shops turned out .17 slugs of varying quality, but according to accounts by such knowledgeable experimenters as Marquart, the first reliably accurate bullets were made by Fred Barnes. Later, Hornady introduced the first mass-produced, high-quality bullet, a little 25-grain hollow-point design. By then other barrelmakers, most notably Douglas and Shilen, were turning out accurate barrels with the little hole.

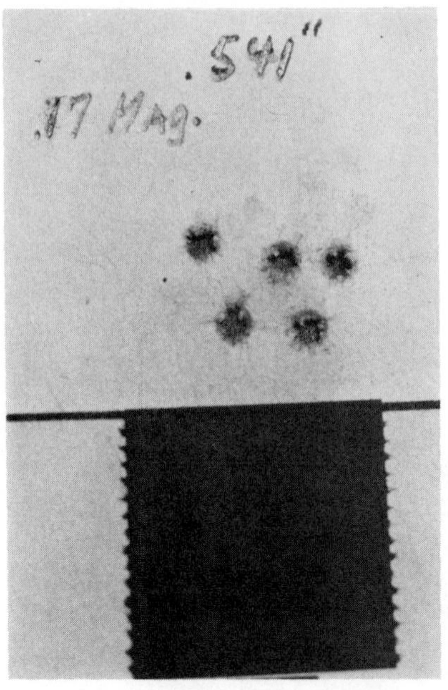

This tiny group, measuring only .541 inch, gives an idea of the accuracy of a good .17-caliber rifle. This one was fired with my .17 Remington Magnum wildcat built up on a Sako action with Douglas barrel. The aiming square is 1 inch across.

Though some cartridges were fearsomely overbore, with such cases as the .250 Savage or .220 Swift necked down, most of the best designs centered around modifications of the .222, .222 Magnum or .223 Remington. My first attempt in the .17 direction was a neck-down of the .222, but at that time good bullets weren't available and I gave up the project as a bum deal. My neighbor and pal Dave Wolfe, publisher of *The Rifle* and *Handloader* magazines, first suggested necking the then-new .223 down to .17. It was a successful idea and was to become the chambering of the first production-made .17-caliber rifle by a major manufacturer. The first rifle in the chambering, custom-built for Wolfe, is now in my collection and still accounts for several dozen prairie dogs each year.

Also during that era Vern O'Brien, a Las Vegas, Nevada, gunsmith, who also happens to be a sharp promoter, designed a cute little trinket of a rifle which he built on the short Sako action and developed a cartridge for it, which he copyrighted as the .17 Mach IV. The round was based on the .221 Remington Fireball cartridge, and he used it on all sorts of game up to and including the big Alaskan bears. When he sold the design rights to his rifle to Harrington & Richardson they marketed it as the Model 317 Ultra Wildcat. But rather than chambering for the Mach IV they chose Dave Wolfe's design, the .17/223.

What with Hornady's new bullet to inspire me, I took another crack at the .17 during the mid-1960s and had Arlie Gardner, the head man at the Douglas Barrel works, chamber and fit a barrel for the .17/222 Magnum. This effort was vastly more satisfying than the first, and I began developing a genuine taste for the hot little numbers. Twenty-three grains of IMR 3031

My wife looks over a prairie dog she downed with an H&R Ultra Wildcat Model 317 in .17 Remington. The scope is a 7.5× Leupold.

powder behind a 25-grain Hornady made it sizzle along at close to 4000 fps, and any crow that got in the way exploded in a puff of fog and feathers.

As the .17s increased in popularity, there reappeared the tired old tales which invariably surface when a new cartridge makes the rounds. This time the drift of the gossip was that the cartridge was hard to load, hard to clean, and prone to excessive fouling. Actually there was a fair amount of truth to the first two charges; .17s were difficult to load because there was no mini-sized powder funnels available. Sifting powder into the tiny necks, sometimes a grain at a time, was a tedious chore. There was also a shortage of .17-caliber cleaning rods and bore brushes. As a result, bore cleaning was seldom well done and barrels frequently remained in a high state of copper and

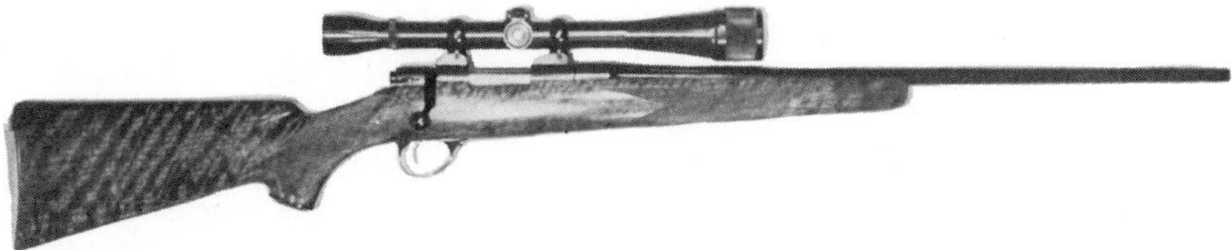

My wildcat .17/222 Magnum, built on a Sako action with Douglas barrel. The beautifully figured walnut stock was made by me, and the scope is a 12× Weaver in Conetrol mounts. This rifle will group close to ½ inch for five shots at 100 yards with good bullets.

I bench-test one of the first rifles in .17 Remington chambering. This rifle, scoped here with a 6× Leupold in Conetrol mounts, produced fine accuracy and with none of the much-touted fouling problems.

powder fouling. In time, powder funnels, cleaning equipment, and neck-turning tools were marketed and these complaints faded away. But as we shall see later, old rumors can return to haunt us.

When I had the .17/222 Magnum built I was concerned about the fouling problem, because of rumors I'd heard and read. But in actual practice they never developed. One afternoon I fired eighty-eight rounds (three sighters, then seventeen five-shot groups) without cleaning, and the last group measured a neat .780 inch between the widest shots. Clearly, the excessive-fouling rumors had originated back in the days of comparatively rough barrels and poorly made bullets.

When Remington introduced the .17 Remington in 1971 I personally applauded their effort. I thoroughly enjoyed the .17s and assumed that the advent of a standardized factory version would make a hit with the varmint-shooting public. Amazingly, however, the shooting press largely ignored the new cartridge or, at best, paid it only lip service. Worse, and quite unfairly I thought, some writers rehashed the old wives' tales about excessive fouling—their philosophy being, I suppose, "If you want to sound like an expert, be negative." When the new cartridge was presented at a Remington writers' seminar, one writer of some repute remarked that although he had never fired a .17-caliber rifle he had *heard* that they tended to foul excessively. To prove that this was not true, Remington technicians took the assemblage of authors out to the bench rest and let everyone shoot to his heart's content. Accuracy remained excellent throughout the demonstration, and the fouling problem never once raised its ugly head. I was delighted with the test results because it seemed apparent that the rumor would be laid to rest for all time. But I was wrong by a mile; when the above-mentioned scribe's report was published he described, to his exclusive authoritative grandissement, how the little .17 would foul a barrel after only a few rounds and destroy accuracy!

A couple of years ago I read another feature-length report on the .17 Remington describing how the fouling build-up of less than twenty rounds would actually cause bullets to keyhole—in other words, to hit the target sideways at 100 yards. I was not surprised that the bullets had keyholed with certain loads—just as the writer described—because I had seen it happen too. I was

This is a very revealing photograph. At upper left is the print of a "keyhole" or bullet that went in sideways at 100 yards. At right is a hole made by a bullet which was tipping slightly as it passed through the target. At bottom is a bullet fragment. These odd-shaped bullet holes were made by .17-caliber bullets which had stripped jackets as a result of being loaded too hot. Unfortunately, some unobservant experimenters have assumed that this type of bullet tipping and keyholing is the result of excessively fouled .17-caliber bores.

dismayed, however, that he had been so blinded by the fouling myth that he failed even to look for the true cause. In truth, the Remington bullets he was using were too thin of jacket, and at top velocities the jacket material strips and causes the bullets to tumble in flight. This is avoided by reducing velocity or using another make of bullet, pure and simple. But the end result of such "reports" has been to turn the public away from the .17s. Only two rifles are (or have been) chambered for the .17 Remington, Remington's own Model 700 BDL and the petite H&R Model 317. I have a notion that in time these rifles will falter by the wayside and the .17 bore will once again be a strictly custom affair.

The .17 Remington is similar to the most common form of the .17/223 but not exactly the same. The neck and overall case length are somewhat larger, but the body length is slightly shorter. Its velocity of 4040 fps is undeniably impressive, and before the re-advent of the .220 Swift, it was the hottest factory round in the business. Sighted in with the point of impact 2 inches above point of aim at 100 yards, it is still close to 2 inches high at 200 yards and a little less than 4 inches low at 300 yards. Beyond there it peters out pretty fast. In the wind the flyweight pill gets blown off course about the same as a slower, but heavier, bullet from a .222.

My most accurate loads have been with custom bullets made by Bill Williams of Cleveland, Texas. The Williams bullets come in a variety of weights and styles and will group within 1/2 inch at 100 yards. My best load is 21 grains of the now-defunct Reloader #11, but 23 grains of Norma #203 will do about as well. The .17s are high-pressure cartridges and seem to build up peak pressures very quickly. Slight overcharges will cause blown primers, so it's a good idea to stay on the cautious side. Also, thick cup primers such as the Remington 7½ should be used exclusively. Standard small-rifle primers are likely to pierce or "biscuit cut" the firing-pin indent.

Perhaps the greatest fun of shooting the .17-bores is the almost total absence of recoil. The rifle moves so little that, if you don't blink your eye, you can see the hole appear in the target or watch what happens to whatever you're shooting at.

13

Varmint Sights

Observers of the current varmint-shooting scene no doubt assume that as the accuracy of varmint rifles improved and the range of varmint cartridges increased over the years there was a corresponding upgrading of optical goods. This is a logical assumption but not an accurate one. A modern shooter will no doubt be surprised to discover that back during the first half of the 1930s, when the .22 Hornet and .220 Swift first came into use, there were telescopic sights available of sufficient magnification and optical quality to do justice to even the finest of today's rifles. In 1936, for example, the year Winchester first made delivery of the Model 70, you could buy a Lyman Targetspot in 8× or 10×. This scope, which was the forerunner of today's Super Targetspot, featured precision adjustment and about as good a look at a woodchuck as anything available today. In other words, precision aiming equipment was available to varmint shooters from the beginning.

Yet, varminters were surprisingly slow to take advantage of the available optics. A few years back when I was researching a detailed history of the .220 Swift I read just about every magazine article that had been written on the subject up to about 1941. One of the things that struck me as most unusual about both the target and varmint shooting done with a Swift in those days was that nearly every account described a rifle equipped with a 2½×, 4×, or, at most, a 6× scope. Higher-magnification target scopes, which would certainly have permitted more exact bullet placement, especially at the longer ranges, seemed to have been all but ignored. I can't claim any first-

Rule No. 1 for rifle scopes: Don't use them to glass for your quarry, or you may find yourself staring down another hunter's barrel. Use binoculars, like this varminter.

hand knowledge of varmint shooting in those days (at the time my idea of formal attire was dry diapers), but conversations with experienced riflemen of the day have explained the prevailing varmint sight situation. First of all, scopes had not become all that common even for varmints. Ordinary factory-standard open sights or "peep" receiver sights were frequently the only sighting equipment even on rifles in .220 chambering. When you take this into consideration it becomes apparent that a rig topped with a 6× glass was a pretty fancy piece of gear. The higher-powered target-type scopes were not at all popular for varmints or, for that matter, any other type of centerfire shooting.

Nowadays we use telescopic sights so frequently, and have become so expert in their use, that we accept them without reservation. But before World War II they were something of a novelty, and many otherwise expert riflemen considered them slow and awkward. The awkwardness was caused in part, of course, by the stock configurations of those days. There was considerably more drop at comb and heel than is considered standard today, and the Monte Carlo comb was virtually unheard of. Thus, with a deep-pitched stock and a high-mounted scope a shooter was inclined to doodle his head around like a turkey peeking over a log. The narrow field of view and short eye relief of target scopes must have presented an almost impossible sighting problem.

And of course there was also the expense factor. The highly competitive scope industry of today produces about the best bargains to be found in any area of the shooting sports. But it has not always been so. In 1940 a Lyman

Super Targetspot retailed for $75. Compared to today's price for the same item this sounds fair enough. But that same year a Winchester Model 70 rifle, which was considered a high-ticket item, sold for $61.25! There were a couple of higher-magnification hunting-type scopes available then, but their prices were truly breathtaking; a Zeiss Zielach 8× sold for $93 and another German-made import, the 10× Ajack, which looked like a cross between a

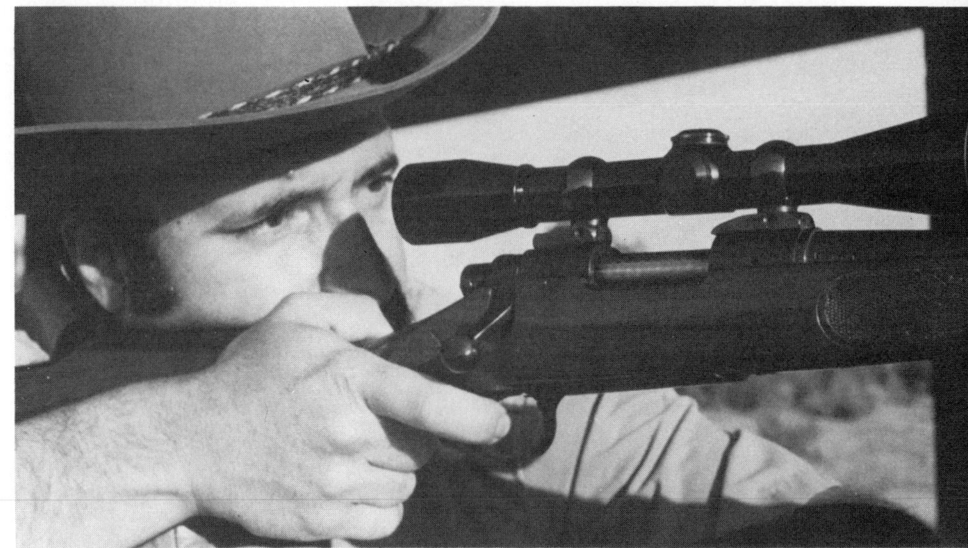

A 6× Leupold in Conetrol mounts, on one of the first rifles made in .17 Remington caliber.

bird bath and a sink pump, commanded a princely $120. This was the equivalent of paying over $400 for a scope today, but the quality of those instruments was only what we expect to pay $29.50 for on today's market. Like most European-made scopes they were fine telescopes but almost worthless as rifle sights.

Before telescopic sights came into universal use on varmint rifles two things had to happen, and they did not happen until after World War II. First, there had to be wider acceptance of all types of scopes. During the war years, American G.I.'s had become accustomed to sophisticated shooting equipment, and upon returning home they were far more receptive to the advantages of telescopic sights than had been shooters in prewar days. Second, there was a need for a good-quality scope that anyone could afford. A fellow by the name of Bill Weaver took care of this. Thus, in 1950 varmint shooters were treated to a tough, accurate 10× scope which retailed for $59.50. It was the Weaver K10, and suddenly the doors to super-long-range varmint shooting were open to everyone.

My first truly varmint scope was none other than one of those K10s. Back in the hills of Tennessee where I then lived, such a scope was hardly a commonplace item, and the local hardware store had to get one for me on special order. It was the first one I ever saw. Delighted with the way it extended my effective range, I sold virtually everything I owned and came up with enough cash to order a Unertl 12× Ultra Varmint glass—again the first of its species I ever set eyes on. I felt that if 10× was good then 12× would be better—and it was. Since then I've never been very shy about using the higher magnifications for varmints or anything else. I've always held that

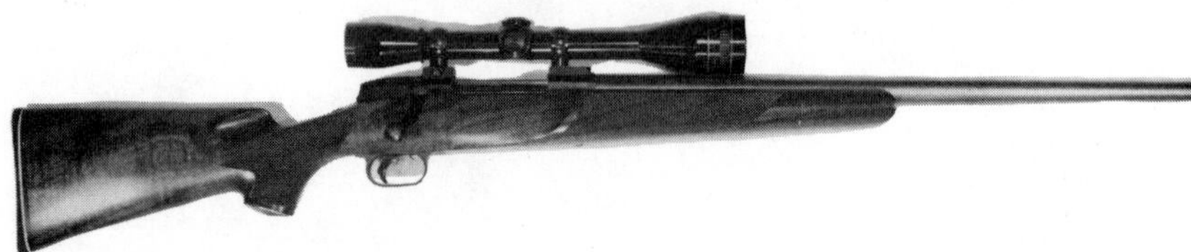

The scope is a 12× Leupold, popular optics among varminters. The beautiful custom-made rifle was built by the Champlin Rifle Company of Enid, Oklahoma. The specially built single-shot action is equipped with a Canjar single set trigger. Note the stiff stainless-steel barrel. Champlin builds custom rigs in any of the popular varmint chamberings.

you can't hit 'em if you can't see 'em. And it takes a lot of optics to get a good look at a prairie pup out at around 400 yards or so. When Bausch & Lomb announced their radically innovative 6–24× target/varmint scope at the unheard-of price of $160.00, in the late 1950s, I mounted one on a target-grade Model 70 in .243 caliber and did thereby considerably upset the local crow population. Though the B&L 6–24× variable is no longer made it is one of the greatest varmint scopes of all time.

I've read, and heard it said, that 10× or 12× is about all the magnification a rifleman can make use of. I don't know who started such a rumor, and if anyone says 12× is all *he* can make use of I won't bother to argue. But I'll willingly argue that most other folks can benefit by more magnification. And in more ways than one.

Until fairly recently, though, 10× was the top magnification in hunting-type scopes. Many shooters were hung up at this magnification level because they didn't like the idea of going to the more cumbersome and rather fragile-looking target-type scopes. I've never considered the target scopes a problem at all, but I sympathize with those who do; the oversize adjustment knobs look vulnerable and the mounting suspension looks like some sort of Chinese torture device, but, in truth, they're a lot more reliable than they appear. Of course the short eye relief and narrow field of view of the higher-magnification models takes some getting used to, but this is overcome with practice. For years I used a 25× Lyman target scope on my pet crow rifle and never lost a shot because of not finding the target in the scope. (But some of my pals who were not accustomed to either the scope or rifle did.) Focusing becomes more critical at the higher powers, but with the focus set for 200 yards the picture will be sharp from 100 yards on out, so there is really no problem.

In the future we're going to see higher magnifications in compact, hunting-style scopes. The Lyman All-American LWBR (Light Weight Bench Rest) 20× set the pace and has been joined by the Leupold 24× and Redfield's 6400 in 16×, 20×, or 24×. These are billed as bench-rest and target scopes but they have a lot to offer varmint shooters, and as a matter of fact, their sales success will depend almost entirely on their appeal to the varmint shooters. In the near future there will be more makes and models of solid, bridge-mounted (hunting-type) scopes available in the 15×-and-up range, and I expect that these, in time, will all but eliminate the traditional "target-style" scopes so far as varmint shooters are concerned.

With but few exceptions I see little purpose in a variable-power varmint scope. The defunct 6–24× B&L scope proved useful in varmint pastures, and to a lesser extent so does Redfield's 6–18× model. But 3–9× and

The Redfield 6–18× variable-power scope can be handy, though in general I prefer the fixed—and high—powers. The heavy-barreled LSA Model 55 is made in Finland and imported by Ithaca.

4–12× contribute nothing that I can see to a purely varmint rifle. If forced to use one I'd just turn it to the highest setting and forget it was a variable. A fellow contemplating, say, a 3–9× scope for his .222 or .22/250 would be better off to buy a straight fixed-power. He'd probably have a better scope and save money too.

But I hasten to point out that variable-power scopes have made some valuable contributions to the overall popularity of varmint shooting. The chap who owns a deer rifle in .243, .25/06, 7mm Remington Magnum, or just about any other caliber you can mention isn't likely to try his gun on distant woodchucks if he is limited by a glass of only 2½× or 4× power. But if the scope happens to be a variable model, and triples its optical horsepower at the turn of a ring, he's likely to get the notion that he can devastate some poor pasture poodle out at the far yardage. Such dual-purpose hunting equipment was only a dream a quarter-century ago but now is as common as holes in sneakers.

It's probably naughty of me to bring this up, but a great truth of our time is that the quest for deer rifles that can do part-time service on woodchucks has resulted in far better deer rifles. How? Let's say our friend was first planning on buying one of the more or less traditional deer rifles in something like .30/30 caliber. But a fast-talking gun salesman fixes him up with a bolt gun in .243 chambering and a snazzy 3–9× spyglass with a pitch about how he can shoot deer in winter and varmints in summer. Regardless of whether or not he goes after varmints, one thing for sure is that he's got a better deer rifle than he first planned on.

Part IV

Target Rifles

14

Smallbore Target Shooting

This game, as its name implies, is limited to rifles chambered for the .22 rimfire cartridge. Virtually every smallbore rifle will be chambered for—and use—the Long Rifle cartridge only. Accuracy development of the rimfire has centered around the Long Rifle cartridge, and match-grade rifle ammo comes in Long Rifle only, though there is some .22 Short match ammo for pistols. American courses of fire include indoor or "gallery" shooting at a range of 50 feet and outdoor matches at 50 yards, 50 meters, and 100 yards.

SMALLBORE PRONE TOURNAMENTS

The most popular outdoor matches are the so-called "prone" tournaments, which are fired entirely from the stable prone position. A prone tournament may last one, two, or four days, most usually two, and during each day's course of fire a shooter will fire four separate events or "matches" at all three distances. Each of these matches includes firing at two target sheets, twenty shots at each sheet. A shot in the bull's-eye or 10-ring has a value of 10 points, so the maximum score possible in each match is 400. The time limit for each target sheet is twenty minutes. After the first "stage" or twenty-minute time period the shooters change targets and then fire the second stage.

The target sheet used at 50 yards and 50 meters is printed with five targets. One of these is a sighting bull, which can be fired at any number of times, and the other four are record bulls, which are fired at five shots each. The 100-yard sheet has only three targets—a sighting bull and two record bulls, which are fired at ten shots each. The diameter of the 10-ring of the 50-yard target is .89 inch, and the tie-breaking X-ring is .39 inch. The 50-meter 10-ring is .787 inch with a .393 X-ring. The 100-yard 10-ring is 2 inches with a 1-inch X-ring.

The firing line of a smallbore prone match. This picture was taken at Arizona's Black Canyon Rifle Range near Phoenix during the 1975 Western Wildcats four-day tournament.

The day's course of fire for a typical tournament will include 50-yard, 50-meter, and 100-yard matches plus the so-called Dewer match, which is twenty shots at 50 yards and twenty shots at 100 yards. During the day, 160 shots will be fired for record, with a possible maximum score of 1600 points. This is why a two-day tournament is called a 3200 match and a four-day tournament a 6400 match. Now, dear reader, this also explains why the Redfield Gun Sight Company calls its two fine target scopes the 3200 and 6400 models. And why did Remington call its target rifle the 40-X? Because the best possible score in any match would have forty X's, or dead-center shots.

In most prone tournaments the first day's matches are fired entirely with "iron" or nontelescopic sights, and scopes are used the following day. A four-day tournament, such as the National Championships held at Camp Perry, will have two days of scopes and two days of iron-sight shooting, fired alternately. On the days when scopes are allowed a shooter may use iron sights if he chooses, but not vice versa.

The rules of the prone position specify that the rifle be held entirely by the shooter with no artificial support, such as a sandbag under the barrel, whatever. The only bracing device allowed is a sling, but a good solid prone position can be amazingly stable. Topflight prone competitors say that their rifle tremor is so slight that when aiming at 100 yards the cross hairs waver over an area scarcely larger than a .22-caliber bullet hole!

To the non-target shooter it surely seems that a marksman able to aim so close would never miss the X-ring, certainly not the 10-ring. But the shooter must deal with a maze of variables. Wind is the major culprit. The relatively light and slow-moving .22-caliber bullet is easily nudged off course by a breeze, and a dead-center aim can—and frequently does—result in the bullet landing in the outer rings. Thus the shooter is constantly evaluating the strength and direction of the wind and making correction. When the wind is especially tricky a competitive shooter may fire nearly as many shots on the sighting bull as he does for record, and sometimes even more.

Another variable which constantly harasses the smallbore prone shooter is his own unconscious effect on the rifle. By tightening the muscles in his shoulder or arm he may alter his hold on the rifle so as to cause the bullet to "jump" out of the 10-ring. And of course there is always the problem of proper trigger squeeze. Actually, good riflemen do not "squeeze" the trigger but exercise a very well controlled *pull.* A trigger let-off that is ill-coordinated or uneven, or victim to any one of the score of trigger-pulling faults, can result in a wide shot. Usually the fault occurs—and then disappears—so instantaneously that the shooter has no idea what has happened except that he sees a bullet hole unaccountably glaring back at him from the 9- or 8-ring.

Though the prone position is not difficult to master, and the targets themselves not all that difficult, the smallbore-prone game is a rough one because it demands fairly lengthy spans of total concentration and requires considerable stamina. Firing 160 for record, plus as many as 100 or even more sighters, is a hard day's work, especially when you're trying to win and must endure under the unyielding pressure of knowing one mistake can cost you the whole match.

Yet perfect scores of 400 are not at all uncommon for a match. In fact, "possibles" with 38, 39 and even 40 X's aren't at all scarce in a tournament of any importance. During the day's shooting, however, even the best shooters will loose a point here and there, so there will be relatively few perfect 1600's, especially with iron sights. There are very few shooters who have scored a perfect 3200 over a two-day tournament, and in all smallbore history only one shooter, early in 1975, ever fired a perfect 6400 in a four-day contest. Now that it has happened, though, and the psychological barriers are down, I expect there will be a rash of 6400 possibles.

THE SMALLBORE PRONE RIFLE

Now that you have a better understanding of the outdoor prone course of fire you'll better understand the funny-looking rifle used in this type of competition and why it turned out the way it has. The rules allow just about any sort of rig the shooter can get to the firing line. There are no restrictions on weight, barrel length, or design features. Of course a rifle can't be too heavy or the shooter couldn't hold it up for twenty minutes. Most rifles weigh about 11 pounds and have 26- or 28-inch barrels. Until a few years ago the rules specified that the weight of trigger pull be not less than 3 pounds—meaning at least 3 pounds of pressure must be applied to the trigger before the sear will release and allow the rifle to fire.

I always felt (and still do) that the 3-pound trigger rule was a good one because it required the shooter to develop a good trigger technique. This is a vital element of marksmanship. Anyway, quite a lot of shooters felt that they would shoot better scores if the trigger-pull minimum was abolished, and the NRA rules committee was prevailed upon to do so. Naturally, scores took a turn for the better. So much better, in fact, that at this writing there is considerable agitation to make the targets more difficult. Some wise heads, however, point out that a return to the 3-pound minimum will eliminate the need for a more difficult target and also bring about a renewed emphasis on the basic principles of marksmanship. Let's face it—until a kid learns how to squeeze a trigger he hasn't really learned to shoot.

Here Lones Wigger, Olympic Gold Medalist and one of the greatest rifle shots of all time, and I look over an experimental Winchester Model 52 smallbore prone rifle. This rifle, which was first announced on a strictly custom basis in 1975, features a stock with removable comb designed by well-known smallbore competitor Herb Hollister. I used this rifle in competition for a few years prior to its announcement by Winchester and consider it one of the outstanding designs currently available. The scope I'm using here is a 25× Lyman Super Targetspot.

The all-time most popular smallbore target rifle is the famous Winchester Model 52. This rifle was first introduced back in 1920 and with relatively few changes over the years has maintained a premier position. The first perfect 6400 score fired in smallbore competition was fired with a rifle built up on a Model 52 action. The first M52 looked a lot like a 1903 Springfield both in profile, sight design, and stock configuration. It was better than anything target shooters had ever seen but was faulted by a too slow lock time. In 1929 the lock time was speeded up, and an even more efficient speed-lock mechanism was introduced in 1937. This was the so-called "B" series. Since the introduction of the "B" series the Model 52 has remained basically unchanged right up until the present.

The "C" series of 1947 had a tremendously improved trigger mechanism, and the "D" series introduced in 1961 had a redesigned stock and elimi-

Here is another Model 52 custom-stocked by me for prone competition only. The high, cradlelike comb allows maximum comfort in the prone position. The rear sight is the new Redfield Mark 10, and the unusual-looking front sight was made by custom riflesmith Womack. The deeply cut and comfortably formed grip promotes extremely uniform shot-to-shot trigger letoff.

nated the clip magazine. The latest M52, the "E" series, offers a choice of stock styles and a choice of different trigger mechanisms, but all in all it's still pretty much the unbeatable M52 of 1937, at least as far as the receiver goes. Everything else has changed radically—barrels, sights, special triggers, ammo, and stock design have evolved so rapidly that a winning combination of a short ten years ago would be woefully inadequate today.

Target shooters, despite their reputation as a conservative, low-key group, are constantly experimenting with their equipment and shooting technique. This has been especially true in the past few years, and I think a lot of their restlessness has been caused by startling developments in the bench-rest game. I can remember my shooting coaches back in the 1950s telling me that a competitor needed only a reasonably good rifle and some reasonably good ammo, for as long as he aligned the sights properly and squeezed the trigger he would win the matches. But twenty years ago virtually every rifle used in smallbore competition looked like every other. In fact, they were all so much alike in all respects that the fellow who aimed and squeezed the trigger right *did* win.

Today, smallbore rifle philosophy has made a complete turnaround. The old saying "My rifle can shoot better than I can hold" is as outdated as "twenty-three skiddoo." Modern coaching and training programs, and intensified competition, have produced a breed of shooter who is almost constantly a jump or two ahead of the best his equipment has to offer. Top-flight competitors are constantly checking their equipment for the slightest sign of breakdown and usually have a couple of spare rifles plus spare iron sights and scopes to use in case they even suspect some form of failure. Very seldom does a topflight rifleman make it through the season without drastically altering his rifle or replacing it altogether.

I've watched competitors grab a wood rasp out of their shooting kits and start slicing away at the cheek rest or pistol grip of their stock right on the firing line. The best shooters are almost constantly changing their rifles in one way or another.

Obviously, the match-winning modern smallbore prone target rifle is most usually a custom affair. Individual demands are so varied that no manufacturer could attempt to touch all bases without having to price his product completely out of the market. Therefore Winchester, Remington, and the West German firm of A. J. Anschutz have maintained a policy of selling

Since many target shooters prefer to build their own stocks, Winchester and other rifle-making firms now supply barreled actions only. This is the Model 52 smallbore rifle which is probably the all-time favorite smallbore action for target shooting.

plain barreled actions which serve as the foundation of a custom rig. However, here of late some manufacturers, especially Winchester and Anschutz, appear to have been watching the evolution of smallbore stock design quite closely and have introduced stocks which represent current design trends. Winchester, for example, now offers on special order only a super-advanced stock designed by Herb Hollister, one of the all-time great smallbore champions. The stock features a comb so high and so far forward that it would be impossible to get the bolt out to clean the barrel if the top portion of the buttstock were not detachable. I used this rifle for two years while it was in the experimental stage and concluded that no amount of "custom" tinkering or reworking would result in a significant improvement. It's *that* good. No doubt, though, in a few years it will be as outdated as pewter dentures. The coming trends, I suspect, will be to wholly fiberglass-and-resin stocks

The popular Remington Model 40-X .22 rimfire smallbore rifle. This rifle can be used for both position shooting and prone competition.

similar in construction to those which have been so successful in bench-rest shooting. Or even possibly toward stocks which are built up on a frame of stiff metal tubing. Try to visualize a stock which is a buttplate, cheek piece, pistol grip, and handstop all connected by a steel bar. . . .

Smallbore barrels have also undergone intense scrutiny in the past decade. Whereas only twenty years ago a .22 rimfire target barrel was looked upon as a fixture that should last forever it is now recognized that barrel life has its

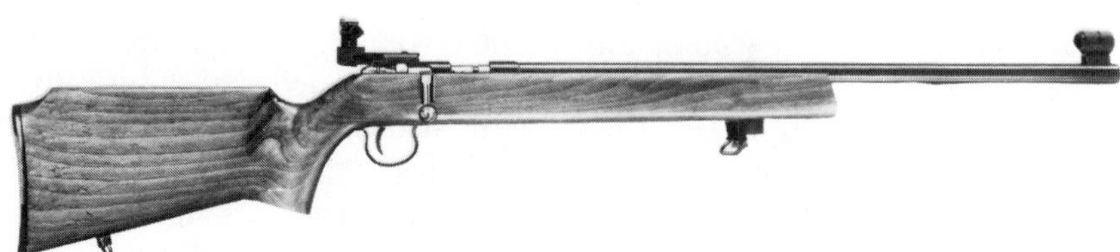

The Savage/Anschutz Mark 10-D is made by the famed West German target rifle firm and is especially well suited as a low-priced starting rifle for beginners.

limits and once that limit is exceeded groups begin to open up. Equally important, it is recognized that despite the care and effort that goes into the manufacture of a barrel, regardless of maker, some barrels come out "more equal" than others. This puzzles barrelmakers and shooters no end, but no one doubts that the best and only remedy for a bum barrel is to yank it out and fit another one.

Usually, worn or unsuitable barrels are replaced by stainless-steel custom barrels made by Atkinson, Douglas, Hart, or McMillin. These beautifully made barrels give a degree of accuracy which is equaled only, in my experience, by certain select Anschutz rifles and Winchester's Model 52 International barrel, a special lead-lapped affair capable of dazzling accuracy. With this barrel on the experimental rifle described above I've grouped ten shots inside ½ inch at 100 yards, with selected lots of ammunition.

The first sign that a barrel is going sour, assuming that everything else is working right, is a tendency to throw wide shots or "flyers." The cause of this, most usually, is a very noticeable ring or groove which has been worn or cut into the bore about ⅛ inch ahead of the chamber. This is caused by the abrasive action of the primer compound and usually becomes evident after about 30,000 rounds have been fired. The common corrective action is simply to remove the barrel from the action, cut off the rear ½ inch or so, and then refit and rechamber. This is far less expensive than fitting a new barrel, but of course there are practical limits as to how many times a barrel can be whacked off.

The best American-made barrels have a total life of 100,000 rounds or over, which means that they will last from five to twenty years. Human nature being what it is, however, smallbore shooters usually get a yen to change barrels—and rifles—well before the barrel is totally worn out. Also, constant advances in barrelmaking technology tend to place better and better barrels on the market, and a barrel will quite likely be obsolete before it is actually worn out in the usual sense.

SMALLBORE AMMO

If one single factor can be said to be responsible for the upsurge in smallbore rifle performance it has to be the vastly improved quality of match-grade ammo. A few years back the house of Eley, a British maker of sporting ammunition, began sending some very interesting rimfire target ammo to these shores. It not only grouped noticeably tighter than anything that had

This instrument is used at the Eley Ammunition Manufacturing Company to test the sensitivity and round-to-round uniformity of the priming composition in smallbore match ammunition. The test is conducted by dropping a metal ball from an exactly known height. The lower the height at which the ball will detonate the priming compound, the greater the sensitivity. The ball is magnetically released and in this photo it can be seen falling about halfway between the release magnet and the anvil. Similar setups are used to test rimfire cartridges and centerfire primers here in the U.S.

been used before, but was markedly less affected by winds. The Eley ammo caught on in a hurry and, quite literally, opened the door to a whole new era of rifle performance. In order to get a clear understanding of the revolutionary effect this ammo had on target shooting, one must consider that before its introduction smallbore target rifle development was virtually nonexistent. The available ammo was the limiting factor, and no matter how fine one's barrel was or how well designed the stock, accuracy was not all that good.

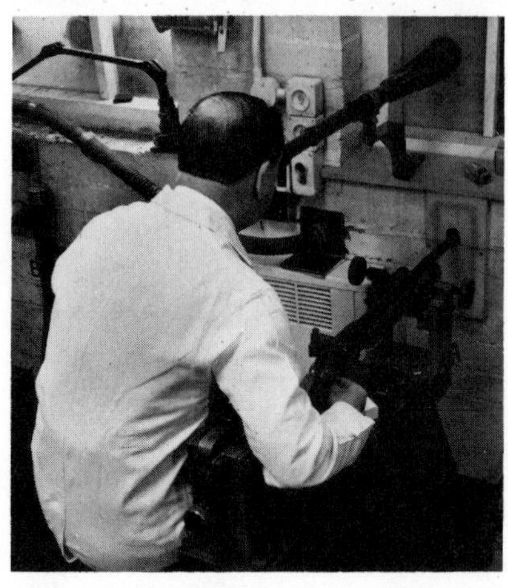

Here an Eley technician samples the accuracy of a production run of Red Box Eley ammunition. The rifle is the British-made BSA Martini held in a machine rest.

With the advent of Eley's best, however, the barriers were torn down; the difference between a *good* barrel and a *better* barrel suddenly became apparent. This stimulated barrelmakers and gunsmiths to try harder. Also, differences in stock design, bedding techniques, and triggers became very much more apparent. In short, "good enough" was no longer good enough, it had to be the best.

Before the coming of Eley, Winchester and Remington had shared the

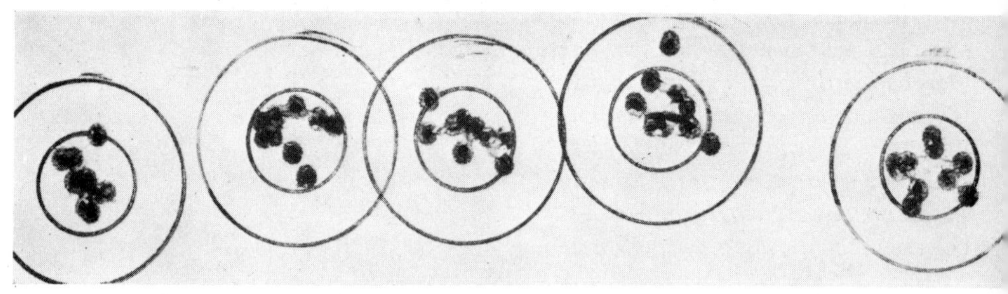

These five ten-shot groups, fired at 100 yards, give you an idea of the accuracy of today's smallbore match ammunition. These were fired from a target rifle held in a machine rest at the Eley factory in England. Since its introduction nearly two decades ago to these shores, Eley ammunition has virtually dominated smallbore competition. However, American manufacturers, especially Winchester, are now producing match-grade ammunition which challenges Eley's best.

rimfire match market, but their sales promptly took a nosedive. Winchester took a pledge to equal the performance of Eley, and after a rather long and expensive research and development program introduced the new Western Gold Super Match. At this writing it's too soon to tell how the Gold Match will fare against the best Eley, but first reports are quite favorable. A fairly important tournament was recently won by a rifleman using the new Western ammo, and perhaps that's a sign of better things to come for American ammo makers.

THE TARGET SIGHT

When Gertrude Stein said "A rose is a rose is a rose," she apparently was not thinking of the individuality of high-performance rifle sights. For, whatever else they may be, a sight is *not* a sight is *not* a sight. But, oh, how competitive shooters wish they were. A generation ago, before the coming of super barrels, hot ammo, and hotter shooters, almost any kind of iron or "peep" sight would pass muster. In fact, that was a time when shooters were not so inclined to question the integrity of their equipment. If a peep sight cost, say, $20, it was expected to be above reproach. In short, the best that money could buy.

But during the great performance upswing of the 1960s, when shooters began squeezing the last possible X out of every target, peep sights in particular came under serious suspicion. The problem was that the sight did not always respond to a turn of the adjusting knobs. A shooter, for example, might suddenly find a rising wind carrying his shots an inch off center on the 100-yard target. Accordingly he would crank four clicks of windage into the sight, expecting the sight adjustment to center up the group again. The next shot, however, would be as far off center as ever. This caused a lot of suspicion. Up until the decade of the 1960s few shooters were aware such problems existed. When equipment, ammo, and shooting talent were so faulty that a shooter was hard pressed to keep his shots in the 2-inch 10-ring at 100 yards, he was not likely to notice that his sight was contributing a ½-inch error of its own. But when ammo and barrels improved to the point that shooters started having a positive idea of where the shots should be going, a bum sight stuck out like a sore thumb.

In past years the old shooter's trick of dealing with "backlash," a sloppy sight response, was to crank the adjusting knob three or four clicks farther than he wanted to go and then reversing the direction the three or four clicks. This tinkertoy technique eliminated some of the "slop" but was not at all foolproof nor as precise as the newly heated-up competition called for. Shooters of a mechanical bent tried testing their sight adjustments with dial indicators reading in thousandths of an inch and were appalled with what they discovered. Some sights, to give an extreme example, not only didn't move when they were supposed to but actually went in a *reverse* direction for the first couple of clicks. Also, it was learned that no make or model was free of defect. Some individual sights were—and are—better than others of the same assembly run. Some clever mechanics found that they could tighten a sight somewhat and hung out their shingles as sight doctors. Other precision machinists even began building finely precise sights selling for over $100 per copy. The latest, and most spectacular, step in the direction of ul-

The new, precision-built Redfield Mark 10 receiver sight.

This receiver sight, the Redfield Model 75, is a popular model for the less expensive target rifles. The retail price is approximately 1/8th that of the Redfield Mark 10.

tra-precision iron sights is the Redfield Mark 10. A virtually handmade affair, this unit is said to have an accuracy of plus or minus 1/32 inch at *100 yards.* If this doesn't impress anyone, then perhaps the $168 price tag will. The previously most expensive iron sights made by Redfield cost less than $50. So who will pay $168 for a little peep sight? You'd be surprised.

The telescopic sights used in the "any sight" phases of rifle tournaments have not, with one notable exception, undergone a radical change over the years. This is simply because the optics and overall quality of the target scopes made by such makers as Lyman and Unertl have always been excellent and quite equal to the demands made on them by serious target shooters. The closest thing to a problem with the exterior-suspension-type target scope is that the scope itself moves when elevation or windage adjustments are made. This is no problem with small changes but when the scope is moved from a 50-yard to a 100-yard zero in smallbore shooting, or from a 600-yard to a 1000-yard zero in bigbore, problems arise. This is because the shooter must alter his head position somewhat, and his cheek contact on the comb.

Here are a couple of popular target scopes. At left the Redfield Model 3200, and at right the new model 6400. I anticipate that bridge-mounted scopes such as the Redfield Model 6400 and Leupold 24× will soon dominate long-range target competition.

Redfield took this problem in hand during the 1960s and produced a target-type scope, the Model 3200, which incorporates *internal* adjustments. Thus the scope eyepiece doesn't move with the adjustment and permits a more constant eye, cheek, and stock relationship, regardless of range. Prone shooters, who are endlessly tinkering with their stock fit, mold or carve the comb cheek piece until the eye is in perfect alignment with the scope when the face is comfortably resting on the stock. Then the iron sight mounting blocks are tinkered with until the rear peep is at the same height as the scope. This allows a constant alignment which pays off in points and X's. When the new 6400 "possible" record was set in 1975 the shooter was using the Redfield 3200 and a stock which had been carefully tailored for an exact fit as outlined above.

There is still room for advances in target scope design. Smaller scopes, for example, which could be mounted lower and offer less "sail" area in the wind, would be a benefit. More exact adjustments can always be used, as can better optics. But there is no great demand from shooters in this direction. Their attention is still on barrels, stocks, and ammo, at least for the moment. When these "problems" are put away you can bet that scopemakers will have to get back to the old drawing board. A target shooter, especially the smallbore-prone specialist, just isn't happy unless he's demanding better equipment.

SMALLBORE POSITION SHOOTING

The most familiar form of target shooting is indoor or "gallery" riflery. It is on the indoor ranges that thousands of high school and college ROTC students get their first taste of disciplined rifle training. These indoor ranges are also the scene of virtually all high school and collegiate varsity rifle competition as well as the training ground for longer-range outdoor shooting.

If it were not for the large number of indoor ranges across the country some avid shooters, especially those living in the larger metropolitan areas, could not enjoy the shooting sports at all. Full-scale outdoor ranges are not always available within a reasonable distance, but indoor ranges are frequently located right down town, in high schools, colleges, National Guard and Reserve armories, gun clubs, and even church basements. Also, more and more commercially run urban ranges are being opened every year. Aside from the convenient location of most indoor ranges, gallery shooting offers special appeal during the winter months and to shooters whose jobs, schooling, and other daytime activities make nighttime shooting attractive. Shooting leagues which involve weekly competition among schools, gun clubs, or industrial teams most often revolve around indoor ranges, especially during the winter months.

Of course, aside from the above-listed conveniences and advantages, there is no overlooking the fact that there are thousands of shooters, both competitors and plinkers, who simply prefer gallery shooting. My first rifle training was in indoor ranges, and during my college days I was a member of the varsity rifle squad, which fired indoors exclusively. Intercollegiate rifle matches, like any other college sport, are singularly intense competitions with rigid training and conditioning schedules. Some of the most determinedly battled and hotly contested rifle matches I've ever been involved in were the tournaments between traditionally rival universities. It is from the college shooters that the military marksmen units "draft" many of their top shooters, and it is these same shooters who provide the talent for our International and Olympic teams. It all starts on the indoor range.

Back when I was a farm lad the closest thing we had to an "official" rifle range was an abandoned one-room schoolhouse. Some shooters in our community raised enough money to buy four bullet traps and during the winter months we'd get together once a week for some practice and informal competition. The affairs were always well attended, I recall, by nonparticipants who claimed, "My eyes ain't what they used to be," but nevertheless crowded close to the glowing potbellied stove and related tales of unsurpassable feats of marksmanship accomplished back when their eyes, I politely presumed, were in more precise working order. In addition to these nonshooting attendants, there were usually a half-dozen or so bird dogs and coon hounds whose invariably wet hides steamed by the stove and lent a pungence which blended well with the characteristic snuff, chewing tobacco, pipe and horse liniment odors of farm folk.

On particularly cold nights the storytellers would crowd so tightly around the stove that very little heat reached the firing line. I recall trying to shoot when my fingers were so cold that I couldn't even feel the trigger. My principal competition was a youngster of almost exactly my age who lived on the next farm. We coached each other, shared our meager resources of ammo if the other happened to be low on funds, and, most important, provided each other with a constant competitive "push." In time the two of us were each four-year lettermen on the same college rifle team and were to become members of crack military rifle teams. The boy-against-boy shooting rivalry which began in that chilly little one-room school gallery reached the ultimate point when we competed against each other for national honors at the U.S. Championships at Camp Perry.

Army veterans may recall firing on indoor 1,000-inch ranges during basic training, and there is also some indoor shooting done at 75 feet, but most indoor shooting, by far, is done at 50 feet. Back when I began shooting, the one and only target used at 50 feet was the old standard gallery card with ten targets. (Later an eleven-target card was introduced which included a sighting bull.) The black aiming bull on this target measures 1.483 inches across and the 10-ring has a diameter of .150 inch (about ⅛ inch).

Until the late 1950s this had been the standard gallery target and was considered pretty tough, especially in the standing position. (I remember when a score of 90 was terrific for the standing position.) However, during the decade of the 1950s, which was the height of the cold war with the Communist-bloc countries, the Russians gave us a hard road to travel in international shooting competitions such as the Olympics. This brought on an intensified interest in International shooting, and a new gallery target, one scaled down from the 50-meter International target, was introduced. This newer target has a black aiming bull 1.395 inches in diameter, slightly larger than the older-style bull, but the 10-ring is only .008 inch, about the diameter of the period at the end of this sentence.

The first reactions to this new target were simple disbelief. In a short while, though, shooters got accustomed to the tiny scoring rings and even welcomed the new challenge. Nowadays virtually all intercollegiate rifle shooting is done on the International or ISU (International Shooting Union) target, and there is no questioning the impact it has had on our world shooting prestige. Perhaps the only noteworthy achievement of my university career was to be the first collegiate rifleman to fire a perfect score of 100 on the ISU target in sanctioned competition. In the prone position, of course. These days, though, a perfect score is not at all uncommon, and I'm sure my modest achievement is seldom noted.

The course of fire of most gallery matches calls for ten, twenty, thirty, and even forty shots in each position—prone, sitting, kneeling, and standing. The sitting position is not used in International competition and is normally not fired in ISU-oriented tournaments. Naturally, since the target sheets have only ten bulls, the shooting is done in ten shot strings, one shot per bull. The time limit is ten minutes per ten-shot string when firing at the conventional NRA target. ISU-type matches allow ten minutes per ten-shot string in the prone position and fifteen minutes in the kneeling and standing positions. Sighters must be fired within these time limits.

Most of the NRA (American Style) tournaments allow either iron sights or scopes to be used, but all ISU matches are for iron sights only. This is because International tournaments are restricted to iron sights only. Likewise, all collegiate and high school matches are restricted to irons only. Actually, the difference between scores fired with iron sights and scopes vary little if at all. Indoor ranges are usually lighted for optimum sight-picture crispness and there are no crosswinds to cope with. (In crosswinds a scope is somewhat more convenient.) So the iron-sight shooter is on a par with the scope shooter, or at least until age begins to take its toll.

A similar but far less common course of fire for American smallbore position shooters is the outdoor events. Fired at 50 yards or 50 meters, these events may be fired on the standard NRA 50-yard target, the NRA 50-meter target (described in the section on smallbore prone shooting), or, more usually, the 50-meter ISU target or the 50-meter target reduced in size for shooting at 50 yards. (These target dimensions are given in the chapter on International target shooting.)

As in gallery shooting, the course of fire may be ten, twenty, thirty, or forty shots in each position, and the time limits are also the same. In fact, the gallery and outdoor courses are virtually identical and the equipment regulations are identical. The big difference is that the outdoor shooter has to deal with the elements, especially wind and variable light conditions.

There is a considerable movement afoot to abolish the variations in outdoor smallbore position shooting and standardize the ISU 50-meter target and course of fire. This would make little difference in terms of shooter participation and would end a lot of confusion. It would also better prepare the U.S. shooter for International events.

THE SMALLBORE POSITION RIFLE

Like every other type of sporting rifle, the gallery rifle has undergone some radical changes in the past couple of decades. Most of these changes have been brought about as a result of sweeping regulation changes designed to make American shooters more familiar with ISU shooting. Back about 1950, when I began gallery shooting, shooters were using a style of rifle that had been in vogue for three decades. The most popular rifle, by far, among the top shooters was the Winchester Model 52, followed by the Remington Model 37. Beginners usually used a Winchester Model 75, a Remington Model 513-T, or one of the medium-weight rifles in target configuration such as the Mossberg Model 144. A few shooters still used the finely built "Walnut Hill" single-shot built by Stevens, and one fellow in our club owned the English-made BSA single-shot rifle. The National Guard and Reserve teams, plus nearly all ROTC units, were equipped with the Springfield M22, a near look-alike of the '03 Springfield service rifle.

The rules of the day didn't allow such fancy accessories as palm rests, hook buttplates, and thumbhole stocks, or at least most tournaments forbade their use, so rifle design tended to be pretty prosaic. The "marksman-style"

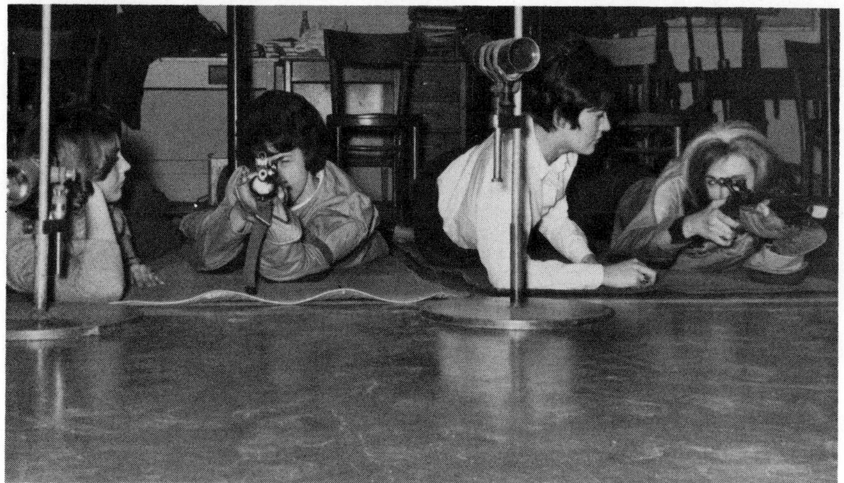

These young ladies are participating in a university physical education class in smallbore riflery. The rifles they are using are Model 52 Winchester target models. Such shooting as this, done on 50-foot indoor galleries, is popular in high schools and colleges.

stock of the Model 52 and other such rifles was quite adaptable for the various shooting positions and was considered about all a rifle needed to—or should—be. Accuracy from rifle and ammo were not held in premium regard because almost any target-grade rifle was capable of "pinwheel" accuracy at 50 feet, and even field-grade ammo was generally considered good enough. Similarly, just about any peep sight would do, because once a rifle was sighted in there usually wasn't much need for further changes. A good trigger was highly regarded, however, and when the C series of the Model 52 was introduced in 1947 its crisp, double adjustable trigger created a sensation. Never before had such a sweet-feeling trigger been available.

Other than once-a-generation improvements such as this, the gallery game rocked along without much change, and very likely would have continued to do so if the Russians hadn't started handing us some bumps in the Olympics. The reasons were simple; American shooters were accustomed to rifles which conformed to American rules. The Russians, and nearly everybody else, took full advantage of the ISU rules and used heavier rifles fitted with palm rests, thumbhole stocks, and all the other features which allow maximum shooter performance. Clearly, the Americans would have to use such rifles if they were to keep pace with world shooting. This meant that upcoming shooters would have to be trained with International-style equipment, and the best way to start would be to allow such rifles in U.S. competition.

The NRA rule book was rewritten, and the rest is history. American shooters, using rifles exactly like those now allowed in U.S. competition, dominate world position shooting. Actually, there is *one* difference: some U.S. tournaments require that the trigger have a minimum let-off of 3 pounds. Other tournaments, though, especially the ISU types, have no trigger-weight requirements, just as in World Class events.

When the rifle restrictions were lifted, it was Katy bar the door so far as development work that took place. The average gallery rifle of the 1950s was, on a scale of comparison, say, 10 percent better than the rifle of the 1920s. Today's rifle, on the same scale, is more like 70 percent better than the rifle of the 1950s!

The most notable rifle to take advantage of the American market under the new rules was the Anschutz, made in West Germany and then imported by Stoeger. The Anschutz had it all; both hook and prone-style buttplate, an adjustable palm rest, a beautifully made thumbhole stock, fine sights, a wonderfully accurate barrel, and a choice of trigger styles and weights. What's more, it was available when the market suddenly developed for such a rifle. Just about the only alternative was a custom rifle, but few stockmakers, and fewer yet do-it-yourselfers, were able to turn out a really good ISU-style rifle. Thousands of existing rifles were fitted with palm rest and hook buttplates, to considerable advantage and score improvement, but the Anschutz rifles ruled the ranges.

There were some other good ISU-style rifles available, such as the Walther, the Finnish Lion, the beautifully made (and expensive) Hammerli of Swiss make, and the Danish Schultz & Larsen, but each of these reached these shores too late or in too small numbers. Buyers of new rifles were buying what the winners were using, and by then the winners were using the Anschutz almost to a man. American manufacturers, true to their conservative nature, either underestimated or ignored the trend and lost out entirely. Of course, target rifles are only a tiny part of the production of major American gun manufacturers, but the prestige a winning rifle gives its maker can be very valuable in the world's marketplace.

At present, Winchester offers a thumbhole-stocked version of the Model 52 called the International Match, and Remington offers their Model 40-X rimfire in similar stock configuration, but the production of each of these ISU rifles is quite low. On a straight, off-the-shelf basis the Winchester International Match is one of the most accurate rimfire rifles ever made. They are built up completely in Winchester's custom shop with special hand-lapped barrels and must meet some pretty stiff accuracy requirements. In gallery position shooting, however, it's the external features that make the difference, and the Anschutz keeps getting further and further ahead. Even the other European manufacturers have about quit trying to keep up. At present the Anschutz line is imported and distributed in the U.S. by the Savage Arms Company.

15

International Target Shooting

The most notable rifle events fired in the Olympics and other International competition are the so-called "Free Rifle" matches. The name comes from their relative *freedom* from restrictions. On the other hand, though, the Free Rifle events are the most demanding of all rifle competitions and require a more highly refined degree of skill and training than any other shooting game. For my money the Free Rifle shooters are the aristocrats of the competitive rifle family. If my children are to become competitive riflemen I will be proudest if they take up this form of shooting.

World Class winners with the free rifle are highly trained athletes who, like other Olympic champions, live in an environment of almost constant coaching and preparation. The winner of the Olympic Gold Medal in the Free Rifle event, you can be sure, is not just a keen-eyed kid who practices on weekends. Instead he follows a day-after-day regimen of honing his physical conditioning—and will to win—to a razor-fine edge. One International champion told me that each day's training involved a several mile run while he formed in his mind's eye the image of a perfect sight picture. As the running became painful to his lungs and body he continued to maintain the mental sight picture as long as he could possibly endure. The reason for this is that the intense pressures of International competition can be equally painful. While the shooter strives for a perfect hold and let-off in the standing position his subconscious is shouting to his whole body, "This is too hard, there's too much pressure, go ahead and settle for a 9 instead of a 10. . . ."

THE INTERNATIONAL COURSE OF FIRE

There are two forms of Free Rifle shooting. One is for smallbore rifles and is fired at 50 meters. The other is for centerfire rifles of not larger than 8mm bore size and is fired at 300 meters. The 50-meter ISU target has ten scoring rings with an outer ring diameter of 162.40mm (about 6.330 inches) and a black aiming bull of 112.40mm (about 4.4 inches). The 10-ring is a tiny

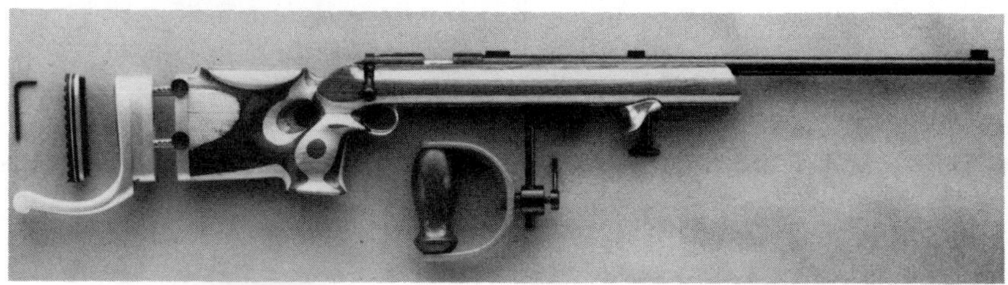

Winchester Model 52 International-style free rifle complete with hook buttplate and palmrest such as used for three- or four-position shooting at 50 feet, 50 yards, or 50 meters. The palmrest is turned sideways for clarity here. These rifles are made strictly on a special-order basis.

Bigbore 300-meter free rifle built by the famous Swiss firm of Hammerli. Hammerli target rifles and pistols are among the most respected and beautifully made equipment in the target-shooting field.

The new Remington 40-XC. The caliber is .308 Winchester. These rifles are designed for bigbore over-the-course competition. The extremely deep forend just in front of the trigger guard is especially helpful in the standing position, but the deep profile offers a lot of "sail" area when the wind blows, thus making it difficult to hold steady.

12.4mm (slightly less than a half-inch), and for dead-center shooters there is a 1mm dot for an X-ring. If you don't think that's tough, just try hitting a pinhead at 55 long paces.

The 300-meter target is an even 1 meter across with a 600mm black aiming circle (about 23½ inches). The ten-ring is only 100mm wide (about 3.93 inches). The X-ring is about the size of a silver dollar.

The course of fire in major International events calls for forty shots each in the prone, kneeling, and standing positions. This gives a maximum possible score of 1200 points. The time limits are: prone, one hour and thirty minutes; kneeling, one hour and forty-five minutes; and standing, two hours. The matches are fired in ten-shot strings, and ten sighting shots are allowed for each position. These sighters must be fired before the record strings are begun.

This International-style shooter is firing a 50-meter free rifle from the difficult kneeling position. The elaborate rifle he is using is made by the German firm of Walther. The wiring in the background is part of an electrical system which changes targets at the push of a button.

All shooting is done strictly with iron sights, but the degree of accuracy achieved is astounding. To put it in terms familiar to the American hunter, these riflemen fire groups from the prone position that would equal putting a bullet in a woodchuck's head at 330 yards *nine times out of ten!* Or, offhand, hitting a chuck over half the time. And with *iron sights. . . .*

The rifles used in the 50-meter smallbore events are the same as those now allowed for U.S. position shooting. The rifle can weigh no more than 8 kilograms (about 17½ pounds), and there are certain rules concerning the shape and size of the hook buttplate, but beyond that the rifles are "free" of restrictions. As in American gallery shooting, the big winning International smallbore competitor who doesn't use an Anschutz is an odd note. The big exceptions are the Russians. They use rifles made in the USSR as a rule, not necessarily because they prefer to do so but because they have little choice.

The centerfire free rifles come in many varieties, however, and if the rifles used aren't out-and-out custom jobs they're at least highly modified factory models. The most successful rifles of recent years have been built around Remington's 40-X actions, and the .308 Winchester has become the most winning caliber. Not too surprisingly, the lines of the 50-meter and 300-meter rifles are quite similar. This allows an easier transition from one rifle to the other, an important consideration when a shooter fires both events.

Here an International-style shooter performs from the standing position, the most difficult position of all. The rifle he is using is the Anschutz, which is the most popular 50-meter rifle used in modern competition.

Actually, aside from the complex stock configuration and the mass of accessories, a bench-rest shooter would feel right at home when inspecting a .300-meter rifle. Actions, barrels, triggers, and ammo loading techniques, not to mention action-bedding methods, have been borrowed from the bench-rest game. Back when I first came in contact with .300-meter rifles many of the rifles used in competition simply weren't accurate enough to put all the shots in the 10-ring no matter how hard the marksman tried. As bench-rest shooting blossomed, however, there was almost a hand-in-hand improvement in free-rifle accuracy. Techniques that proved successful on the bench range would show up on the ISU range a year or less later.

Unfortunately, the day of the great free rifles may be passing. International shooting has very powerful political overtones, and nations that can't field a winning squad in any given event would just as soon scratch the event and dream up another game at which they might fare better. Many would like to see the 300-meter done away with in particular because it gives the winner more prestige than any other shooting event.

16

High-Power Target Shooting

Napoleon called artillery the "queen of battle." If so, the high-power rifle must be the king of target guns, and the high-power competitor the crown prince among riflemen. If a psychologist were to run a personality profile on various types of target shooters I'm sure he would find that the high-power rifleman possesses a greater degree of flair, boldness, and individuality than other breeds of target shooters. This is because the high-power course of fire demands greater versatility of the competitor and more shot-after-shot decision making.

The High Power National Match course of fire calls for ten shots to be fired from the standing position at 200 yards, ten rapid-fire shots shot from the sitting position at 200 yards, ten rapid-fire shots from the prone position at 300 yards, and finally twenty slow-fire shots at 600 yards from the prone position. Telescopic sights are *never* allowed, iron only.

The rapid-fire stages have a time limit of sixty seconds at 200 yards and seventy seconds at 300 yards. This is known as "bolt gun" time. If the match is for military autoloaders such as the M-1 Garand or the M-14, the time limit is reduced to 50 and 60 seconds for the two ranges. Firing ten aimed shots in sixty seconds is every bit as tough as it sounds. As a matter of fact it's even tougher. Here's why. The rules specify that when the command to commence firing is given the shooters must be *standing up!* Therefore, *within* the time limit the shooter must get down into the prone or sitting position. Also, as if that didn't consume enough time, the shooter has to *re-*

load sometime during the time limit. With what time is left the shooter must aim, squeeze the trigger, recover from the recoil, cycle the bolt, and aim again ten times. A really good bolt-gun shooter can operate the bolt so fast it's difficult for the eye to detect the motion. Some speedy shooters actually finish the string with as much as ten or fifteen seconds to spare! In-

A more or less typical bigbore "over-the-course" bolt-action rifle. The action is a Model 70 Winchester, which virtually dominates bigbore competition, fitted with a stainless-steel Douglas barrel in .308 Winchester caliber. The laminated walnut stock is the popular Roy Dunlap design, which has proved to be especially adaptable for prone, standing, and rapid-fire shooting. Sights are Redfield Internationals.

credible as it may sound to non-target shooters, a good high-power shooter may rip off a couple of shots, take a look through his spotting scope to see if the point of impact is where he wants it to be, and, if necessary, make the mental calculations and sight adjustments needed to get the group in the 10-ring.

A well-rehearsed rapid-fire shooter is a remarkable athlete to watch. No motion is lost or wasted, and despite the almost machine-gun-like burst of fire he puts out, the entire ten shots may be in an area smaller than your hand. During the rapid-fire stages it is not at all uncommon for several competitors to have all ten shots inside the 7-inch 10-ring with several of them in the little 3-inch X-ring.

Very few tournaments allow any sighting shots whatever during the 200- and 300-yard stages, so the shooter has to have an absolute knowledge of his rifle and how to set the sights for each range. Likewise, he had better be good at judging wind velocity and know how much a given velocity of wind from any direction will affect the flight of his bullets.

A few years back when I was firing in a Regional High Power tournament I got hot on the 200-yard-fire stage and socked in a tight group which scored a "possible" 100 with eight X's. The military "SR" target was new then and it looked as if I had a good chance to set a national record if I could hold the second string in the 10-ring. Word that I was on a hot streak spread up and down the firing line, and by the time the targets were cleared for the final string there was a fair-sized crowd of onlookers behind my firing point.

The second string was even better than the first and I ripped off a tight

Here I run off a rapid-fire string with a custom-stocked Model 70 bolt gun in .308 Winchester caliber. The rapid-fire string calls for ten shots in sixty seconds. This means that the shooter must start off from a standing position, get into a proper sitting position, and even reload once during the string.

little group that clustered around the X-ring. But the target crew scored only nine hits! I challenged at once. There was no way I could have missed the target, there were no hits on targets to either side of mine, and at least half of the onlookers, including the scorekeeper, had counted ten shots. Clearly the missing shot was a "double"—had gone through another hole. Nevertheless, my challenge was lost and I was scored a miss. The pit officer could see only nine holes and had no other choice.

The reason I tell this sad tale is the strange irony which occurred exactly a year later. It was the same Regional tournament, and, as had happened a year earlier, my first rapid-fire string was a "possible" with a healthy bunch of X's. On the second string, however, my clip fouled when I was reloading and I lost so much time getting the magazine cleared that I could fire only nine shots. Yet when the targets came up for scoring I was credited with *ten hits!* There were no wide shots from either side that could be determined, but there were definitely ten holes in my target. Again I challenged the score and even showed the range officer the leftover round. But, again I lost the challenge and was told my score would stand as originally given. I tried to challenge again but to no use. Second challenges are not allowed and my score was the highest of the tournament. Finally I accepted the score because I had no choice, but I refused to accept the trophy or the other prizes. I don't guess I'll ever stop trying to figure out where that extra shot came from. . . .

At 600 yards the shooter is allowed two sighters before beginning his record string, but after that every shot counts. He judges the direction and strength of the wind by watching the range flag and by watching the mirage (rising heat waves) through his spotting scope. An experienced shooter can take into account a complete switch in wind direction, make a few mental calculations, make the necessary sight change, and get the very next shot right in the bull's-eye. The 600-yard target has a black aiming circle 24 inches wide (which looks mighty small at 600 yards), but the 10-ring is only 1 foot wide and the X-ring is a mere 6 inches. Even so, it is not too unusual for a shooter to get all twenty shots inside the 10-ring with more than half in the X-ring.

Most tournaments will double the above-described course of fire so that the shooter fires at least twenty shots standing and two ten-shot rapid-fire strings at both 200 and 300 yards. This is a punishing exercise, but this is also why high-power shooters are the cocks of the target-shooting flock. No other form of rifle competition calls for such a varied performance or mastery of so many different shooting skills.

THE SERVICE RIFLE

As its title implies, the high-power target rifle fires a centerfire cartridge. The rifles allowable in high-power competition fall into three distinct classes: Service Rifle, NRA Match Rifle, and Any Rifle. This last one, the "Any" rifle, is a more or less odd duck which is usually used only in long-range matches, so we'll discuss it later in the section "The Long-Range Target Rifle."

The matches for service rifles are restricted to the use of the M-1 Garand

A lineup of past and present service-type bigbore target rifles. At top is the great prewar favorite, the 1903 Springfield with type C (competition) target stock. In the middle is a National Match Garand M-1, which is still widely used in competition. At bottom is the M-14 in National Match version. The M-14 has proved to be a spectacular performer on the target range.

rifle of World War II and Korea fame, which is chambered for the .30/06; the M-14, which fires the 7.62 NATO round (.308 Winchester); and, as of just recently, the M-16, which uses the little 5.56 cartridge known in civilian circles as the .223 Remington.

Matches which are limited to service-type rifles are usually sponsored by the Director of Civilian Marksmanship, a government agency connected

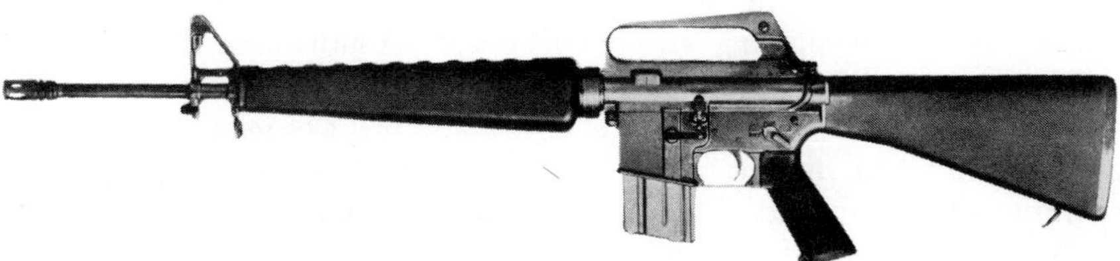

The M-16 is perhaps the service target rifle of the future. However, the small, light 5.56mm round does not do well at the longer ranges in its service form.

with the military, whose function is to promote military-oriented marksmanship. They supply support to such matches in the form of free ammo and will even lend service rifles to civilian gun clubs.

Most serious high-power competitors, however, own a service-type rifle. The Garand is the rifle most commonly owned and used by shooters because they have been sold to civilians by the DCM and commercial outlets. The M-1 most often used in competition is a far cry from the rifle G.I. Joe slogged across Europe with, however. Called the National Match grade, it is specially built for competitive shooting and finely tuned for accuracy. The only identifying external characteristics are somewhat different sights, and the letters NM stamped on the barrel and some other parts. The "innards," though, are a whole new ball game. In addition to being built of specially matched parts, the receiver has most usually been glass- or resin-bedded into the stock, and several other alterations can usually be found here and there.

Since many shooters own a Garand but prefer to use the .308 cartridge, it is permissible under the rules to alter the M-1 so that it fires the .308 rather than the .30/06.

Veterans who shouldered the M-1 during World War II or the Korean disagreement probably remember it as a hard-kicking, heavy, generally disagreeable gadget whose only redeeming quality was its ability to stand up under terrific abuse and keep pouring the lead out. Target shooters tend to view it as a temperamental affair, highstrung as a June bride and capable of all sorts of mischief. When I fired on a military rifle team back in the 1950s I was equipped with four rifles. Two were Winchester Model 70 target rifles (one in .300 H&H caliber for long-range matches and another chambered for the .30/06, which was used in some "over-the-course" events), and two match-grade Garands. The idea of carrying two Garands was to have an extra handy in case one went sour. And go sour they would, throwing wild shots all over the place. The loss of accuracy could result from any number of ills but it happened often enough that my marksmanship unit employed two armorers just to keep the team's M-1s doctored and in some sort of decent shooting order.

My own opinion of the M-1, then and now, was a sort of love-hate relationship. I loved competing with one if it was in tournament trim. I could belly down on the 600-yard line and eat up the bull's-eye to a fare-thee-well, content that the Garand was the highest achievement of man's mechanical genius. But when shots start walking up the target—generally a sign of operating-rod complications—I'd go screaming to our armorer with vile oaths, insisting that the M-1 was a tool of Satan and anyone who would fool with one should have his head examined.

The M-1 was designed as a weapon of war—make no mistake about it. Of course its designer, John Garand, had certain accuracy requirements in mind when it was being developed, but it certainly wasn't designed for the target ranges. Yet the accuracy that can be coaxed out of one is astounding. A couple of years ago my shooting pal Paul Wright of Silver City, New Mexico, fired twenty-two consecutive shots inside a 20-inch circle at 1,000 yards with an M-1! This translates into firing twenty-two shots inside an inch at 100 yards. Of course this is far better performance than most shooters and M-1s are capable of, but it pretty well illustrates the point that the old Garand is very much capable of cutting a wide swath on the target range.

The rifle that made the M-1 obsolete as a military rifle, the M-14, has pretty much done it in as a target rifle as well. Back when the M-14 was introduced (I first saw it fired in 1957), target shooters started wringing their hands and claiming that Service Rifle competition had just taken a giant step backward. After all, they pointed out, the M-14 was a tiny little thing, too light and too short of barrel for good accuracy, and, worst of all, by a simple alteration of the fire selector it became a fully automatic rifle—a machine gun. "Now how," they asked each other, "can a machine gun ever be accurate enough for target shooting?"

What they failed to take into account was that almost exactly the same laments had been chanted when the M-1 replaced the beloved '03 Springfield.

Within a very short while, the time, in fact, required to develop an M-14 in National Match grade, the little newcomer was completely rewriting the record books. It proved not only more accurate than the Garand but also considerably less temperamental. Much of the accuracy has centered around the ammo. Lake City Arsenal, for example, produced some match-grade ball ammo that was considerably more accurate than any government ammo ever made before anywhere. I tried some of the 1962 production run in a

Here I shoot a National Match M-14 rifle in the standing position. The extended magazine makes for a convenient arm rest. This is only one of the reasons the M-14 outclassed earlier service rifles such as the M-1 Garand and the earlier 1903 Springfield.

bench-rest rifle chambered for the .308 and got some 100-yard five-shot groups that measured less than ½ inch between the widest shots. Accuracy such as this can be bested only by the most carefully assembled handloads.

Other factors which favored the winning performance of the M-14 was its mild recoil and the twenty-shot magazine which extends some 3⅝ inches below the stock's belly line. In the standing position the magazine box can be used as a sort of palm rest, and with the elbow rested on the hip the rifle can be more rigidly supported than is possible with the ordinary "offhand" stance.

The only thing wrong with the M-14 as a target rifle is that it can be fired fully automatic. This brings on all sorts of complications and has even caused some hard feelings among civilian shooters. According to federal law it is illegal to own a machine gun, without a lot of licensing and red tape. Thus civilian shooters were forced to use their Garands in Service Rifle matches against military teams equipped with the decidedly more accurate M-14s. The Director of Civilian Marksmanship has helped out by lending M-14s to some civilian rifle clubs, but these are usually not Match grade rifles; and besides, a winning competitor has to virtually "live" with his rifle, and this is all but impossible under most club programs in which, say, twenty shooters must share half that many rifles.

The solution to this dilemma has come about just recently in the form of commercially made M-14s. These rifles are identical to military M-14s—in fact, they are made up mostly of surplus parts—except that the receiver is made so that the rifle cannot be converted to full automatic fire. Aside from that they look and operate exactly like G.I. M-14s and are perfectly legal for Service Rifle competition. An outfit in Devine, Texas, started making commercial M-14s, called the M-14A1, a few years back and was even granted the use of the name "Springfield Armory." This firm is now located in Illinois and makes both standard and match grade rifles. I use one of these in competition and have gotten some fine scores. I once fitted it with a scope so I could bench-test it for accuracy and got several five-shot groups at 100 yards that measured under a minute of angle.

The final and latest service rifle allowable in competition is the newfangled M-16. This is the rifle, you'll recall, that created such a flap in Vietnam when reports filtered back that it would jam in combat. Its cartridge, the 5.56 or .223 Remington, you'll also recall, got a lot of publicity from Vietnam newsmen who said that the bullet tumbled over and over in flight and had a "buzzsaw effect" on the enemy. This of course is absolute nonsense, the drivel of a correspondent who was long on imagination but short on gun savvy. A bullet that tumbles in flight has limited range and no accuracy whatever.

So far the M-16 has met with only mixed success as a target rifle. Despite its Buck Rogers profile it can be accurately aimed and fired, and the nonexistent recoil makes it pleasant to shoot and easy to control in the rapid-fire stages. But the short, 55-grain bullet, despite its nearly 3200 fps muzzle velocity, can't get the job done out at the 600-yard target. It is too susceptible to cross winds, and the rapid loss of velocity beyond 300 yards simply takes the spunk out of the slug.

Back about 1970 or so I helped design a match load for the M-16 which utilized an 80-grain bullet. I understand that considerable experimenting has been done with this load, which requires a fast-twist barrel to stabilize the long projectile, but I can't say what progress has been made. There is also some talk of a special shorter-range course of fire for the M-16, but to my notion the soul of high-power target shooting is the long-range events.

Needless to say, Service Rifle events are fired with the original metallic sights only (except the M-16, which can be fitted with a more suitable metallic sight), and the rifles must be fully operational as originally designed. The sling must be of standard military web or leather design, and the trigger pull cannot be adjusted to fire with less than 4½ pounds pressure.

THE NRA MATCH RIFLE

The NRA Match Rifle, as it's called in the rule book, can be just about any sort of a rifle as long as it is not used with a telescopic sight, palm rest, or hook butt plate and has a 3-pound-minimum trigger pull. Actually, though, the NRA Match rifle is more often called an over-the-course rifle and is almost always a heavy-barreled bolt-action rig with a five-shot magazine and peep sights. It is guaranteed to separate the real shooters from the dilettantes. The course of fire where it is used demands speed and flexibility as well as accuracy, so a really good over-the-course rifle will warm the cockles of a rifle lover's heart be he target shooter or not.

The all-time great over-the-course bigbore target rifle is the Model 70 Winchester. This rifle is built on the same basic action as the standard Model 70 sporting rifle but has a heavy barrel and a marksman-style stock designed for match shooting. This rifle was first introduced way back in the early 1930s and is still a standard Winchester catalog item. It has been mod-

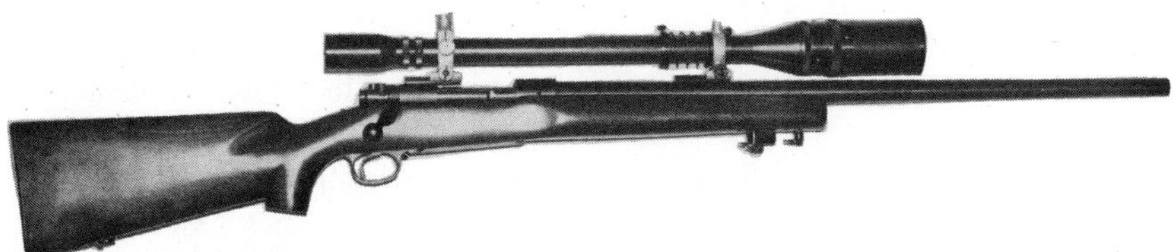

The standard Winçhester Model 70 target rifle is one of the all-time favorites for both over-the-course shooting and 1,000-yard competition. Model 70 target rifles and rifles built on Model 70 actions have won more bigbore competitions than all other makes put together. This rifle is topped off with a Unertl 15× scope for 1,000-yard shooting.

ified extensively since it was introduced, especially back about 1964, and the various changes have kept them very much up to date. The current production, which is available in either .30/06 or .308 Winchester, is, as always, the rifle to beat in any match.

As one might guess, however, the very finest bigbore over-the-course rifles are custom affairs with stainless-steel barrels by the best barrelmakers and custom-made stocks. Almost without exception, though, the winning rifles will be built around a Model 70 action. It might be argued that only the best shooters use the M70 action and therefore it will inevitably be the winning action, but either way you look at it there's no arguing with results.

Reasons given for the overwhelming success of the M70 action for over-the-course target rifles center around the superb trigger mechanism, the speedy lock time, the inherent accuracy of the action, and the fact that the receiver has a fairly large, flat bottom. This last takes some explaining. A high-power cartridge such as the .30/06 has a torqueing or twisting action on a gun when the bullet plunges against the rifling. Some experimenters say this sudden twisting jolt can alter the position of the receiver in the stock recess and create small bedding changes after each shot. The best way to resist these changes is to use a flat-bottomed receiver which offers a solid resistance against radial pressure. The need for this type of bedding structure increases as the power of the cartridge increases, and this helps explain why the Model 70 has been so overwhelmingly successful with the magnum-caliber rifles used for 1,000-yard shooting.

Of course, there are other flat-bottomed actions which do not seem to do at all well for target rifles. An example is the common Mauser '98. Despite the easy availability and low cost of a usable '98 action, very few of them are used for target rifles and even fewer are successful. The long, lumbering lock time pretty much rules out any possibility of fine accuracy in a hand-held rifle, and the midsection weakness of the Mauser allows too much flexing to properly support a heavy barrel.

The same pretty much goes for the popular 1903 Springfield. Though it's a sentimental favorite, especially among retired military shooters, there's no getting around the fact that the poky lock time and flimsy rear section rule it out as a contender. Nostalgia is great—but winning is better.

Rifles which have considerable possibilities as over-the-course contenders are the Remington 40-X and the Swedish-made FFV, formerly known as the Husqvarna. Both of these have a round-bottomed receiver, which scares off many of the top shooters, but on the plus side they have extremely fast lock times and the FFV has the slickest-working bolt you'll ever feel. This feature is of considerable advantage in the rapid-fire stages.

The Ruger Model 77 bolt-action also has considerable possibilities as the basis of an over-the-course rig, but it would first be necessary to devise a means of clip-feeding the magazine. This would be little problem for a clever gunsmith. The action which has the greatest potential of unseating the Model 70, though, is the Shilen. It has super-fast lock time, is as slick as a fudgecicle in July, and has the biggest, widest, flattest receiver bottom in the Kingdom. Until 1975 it was made only as a single-shot and gained a terrific reputation as a winner in bench-rest competition. Just before I wrote this section, however, Ed Shilen, the designer and manufacturer, showed me a magazine version. The next step would be to mill a clip slot into the top of the action bridge and it would be fully operational as the heart of a super-performance bigbore target rifle.

How good do over-the-course rifles have to be? A few years ago, quite honestly, they didn't have to be so hot at all. The targets were big, and a rifle that could group in a piepan could get by. When the bigbore targets were revamped, however, accuracy became a vital factor. The 10-ring of the target used for the 200- and 300-yard events is 7 inches across. The X-ring is a mere 3 inches across. The 10-ring of the 600-yard target is a foot across, and the X-ring is only 6 inches. This means that a rifle has to be at least capable of minute-of-angle accuracy. But there's more to it than this. A rifle that will just barely get five shots inside a 1-inch circle at 100 yards will never get five shots inside 6 inches at 600 yards. It just doesn't work out that way.

A rifle capable of 6-inch groups at 600 yards will most usually group well under ½ inch at 100 yards. To add another complication, consider that the bigbore match rifle must group *twenty* consecutive shots (plus two sighters) at the 600-yard stage. Needless to say, most shooters are not able to shoot this well, especially with iron sights, regardless of their rifle's capabilities.

But personal marksmanship notwithstanding, if the rifle won't shoot MOA at 600 yards the shooter is fighting a losing battle from the start.

The best over-the-course rifle in my target battery is the .308 illustrated a few pages back. It is built on a Winchester M70 action with a Dunlap-designed laminated walnut stock and 26-inch Douglas stainless-steel barrel with 10-inch twist. Firing from a bench rest with a target scope, this rifle will, and has, fired five-shot groups at 100 yards that measure less than ¼ inch between the widest shots.

Aside from sheer accuracy a top-grade bigbore target rifle must be absolutely stable. Any tendency toward temperamentalness or odd quirkiness, no matter how accurate the rifle may otherwise be, is absolutely verboten. Trying to shoot a super-accurate but contrary rifle is like living with a beautiful sex-goddess who has an I.Q. of 49; the romance is fascinating at first but it quickly becomes a drag. The above-mentioned M70 is exactly what the over-the-course rifle should be: every shot out of the barrel goes exactly where it should. It doesn't matter if the barrel is cold, hot, clean, or fouled. There is no "walking" or angular stringing as the rifle heats up, and the last round of a twenty-shot string goes exactly where the first shot goes. To test rifles for this capability I fire twenty-shot groups from a bench rest. A rifle that will keep all twenty shots under an inch is worth taking to the matches, but a really great rifle will drill them all in close to ½ inch.

Keep in mind that the bigbore competitor doesn't get any sighting shots over much of the course. He needs a rifle which will faithfully put the first shot, and every shot thereafter, right where it is supposed to go. The degree of difficulty, for both rifle and rifleman, can probably best be expressed by comparing the 600-yard bigbore event to the 100-yard smallbore event; the X-rings are 6 inches and 1 inch respectively, thus they represent a perfectly scaled angle of departure (one inch at 100 yards equaling 6 inches at 600 yards). Likewise, the 10-rings are 12 inches and 2 inches respectively. The black aiming circle of the 600-yard target is only 2 feet across, however, while the 100-yard bull, or black aiming circle, is 8 inches across. Thus the bull, as it appears to the bigbore shooter, is only half as big as it appears to the smallbore rifleman. For both, the course of fire calls for twenty shots for record within a twenty-minute time limit, plus two extra minutes for two sighters at 600 yards. The smallbore competitor can fire as many sighters as he wishes any time he wishes. If the wind shifts while he is firing his record string he can go back to the sighter and see what sight changes are required. After he has satisfied himself that he has made the correct adjustments he then goes back to the record bull. Obviously, he never learns, nor has to learn, to become a really expert wind doper. His "decisions" need not be final because he can always fire some test shots on the sighting bull.

The bigbore shooter, on the other hand, gets only two sighting shots at the beginning of his string and after that he's strictly on his own. No matter how much the wind shifts, every shot is for record. He must evaluate the changes in wind direction and velocity, calculate how much the flight of the bullet will be affected, and make a positive sight change, knowing that right or wrong his next shot will be for score. This explains why successful bigbore shooters must have a certain extra flair and boldness.

Also, a wide range of versatility is demanded of the bigbore target shooter and his rifle. Slow, contemplative shooting from the prone position at 600 yards is one thing, but ripping off ten shots in the space of one minute (50 seconds in Service Rifle events) from the sitting position at 200 yards is quite another. Likewise, a fast-handling magazine-fed rifle which will allow such high-speed performance doesn't sound like a rig that could—or even should—be expected to drill a string of shots into the X-ring at 600 yards. But they do.

The rifle must incorporate a stock design which allows a stable and comfortable position for offhand shooting (standing), fast handling characteristics for both prone and sitting rapid fire, and finally, precision handling and aiming for prone slow fire. These demands call for a certain compromise of design features, of course, but the better designs are surprisingly adaptive to all positions. One of the best designs ever worked out is the popular Roy Dunlap stock. Dunlap no longer makes either rifles or stocks, but his design is still available from other gunsmiths. Also, just for the record, the basic marksman-style stocks on Winchester M70 target rifles and the Remington 40-X are very good for over-the-course shooting and hard to improve on. In fact, some far-out custom stocks I've seen aren't nearly as good.

Next to a hunting rifle, the bigbore target rifle gets more abuse from the elements than any other. The firing points are never covered, and, true to military tradition, rain is seldom considered just cause for calling a match. So rifles need to be well waterproofed in and out. The epoxy or polyurethane finishes do the best job as far as keeping water out of the wood and also keep the stock from getting darkened and weakened by oil or sweat. Of course, resin-type bedding materials with either fiberglass or metal-particle fillers are used on virtually every bigbore target rifle you're likely to find. This contributes greatly to accuracy and stability and also serves to waterproof the inside stock surfaces and help avoid warping if water seeps in.

Several years ago I used a nicely accurate rifle that was bedded in the traditional way with metal closely fitted in the wood. As will inevitably happen, it rained on the day of an important regional tournament and the rifle was exposed to several hours of on-and-off drizzle. Toward the end of the day, when we had moved back to the 600-yard line, that rifle began doing some strange things. The two sighting shots never hit the target, and neither did the next five shots for record. I just gave up and left the line, vowing never to use another unsealed rifle in competition—a promise to myself which I've faithfully kept over the years.

If you inspect the barrel bedding of a properly made bigbore target rifle you'll notice that there is a gap of about ⅛ inch between the barrel and the forearm. This is "free floating" with a vengeance, but serves purposes other than simply allowing the barrel to "float" or vibrate freely. The wide gap allows air to circulate around the barrel and cool it more efficiently during the rapid-fire events. It also allows rainwater to drain out before it has a chance to soak into the wood. Don't laugh, it really works.

Sights for the bigbore target rifle also require more than just casual consideration. Of course it's obvious that the micrometer adjustments need to be as precise as possible, what with all the adjustments for the different ranges that's required, not to mention the unending corrections for wind changes. But a sight that's good for, say, a smallbore target rifle might not pass muster on a high-power rig. Recoil causes the complications.

A few years back a shooting pal of mine paid a cool hundred smackers for a handmade, ultra-precise rear sight for his bigbore target rifle. Similar sights had made a big hit with smallbore shooters, and it looked like a good thing for an over-the-course rifle. But as it turned out it was too much of a good thing—literally. The sight got its precision by means of comparatively massive component parts. The total weight was about three times that of rear sights commonly used. After only about three hundred rounds the beautiful sight snapped off the receiver and fell into the dust. The static inertia of the heavy sight resisted the recoil movement and the two base screws sheared off. He finally got the sight to stay put but only after silver-soldering the base to the receiver and pinning it with hardened-steel pegs. The Redfield Olympic and International receiver sights are light enough to "ride" with the recoil and still offer ample precision of adjustment. Even so, it's a good idea to check the fit of the moving parts every so often, because the constant battering effect of recoil will make them sloppy and unreliable in time.

The front sight is like the rear, only more so, in regards to the battering of recoil. The most successful front sight is the Redfield International Big Bore

This is the popular Redfield International Match bigbore front sight. The sight is made of lightweight alloy so that it will effectively "ride" the recoil of a bigbore rifle. If the sight were made of heavier material the static inertia would, in time, tear the mounting loose.

unit. It's made of a lightweight alloy which "rides" the recoil and stays put. The various inert elements which come with the sight include different post and globe apertures which will suit anyone's taste. For the more sophisticated shooters (and those who think they are), a West Coast firm markets

This front sight is equipped with a spirit level so the shooter can make sure that the rifle is held uniformly. Shot-to-shot variations in the vertical angle of the rifle can result in a wide displacement of the point of impact at long range.

a front sight similar to the Redfield model which has a built-in spirit level. The idea of this is to avoid canting the rifle and thus ensure less aiming error over the longer ranges.

Back when I began high-power target shooting the choice in calibers was simple; the rules of the day allowed only the .30/06, which at that time was the standard military service round. When the .308, or 7.62 NATO as it is known in Army circles, became the standard service cartridge the rules were changed to allow either the .30/06 or the .308 Winchester. More recently, when the little 5.56mm became an official military cartridge, the rule makers threw in the towel and said, "Oh, what the hell, let's use any caliber we want." Service Rifle matches still must be fired with service calibers, but the bolt gun can be chambered for whatever turns you on.

Actually, the new rules have had very little effect on the cartridges used in bigbore competition. During the years when only .30-caliber rifles were used there was a great deal of development work done by the various bullet makers toward turning out super-accurate .30-caliber competition bullets. As a result there are any number of fine .30-caliber target bullets by different manufacturers, but very few in other calibers. Thus high-power target shooters are pretty much forced to use a .30-caliber rifle whether they want to or not. This not only goes for handloaded ammo but for factory loads as well. For many years the only factory-loaded match ammo, not to mention G.I. ammo, has been in .30 caliber.

Not that there's anything wrong with .30 caliber anyway. The .30/06 is a fine performer, and the .308 is one of the most inherently accurate cartridges ever developed. I personally use a pair of perfectly matched bigbore rifles built up on Winchester Model 70 actions with 26-inch Douglas stainless-steel barrels and Dunlap-type stocks. The main idea of a matched pair of target rifles is to have a spare in case something breaks or gets out of order. (This has never happened since I started carrying an extra.) The only difference is that one is chambered for the .308 Winchester round and the other is a .30/06.

The .308 is slightly more accurate, has somewhat less recoil, and is speedier in the rapid-fire stages because of the shorter bolt travel. Therefore it is my "Number One" rifle. However, if the wind is blowing particularly hard on the day of the match I'll use the .30/06. The higher velocity of the '06 results in significantly less wind drift when the wind velocity is above 10 miles an hour, especially at the 600-yard range.

Though I confess to a fondness for "working up" loads and experimenting with different combinations of bullets, propellants, primers, etc., I remain rigidly inflexible with my bigbore loads. Continuous experiment with match ammo and loads will invariably result in a mix-up at the worst possible time. I can think of a dozen or more instances where I've encountered a woefully disappointed shooter whose only excuse for a poor score was "I took the wrong ammo to the firing line," or "I picked up the wrong batch of loads."

My standard short-range load for the .308 is 40 grains of No. 4895 powder behind a 168-grain bullet. For long range I use 48 grains of No. 4350 behind a 185-grain Lapua. For the .30/06 I stick with 48 grains of No. 4320 behind the 180-grain Sierra Matchking. Any time I notice a falling off of accuracy I don't tinker with the loads trying to find a cure for an ailing rifle. This just leads to more complications. Instead, I find out exactly what's wrong with the rifle and get it fixed or replaced. A competitive shooter can never do his best if his concentration is befouled by worry over a sick rifle.

Also, there's no room for such little handloading niceties as neck sizing and "optimum" bullet seating depths. I full-length-resize the brass at every loading because I want slick, effortless feeding during the rapid-fire stages. Also, the magazine length of most target rifles, especially service rifles, dictate bullet seating depth. The cardinal rule is *uniformity,* and the competitive shooter who can accomplish this with his handloads doesn't need to worry about anything else.

The closest thing to kicking the .30-caliber habit in bigbore target shooting has come in the form of a pair of 7mm (.284-inch) match-grade bullets by Hornady and Sierra. In fact, these two are catching on so well that there will probably soon be other 7mm target slugs by other manufacturers. The advantage, if it can be called that, of the 7mm over the .30 caliber is that bullets of the same weight range have a higher sectional density and ballistic coefficient. This in turn results in less loss of velocity and more resistance to side drift caused by crosswinds. Thus you get the advantages of a long, heavy bullet combined with the milder recoil of a lighter bullet. (Of course there's a practical limit to this, and it appears that 6.5mm or perhaps .25 caliber is about as small a diameter bullet as can be used "over the course" without running into other problems.)

Surprisingly, perhaps, the wind-bucking advantages of the new 7mm bullets is not so important at the longer ranges as at the shorter. At 600 and 1,000 yards the shooter has time to consider the shot-to-shot changes of wind conditions and make the necessary sight changes. During the rapid-fire stages at 200 and 300 yards, however, a gusting wind can be a difficult problem. The shooter cannot stop before each shot and consider any changes in wind value, and on gusty days the rapid-fire strings are just that—horizontal strings of bullet holes tattooed across the bull's-eye. Matches are often won or lost because of a difference in the X-count, and when you're dealing with a tiny 3-inch X-ring it isn't difficult to lose X's to the wind. The bullet with the best wind resistance will automatically take "windage spread" out of groups and save valuable X's. It's as simple as that.

Model 70 with Atkinson stainless-steel barrel in .280 Improved Remington caliber. The rear sight is made by John Wilkes of England.

Cartridgewise, the best choices in a 7mm over-the-course rifle are the .280 Remington, the 7×57 Mauser, and the 7mm/308. This last one is simply the .308 Winchester necked down to 7mm. Some versions of this wildcat round retain the existing shoulder angle and others have the shoulder set back somewhat in order to have a longer neck. The 7mm/.308 would be the best choice for a short throw action, and the .280 Remington is the best bet for a full-length action. Actually, the .280 Remington is so little known, especially among target shooters, that some bigbore shooters are having rifles barreled and chambered for what they call the 7mm/06 without realizing that this is one and the same thing as the .280. Call it what you will, .280 or 7mm/06, it makes a superb bigbore target cartridge. The 7×57 doesn't have quite as much steam but still must be used in a full length action so is at a disadvantage to both the 7mm/308 and the .280. The near-defunct .284 Winchester combines short case length with good velocity, but the fatheaded, rebated rim case would cause feeding problems in many rifles. This pretty much eliminates it from serious consideration.

A 1,000-yard range. The targets, which are 6 feet high and 6 feet across, can just barely be seen in the background. Each of the shooters shown here is accompanied by a scorekeeper.

THE LONG-RANGE TARGET RIFLE

The American long-range target rifle has a reputation for excellence which dates back to 1879. That's the year a cocky branch of Irish Crackshots, who had been beating Europe's best on a regular basis, challenged "The Riflemen of America" (not knowing that the National Rifle Association had been formed just two years before) to a rifle tournament for the championship of the English-speaking world.

Actually, the Irish were already of the notion that they were the champions of the world, but they felt they ought to beat some Americans before they started bragging about the title. It looked like a pretty safe challenge, because as far as they knew there wasn't even a recognized U.S. shooting

This gives an idea of the size of a 1,000-yard target. The 5-ring or bull is 36 inches across, the V-ring is 20 inches. At over half a mile it looks like a flyspeck. The rifle is a Model 70 in .300 Winchester Magnum with Redfield 3200 20× scope in place. A little further on you'll see me using it with iron sights.

team, and also there weren't any rifles in the U.S. capable of target performance at the ranges the challenge called for: 800, 900, and 1,000 yards.

But cockiness was by no means the exclusive domain of the Irish in those days, and a bunch of American shooters, calling themselves the "Amateur Rifle Association," accepted the challenge without batting an eye and agreed on the date of September 26, 1874, for the big shootoff for the "World Championship." That gave the Americans about a year to design and manufacture long-range target rifles and learn how to use them.

In that day and age, breechloading rifles had become fairly common, but muzzleloaders were still considered to be considerably more accurate. The Irish team, for example, was equipped with superb muzzleloaders built by none other than the great Dublin gunsmith John Rigby. Nonetheless, the Remington and Sharps companies, which had taken on the task of making rifles for the American team, elected to build breechloaders. This decision brought on considerable opposition among some American shooters, who voiced the opinion that using breechloaders was tantamount to giving the match to the Irish and therefore nothing short of an act of treason.

When the day of the great event arrived, thousands upon thousands of spectators made their way to the scene of the contest. The New York *Herald* had run a series of front-page features on the coming match and whipped emotions to a frenzy. The crowd was prepared to worship the American team if they won or hang them if they lost.

The American team won the 800-yard event by a score of 326 to 317, but at 900 yards the Irish won 312 to 310. This narrow margin would have been wider if one of the Irish shooters had not fired on the wrong target and been scored a miss. (His shot was a bull's-eye, by the way.) The Irish won again at 1,000 yards, 302 to 298, but the final score, thanks to one hapless Irishman, was Americans 934, Irish 931.

Thus began a tradition of long-range marksmanship which continues today. The scene of the great match was Creedmoor Rifle Range, and those magnificent breechloaders came to be known as "Creedmoor" rifles, a term which is still very much alive today. (Ask a target shooter if he has ever been "Creedmoored.")

The days of the great Creedmoor matches are gone, and the closest thing that is still fired in modern competition is the Palma Match. Just as was the case back in the Creedmoor days, a select team of long-range marksmen (all chosen on the basis of their performance at the National Matches) compete against the teams of other English-speaking countries. The course calls for two sighters and fifteen shots for record each at 800, 900, and 1,000 yards. The host country provides the rifles and ammo for all shooters, and in recent years the Palma has been fired with Winchester Model 70's, S.M.L.E. Enfields, M-14's, Musgraves, etc.

Modern long-range target shooting is fired from the prone position only (how else?), and the famed Wimbledon Trophy Match fired each year at the National Championships Matches sets the style for virtually all 1,000-yard competition. A typical course of fire is twenty shots for record with two or three sighting shots allowed and a total time limit of thirty minutes.

Here I am at the 1,000-yard Black Canyon Range near Phoenix, Arizona. Each shot is carefully plotted and recorded, along with the prevailing wind and light conditions for future reference. This rifle is my Winchester Model 70 with Atkinson stainless-steel barrel in .280 Remington Improved, also illustrated a few pages back. The scope is a Redfield model 3200 and the laminated walnut stock was made by me.

The target has a 36-inch black aiming bull, but at 1,000 yards it looks like a flyspeck (like aiming at a 3½-inch black spot at 100 yards). It has a high value of 5. The tie-breaking V-ring is 20 inches in diameter and the 4-ring is a nice, fat 54 inches across.

There is not much variation in 1,000-yard events except in the classes of rifles. The standard over-the-course bolt-action rifle is often used, and most 1,000-yard tournaments have a special classification for service rifles—the M-1 Garand or M-14. The most interesting events, however, are the "Any Rifle" events. There are practically no restrictions on the "Any" rifle and like the smallbore prone gun, it has become a highly specialized piece of equipment developed for the sole purpose of getting a bullet inside a 20-inch circle at nearly three-fifths of a mile.

Caliberwise, you can use just about anything you like, but practical considerations keep one's choice within certain limits. The most popular cartridges in the Any Rifle classification are the .300 Winchester Magnum,

Here I fire at 1,000 yards with an iron-sighted rifle. This rifle is my Winchester Model 70 with Douglas stainless-steel barrel in .300 Winchester Magnum caliber. The laminated stock was made by me, and the sights are Redfield International. The "awning," a black elastic tape spanning the barrel, is used to keep heat waves rising from the barrel from interfering with the sight picture. Over a 22-shot string these magnum barrels can get mighty hot, and the heat waves, or mirage, become a serious sighting problem.

7mm Remington Magnum, and .30/338 (a .338 Winchester Magnum necked down to .30 caliber). This last round enjoyed considerable popularity a few years ago, before the introduction of the .300 Winchester Magnum, but now it has nothing to offer which makes it worth bothering with. The .300 H&H Magnum once enjoyed a long run of popularity, and there was a time when the Winchester M70 bull gun in .300 H&H chambering was almost the standard Wimbledon rig. At this writing, though, the Model 70 target rifle is not offered in a magnum caliber. The only over-the-course target rifle available in belted magnum chambering is Remington's Model 40-XC. It can be had in, among other calibers, .300 Winchester Magnum, 7mm Remington Magnum, and even .30/388.

The idea of using a big magnum caliber for a long-range rifle is simply to get the bullet downrange in a hurry. The trajectory is flatter, of course, but more important is the fact that the faster bullet is less affected by wind. Long, streamlined, relatively heavy bullets are also less affected by wind, but it takes a big caseful of powder to pump them up to a substantial velocity level. One of the most popular 1,000-yard target bullets is Sierra's 190-grain Matchking. In .300 Winchester Magnum chambering this bullet can be loaded up to a muzzle velocity of about 2900 feet per second. Even at this velocity level the bullet will be carried off-course 6 feet by a 10-mile-per-hour crosswind.

For comparison, the maximum velocity you can get out of a .30/06 with the 190-grain Matchking is about 2700 fps. At this starting-out velocity a 10-mile-per-hour crosswind can carry the bullet a little over 81 inches off course. The importance of this 10-inch difference in wind effect is more than apparent when you consider that the width of the 5-ring (from the V-ring to the 4-ring) is only 8 inches!

Of course there are limits to how much of a good thing a shooter can stand. A few rifles have been chambered for behemoth rounds such as the .387 Weatherby necked down to .30 caliber. The velocity really gets impressive—but so does the recoil. When firing from the prone position a shooter gets to savor every ounce of kick a rifle has to offer, and over a twenty-two-shot course one can get downright punchdrunk. Even shooters who claim they are not sensitive to recoil fail to take into consideration that recoil has a fatiguing effect and fatigue is one of the most difficult problems the long-range shooter has to combat. I figure I can handle about as much recoil as anyone, but when I come off the 1,000-yard firing line I feel as if I've been pulling a plow all day.

Recoil can be absorbed by a heavy rifle, but there is, again, a practical limit on how heavy a rifle you can support in the prone position for up to half an hour. My heaviest rig, with scope, weighs 16 pounds, and this is just about the outside limit for most shooters. Actually, about 13 pounds maximum is better for the average competitor.

The most popular action for the 1,000-yard rifle is the Winchester Model 70 by a wide margin, with the Remington Model 700 and Model 40-X fol-

Who says the big magnums won't shoot? This five-shot group fired at 100 yards measures only .356 inch and was fired with my Model 70 in .300 Winchester Magnum.

lowing. You'll occasionally see Mauser, Springfield, or Pattern 14 and 17 Enfield actions used but this is usually a lost cause from the beginning. Certain sleeved actions, especially a sleeved 40-X receiver, perform well, but specialized actions such as the flat-bottomed, single-shot Shilen DGA model will probably prove to be the most accurate performers of all.

Choosing a barrel for a 1,000-yard rifle presents the same problems as selecting any other target barrel. Accuracy comes first, last, and always. This means a heavy stainless-steel tube by one of the top makers and a top-drawer fitting job by someone who knows what he's doing. A winning rifle should be capable of grouping twenty consecutive shots inside 15 inches at 1,000 yards. This interpolates to something like keeping twenty shots inside 1 inch at 100 yards. The most accurate long-range rifle I've ever owned, or used, is a

.300 Winchester Magnum with Douglas barrel on a Model 70 action. Five-shot test groups fired from a bench rest at 100 yards have measured as small as .300 inch between the center of the two widest shots. And, for the record, I consider this none too accurate for a long-range tournament rifle.

Barrels, unfortunately, are always a heartbreaking proposition on the magnum-class target rifle. It seems that no sooner do you fit a barrel, get some sight data and some practice, and fire a few matches than suddenly the bore is washed out. The big powder charges generate a hellish heat, and high temperature is sure death on gun barrels. I once kept a careful record of the rounds I put through a .300 Magnum with stainless-steel barrel. The sum total of its accuracy life was a brief *613 rounds!* Some rifles, for some reason, seem to keep going for upwards of 2,000 rounds, but 1,000 seems to be about the average.

Stocks on rifles used only for long-range prone shooting are quite similar to those on the smallbore prone target rifle. After all, the position is the same and so is the general approach to dealing with the course of fire. The prone stock is designed for maximum shooter comfort over a fairly long time span. The standard Winchester Model 70 target or "Marksman" stock is fairly good for the job, and so is the standard Remington 40-X. Much better,

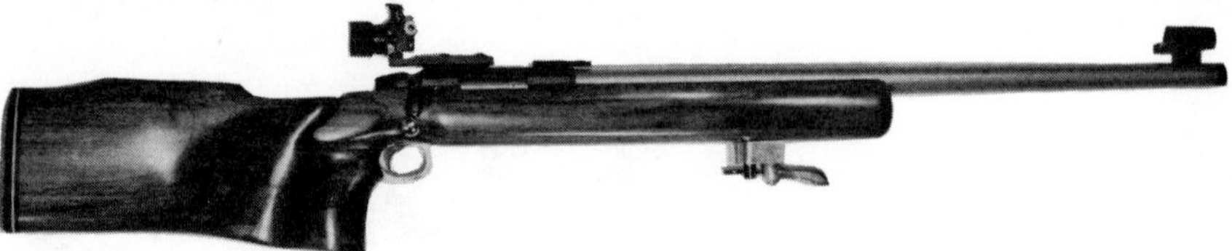

This is one of the most accurate 1,000-yard prone rifles in the world. It is built up on a Shilen single-shot bench-rest action with a Shilen stainless-steel 28-inch barrel in .300 Winchester Magnum caliber. The stocking is in laminated walnut by target stock specialist Jim Cloward of Seattle, Washington. The rear sight is by Anschutz and trigger by Canjar. This rifle has grouped five shots as small as .3 inch from a bench rest at 100 yards, and ten shots under 10 inches at 1,000 yards.

however, are stocks with higher combs, comfortable cheek pieces, and custom-fitted, palm-filling pistol grips which position the shooting hand so the trigger finger will feel just right. Probably the best 1,000-yard target stocks are those made by Jim Cloward of Seattle or P. J. Wright of Los Angeles.

Since the typical 1,000-yard tournament includes matches for both scope and iron sights, the rifle must be fitted with a removable set of each. As with any other type of target shooting the competitor wants iron sights with absolutely reliable adjustments. After the specified sighting shots are fired, no further sighters are allowed and the competitor has to really get serious about his adjustments. Every time he cranks a few clicks into the adjustment knobs he wants to be sure that the sight responds. What all this boils down to is that the iron sights that are best for any other target shooting are also probably the best for long-range competition. Like most bigbore shooters, I use the Redfield International Match receiver sight and front sight, but as soon as something better comes along I'll grab for it. There's always room for improvement, especially in the area of target sights. Competitive shooters have a deep-seated and, frankly, well-founded mistrust of nearly all sighting equipment.

From the standpoint of scope sights, however, the mid-70's have produced two excellent optical instruments for long-distance aiming. These are the new Redfield 6400 scope and the Leupold M-8 24× AO. Target shooting at 1,000 yards calls, of course, for a target-type scope, but heretofore there have been certain complications. First of all, the high-magnification target scope with its short eye relief and flimsy mounting system was never designed for a heavy-caliber, hard-kicking rifle. Back in the late 1950s when I was a member of a military rifle team, I fired a team match at Camp Perry with a .300 H&H Magnum fitted with a 15× target scope that had been mounted too far to the rear. My short-necked team mates had no problem, but I'm a natural-born stack crawler and when I flopped into position the sharp edge of the ocular ring was less than an inch from the bridge of my nose. Ordinarily I would have repositioned the scope, but sliding the scope forward in its mount could have shifted the point of impact. It was a team match, with no sighting shots allowed, so I had to leave it the way it was. Every time I pulled the trigger on the rig I got a whack across the nose that felt like Jack the Ripper was going after me with a meat cleaver. By the time my twenty rounds were used up I was in a pool of blood and there were tears in my eyes as big as pumpkins. I handed the rifle over to the coach, told him that as far as I was concerned he could just count me out the next time we had to use that rifle, and headed for the first-aid station.

From the standpoint of accuracy mechanics there has always been something disagreeable about mounting a target scope on a rifle barrel. It's even worse to mount the scope partly on the barrel and partly on the receiver. Worst of all is when the rifle happens to be chambered for a big centerfire cartridge that gets the barrel too hot to touch. Thermal expansion can cause a barrel to do rather strange things, and it doesn't help a bit to have a scope attached that wants to bend one way while the barrel wants to bend another way.

The two new scopes by Leupold and Redfield solve all of these problems in one grand swoop. They are short and thus mount entirely on the receiver. The barrel is then free to do its own thing. The eye relief is about 3½ inches and thus offers plenty of protection against excessive bloodshed. They both have convenient target-type adjustments, come in a high magnification range, and, as an extra bonus, offer a field of view considerably wider than some traditional target scopes of the same magnification. This makes it easier for the shooter to study the mirage and detect any changes in wind direction or velocity. I predict that within a few years these receiver-mounted scopes will be used on most long-range target rifles.

All of the above data has dealt almost entirely with the so-called "Any Rifle" classification of competitive arms. While these guns are quite spectacular in caliber, proportion, and purpose they are by no means the only type of rifle that can be used at long range. Many bigbore shooters fire the 1,000-yard events with the same rifle they use for over-the-course high-power tournaments. In fact, some tournament programs specify that the 1,000-yard match is part of the course and will be fired with the same rifle used in the other matches. Likewise, there are events and classifications which specify that only service rifles, an M-14 or an M-1 Garand, are to be used. Sometimes the scores fired with the little .308 Winchester cartridge in a good M-14 make the magnum shooters stand back and take notice. During the 1974 National Matches at Camp Perry, to give a sterling example, the Wimbledon Cup match was won by a perfect score of 100 with 19 X's. The winning rifle was a sleeved, custom-barreled, custom-stocked Remington 40-X action rifle in .300 Winchester Magnum caliber. The Service Rifle division of that same match was won with a perfect score of 100 with 14 X's! Not much difference, is there? On different occasions I've seen as many as 19 V's fired with the M-14.

In order to use a standard over-the-course bolt gun for 1,000-yard work all you need to add is a set of bases for a target scope. This is exactly why nearly all bolt guns you see are fitted with bases. If you feel pretty salty you can always fire the "any sight" or scope event with irons. In fact, surprising as it may seem, iron-sight scores usually run neck-and-neck with those fired with scopes. My iron-sight scores tend to run about 2 V's less, on the average, than my scope-sight tally. Again using the 1974 National Matches as an example, the winning score of the Leech Match, a 1,000-yard event for iron sights only, was a perfect 100 with 20 straight V's—better by a V than the winning scope score!

The modern long-range target rifle is about twice as good as they were in the decade of the 1950s. The big difference is due to tremendous improvements in barrels and bullets. Also, shooters are much better than ever, and they are demanding better equipment. I think long-range rifles will get even better in coming years. Already high-power shooters are discussing a more difficult 1,000-yard target—one that will have a 10-inch X-ring and a 20-inch 10-ring.

17

The Silhouette Game

Unfortunately, there has always persisted a fundamental difference in shooting philosophies between average hunters or sport shooters and the serious target shooter. There are several reasons for this. One is the fact that the maze of equipment deemed necessary for target shooting tends to scare off a lot of beginners. Also, there's no denying the snob attitude of some target shooters. This makes communication between the groups difficult if not downright impossible. There is even a "reverse" snob effect among hunters and plinkers toward target shooters. I can't help comparing this situation with the attitude of those who like classical music and those who don't. Those who don't care for fine music simply haven't bothered to learn anything about it. On the other hand, classical music lovers never seem interested in spreading the good word.

At last, though, thanks to a relatively new shooting game, the hunter, plinker, and serious paper puncher may have found some common ground on which to unite. The name of the game is Metallic Silhouette or, in Mexico, the country where the game originates, *Siluetas Metálicas*.

Basically, the silhouette match is a course of fire for hunters. The targets are full-size, or nearly full-size, metal profiles of chickens, javelinas, turkeys, and sheep. There is no bull's-eye; a hit is a hit and a miss is a miss. The targets are set on posts, or pedestals, and if the bullet knocks it over, the shooter gets one point. If the profile doesn't fall over—even if hit—he gets nothing. A simpler scoring system is hard to imagine.

What's more, the rules of the game all but eliminate fancy target rifles. Palm rests, hook butt plates, thumbhole stocks, padded shooting jackets, and slings are forbidden. The rifle can weigh no more than 4 kilograms (8 pounds, 13 ounces) plus the weight of the sights, and all shooting is done

A range officer places silhouettes of the turkey, or guajolote, *on the pedestal. The* guajolote *are fired at from a range of 385 meters and are considered by most shooters the toughest to hit.*

from the offhand position. The idea of the rules is to eliminate target-type rifles and thus leave the game wide open for standard hunting rifles. It's a good rule.

The ranges are 200 meters for the chicken, 300 meters for the javelina, or wild pig, 385 meters for the turkey, and 500 meters for the bighorn sheep. The profiles are set up in groups of five at each range and the competitor has only two and a half minutes to fire at the five targets. One shot is fired at each profile, left to right, and if, say, the third shot knocks over the number 2 profile it's a miss. Once the match is under way no sighters are allowed and sight changes from one range to another are done "cold turkey"; *every shot counts.* But after all, a hunter shooting at a live turkey or sheep wouldn't get a practice shot; and that's the spirit of silhouette shooting.

The game got started years ago in Mexico, where the shooting was done

The javelina profile, fired at from 300 meters.

at live targets. A local impresario would tie a goat, chicken, or some other edible target out at some near-impossible range and sell shots at it. Whoever hit the target claimed it and carried it home for table fare. Needless to say, the shoot manager had to make sure that the range was so difficult that quite a few chances would be sold before a lucky bullet found its way to the hapless prize. The rules varied in different locales, but in most places a visible spot of blood on the target was considered a winning hit. Shooters sometimes took advantage of this rule by aiming at the general area in front of the target, hoping that the resulting spray of gravel and bullet fragments would at least draw some blood. After such a "spray" shot the animal would be carefully searched hair and feather for a tiny speck of blood. Even in a modern silhouette match, by the way, it is perfectly legal to bounce a bullet off the ground, but there is little chance of rock fragments toppling the heavy profile.

The animal-shooting game became so popular among the Mexicans that they began to lay some universal ground rules as to distances and time limits, and metallic profiles replaced living targets. Since it was definitely a game for hunting rifles and cartridges, the metallic profiles were made heavy enough so that it would take a heavy blow to knock them over—just as it takes a pretty powerful rifle to down a bighorn sheep at 500 meters (550 yards). The present rules call for a minimal caliber of 6mm, but it actually takes more steam to knock over the heavy sheep profile than most 6mm (.243 bore size) bullets have to offer.

The rules also allow a coach or spotter to watch through binoculars or telescope and tell the shooter where his shots are hitting. This is a reasonable and valid rule, because a hunter is also apt to have a guide or hunting companion helping him out when he shoots at live game.

The game became so popular in Mexico that regional shooting leagues were formed which operated much like our American bowling leagues; teams and individuals competed against each other on a regular basis with the winners advancing to state and national tournaments. It was only natural that some American shooters would travel south of the border to see what the Mexicans were having so much fun at, and before long there were silhouette ranges on the U.S. side of the border. Once word of the new game began to spread it became the fastest-growing target sport in America.

Probably the secret of its success is its difficulty. No one likes to be exposed as a poor shot, but when the target is damn near impossible and everyone is missing there isn't so much personal embarrassment. Also, it's a great spectator sport. There's no such thing as waiting for a target to be scored. If the target falls over everyone knows it at once. There's a resounding "clank" of bullet striking steel plate and the target topples from the perch amid great cheering or jeering from the onlookers. Sometimes a hit target teeters for a breathless moment before falling, and occasionally it remains on the post for a scored miss. All this adds to the excitement and spirit of the game and certainly adds spectator appeal. Even so it is difficult for the spectator to remain just an onlooker for long. Pretty soon he gets the idea that he (or she) can hit—or miss—as well as the guys and gals he's watching, and from that moment on he's a gung-ho silhouette marksman.

In silhouette shooting a spotter is allowed to tell the shooter where his shots are hitting. Here a spotter, whose shirt proclaims that he is a member of the Guaymas, Mexico, silhouette shooting team, tells the shooter what is happening to his shots. This is the Three Points range near Tucson, Arizona.

By and large there is nothing special about the average silhouette rifle. The rifle rack at a typical tournament could be just as easily the sales rack at any gun shop. There are Winchesters, Rugers, Remingtons, surplus Mausers and Springfields, autoloaders, pumps, and even lever guns. Some show the use and abuse of many years of hunting, while others glow with the pristine newness of rifles that never venture beyond the target range. In many cases it is apparent that the rifle in use is one that the shooter happens to be very fond of rather than one he feels he can win with. After all, it's a fun game and a great way to practice with an old friend that might otherwise rust away in the back of a closet.

The most popular off-the-rack rifles for silhouette shooting are the Winchester Model 70, the Ruger Model 77, and the Remington Model 700. Being great long-range hunting rifles, they are naturally also fine silhouette rifles. Each has an adjustable trigger which can be set for a crisp letoff (a definite aid to offhand shooting) and generally offer more accuracy than the average shooter can take advantage of. The best choice in calibers are .308 Winchester, .30/06, .25/06, 7×57, .280, and other rounds in this general category. The magnum rounds such as 7mm Remington Magnum or .300

Winchester Magnum aren't good choices, because the recoil is a bit much and sooner or later they are going to cause the shooter to flinch or jerk the trigger. Either of these conditions will be the ruination of good offhand shooting.

On the other side of the coin, one cannot avoid recoil altogether. Some shooters have attempted to reduce recoil as much as possible by using such mild kickers as the .243, 6mm Remington, etc., but their long-range punch is somewhat on the light side and will not always topple the heavy sheep from its perch. The .257 Roberts or .25/06 Remington is about as light as one can go, caliberwise, and be sure of adequate "knock-over" power. In a more practical sense, though, the 7mm (.284 inch) and .30 calibers have the great advantage. This is simply because of the super-accurate, high-ballistic-coefficient target-type bullets available in these two bore sizes.

Most silhouette shooters use handloaded ammo, and the most accurate loads utilize match-grade bullets such as made by Hornady, Winchester, Lapua, Nosler, Sierra, etc. The built-in accuracy of these precision bullets is of vital importance, obviously, but match-grade bullets are also built to a super-streamlined shape which helps maintain velocity at the longer ranges and resists the bad effects of crosswinds. The single most popular silhouette round is the .308 Winchester, and the 168-grain match bullets are most often loaded.

Some shooters use the 168-grain match bullets for the shorter range, then go to a 185- or 190-grain bullet for the long range. The idea is not for additional "knock-over" power, as one might suppose, but, rather, for the additional wind-bucking advantage one gets from the heftier slug.

While the .30-caliber cartridges are currently the most popular choices, I think there is going to be more and more emphasis placed on the 7mm bore size. The 162-grain Hornady 7mm match bullet has a higher ballistic coefficient than any of the 168-grain .30-caliber bullets and is thus less affected by wind, especially at the longer ranges. It and similar 7mm bullets may well be the big winners in future years. If I were contemplating building a super silhouette rifle I would be very much inclined to favor the .280 Remington, 7×57 Mauser, or a wildcat based on the .308 Winchester necked down to 7mm. This latter would be the first choice if I were using a short action such as the Remington 700.

Since silhouette shooting is done entirely from the offhand position, some shooters tend to discount the need for finely accurate rifles, their reasoning being that a minute-of-angle rifle can't be of any special benefit to a shooter who can't hold inside a 6-inch circle at 100 yards. Actually, a finely accurate rifle is always an advantage no matter how poor the shooter's marksmanship. A pretty good bolt-action hunting rifle, when fired from a rest, will group five shots in about 2 inches at 100 meters. This does not mean that it will shoot inside 10 inches at 500 meters. More likely, group sizes will run around

15 to 20 inches. This means that no matter how carefully a shooter aims at the 500-meter target his bullet may hit up to 8 inches or so from where he aims. The sheep profile is approximately 12 to 14 inches deep from back to belly line, so this means that a shot could very easily miss even with a dead-center hold. Therefore, a match-winning rifle needs to be capable of grouping close to 6 inches at 500 meters. Such a rifle will group five shots inside ½ inch at 100 yards.

When you talk about this kind of accuracy you're talking, with few exceptions, about specially built, custom-barreled rifles. The beginner will have no use for such fancy equipment, and may not even want it, but as his skill improves he begins to think about some sophisticated rifle features that might boost his score a bit. The rules prevent anyone from getting too carried away, but there is plenty of room for some worthwhile touches. The goals for a custom, semi-custom, or do-it-yourself silhouette rifle are (1) maximum accuracy, (2) maximum shooter comfort and efficiency within the rules, and (3) a mechanical unit which offers top accuracy when firing from the offhand position. The first two requirements are clear enough, but the last one needs some explaining.

A rifle which may give excellent groups when fired from a bench rest, and even feel great in the offhand position, may actually contribute more of a handicap than the shooter realizes. No shooter can hold a rifle perfectly still, and I do not know of a shooter who can even hold the cross hairs on any of the profile targets for more than a brief moment. Despite our best efforts the cross hairs dance such a nervous jig that good offhand shooting becomes a matter of developing sharp reflexes and a finely honed coordination between eye and trigger finger. When the sights come to bear on the target there is only an instant for the signals to flash from the eye to the finger. It is a lightning fast response and the rifle's firing mechanism is a vital link in the chain of events that must occur before the cross hairs wander off the target. Rifles with a slow, sluggish lock time (the time lapse between the sear release and the primer detonation) tend to slow down this chain of events and cause the bullet to get to the wrong place at the wrong time. This is why good "follow-through" is a vital part of good shooting, to minimize the effects of sluggish lock time and allow the bullet to get out the barrel. Mausers, for example, have a too leisurely firing-pin fall, and so do Springfields, Enfields, and just about any rifle of military origin you can name. Actually the difference between a fast striker fall and a slow one is only a matter of a few microseconds but in this fraction of a second a nervous rifle can jiggle quite a ways. This is why the best silhouette rifles are built on the fastest actions.

The standard Remington Model 700 has one of the quickest lock times of commonly available centerfire rifles. For this reason, plus its inherent accuracy and good trigger, the Model 700 is used as the basis for more custom silhouette rifles than any other design. There are two versions of the Model

A shooter draws a bead on one of the distant silhouette targets. His rifle is a rebarreled Model 700 Remington.

700 action: the long model used for rifles in .30/06, .270, 7mm Remington Magnum, etc., and the short job used for rifles in .22/250, .243, .222, etc. The short model is more desirable for target rifles because the lock time is faster (thanks to the shorter and hence lighter firing-pin shank) and because the shorter length makes it more rigid. The shorter model is necessarily limited as to the cartridges that can be used with it, but this is no problem because the .308 Winchester, the single most popular silhouette cartridge, is a perfect match for the short 700.

Only a couple of weeks before I wrote this, Ed Shilen, the well-known maker of custom rifle barrels, showed me a new version of his super-accurate bench-rest action which features a four-round magazine. When he gets this new action on the market it should be about the best possible choice for the basis of a super-dooper silhouette rifle, not to mention a tack-driving varmint or hunting rifle.

Another good choice for the basis of a winning rifle is the old favorite Winchester Model 70. It is, in fact, probably the *best* choice with cartridges such as the .30/06, .270, .280 Remington, .25/06, etc. The same features that make it a favorite among long-range target shooters are no less important on the silhouette range. The only thing going against it is the unnecessary length and weight if a short cartridge is used.

The distribution of weight is an important factor in any sporting arm, but doubly so in a silhouette rifle. The overall balance of the rifle must favor maximum holding stability and at the same time help keep fatigue to a minimum. This means that more than passing thought must be given to just where the allowable 8 pounds and 13 ounces can best be used. Most shooters agree that as much weight as possible should go into the barrel. This way the barrel can be stiffer and more accurate. Also, it's better to have a short, thick barrel than a longer one. Remember, the shorter the barrel, the quicker the bullet gets out of the muzzle, and this aids offhand shooting. For this reason it is not unusual to find silhouette rifles with thick, stubby barrels no longer than 20 inches. I personally consider 25 inches the maximum length with 23 inches being about ideal.

Many, if not most, "custom" silhouette guns are merely commercial rifles which have been fitted with top-grade match barrels in an effort to improve on the original accuracy and to bring the weight up to the allowable limit. Stocks therefore are usually the original factory wood, but it's a good bet that the action has been resin or "glass" bedded. Sometimes the butt section will be sawed off or drilled out to remove weight, and the forend is also likely to be trimmed down or hollowed out. Those shooters who go to the bother and expense of a custom stock tend to favor a higher-than-usual comb and cheek piece but somewhat more drop at heel than normal. This apparent contradiction of design feature allows an erect head position which is more comfortable in the offhand position. Also, the pistol grip is usually closer to the trigger guard in order to maximize trigger control. This general design is great for offhand shooting at stationary targets but wouldn't be so hot for a running target.

There are no restrictions or minimum weights for triggers, and this tends to allow some shooters to mislead themselves. The common notion is that it's easier to shoot a "hair" trigger, but some silhouette shooters have learned from bitter experience that this is not necessarily true. It takes a lot of practice to get used to a trigger that releases with only two or three ounces pressure and I've seen plenty of rifles fire before the shooters really wanted to. At the first Silhouette National Championships in Tucson in 1973 a shooter bragged to me about how he had managed to work his trigger down so that it fired at the touch of a feather. Not more than five minutes later he went up to the firing line, chambered a round, and was in the act of raising the rifle to his shoulder when his finger brushed the trigger. The bullet hit the ground about fifteen feet in front of him and he was scored a "miss" for that shot.

Actually, a 2-*pound* trigger is a lot lighter than it sounds, and I think this is a good trigger weight for the silhouette game. One may eventually go to a lighter trigger, but it's best to go about it a few ounces at a time.

SILHOUETTE OPTICS

The great bone of contention among silhouette shooters is the best scope for the game. The rules allow any kind of sight of any weight or magnification, and just about every conceivable combination has been tried. Personal opinion counts for a great deal, and discussions on what constitutes the "ideal" sight is likely to shed more heat than light. Most of the American scope manufacturers are having a whack at designing a scope purely for silhouette shooting, but the game is still too new for anyone to positively say which scope is best. Everyone is at least in agreement that the most important single feature is *positive* adjustments. This means adjustments that can be turned to any of four different settings and then returned to another setting time after time without loss of precision. This is vitally important because, as you will remember, sighting shots are not allowed in a silhouette match and when a shooter sets his scope for one of four ranges he wants to be absolutely certain that the cross hairs are pointing where the bullet will strike. This single factor is more important than magnification or optical quality.

The choices of magnification range from 4× to 10× among most silhouette competitors. Some shooters prefer the lower powers because the *apparent* holding error or wobble is less. Of course the rifle is going to tremble the same no matter what magnification, and I personally prefer an 8× or 10× scope. This gives a sharper look at the target. The only real disadvantage to the higher-power scopes is that they are somewhat longer and have larger objective-lens bells. This is a disadvantage in a crosswind because the greater "sail" area makes the rifle harder to hold steady. The ideal silhouette scope, to my notion, would be about 8×, have a ¾-inch tube with a small objective lens, and, naturally, would have ultra-reliable adjustments. Such features as great light-gathering power and optical crispness can be sacrificed. When you aim at the sheep across 550 yards of boiling mirage, optical fineness doesn't mean much anyway. It's about like trying to read a newspaper through the bottom of a catsup bottle.

There will be dramatic improvements in silhouette rifles within the next few years. Improved sighting equipment, which is just around the corner, will in turn reveal a need for better stock design, which in turn will spur greater emphasis on barrels, triggers, and actions. Someday a silhouette shooter is going to put it all together and knock over all the targets. But until both rifles and shooters are vastly improved, a score of 40 out of 100 will continue to win most of the marbles.

18

Bench-Rest Shooting

The average sport shooter or hunter is more likely to have at least a basic understanding of bench-rest shooting than any other form of rifle competition. This is because of the articles which turn up on bench shooting from time to time in the various shooting magazines. Unfortunately, though, these same articles have had the effect of creating a band of separation between bench-resters and other shooters and causing many good folks to look on the bench-rest shooter as a sort of weird case who dreams up completely unrealistic contraptions in the name of better accuracy. The journalistic race, regardless of breed, tends to put the emphasis on the unusual or spectacular, and as a result most bench-rest articles devote considerable space to 80-pound monstrosities that must be wheelbarrowed to the shooting bench. Also, there is the tendency to make some of the small groups fired seem like near-impossible achievements that can never be equaled again. By the time Mr. Average Guy gets through reading such an article he feels that he has no place with such a bunch of space-age miracle workers. What those spectacular-sounding articles failed to tell him, however, is that those 80-pound monsters are allowed in only a few matches and seldom win anyway. Also there is little mention that lots of women, young and old, and even sub-teenage kids frequently shoot and *win* in bench matches. And that from the standpoint of recruiting new shooters the bench-rest game offers the beginner an opportunity to succeed on a state or national level much faster than any other competitive rifle sport.

Interestingly, though bench-rest shooting is the most modern form of riflery it is also one of the oldest. In Colonial America, for instance, and in Europe even before, shooters—especially gunmakers—tested their rifles by seeing how close they would group at a given distance. Grouping ability, then as now, is the fundamental indicator of any rifle's accuracy, and riflemen have long sought to discover and eliminate the factors which cause a bullet's path to stray from that of the preceding bullet. Obviously, the first step in this direction was to eliminate, as far as possible, the basic human errors of holding and aiming a rifle. In earlier times this was accomplished by the use of heavy timber benches to support the rifle. More recently, even more stable benches of concrete have become the rule.

My 13½-pound Heavy Varmint bench rifle. The action and heavy stainless-steel barrel are by Ed Shilen. The fiberglass thumbhole stock is also by Shilen, and the rig has a 2-ounce Remington trigger and 20× Lyman scope. Caliber is .222 Remington. This is a standard bench-rest setup with sandbags and concrete shooting bench.

Before World War II there was very little formalized bench-rest competition. Most activity in this direction was by individuals like C. W. Rowland or the great experimenter Dr. F. W. Mann. Also, some rifle and ammo manufacturers, especially the makers of military small arms and ammo, used both bench and machine rests to test their products. But most shooters were content to just observe or read about these bench-rest experiments and, whenever possible, take advantage of the results. The most famous rifle group of the era was the fabulous "Rowland Group" of 1901; ten shots fired with a single-shot .32/40 at 200 yards and measuring only .725 inch from center to center of the widest shots. To me the .725 Rowland group is fascinating not only because it was a good group, but because it emphasizes the very slow progress in accuracy development over the following fifty-year period and because it actually had the effect of cowing other experimenters. Any number of articles dating from the between-the-wars period refer to the Rowland group as "unbeatable." This was without consideration of the fact that the Rowland group was not fired in competition and as such was only a selected sampling from hundreds of other test groups fired by Rowland. For all anyone knew, a barefoot lad in the hills of Tennessee might have lucked into a ten-shot group even better.

Immediately after the second big war some shooters in the Northeastern states decided to come to grips with the problem of getting all the bullets to go in one hole and began a series of bench-rest competitions. This handful of shooters formed the nucleus from which grew the National Bench Rest Shooter Association (NBRSA) and the International Benchrest Shooters (IBS) organizations. To today's well-read and sophisticated shooters, looking back on the bench rifles of 1950, it must seem incredible that such a ragtag collection of rifles and ammo represented the most up-to-the-minute thinking of only a quarter-century ago. But they learned fast.

Under the rules of the early days almost anything was allowed. This was a good rule for its day because during the formative years no one was very sure which way the search for accuracy would lead and it was necessary that there be no restrictions on design. In time it became apparent that if continued accuracy development was centered around the heavy, unrestricted rifles the end result would be meaningless. In other words, what's the point of developing a varmint rifle for nailing chucks at 500 yards if it's too cumbersome to take on a chuck hunt? Also, the big-rifle game was not attracting many newcomers, and new blood is essential to the survival of any activity. A forward-looking group of NBRSA members therefore devised a set of rules and specifications, especially weight restrictions, which brought about far more practical rifles. These are the so-called Varmint Class of bench rifles. The effect these rule revisions had on the future of bench shooting cannot be underestimated. It is very easy to speculate that the sport may have fallen apart altogether or at least experienced virtually zero growth, especially when you consider that unrestricted rifle matches make up only a a very small part of the current shooting calendar.

The Varmint Class bench rifles are the Heavy Varmint, which can weigh no more than 13½ pounds with scope, and the Light Varmint, which can weigh no more than 10½ pounds with scope. Though the allowable weight is the most distinguishing characteristic of this class of rifles, there are other regulations which specify, in a general way, overall design and mode of firing. For example, unlike the unlimited class, they have to *look* like rifles, and they cannot be fired from a mechanical rest or holding fixture, only sandbags. In other words, the shooter has to aim the rifle and pull the trigger for each shot.

The information yield from this class of bench rifle has been tremendous. Shooters and riflemakers have learned how to build a high degree of accuracy into a reasonably portable rifle, and this is the original goal of bench shooting. When the Varmint Class was created, some experimenters voiced a fear that the lighter classification would sidetrack the ultimate accuracy goal, but as it turns out the modern 13½-pound Heavy Varmint rifles will group just about as well as the unrestricted "iron masters." Not only that, the Light Varminters shoot just about as well as their big brothers!

A similar rifle is the Sporter Class, which, like the Light Varmint, has a maximum allowable weight of 10½ pounds but in addition must be .23 caliber or larger. The idea here was to move away from the .22-caliber cartridge

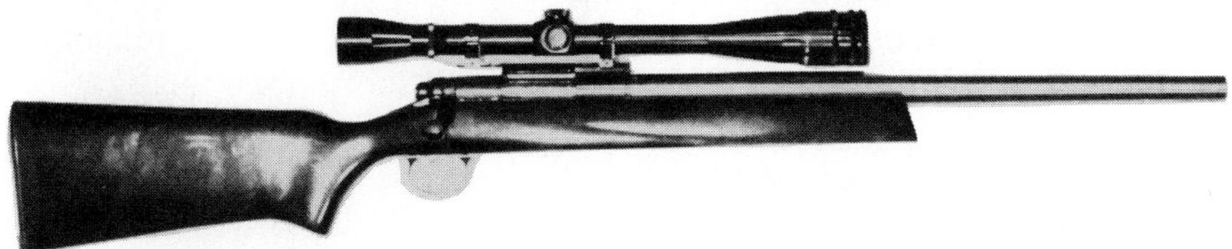

My bench-rest Sporter Class rifle. Built on a Remington 40-X action, the 10½-pound rifle has an Atkinson stainless-steel barrel chambered for the 6×47 cartridge and an all-fiberglass stock made by Chet Brown of San Jose, California. The scope is the popular Lyman Lightweight (LWBR) Bench Rifle in 20× magnification.

which dominated bench shooting and stimulate some experimenting with the larger bore sizes. Since a legal Sporter Class rifle conforms to Light Varmint rules it is not uncommon for competitors to use their Sporter Class rifles in Light Varmint matches. This streamlines your traveling kit by one rifle and qualifies you for two events for the price of one gun.

A fourth classification of bench rifle is the so-called Hunter group. As the name implies these rifles are close look-alikes of the rifles we deer hunters carry afield. Under the rules the stock cannot be over 2¼ inches wide (which is still pretty wide), the rifle must have a working safety and a workable magazine which holds at least two cartridges, must weigh no more than 10 pounds with scope, must be 6mm or larger in caliber, and can't have a scope

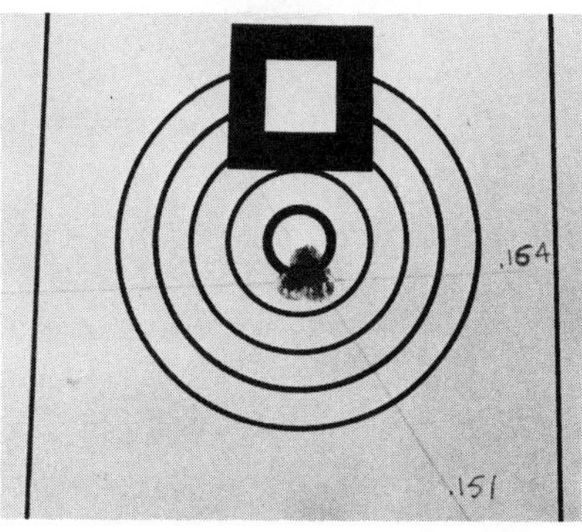

This group, which measures well under .2 inch, was fired in actual competition with my Sporter rifle. This is a five-shot group fired at 100 yards. By the way, it did not win the match.

of over 6× magnification. In short, what these and the other rules defining the Hunter Class rifle are meant to do is direct accuracy development efforts toward rifles which the average American hunter uses. Also, the Hunter Class is an excellent threshold for newcomers into the world of bench-rest shooting. If a fellow thinks he has a tack-driving deer rifle he can enter it in Hunter Class matches without fear of being outclassed by expensive equipment and high-power target scopes.

Another feature of Hunter Class competition which makes it more familiar to the average sport shooter or plinker is that the objective is to aim at and hit a definite target rather than put a series of shots into a small group. The target card has six bulls, which includes one sighting bull; and one shot is fired at each of the five record bulls. The 10-ring is only a tiny dot, and a hunter rifle that can make a center hit is not just a tack-driver but a pin-driver.

The most exotic class of bench rifles is, of course, the Unlimited guns. These can be of any caliber and any weight, and can be fired from mechanical "return-to-battery" rests. The only rule of note is that they must be fired by manually pulling a trigger, or at least something that looks like a trigger. When it comes to poking bullets in the same hole these rifles get right down to the real nitty-gritty. An interesting device allowed for unrestricted rifles is the so-called "return-to-battery" rest. These are heavy, complicated-looking rests which hold the rifle in a highly uniform shot-to-shot position. They are so positive, in fact, that once the rest is adjusted so the rifle is correctly aimed at the target, the shooter no longer needs to look through the scope to see where the cross hairs are pointing. He can just keep pumping ammo through it while he chats with his next-door neighbor. All he has to do, aside

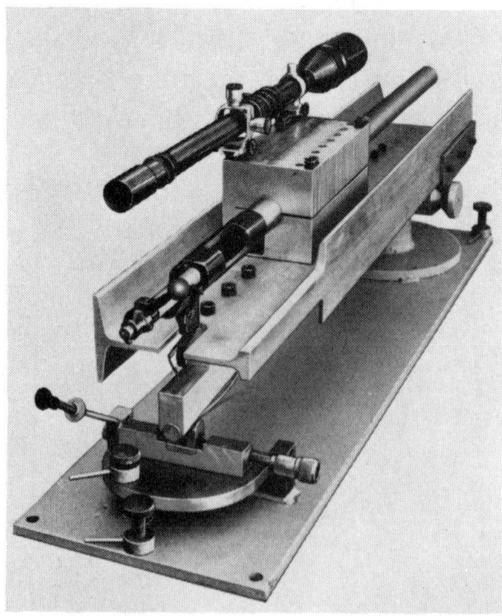

This is one of the so-called "iron monster" bench-rest rigs used in unrestricted competition. The scope is a Unertl and the action is a Remington Model 40-X. This particular rig is used by the Hornady Manufacturing Company to check the accuracy of its bullets.

from loading and pulling the trigger, is shove the rifle back to the forward stop, or "battery," after it recoils. This is not so foolproof as it sounds, though, because a wind shift while the rifle is locked in on target brings an obvious complication. The shooter has to wait for the right wind condition to return or reset the mechanical rest. Many unrestricted-class rifle shooters forego the return-to-battery rest altogether and use sandbags. This requires careful aiming for every shot, but most shooters are accustomed to this chore anyway and the sandbags offer a bit more flexibility.

Some of the unrestricted rifles simply look more or less like overgrown rifles, some are vaguely identifiable as rifles, and some look like just about anything *except* a rifle. This latter batch includes the "iron monster," which is a barreled action bolted to a length of structural I-beam steel. There is no way of getting ahold of these things so they are strictly a return-to-battery proposition. As a purely shooting machine they are hard to beat, and for that reason are used by some bullet manufacturers for accuracy-testing their products. Fired in a test tunnel they can produce some ridiculously tiny groups.

BENCH-REST COURSES OF FIRE

Tournaments for Light and Heavy Varmint rifles or the Sporter Class usually consist of five five-shot matches at both 100 and 200 yards. Occasionally 300-yard matches will be fired, but not in National or Regional Championships. There is also a "warm-up" match at the beginning of each day's shooting, or at the beginning of firing at a different range (as when going from 100 to 200 yards, etc.), but these warm-ups don't count in the official tally. The smallest group I ever fired in bench competition was in one of these warm-up matches, so all I won was a "Way to go!" from the other shooters.

The time limit for the five-shot matches is seven minutes, except for the first match of the day or the first match after a change of distance, in which case the time limit is ten minutes. The big unrestricted rifle matches call for five ten-shot groups at each range, and the time limit is twelve minutes. For the first match of the day the time allowed is stretched to fifteen minutes. The purpose of the additional time for the first events is to allow shooters enough time to get their rifles zeroed and tend to any other necessary tinkering.

Each target sheet has two targets, one for the five or ten record shots and the other for sighters. A shooter can shoot at the sighters as many times as he likes, but of course the time limit imposes its own restrictions. Spectators and first-time shooters are often shocked to discover that rather than shooting slow and deliberately bench-rest shooters may rattle off their five shots in as little as *thirty seconds.* In fact, some shooters in an effort to speed up their shooting have had special actions made with a left-side loading port.

This way they can work the bolt with their right hand and stuff ammo in the rig with their left. Surprising, isn't it?

Despite a popular but somewhat misguided notion, bench-rest shooting does not, by a long shot, have the shooter error removed, and it certainly isn't free from the effects of wind or mirage and the spooky score of tribulations that make bullets land at odd places. Bench-rest champions are shooters who by luck or experience are able to "read" the atmospheric shenanigans taking place between the muzzle and the target and take appropriate action. In a constantly changing wind condition, for example, a shooter may have actually aimed at five different places on the target in order to get his shots to go in one neat little hole. Other shooters, rather than playing the conditions, wait until the breezes are more or less stable and rip off as many shots as possible before the conditions change. Often you'll see a shooter anxiously watching the wind flags and hoping his pet "condition" will return before the time limit is up. If it were not for the time limits some shooters would dawdle all day. Back in 1931 when C. W. Rowland was striving for one of his super-tight (for his day) groups, he fretted away five hours firing a ten-shot string.

The 100-yard bench-rest target has a 1-inch aiming square (2-inch square on the 200-yard target, etc.) surmounting a more or less traditional targetlike series of rings. It doesn't matter where the group is placed, however, as long as it's inside the boundary lines. When the black aiming square first came into use on bench targets it was thought to be the most precise way to aim with a telescopic sight because it can be neatly quartered with the cross hairs. More recently, however, many shooters, including myself, have preferred to aim directly at the center circle on the round target. There are a couple of good reasons for this. First of all, the ½-inch center ring is a good aiming spot, especially with scopes equipped with a ⅛- or ¼-inch dot reticle. You just center the dot in the ring. Also, it is a good idea to zero the scope so that the dot or cross hairs are exactly on the bullet hole. This makes it easier to "chase" bullet holes. Let's say the first shot of the record string doesn't hit where it was supposed to. This means that the rest of the shots will have to be aimed at the errant hole. With the rifle zeroed on the point of impact this "chasing" is much easier than when the zero is set for aiming at the square and bullet placement is in the rings an inch or so away. In order to allow even more precise cross-hair-on-bullet-hole zero Lyman now offers their great 20-X All-American scope with ⅛-minute adjustments. With this scope you can, at worst, zero to within 1/16 inch of where the bullets are *supposed* to hit.

BENCH-REST EQUIPMENT

The restricted-weight rifles, especially the Sporter and Lighter Varmint classes, are marvels of clever design and construction not just by virtue of their pinpoint accuracy but in the way weight is utilized where it will do the most good. Of major importance so far as accuracy goes is a good stiff barrel. Thus the idea is to use as much barrel as possible and as little as possible of everything else. This has led to a considerable hollowing out of wooden stocks, until they are sometimes little more than thin shells, but there is obviously a practical limit to this. Back about 1970 a couple of San Jose, California, shooters and gun tinkerers, Chet Brown and Lee Six, turned the bench-rest world on its ear with the introduction of a super-strong but ultra-lightweight rifle stock made entirely of fiberglass cloth and epoxy. These stocks, in one quick chop, offered lightness and a higher degree of stability than wooden stocks. This eliminated much of the bedding problem which has so long plagued stocks of wood. About that same time, Unertl and Remington started making target-type scopes which were short enough to mount on a rifle section and combined light weight with high magnification. Not long after, Lyman introduced a 20× hunting-type scope which weighed under a pound and created an immediate sensation. Thus, with about a pound in scope and rings plus a stock weighing only 2 pounds there is still 7½ pounds left for a pretty healthy barrel and action. Even so, barrel weight is used up in diameter rather than length. Barrel length in itself adds little, if anything, to accuracy, but stiffness does. The rules say that the barrels can be no more than 1¼ inches in diameter at the rear end, and from a point 5 inches or less from the breech must taper toward the muzzle. The minimum allowable taper would result in a barrel diameter no larger than 9/10 inch at a point 29 inches from the breech. Taking full advantage of these rules and allowing for the weight of the action results in a barrel length of about 20 inches.

With 3 extra pounds to play with Heavy Varmint riflemakers can be less choosy about scope weight, stocks, and barrel length, but during the past couple of years a mighty interesting innovation has been turning up. This is the use of a single rifle with two or three interchangeable barrels. This way the shooter meets the specifications of the Light and Heavy Varmint class, plus Sporter, by simpling screwing in a barrel of the correct weight and caliber. This can be done by means of a barrel vise which clamps to a car bumper and a compact little action wrench which slips into the action's lug slots.

In practical terms, the idea is a great one because it lightens a shooter's traveling kit by two rifles. However, to this writer's mind it represents a milestone in accuracy development for reasons which have nothing to do with convenience. I'll try to make it clear. First of all, no serious bench shooter would go for a swap-barrel rig if he thought it would cost him the slightest bit of accuracy in any of the classes, especially the Heavy Varmint matches. The acceptance of the multiple-barrel rig by some of our very best shooters indicates a recognition on their part that the state of the art of accuracy has been refined to the point that virtually everything known about stocking, bedding, and scoping for accuracy can be utilized in a 10½-pound rifle! Twisting in a heavier barrel for the Heavy Varmint events makes the rifle rest more solidly on the sandbags, and a little easier to shoot, but the real accuracy difference is slight.

These developments underscore the wisdom and farsightedness of the men who moved in favor of the Light Varmint class of rifles a few years ago. Their goals are being reached in more spectacular fashion than most of them dared hope. The real winners in the long run will be the average hunters and sport shooters.

The firing mechanism of the bench rifle has always been an area of particular interest. Since it is the core of the accuracy unit, it is one of the primary causes of good or bad accuracy. Back in the early days of bench competition, shooters and rifle builders tended to use whatever actions were available. Since the familiar old '98 Mauser was about the cheapest and most available it was one of the most often used. When shooters began to discover the causes of poor accuracy one of the first things they learned was that the syrupy striker fall and flimsy barrel support of surplus military actions, or commercial actions of that genre, contributed nothing to fine accuracy. This created an overreaction in the opposite direction, and during the 1950s some custom riflemakers turned out some specially made actions that looked more like precision-turned nail kegs than anything that belonged on a rifle. Yet they served their purpose most admirably and permitted some significant steps in the discovery of fundamental accuracy principles. Once these were understood it was possible to evolve actions of more modest proportions. One action, the Remington Model 700, and its close kin, the Remington 40-X, 722, XP-100 and 600s, are so widely used on today's Varmint and Sporter class rifles that they virtually begin and end the topic. At least half the rifles at any shoot will be built up on the above-listed Remingtons or a modification thereof. At the 1974 NBRSA Varmint rifle championships, for example, two-thirds of the top twenty Heavy Varmint rifles were built up on the Remington design. The reason for this is that it offers quick lock time, a very rigid stocky profile, almost perfect symmetry, relative lightness, and a simple contour which is relatively easy to stock or sleeve. Too, of course, they are reasonably cheap and easy to come by. There are other mass-produced actions which may claim two or three of these features but none quite gets them all together in such a handy little package.

A singular advantage of the Remington is its roundness, which makes it especially convenient for sleeving. This phenomenon of recent years is the practice of slipping an action receiver inside a larger metal tube to add stiffness and bedding control. If I had to say which was the greater advantage, I'd have to go with bedding. Of the above-mentioned Remingtons used in the 1974 Championships over half were sleeved.

These sleeves, which can be no longer than 15 inches, are almost always of aluminum or aluminum alloy, because of the weight factor, and may be cast, extruded, or machined from solid stock. Some are perfectly round and others, such as the ones made and fitted by Ed Shilen, may have a flat bottom and sides. The sleeve is bored so that the round Remington receiver slips snugly inside and the two are joined by epoxy glue. The two thus become virtually a single unit and it takes a temperature of nearly 400 degrees to cause the glue to let go.

A sleeve will double or triple the bedding area of an action and thus distributes the job of supporting a heavy barrel over a much wider area. In the case of flat-bottomed sleeves, such as the Shilen, the problem of proper bedding is vastly simplified. Many experienced bench shooters prefer a round action, such as the Remington, or a round sleeve because they feel that the shape contributes to accurate bedding. I personally hold almost the opposite view. The flatter the bottom of an action is the better I like it, especially in heavier calibers which are more prone to twist an action in the stock. Over the years I've read a dozen or more articles, all different, on how to go about bedding a round receiver, and it occurs to me that the reason there is so much discussion on the subject is simply that a round receiver is so tricky to bed properly. I really take my hat off to the fellows who can do it right. Of which, by the way, there are not too many.

Of course all sorts of other makes and models of commercial actions are used, or at least have been tried, with varying degrees of success. The cute little Sako Vixen action, for one, comes in a stiffened-up version with the magazine cut blocked in, and every once in a while one turns up on a finely accurate Light Varmint rig. They have a quick hammer fall and offer a slight weight advantage but don't sleeve nearly so easily as the Remington and in their natural state don't tend to support a heavy barrel as well as one might wish. This tendency, plus their rather restricted bedding contact, brings on more problems than some shooters want to bother with. If an even lighter Varmint rifle class were to be created, with, say, a 9-pound weight maximum, the Sako would really come into its own.

A newcomer to bench shooting of recent months is the Swedish-made FFV action. This descendant of the famous Husqvarna line has a snappy lock time and a nicely rounded receiver which lends itself to all sorts of fancy bedding and sleeving operations. When the Swedes learned that bench shooters were casting admiring glances at their action they promptly produced a solid-bottomed bench-rest version. My carrot-topped pal L. E. "Red" Cornelison nailed down second place in the 1974 NBRSA Heavy Varmint nationals with a rifle built around one of these sturdy chunks of Swedish steel and there is no question that more and more of them will be used in the future.

I expect the legions of Model 70 Winchester fans are perpetually distressed that their pet design has such a paltry standing among the bench-rest clan, but the simple fact of the matter is that the M70 is too long and unnecessarily heavy for the job. It has a wonderfully quick striker fall, however, and its inherent accuracy is well known. If Winchester had, like Remington, chosen to court the accuracy buffs by producing a solid-bottomed version of the M70, perhaps in a shortened form, the current action picture would no doubt be different.

Of the actions built especially for varmint-weight bench rifles those built by Ed Shilen and Bob Hart are the best known and the most successful. Neither of these is exactly what you'd call a mass-produced item but they are turned out in at least enough numbers to make them reasonably available.

The popular Hart actions, which are strictly single-shot but come in various sizes and weights, are of cylindrical shape, which Hart prefers, and except for the dimensions are reasonably similar to the Remington action. In fact, Hart uses a Remington bolt in his actions. His Varmint actions are characterized by a bridgelike fixture which extends forward from the receiver ring and supports the front scope mount, thus eliminating the need to attach a target-type scope to the barrel. Like the bolt, the Hart trigger is Remington-issue.

The Shilen action represents the opposite extreme in bedding philosophies. It is 8 inches long, about 1⅜ inches wide, and dead flat on the bottom. Like Hart, Shilen uses a Remington trigger mechanism (which comes in standard or 2-ounce pull weights, or can be substituted entirely by one made by Canjar), but the rest of the rig is his own make. For a mechanism designed purely for the achievement of accuracy it is a surprisingly good-looking affair with a faceted, three-sided top contour and a neatly matched bolt sleeve.

Some time back I had a vision that the broad-bottomed Shilen action would make a great beginning for a magnum-class 1,000-yard target rifle and had him build and barrel his bench action for the .300 Winchester Magnum. After stocking by Jim Cloward, the Seattle-based target-rifle specialist, the rig, to my profound joy, shoots five shot groups at 100 yards measuring as small as 3/10 inch between centers of the widest shots with an experimental batch of 190-grain Winchester match bullets.

About the only criticism of the Shilen action I've heard is that the wide, flat receiver bottom does not end bedding problems as it was meant to do, but in fact causes some unique problems of its own. The example given is that it is impossible to perfectly mate flat surfaces and the bigger the surfaces the more irregular the contact. I get a chuckle out of this one, mostly because it's the sort of notion that shooters like to dream up just for the sake of finding fault. Apparently no one stops to consider that a *round* receiver is, for bedding purposes, a form of flat receiver, or that in the geometric sense a cylinder is a flat plain with only the dimension of curvature added. Let me explain. Consider a flat piece of paper. Now, lift the paper by its edges so that it curves, or even roll it into a tube, and visualize "bedding" or mating this form with an opposing surface. Obviously, the problem, round or flat, is the same. It's just that the flat is easier to deal with.

Of course arguing about such points as these makes for lots of enjoyable conversation, and as some wisehead once put it, "A difference of opinion is what makes horse races."

The barrel, needless to say, is the real heart of a bench rifle. No matter how perfect everything else is, if the barrel is no good a rifle just won't shoot a tight group on a reliable basis. This, considering the ever-tinkering dispositions of most bench shooters, is an irony of near tragic proportions. He can tinker with the bedding, the trigger, and the sights and experiment with his ammo till old Hector turns gray and dies, but the barrel remains almost unalterable with solitary orneriness. If it won't shoot it won't shoot, and tinkering isn't liable to help. There's no choice save buying a new barrel.

There's not much point in my giving my views on which makes of barrels give the best accuracy. A look at a list of the equipment used by winning shooters repeats itself with liturgical monotonousness: Atkinson, Hart, McMillan, Shilen, with an occasional Douglas or Garrott. The Remington Model 40-X BBR Light and Heavy Varmints are the only factory-made rifles that are designed to meet bench specs. These of course carry Remington-made barrels (which are specially made in the custom department) and are about the only barrels from a big-name manufacturer that ever make it to the win columns.

I harbor a suspicion that some of the lead-lapped, hammer-forged barrels made by Winchester could cut a fat hog in the centerfire accuracy department, but these are all relegated to use on Winchester's finest. The FFV people, now that they've wetted their feet with a bench action, are just liable to try their hand at peddling some bench-weight tubes of their own hammer-forge manufacture. The results, though, are only a guess at this time.

Whereas "only your barrel maker knows for sure" when it comes to the rifled tube, everyone gets in his licks when it comes to stocking the bench rifle. Choice of bedding techniques are individualistic as preferences for the opposite sex, and few shooters are content until they've bedded, rebedded, scraped, tuned, and glued their stocks until, for better or worse, their distinctive brand of craftsmanship is firmly implanted.

A discussion of stockmaking for any breed of rifles save bench guns covers a wide area—woods, shapes and finishes, etc. But when it comes to bench rest the conversation is centered almost entirely around bedding, that mysterious fit of barreled action to wood which is held responsible for causing all sorts of funny business. Much of the problem of achieving an accurate bedding job arises from the basic instability of wood. Dry or wet weather can cause wood to flex and bend and thus cause bedding shifts which reveal themselves in the form of enlarged groups. Bedding an action in "glass," a hard and stable bond of glass or metal particles in a space-age resin, is a well-known way of fighting the bedding problem, and here of late the practice has been extended to stocks made up entirely of glass and epoxy.

A stock of solid glass and resin would be impossibly heavy, so they are made as a thin-walled shell filled with a light plastic foam. Lovers of nicely grained wood are somewhat repelled by the sight of the brightly painted fiberglass stocks, but from the performance standpoint the writing is on the wall. The day of the fiberglass stock is here.

A very interesting bedding innovation is the practice of "gluing" the barreled action into the stock. If variations in action screw tightness, irregular fit, or shifting of the metal in the stock lead to poor accuracy, then it follows that the best thing to do is fasten everything together so that it becomes one mechanical unit. Some shooters are doing exactly this and getting spectacular results. With epoxy glues the bond is weld-tight and damn near permanent. Once the barreled action is stuck in the wood it can be removed only with a torch. Some shooters glue the action itself into the stock, and others glue only a 4-inch section of the barrel just ahead of the receiver. This leaves the barrel free to float on one side and the action to float or otherwise do its thing on the other. This basic principle was pioneered and proved with Unrestricted class bench rifles which were "bedded" simply by clamping the barrel in a metal block which, in turn, is attached to the stock or whatever serves as a stock. The technique is workable but isn't all that practical for rifles in the restricted-weight classes. "Gluing" the barrel in the stock is an application of the same principle, however, and is completely feasible for the Varmint class bench game. Bench shooters, being only human, tend to resist radical changes in their habits, but they're also great at copying the equipment used by the winners. In other words, the day of the great "glue-in" is here.

Cartridgewise, the designs and variations that have been tried by bench shooters absolutely boggle the mind. Yet, despite all the wandering about in the ballistic wilderness the unadorned little .222 Remington case continues to collect more baubles than all the others put together. The unparalleled success of the triple deuce has been a crown of thorns for dyed-in-the-wool wildcatters who remain unconvinced that they can't beat any factory design, so, just as sure as the .222 will keep on winning, there will be an unending parade of wildcats. One of these days someone may conclusively prove that he has designed a better round, and just between you and me and the gatepost, I'm looking forward to that day. A round that beats the .222 will represent genuine progress.

A while back the .308 Winchester round enjoyed a flash of popularity among bench shooters and accounted for some record-setting scores. The

.308 is wonderfully accurate, but this was only partially responsible for its popularity. Other reasons were the fact that the heavier bullet was less likely to be blown astray by passing winds and, most important I feel, because a superbly accurate bullet was commercially available in the form of Sierra's 168-grain International Match hollow-point. As highly accurate .22-caliber slugs became more available, most notably Remington's bench bullet, the .30-caliber trend went into a decline. And too, the recoil generated by the .308, even with mild loads, was beginning to get to some shooters. The usual bench-firing technique calls for very slight shoulder contact at the butt and almost nonexistent pressure by the trigger-finger hand on the grip. This means that even a moderately recoiling rifle has a running start before it smacks you and a severe case of flinchjerk can result. Nowadays about the only place the .308 is still popular is in the Unrestricted class where return-to-battery setups are used.

The Sporter class demands a caliber larger than .22, but most shooters get by with as little as possible in the form of the .222 Remington Magnum case necked up to 6mm. Known as the 6×47 (for 47mm length), it is far and away the big favorite for the Sporter class. I use this round for the Sporter class myself, and think it's as sweet as strawberries and cream, but from the standpoint of general use it's a total failure. With a 75-grain bullet it will only turn up to about 3000 feet per second, which means that at best it would only rate as a third-class varmint-hunting round. It has, however, the distinction of being one of the very few wildcat cartridges chambered for in a factory-made rifle. Remington will sell you a 40-X all ready to go, but you'll have to make your own music when it comes to ammo.

It has been an axiom among bench-resters that the best bullets are the homemade variety swaged on expensive finely built dies by such gifted machinists as Pat McMillan, Bob Simonson, or a chap named Rorsch, to name a few. The do-it-yourself operation involves selecting jackets, forming cores, and swageing the bullets themselves, and, despite the prevailing lay opinion, is by no means an endless source of low-cost bullets. Most owners of excellent swageing equipment would willingly escape the chore if only high-grade commercial bullets were available. In fact, that long-awaited day is all but here. Constantly pressured by precision accuracy buffs, custom makers such as Sierra, Speer, and Nosler have refined their product so that it rivals the best homemade efforts. Remington even uses custom dies exactly like those used by do-it-yourselfers in the making of their well-thought-of bench bullets. Winchester has just introduced a line of match bullets which follows the same strategy.

Another factor which has contributed to recent accuracy developments is improved primers. Until only recently this component was largely overlooked as a contributor—or detractor—to fine accuracy, but the effect it can have is startling. As manufacturers began to realize the promotional benefits of bench-match-winning components they made more serious efforts toward turning out highly uniform primers. As a result the primers of right now are better than those of only five years ago. Omark-CCI, for example, even makes a special bench-rest primer for the accuracy trade. These were used by "Mac" McMillan when he shot his world-record .009 inch group.

All this industrial intervention here of late is proof most positive that the bench-rest game is serving the goals outlined a quarter of a century ago when a few guys got together to see who could shoot the smallest group. We have reached a level of accuracy they scarcely imagined, and the benefits have overflowed into virtually every area of the shooting sports. Even the Holy Grail of riflery, the one-hole group, is so close that the most skeptical now admit that it's only a question of time. . . .

Part V

Custom Rifles

19

Custom Stocks

The single most visible feature of a custom rifle is its stock. The stock alone, as a matter of fact, is so much the embodiment of a custom rifle that it is generally considered the only thing that needs to be changed in order to elevate a rifle from the humdrum masses into the rarefied air of the custom or "bespoke," as the English say. You can change a rifle's barrel a dozen times over or add exclusive metalsmithing touches until you've got a fortune invested in skilled gunsmithing, but as long as the original factory-issue stock remains you'll have a hard time convincing most people you've got a custom rig. On the other hand, leave every scrap of metal just the way it was originally built, but put on another stock, and the whole shebang instantly becomes a bona-fide custom rifle.

And, need I add, our top-drawer stockmakers are the heroes of the custom-gun world. Such names as Al Biesen, Jerry Fisher, Len Brownell, Dale Goens, Clayton Nelson, Earl Milliron, and Monte Kennedy are household words in the shooting world, even among shooters who have never had an opportunity to admire their work firsthand. This is a result of the considerable publicity given custom stockmaking over the past several years.

Actually there is a fairly widespread disagreement over what constitutes a truly custom stock job, even among stockmakers themselves. In the traditional British sense a "bespoke" stock is one that is made specifically to fit a certain individual. Its custom elements are obvious because while it perfectly fits the individual for whom it was made it does not fit other shooters.

However, this extremely close tailoring is, even in the best circles, relegated almost entirely to shotguns. Since rifles are aimed rather than pointed there is no need for a very high degree of exactness in regards to length of pull, drop at comb, cast-off or cast-on, etc. If the length of pull is somewhere in the 13¼-inch to 14-inch range and the comb high enough to allow a good look through the scope, there isn't all that much to add in the way of individual fit. Or to express it another way, let's say a man of more or less typical height somewhere between five foot eight and six foot four with matching

The custom stocking on this Winchester Model 70 was done by Jim Cloward, Seattle, Washington. Cloward is best known for his target-shooting stocks and accessories but his sporter-rifle styling and workmanship is first-rate.

arm and neck length, and ranging somewhere between 125 and 250 pounds, has a custom rifle stock which is made to measure in every detail. It would point quite nicely for him, no doubt about it, *but* it would feel just as good to an overwhelming majority of other men who fall within the broad height and weight class described above.

In my gun rack are fourteen custom hunting rifles stocked by some of the greatest stockmakers in the business. The lengths of pull range from 13½ to 14 inches and the heights of comb, as per my usual specification, are "high enough to just clear the bolt." Custom-made for me, yes, but just about everyone who shoulders any of these rifles goes into a near swoon about how well they seem to fit *him* personally.

Custom stockmakers have pointed out to me that while they agree that primary dimensions such as length of pull are indeed not so exacting on a rifle as a shotgun, what they strive to build into their stocks are such custom features as high, full combs, gracefully curved and comfortably cross-sectioned grips, and comfortable-to-hold forends. Now right here we get into the real crux of the beauty of a great "custom-made" stock: It's not so much that great rifles are custom-fitted as it is that good stockmakers know how to make a stock that feels great—to nearly everyone! Add this talent to an ability to express these features in graceful harmonious lines, combined with fine craftsmanship, and you have a *great* stockmaker.

Thus, when employing the services of a skilled stockmaker we are buying his knowledge of what features contribute to both shootability *and* beauty

Bob Winter, a first-rank custom stockmaker from Menno, South Dakota, puts the final touches on a stock made of "quilted" maple.

and his ability to execute them in wood. "Custom" features are, in the main, the customer's personal desires in regards to checkering pattern, type of butt plate, extra fittings, etc.

More than once I've had custom stockmakers tell me how they've received very exacting dimensions from customers specifying measurements for everything from length of forend to width of grip cap. If these dimensions detract from the shootability and beauty of the finished product they may persuade the customer to change his specifications or refuse the job altogether. Just as often, however, they quietly go ahead and do it their own way, and almost invariably the customer is as happy as a hog in the corn crib.

Just for the record, though, there are stocks occasionally made which definitely cater to an individual's physical characteristics. Left-handed stocks which have the cheek piece on the right side of the butt section are an example of these (though this feature is now available on some mass-produced rifles), as are lengths of pull, which, at much less than 13 or over 15 inches, are obviously made for a shorter or taller than average person or perhaps a specific type of shooting. The most notable examples of this kind of custom stockmaking are those stocks which are made for a shooter with such physical handicaps as the need to aim with the left eye and shoot from the right shoulder, or a missing trigger finger that requires a grip shaped to allow more efficient trigger control by one of the remaining fingers.

Another area of considerable discussion and disagreement as to custom stocks are stocks completely hand-cut from solid blanks and those semi-inletted and semi-shaped by machine. This has been a more or less touchy subject with many professional stockmakers and deserves some discussion.

A rough-shaped octagonal barrel blank, Mauser action, and block of French walnut to be used by Duane Wiebe for one of his stock jobs.

Much of the strong feeling in this area results from the natural resentment of professional stockmakers toward do-it-yourself amateurs who fit a nearly finished machine-made stock to a barreled action and claim they have

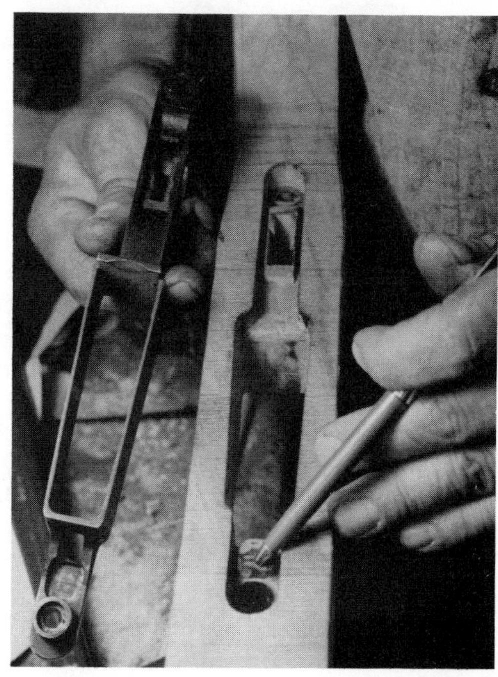

Detail of the inletting process as done by Duane Wiebe. This is a Mauser, so the trigger guard is inletted before the barreled action. The black "spotting in" agent can be seen in the inletting.

a "custom" rifle. I tend to sympathize with this resentment—up to a point—especially in the cases where the machine-shaped stocks are so nearly finished that there is very little way the do-it-yourselfer can affect the shape of the finished product. But on the other hand there are semi-inletted blanks available which are so grossly oversized that the craftsman, either professional or amateur, has complete authority over what the stock will ulti-

Wiebe at work on another of his custom jobs. Notice the Mauser action has a tang safety fitted.

mately look like. In these cases it is impossible to tell if a stock was made from a solid block or a machine-inletted blank, so I don't see that there is any cause for quarrel as to whether the product is truly "custom" or not.

Here of late quite a few of the very best-known custom stockmakers have gone to making some of their own stocks from machine-inletted and shaped blanks. The question is, do these stocks qualify as truly custom jobs? The answer, in my opinion, is an unqualified yes. Here's why: First of all these stocks are usually machine-shaped by the stockmaker himself on his own equipment or at least made to his personal pattern. Every top stockmaker has characteristic lines and style which identify his work. By and large it is these individual stylistic features which attract a customer to a particular craftsman. Therefore the customer is getting what he expects whether the stock is entirely done by hand or roughed out on a machine. In fact, if the machining process saves time which in turn is passed along to the customer in cash savings, then I say more power to them. And besides, I've seen beautiful custom stocks made by top-of-the-line craftsmen from semi-finished blanks which in no way could be distinguished from those carved from a block. Remember, it still takes a lot of hard work to inlet and final-shape a semi-finished job. And remember too that most "custom" features are in the

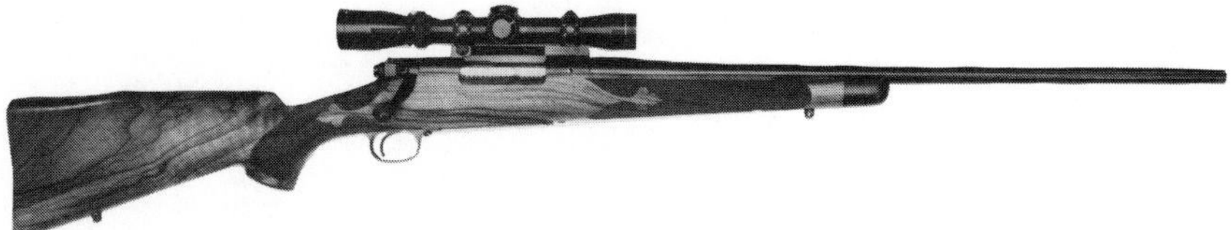

A Duane Wiebe stock job, this one for a Model 70 Winchester. The wood is a magnificent piece of English walnut.

area of fittings, checkering, etc. There are those, of course, who will always insist that a truly custom stock has to be hand-carved from a solid chunk of wood, but in recent years so many professional custom riflemakers have bought or built their own stock-duplicating machines that this long-held opinion is no doubt dying out fast.

CRAFTSMANSHIP

In plain truth, there are so few really great stockmakers, and their lifetime output is so small, that a pretty small percentage of shooters, even the more avid rifle lovers, ever get to actually see and handle the best in custom rifles. Sadly, for the most part the closest most of us ever get to the real thing is the pictures published in various shooting publications. We can see by the pictures that the lines of the stocks are mouth-wateringly beautiful, and we read that the wood-to-metal fit is so close that a cigarette paper can't be slipped between, but there is very little way that we can ever be made to appreciate the *detail* work of a great stock without personal inspection. Thus, unfortunately, even though the fame of a talented and skilled stockmaker may be known from Kalamazoo to Kenya, there will be very few of us who ever get a chance to see how great his work really is.

Frequently great stockmakers are applauded in print for their beautiful, razor-sharp inletting. To be sure, fine inletting is something to be admired, but you'll no doubt be surprised to learn that inletting a stock so closely as to look like the metal grew in the wood (as some writers like to put it) is only one of the skills mastered on the way to becoming an outstanding stockmaker. There are many other things to be looked at before a stockmaker can be judged truly outstanding. The way the ends of the cheek piece blend into the butt section is an example. Do they just fade away haphazardly or is the detail of the curve maintained until it is all but invisible? Are sharp edges really sharp, and are flat surfaces really flat? It has been said that only another stockmaker can truly appreciate the detail work of a top craftsman. This is in large measure true, because who knows how difficult something is until he's tried it?

I'm of the opinion that really fine detail work is coming more and more to

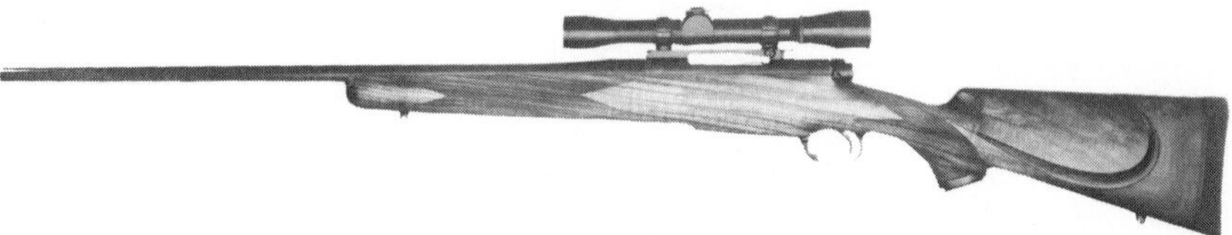

A Winchester Model 70 rebarreled to 7mm Remington Magnum featuring a custom-built five-shot magazine. The stock work, by Earl Milliron, is absolutely classic.

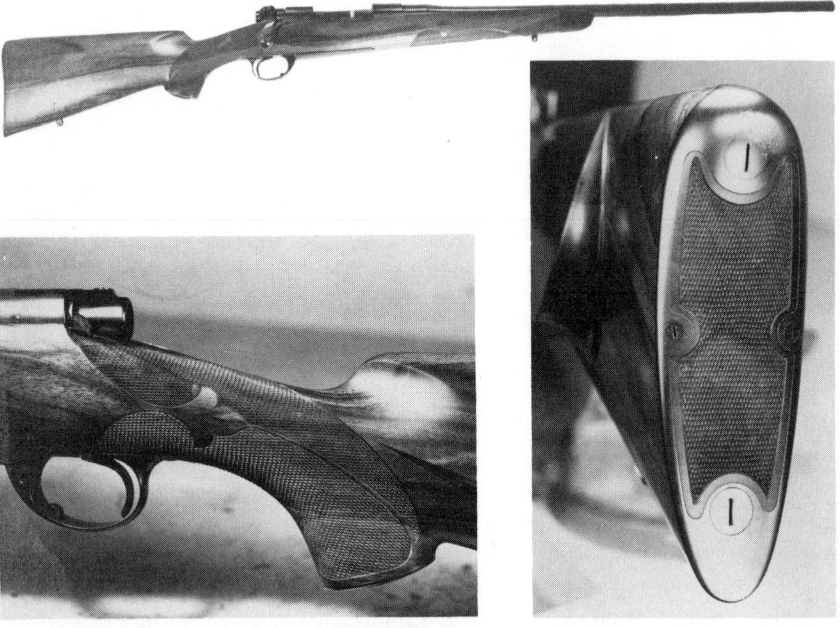

A magnificent restocking job by Gary Goudy done for me on a Model 70 Winchester rebarreled to 6mm Remington. The trigger guard is by Ted Blackburn. The wood is a tight-grained and richly textured piece of French walnut. The difficult checkering pattern is flawless. The fitting of metal to wood is absolutely perfect. Notice on the butt-plate detail that the screwdriver slots in the screw heads do not run the full width of the screw head. This is a clever touch.

the fore in modern stockwork. As a budding stockmaker's style matures and "sets," he tends to put more and more emphasis on his detail work. Also, with the development of what we call the modern "classic" style there has been, here of late, a decreased emphasis in the way of development of basic forms and more effort towards detail.

Nearly every one of our finest stockmakers works in what is commonly referred to as the *classic* form. The only problem here is that no one has come up with a really good definition of a classic stock. They are a lot like beautiful women; you always recognize them when you see one, but they are hard to describe. Also like beautiful lasses, "classic" stocks can vary greatly from one to the next but still fit the type. This is another reason the classic is so hard to describe. Stocks by, say, Jerry Fisher are quite different from those made by Al Biesen, but both are examples of the classic school.

Dale Goens of Cedar Crest, New Mexico, is widely considered one of the world's all-time great stockmakers. Here he sands a beautifully textured piece of French walnut.

If I had to propose a working definition of the classic style I'd say it combines extreme shootability with clean, graceful, and well-proportioned lines. Every line and feature goes somewhere and does something and complements every other line and feature so that the total effect is one of subtly balanced curves and straight lines. *Nothing is there that isn't needed!* This last rule, needless to say, eliminates such purely ornate features as shovelbill forends, cow-catcher grip caps, and rollover cheek pieces.

A little-known fact about the classic style, by the way, is that it is the most difficult form to master. They are not plain stocks by any means, certainly not in the sense that an ordinary mass-produced stock is plain. They are, in fact, a very rich combination of subtleties which confound all but the most discerning eye. I know of some stockers who have tried for years to master the classic form but cannot, by their own admission, get it right. I know of

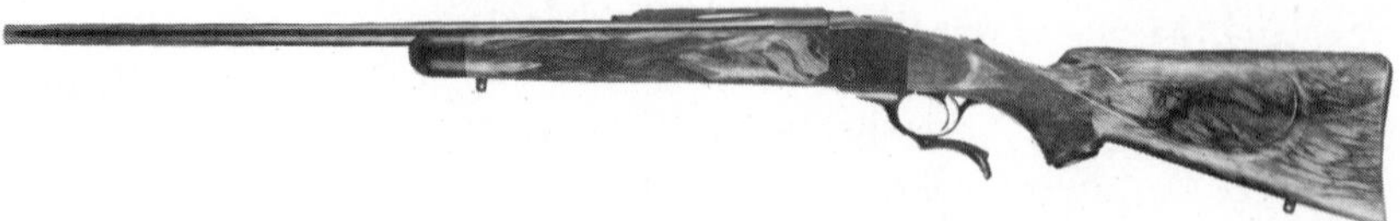

A Ruger Number One single-shot restocked by Dale Goens with exhibition-grade French walnut.

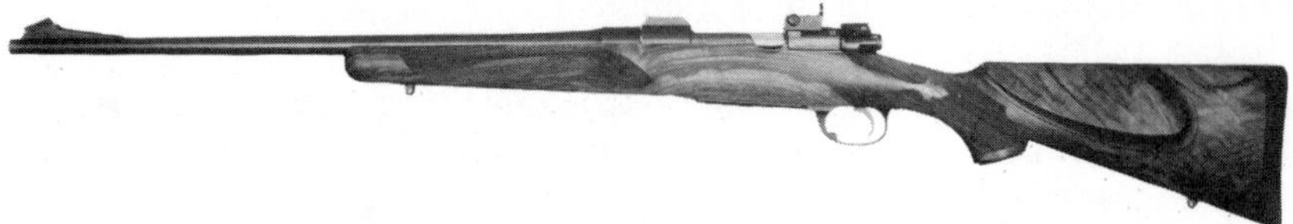

Earl Milliron stock on a Mauser action rebarreled to .306. Extremely clean but graceful lines are a hallmark of Milliron's craftsmanship.

A Leonard Brownell stock in French walnut on a Mauser action.

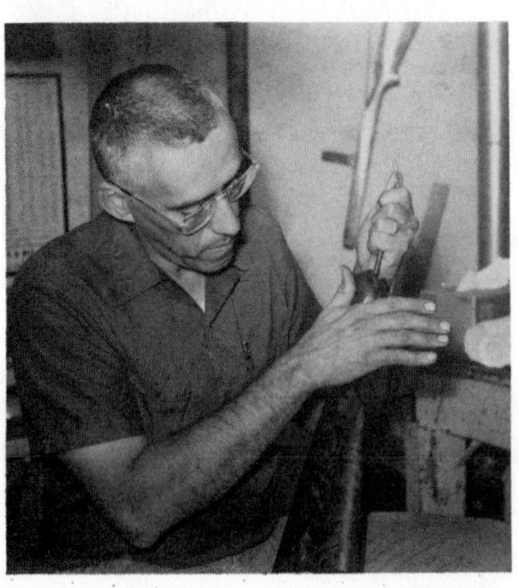

This is stockmaker Mike Conner, a former resident of New Mexico who now lives in Alaska.

Leonard Brownell of Wyarno, Wyoming, is one of the country's leading classic-style stockmakers and is responsible for the beautiful styling of the Ruger Model 77 and Number One single-shot rifles.

quite a few others who claim to make "classic" stocks, but in fact they are only making *plain* stocks. Just because a stock doesn't have a Monte Carlo comb, teardrop grip cap, thumbhole grip, and rollover cheek piece doesn't mean that it is a classic—not by a hell of a ways. You don't judge classics by what they don't have but, rather, by what they *do* have.

There is also a fairly widespread misconception that the classic style is nothing more than an attempt to perpetuate the stock designs of the better-grade rifles made both here and abroad during the era between the two great wars. This is far from the actual case. In truth, the classic form is a highly dynamic style which has changed tremendously over the years. The

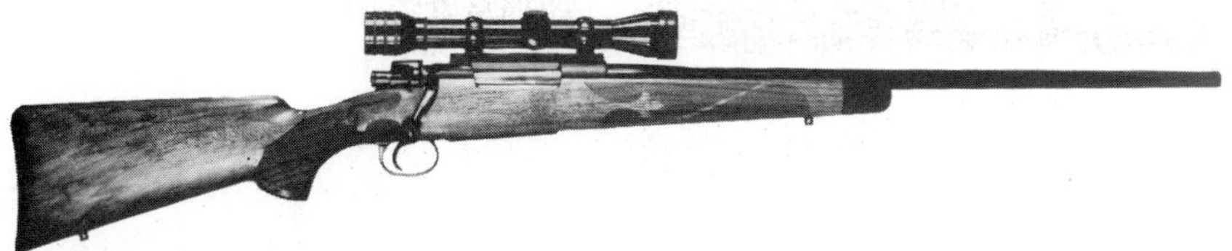

This French walnut stock by Mike Conner is on a Mauser 98 action.

"classics" of the 1920s and '30s, both those made here by such custom firms as Griffin & Howe and those of the great English firms, are easily distinguishable from today's classics. They had thinner combs, greater drop at both comb and heel, and less generous application of stylish detail. The classic style as now produced by our top craftsmen is *definitely* a post-World War II development.

CHECKERING AND CARVING

Another distinctive feature of the modern custom stock is the special emphasis placed on ornate and beautifully executed checkering patterns. This is not only a phenomenon of fairly recent times but also a distinctly American one. The purpose of checkering, in the traditional sense, is to provide a nonslip surface where the stock is grasped by the hands. But, as has been amply proved, it can also add a highly decorative touch to a stock and provide a handsome showcase for the skills of the craftsman. It is in this latter respect that the art of checkering has gotten so much attention in recent times. In fact, the art of checkering has been elevated to a position of such prominence that it has become, like engraving, a specialized field quite indepen-

Ace stockmaker Gary Goudy of Menlo Park, California, at his checkering cradle.

dent from the rest of the gunmaking crafts. Quite frequently, custom stockmakers negotiate the cost of a checkering job separately from the rest of the stocking job because they view it as a distinctively separate operation and therefore offer a wide variety of checkering patterns. Or to put it in money terms, which is usually the clearest way to make a point, if you expect to pay a premium to have a stockmaker "create" for you a uniquely different and beautiful stock design you can also expect to pay a premium for the creation of a beautiful and/or ornate checkering pattern.

It has not always been this way. In past generations checkering was viewed from the completely utilitarian standpoint. This is especially evident in British and Continental gunmaking. The finest woods might be used, beautifully inletted and finished, with the metal engraved to a fare-thee-well, but checkering patterns never showed the least bit of flair. As a matter of fact, the task of checkering a stock is, in many gunmaking areas, looked on as a job for women or apprentices. In a gunmaking center in Italy I once visited, gunstocks were taken home by women and checkered on a piecework basis. The checkering was poor but no one seemed to care in the least even though great care was lavished on the rest of the gun.

Even the great English gunmaking firms have never paid much attention to upgrading their checkering or even to making it equal in quality to the rest of the mechanism. I've inspected otherwise superb British doubles which had plain, uneven checkering with more than a few runovers at the borders. In fact, of the scores of great British guns I've inspected I've yet to see one with a checkering job that I couldn't beat in a six-hour working day. (And I ain't that good myself.)

Fancy checkering seems to have come into its own on best-grade U.S. shotguns back around the turn of the century. The skill was increased on high-grade Ithaca, Parker, Fox, etc., shotguns and eventually began to spill over into the area of rifle stocking.

Elaborate checkering has become an especially effective decoration for the modern classic stock because the fancy patterns and conservative stock lines tend to complement each other. Like anything else, though, large and fancy checkering patterns had better be done to near perfection or they look miserable. The most often heard index of good checkering is that the edges of the pattern be completely free of runovers. Since checkering wood is done with a back-and-forth filing motion with a small multi-toothed tool it is easy for one to "jump" the boundary and leave a runover. Thus a pattern with no runovers is evidence of a high degree of skill. The emphasis which has been placed on runover-free checkering has, in turn, brought about an ever increasing demand for borderless patterns. Traditionally, a molded or carved border around a pattern is to give the checkering a more or less framed appearance which highlights the pattern and takes away some of the plainness. But it can also be used to cover up runovers, and for this reason borders have largely come into ill repute. A stockmaker dare not put a border around his checkering lest someone accuse him of hiding a shaky hand with the checkering tool. In some instances this is unfortunate, because some simple point patterns are definitely improved by the addition of a well-done border. One stockmaker who has the nerve to use a border where it's needed is young Bob Winter of Menno, South Dakota. Bob is an extremely conservative stylist who makes some of the most cleanly beautiful stocks you'll ever see. Even cheek pieces are too racy for Bob's taste. On a .25/06 custom job he made up for me a while back he used a simple but classy point pattern with a border on the pointed ends of the pattern. It probably took nerve to do this because he no doubt wanted to show me that he was capable of runoverless borders. But his good taste told him that a border was needed to add just that certain something to set off the pattern. He was right; in fact, I'd almost forgotten how nice a cleanly cut border can be.

In this same vein the major rifle manufacturers no doubt got tired of hearing, year after year, about how great the borderless checkering was on fine custom stocks. In the early 1970s when Remington and Winchester developed highly automated, high-speed checkering machinery they naturally made a big thing out of the fact they now produced neatly cut *borderless* checkering. But wouldn't you just know it, their neat and stylish point patterns are just a little *too* plain and really need a border to set them off.

Another feature of custom checkering which gets lots of comment is the size of the diamonds. This is determined by the number of lines, or rows, of checkering there are to the inch. The fewer lines there are to the inch the larger and more deeply cut are the individual diamonds. Generally, the checkering on factory-made rifles is somewhere between sixteen and twenty lines to the inch. There are several reasons for this. First of all, checkering of this size, which is considered rather coarse-lined, is relatively fast and easy to cut. Second, the rather open-grained wood commonly used on factory rifles will usually not tolerate checkering much finer than twenty to the inch. The open grain causes smaller diamonds to chip off easily. And third, coarse checkering is generally considered to have a better "bite" or non-slip quality.

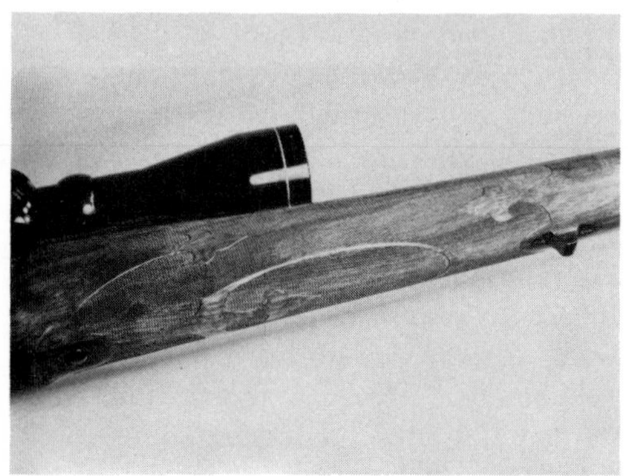

Detail of the almost unbelievably perfect and beautiful checkering pattern done for me by Duane Wiebe on a Model 70 rebarreled to 7mm Remington Magnum. This is one of the most difficult checkering patterns imaginable and could be handled by very few stockmakers. The checkering is 32 lines to the inch.

Finer-line checkering, usually twenty-four to twenty-eight lines to the inch, is more favored for fine custom stocks because it is neater-appearing, is more delicately stylish to look at, shows off the skill of the craftsman, and, most of all, is more suitable for fancy patterns. And too, fine-line checkering, being more shallow, tends to reveal the natural color and figure of the wood better than coarser stuff. Since top stock craftsmen almost always work with dense, tight-grained wood there is little problem with the fine-line diamonds chipping or flaking off. One of the most magnificent checkering jobs I've ever seen is on a custom stock made for me by Duane Wiebe of Pleasant

Hill, California. The ultra-elaborate pattern is done in super-difficult thirty-two lines to the inch in a dense piece of California English walnut. Such fine-line checkering is usually relegated to the fill-in in skeleton grip caps, etc., but Wiebe is one of the few stockmakers skilled enough to fill a whole pattern with the tiny diamonds.

A common complaint against extra-fine-line checkering (twenty-two lines to the inch and up) is that it does not provide as good a gripping surface as coarser checkering and that it damages easily and is hard to repair. As you no doubt suspect, these charges are usually hurled by frustrated stockmakers who simply can't master the more delicate technique. Of course fine checkering does not "bite" as well as coarser diamonds, but that's not the point anyway. Fine-line checkering is a showcase for good workmanship—first, last, and always. And besides, no one is going to drop his rifle because the checkering is fine rather than coarse. By and large, the chief function of any checkering, coarse or otherwise, is decorative. But for the record, fine-line checkering does *not* damage more easily than coarse, and when it does it's even *easier* to repair.

Just how much more elaborate checkering patterns may become is hard to say. Until a few years ago I thought they had gone about as far as they could go. But then Duane Wiebe arrived on the scene with his incredible layouts and suddenly it was a whole new ball game.

Buying custom stockwork is a lot like investing in engraving or other art

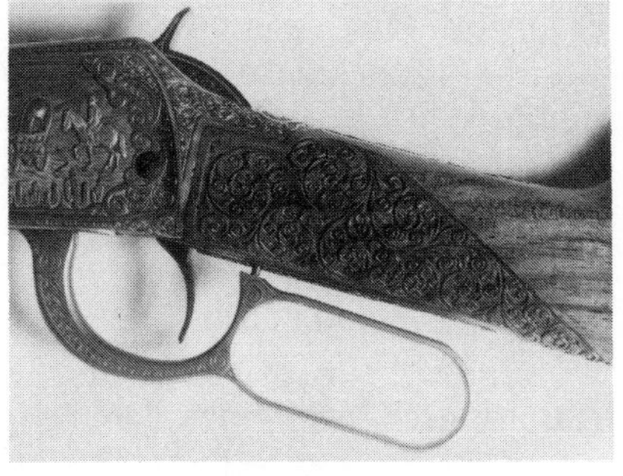

Ordinarily I do not favor carving on gunstocks because it is usually not at all well done. This work, however, done by the Pachmayr Gun Works, is an outstanding exception. The delicately cut scrollwork complements the engraving very nicely.

forms. If the work is good it will steadily go up in value. Stocks which feature elaborate checkering by skilled and well-known craftsmen will, in my judgment, increase in value at a faster rate. The more elaborate patterns will always be the scarcest, and this will make them the most desirable in years to come. So, like everything else on this earth, the more you put into it the more you get out of it.

On the subject of stock carving there really isn't much to say—it's almost a dead issue. The biggest reason for this is simply that there aren't that many really skilled carvers around. Another good reason is that there isn't much demand. Firearms connoisseurs who could afford really good carving are spending their money for checkering. My personal attitude is that I wouldn't care for carving unless it is absolutely first-rate. But first-rate carving, even if you can find someone to do it, is expensive and I'd rather put the money in engraving.

Now that fine checkering is in so solid with the custom-gun-buying crowd there is a noticeably snooty attitude toward decorative carving. I don't think this is entirely fair because I've seen some carving that is truly beautiful and which I'd love to own. Some of the scroll carving done on the early presentation Winchesters was exquisite and obviously done by a highly skilled engraver—most usually the same hand that did the metal engraving on the same rifle. Needless to say, examples of this sort of carving are highly desired by collectors and don't come cheap. The best carving one could get these days would no doubt be done by metal engravers. Likewise, the most attractive patterns, to my notion, would be delicate scroll or floral patterns similar to the patterns used in gun engraving. The traditional European-style stock carving featuring prancing nymphs and grinning satyrs somehow just doesn't turn me on.

Stockmaking, probably more than any other facet of the gunmaking arts and skills, is nearly the exclusive domain of American craftsmen. There are upwards of a dozen U.S. stockmakers whose names and reputations are known around the world—I've heard them discussed in such diverse places as Johannesburg, Sydney, Tehran, London, and Madrid—but I've yet to hear of any outstanding non-U.S. craftsman or see examples of his work. In Iran I heard of a stockmaker who is supposed to make copies of Al Biesen stocks, and in South Africa I was told about a fellow who turned out copies of the Bob Owens style. But these only emphasize the paramount position held by U.S. stylists.

Interestingly, and perhaps more than a little sadly, most stocks now being done in England and on the Continent, on both factory and custom rifles, are copies of the very worst in American styling. You guessed it—white spacers, Monte Carlo combs, flared grip caps, the whole works.

Luckily, at least as far as U.S. stockmaking goes, the future of fine stockwork is well secure with some really terrific new craftsmen coming along to join the old guard. Mike Connors turns out a trim, well-styled sporter in a solid, craftsmanlike way learned from his mentor Dale Goens. Engraver Winston Churchill has a flair for graceful curves and almost unbelievable detail. Gary Goudy combines exquisite detail work and superb checkering. Duane Wiebe is a master metalsmith as well as master of many stock styles and turns out the most magnificent checkering we're likely to see. And young Bob Winter will probably become known as the most classic stylist yet.

20

Custom Metalsmithing

The general concept of a "custom" rifle is one that has simply been restocked with fancy wood and styled to suit the client's taste and physical dimensions. How often, for example, have you run across a so-called custom rig that is nothing more than a standard commercial or surplus military rifle that has been "customized" by no other effort than a new stock and a fresh blue job?

A truly customized rifle may include any number of alterations in the basic metallic unit, put there for the purpose of improving functional efficiency, ease of operation, and overall appearance. Sometimes these changes are quite apparent, as in the case of a reshaped bolt knob or trigger guard. And sometimes they are subtle, such as a reduced receiver ring or narrowed tang. Sometimes they can't be seen at all, like a lightened firing pin or a magazine box reshaped to ensure better feeding.

Too, in the interest of distinguishing between wheat and chaff, there can be considerable difference between a simple alteration and a *custom* alteration. Consider a bolt handle on a surplus '98 Mauser rifle. The owner wants to use a scope on the Mauser, so the bolt handle has to be turned down out of the way. He takes it to a shop where the resident gunsmith forges the original handle down to a low sweep which will clear the scope, or perhaps the original handle is whacked off and a new one welded on. Obviously the bolt has been changed, but is it truly customized? Not necessarily. In fact, based on the actual number of bolt alterations done, the odds are better than *five thousand to one* that the bolt job is not an honest custom effort. This is because simply changing the angle of the bolt handle to clear a scope is only a utilitarian function. But, on the other hand, if the overall shape of the bolt handle shank and knob have been reworked so that it is pleasingly

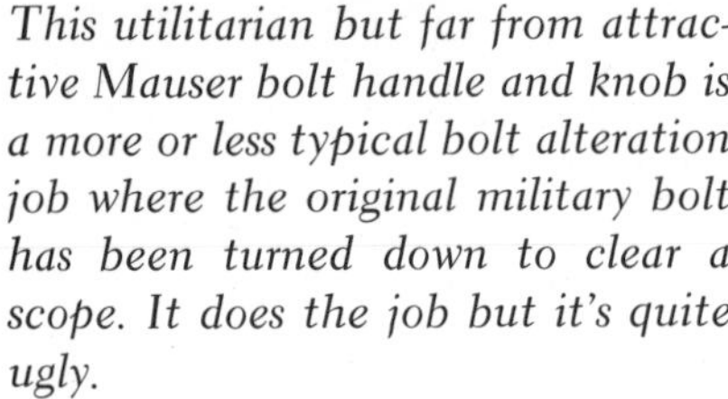

This utilitarian but far from attractive Mauser bolt handle and knob is a more or less typical bolt alteration job where the original military bolt has been turned down to clear a scope. It does the job but it's quite ugly.

In contrast, this is a gracefully reshaped and sculpted bolt handle for a Mauser. Notice the neat checkering on the bolt knob and also the Model 70-style safety. This work was done by ace rifle builder Al Biesen of Spokane, Washington.

graceful and, just as important, blends in with the overall lines of the rifle, it takes on the aspect of a truly custom effort.

While we're talking about bolt handles, let's say that a gunsmith is trying to turn out a lightweight rifle so he drills a hole in the bolt knob to get rid of some excess steel. Is this a custom touch or only utilitarian? A hole in a bolt knob is never pretty, so the custom craftsman hides the hole by means of a thin, perfectly fitting plug. You can't even see the results of the work, but it contributes to the overall efficiency of the rifle without distracting from its appearance. Subtle touches such as this are the essence of high-quality custom work.

Most gunsmiths, both professional and do-it-yourselfers, tend to have too much reverence for the original factory configuration of actions, barrels, and accessories. This is apparent in the way they shy away from altering or cutting away metal even when the advantages are obvious. Probably the all-time classic example of this is the tang on Mauser receivers. As everyone who has ever glanced at a Mauser knows, the tang has a full-length groove for the sear. When the action is inletted into the stock this groove must be continued into the wood for a distance or the bolt cannot be drawn fully to the rear. Cutting such a groove right on top of the stock harshly interrupts the natural lines of the grip area and eliminates any possibility of a clean contour. The solution is so simple as to be laughable. The top of the tang should be slanted off so that the groove disappears at the rear edge. It takes about five minutes with a file. Not only is the groove in the stock eliminated but the lines of the receiver flow more gracefully into the wood.

This is an example of the nice little touches that make for fine custom gunsmithing. In front is an original Mauser action tang with the unsightly groove cut in the stock for the cocking piece. In the background is an otherwise identical Mauser tang which has been reduced in profile for a more pleasing union with the stock.

Another offender in this area is the big, flat tang on Model 70 Winchester receivers. The Model 70 is one of the best possible actions to build a custom rifle around, but some changes are necessary. The overly wide tang, if you've ever noticed, just sort of sits on top of the grip like a big blob. Stylistically

Another classy custom metalsmithing feature. The Model 70 tang in the foreground has been reduced in size so it fits more neatly into the custom stock. The original Model 70 tang in background, as you will notice, is much larger, does not fit well into the stock, and tends to dominate the grip area. Also notice the neatly reshaped and checkered bolt release on the stock in foreground. The original shape of the bolt release, a simple metal stamping, is seen on the rifle at rear. Again, this is a stylish touch.

it's an eyesore because it dominates rather than blends into the wood. Therefore a savvy custom riflemaker trims it down to a graceful shape which fits *into* the stock and doesn't just lie on top. Likewise, the Model 70 trigger guard and floorplate unit, though one of the best-looking commercial designs ever offered, is hardly acceptable for a fine custom rifle. The slab-sided guard bow is in need of recontouring, and the floorplate can always stand dressing up around the edges. The best treatment is to throw it away and start all over with a completely custom unit with straddle-butt floorplate and guard bow release such as those made by Ted Blackburn.

The same goes for virtually every other rifle design, either commercial or military surplus, that a custom rifle is likely to be built on. The white metal trigger-guard units on Remington 700s, Ruger 77s, FFVs, etc. would never pass muster on a good custom rifle and must be built from scratch. Mausers are particularly offensive, especially the surplus models with the hole in the

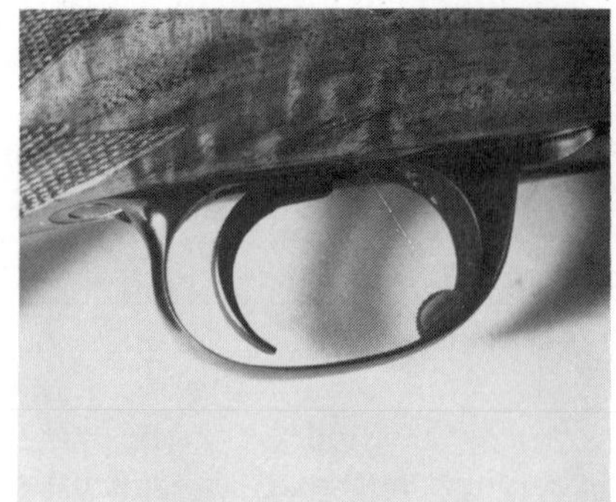

The styling of some surplus military trigger guards such as this Model 98 Mauser is ugly, but the skilled metalsmith can convert it into a work of art. The trigger guard has a floorplate release in the front of the guard bow. This is good gunsmithing.

front of the guard bow. The best of the lot are the Model 1909 Argentine Mausers built by the old-line German firm of Deutsche Waffen und Munitionsfabriken (DWM). These have a hinged floorplate with a release in the bow. But still, considerable work is required to make them fit for a custom rifle. The bow has to be reshaped to a more graceful contour, a release button has to be made and attached, deeply stamped serial numbers must be erased, and the floorplate must be replaced or extensively reworked. As with all mass-produced rifles the floorplate is slightly narrower than the magazine box outline. On a custom rifle, however, the floorplate should slightly lap over the box inletting. This looks better and forms a protective seal. A subtle touch to be sure, and adding upwards of $50 to the total bill, but certainly worthwhile.

By now the prospective custom rifle customer is no doubt becoming pretty impressed with the amount of work that must go into the action

This nice little metalsmithing touch on a Mauser bolt release involves fitting a checkered steel thumb tab for better appearance and operation. Simple as it appears, few gunsmiths really have the skill or know-how for this type of work.

alone if it is to serve as the basis for a fine rifle. But there's still a lot to be done. Let's consider a plain Mauser action. First of all, the knowledgeable riflemaker will determine if the proposed action is tough enough in its present form. Many of the earlier military and commercial versions are quite soft and therefore unsuitable for modern high-intensity cartridges. The thrust actually mashes the locking lugs into the receiver steel and after a few rounds a condition of excessive headspace develops. Unfortunately, this condition is most prevalent in the better-finished actions such as those made by DWM, Oberndorf, etc. This doesn't mean that the actions are useless, but they will have to be properly heat-treated by a specialist in order to bring them up to suitable hardness. Most gunsmiths do not attempt the exacting process of heat-treating a bolt and receiver but, wisely, farm out the work to large heat-treating firms that are properly experienced and equipped for the job.

This custom work on a Mauser action by Herman Waldron shows the custom-styled trigger guard, Model 70-styled safety, and beautifully rebuilt bolt handle with checkering.

If the receiver has a large receiver ring, the riflemaker may first want to grind down the outer radius so that it matches the side rails. This eliminates the bulbous front-end contour and allows better stock lines, and it also reduces weight. A properly ground receiver ring leaves a full-diameter crest at the top of the ring just wide enough to flare into the scope-ring base. This looks good and leaves plenty of metal around the locking-lug recess.

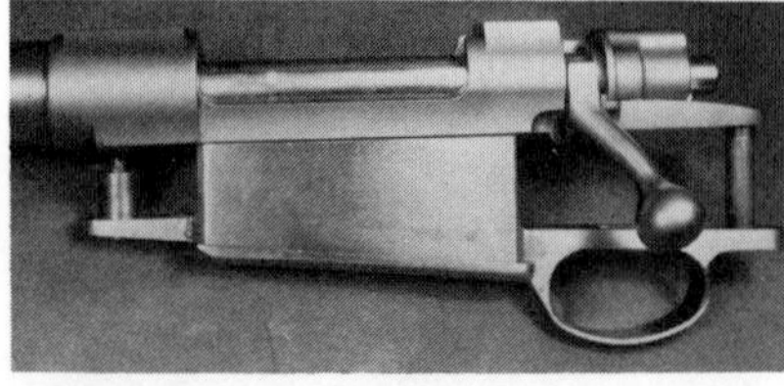

This is custom metalsmithing at its most elaborate. This true "mirror-image" left-hand Mauser action was completely built by Fred Wells of Prescott, Arizona.

After any necessary hardening the locking lugs are checked to see that they bear fully and evenly against the lug recess shoulder. Heat treating can cause enough warpage to result in uneven contact, but, at any rate, surprisingly few sets of lugs bear evenly anyway. A sharp rifle specialist will lap them into full contact. The lapping operation also serves to smooth up bolt operation on the opening and closing (up and down) strokes.

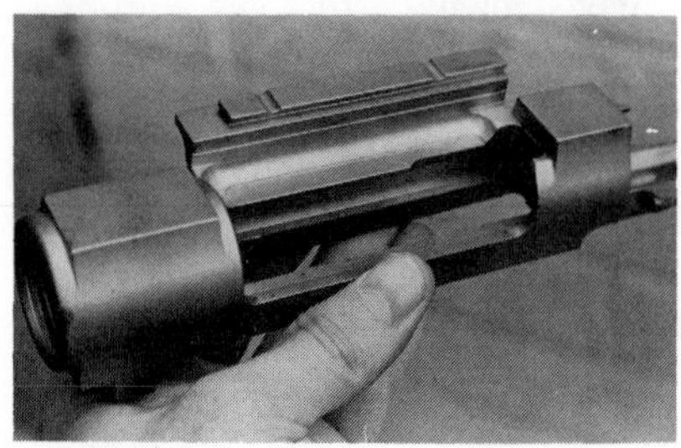

This detail of the receiver of one of the left-hand Wells Mauser-type actions shows the popular double square bridge configuration favored by Wells and also the built-in, offset scope base.

Also, the front of the bolt needs to be turned and lapped so as to remove any gas-cut pits and to square up the fore of the bolt with the centerline of the action. This ensures full, even contact against the cartridge-case head and eliminates lost firing-pin motion and a possible degree of action flex. If the rifle is to be chambered for a magnum-class cartridge, the bolt face must of course be opened up for a larger rim diameter and the extractor altered accordingly.

Next the inside of the action and the surface of the bolt must be cleaned out. This means polishing away tool marks until the surfaces are dead smooth. Also a new bolt handle must be attached and, unless it is to be engraved, the knob will be nicely hand-checkered. Machine knurling will *not* do. The original safety, which will not work with a low-mounted scope, is thrown away and a front-to-rear-motion safety similar to the Model 70 Winchester installed. This is the all-time best in my opinion but requires some pretty fancy know-how to install on a Mauser bolt sleeve. The alternatives are a commercial low-sweep safety lever which simply replaces the original high-sweep tab or a shotgun-style tang safety or a side tang safety which attaches to the trigger mechanism. There are fancy variations on all of these, of course, but for my money the Model 70 safety conversion is the best combination of convenience and safety. (It blocks the striker fall and thus prevents "safety-on" jar-offs possible with trigger-block safety designs.)

Next problem to deal with is that bulky bolt release. Not a lot can be done here, but the finger tab should be checkered for a better grip or, better yet, the tab completely replaced with a somewhat larger and better-styled tab. Neatly hand-checkered, of course. And of course the tang needs to be cut down as described earlier.

The next major project is coming to grips with the trigger-guard assembly. Unless a new unit like the Blackburn assembly is used the custom riflemaker has to begin a rebuilding job at square one. The guard bow has to be reshaped, a floorplate release installed, and whole new hinged floorplate fitted. The original action screws will never pass muster, and the new store-bought replacements aren't much better. This means handmade screws with heads that fit inside the screw wells with hairline closeness. Some smiths use long-headed screws at this point which can later be cut and trimmed flush and "north & south" slots cut. The importance of the trigger-guard assembly to a rifle's entire appearance cannot be overstated. It is the focal point of the rifle's entire underside and is a dominating factor in stock styling. In short, it can nearly make or break the overall effect of a custom stock. Needless to say, a fellow can get quite a few man-hours tied up in the trigger guard alone, especially in milling a new floorplate.

Here are the three steps in the construction of a custom trigger guard as done by Herman Waldron of Pomeroy, Washington.

With the trigger guard and magazine unit completed, the next step is to make whatever alterations are necessary for smooth, foolproof cartridge feeding. This is sometimes simple but at other times it can be exasperating, especially when the action is being opened up to accommodate the fatter magnum cartridges. The rails have to be opened, and the underside bevel altered just enough to elevate the cartridge so the bolt will get a good bite.

But at the same time the cartridge shouldn't come up so far that there is a possibility of its popping out of the box and creating a double feed jam. With the feeding properly adjusted and polished a cartridge will snake out of the magazine and into the chamber with scarcely more effort than it takes to work the bolt when the rifle is unloaded!

So, after three or four days of work the action *alone* is pretty well ready for rebarreling. The remaining touch is drilling and tapping for scope bases or, in the case of a deluxe effort, the building and fitting of custom rings and mounts. Sometimes these are reworked commercial models, but some of the top metalsmithing specialists make a completely custom unit. Usually they are quick-detachable, lever-release designs which look mighty handsome but don't add too much in the way of practical convenience. The simple truth is that quick-detachable models are seldom detached—quickly or otherwise. But like an extra pair of socks, they're handy if you should ever need them.

A Wells receiver with a Griffin & Howe-type detachable scope ring set in place. This is top-class metalsmithing.

Model 70-styled trigger guard and scope ring bases as done by Herman Waldron.

From the standpoint of appearance, most custom scope-mount makers strive for exceptionally low, unobtrusive bases. This way when the scope is detached the bases don't stick up like sore thumbs as do commercial bases. The ultimate step in this direction is a base system built integrally with the receivers such as the Wells custom actions.

But there's still more to be done! After the barrel is fitted, a stock made, and the metal blued, the custom riflesmith goes back into the action and polishes out the inside surfaces: magazine box, rails, and feeding ramp. The blueing process has a way of tightening up a slick action somewhat, and the polishing is necessary. In the case of old-fashioned rust blueing the inside needs to be polished just to eliminate the traces of blue that overlapped onto bright-metal areas. Getting into all those nooks and crannies is a tedious hand operation and, again, the hours mount up. And too, of course,

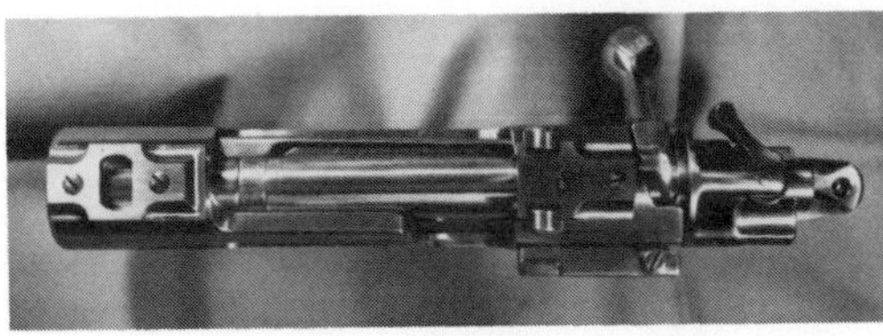

Top view of the custom scope bases by Herman Waldron.

the bolt is usually polished and jeweled. The final touch is the installation of a modern, adjustable, single-stage trigger. Then at last the rifle is ready for a final test firing and sighting in.

When this much action work is done by a top craftsman the final bill can be downright breathtaking. A tab running hard on to the half-grand mark just to get a $35 surplus Mauser in top form can come as quite a jolt, but even at that most custom metalsmiths are only equaling what might be considered semi-skilled labor wages in other lines of work.

Of course if a fellow really wants to see a custom metalsmith strut his stuff all he has to do is have an action shortened or lengthened. Let's say that you want a trim little .22/250 varmint rifle built on a Model 70 action. But the thought occurs to you that the mechanism is longer than necessary for the stubby round and wouldn't it be nice if the whole works were scaled down to size. There are, as it turns out, a few metalsmiths who are set to do just the sort of job you want. Fundamentally, the job involves cutting a section out of the receiver, bolt, striker rod, magazine, floorplate, etc., and welding the two halves of everything back together. Needless to say, this is a tedious operation requiring a high degree of skill and know-how. When done by a top craftsman there is virtually no way to recognize—except by the shortened length—that the metal has been sawed and welded. Young Ronald Lampert, one of the country's top metal specialists, accomplished the double-barreled feat of splicing the amputated portions of a cutoff job into a second action, thus converting a standard-length model into a magnum version. These build into an especially fetching matched pair of rifles for extra-large and extra-small game. The set he did for me are chambered for the .375 H&H and .250 Savage! Very cute indeed.

The above-described metalworking features are particularly notable because by and large they are products of *modern* gunsmithing. All of these techniques, to be sure, existed before World War II and are commonly seen on the better custom rifles from that era. However, one is likely to find them only on a more or less piecemeal basis. It hasn't been until the last couple of decades that modern custom riflesmiths really started putting it all together.

The ultimate in custom riflesmithing is achieved by the handful of master machinists who make an action entirely from scratch. By and large these have been aimed at the specialty market. Before Savage and Remington offered bolt-action rifles in southpaw configuration there were a few limited-issue left-lift jobs turned out by small custom shop craftsmen. One of the best-known custom actions was a sturdy and nicely turned-out falling-block single-shot affair by Wilbur Hauck. These were especially popular among varmint-shooting single-shot fans who wanted something a little more sophisticated than the Winchester High-Wall and Low-Wall Models. This market was pretty well plugged up, however, with the Ruger Number One single-shot and now the Browning Model 78.

One of the currently most active makers of custom actions and rifles is the Wells Rifle Shop of Prescott, Arizona. Fred Wells and his son, Rube, are top-flight craftsmen and machinists who specialize in magnum-length actions in either right- or left-hand configuration. Though they will make short or standard-length actions if that's what the customer orders, the main thrust of their business is directed toward filling the void created when production of the big Brevex Magnum Mauser actions was dropped a few years back. The Wells boys like big cartridges such as the .378 Weatherby Magnum necked down to .35 caliber or clodbusters such as the .460 Weatherby case necked out to .50 caliber! As actions long enough to house such rounds became harder to come by the Wells team simply started making their own. Basically these are on the tried and proven basic Mauser design, but they jazz them up with integral scope-mount bases for either side- or top-mounted rings. The side mount is an especially clever rig in that it utilizes the classy Griffin & Howe-style lever-lock, quick-detachable ring assembly. The unit is extra rigid, however, because the base is actually part of the receiver wall. The Wells trigger-guard unit, which like the original Mauser design is a one-piece guard and magazine box unit, is machined from a single block of steel. Needless to say, such work is time-consuming and very expensive, but for those who truly want custom work it's the only way to go.

During the 1950s and '60s there was a good bit of activity among skilled machinists in the direction of developing and producing massive single-shot bolt-actions for bench-rest competition. A few of these, usually one-of-a-kind specimens, are still turned out from time to time, but the market is pretty well handled by the actions made on a more or less commercial basis by Hart and Shilen.

Custom action building always has been and always will be a super-specialized field. There are very few craftsmen with the equipment and know-how to turn out a complete action, and not a whole lot of shooters willing and able to lay out the $1,000 on up this sort of work costs.

21

Engraving

Back when I was teaching at a Southeastern university (I'm sure they prefer I leave their name out of it) I was acquainted with an instructor from the Art Department who was something of a firearms buff. Our association almost came to a tragic end one day, however, when I showed him a nicely engraved little double. Since he was an art teacher I naturally supposed he would be delighted with the graceful and skillfully cut pattern. But when I lifted it out of the case he launched into a tirade on how guns were supposed to represent fine engineering and mechanical craftsmanship but *never*, he said, any form of artistic display. When he stopped to catch his breath I pointed out that he, of all people, should be aware that the desire to embellish one's weaponry was probably man's very first artistic endeavor. Then I went on to point out that throughout the ages swords, spears, daggers, arrows, and finally firearms have been considered an especially desirable and appropriate showplace for carving, etching, sculpting, and engraving. In fact, some of the world's great art treasures are ornately carved guns. The Metropolitan Museum of Art in New York, for example, has an entire section dedicated exclusively to priceless masterpieces of firearms decoration. But none of this made any impression on the art professor and he went off in a huff. (But then, come to think of it, he always was in a huff.) Possibly, his viewpoint may reflect the thinking of a considerable percentage of gun lovers.

Another, more common, viewpoint or impression is that great gun engraving is at least a dying if not already dead art. A couple of weeks before writing this I read a human-interest feature in a local newspaper about an area resident who was something of a gun engraver. Whenever newspaper writers chance to get on the subject of guns, either from the positive or the negative viewpoint, the overwhelming likelihood is that they'll miss the point entirely or get the whole episode wrong—usually both. Well, anyway, the subject of this write-up was a retired jeweler who happened to have a few engraving tools lying around and decided one day to pick up a few bucks engraving guns and at the same time rescue the dying art from total extinction. According to the story the art of gun engraving would pass forever with the passing of the old jeweler and thereafter join ancient Egyptian embalming as a lost art.

Balderdash!

Just as modern shooters are blessed with better barrels, bullets, actions, stocks, and sights, we've also got better engravers than ever before, and a lot more of them. The whole idea of the "Old Master" is something of a myth too. Winston Churchill, Lynton McKenzie, Frantz Marktl, Bob Swartley, to

This absolutely superb engraving was done by Winston Churchill of Ludlow, Vermont. Churchill's anatomy and execution are flawless, as are the layout and execution of his scrollwork.

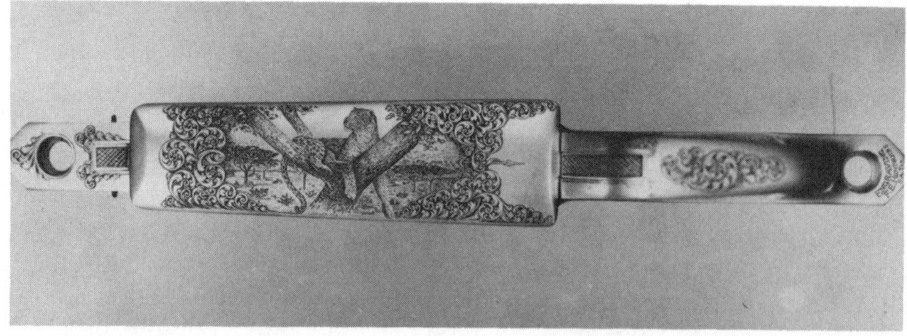

This extremely eye-catching engraving was done by Frank Hendricks of San Antonio, Texas. Hendricks is a master of innovative design and execution who offers a wide variety of engraving styles. This work was done on a Champlin rifle floorplate.

name a few, are scarcely more than pink-cheeked school lads, but they can engrave the pants off a roomful of Old Masters.

Good engraving, and I emphasize *good* (poor or mediocre engraving is worse than no engraving at all), does a number of worthwhile chores. First of all, of course, it decorates a rifle and makes it even more interesting and enjoyable to look at. Also, a well-engraved firearm can be a surprisingly pleasant companion to the lonesome or bored hunter. Occasionally when the hunting is progressing slowly, or when stuck in an unproductive shooting stand, I've passed the hours quite agreeably by studying the engraving on my rifle or shotgun. Each line, curve, and shading can be a source of considerable fascination.

Another function of *good* engraving is its ever-increasing value. Like many other art forms it frequently represents a smart cash investment because the worth may double every few years. (The flaw in this reasoning, though, is the same as art investment: the purchaser becomes so fond of the art that he can seldom bring himself to part with it.)

Actually, from the investor's standpoint, gun engraving is a pretty sound way to sock away some security for the future, but there is little likelihood that a gun engraver will be an overnight sensation whose work will double in value a thousand times over. I'm reminded of some of the "pop" artists of recent years whose goofy drawings of soup cans and cartoon characters have caught on with the "in" crowd and fetched ridiculous sums. These are usually artificial situations which can result in considerable cash loss to the investor. The "in" crowd will eventually be the "out" crowd and their darlings will be forgotten.

Fine gun engraving, on the other hand, represents an almost unfailingly sound investment because the work represents a sincere and highly skilled effort that will never at any time be worth less than when it was completed. In fact, in past generations engraving has been considered to hold a value intrinsically its own. In other words, unlike paintings, even if the artist is completely unknown, the quality of the work establishes its worth.

Here of late, however, the work of certain individuals is tending to create a special interest among collectors. The work of the late Rudolph Kornbrath, for example, is highly prized because he was one of the all-time great masters. Today's engravers are getting a lot more individual attention and publicity than engravers of the past, and this will no doubt have an effect on the ultimate worth of different works. Gun engravers tend, as a group, to be of a rather retiring nature and not inclined to promote themselves, but here of late I've noticed more of a tendency to step forward and promote themselves. This will not only increase the immediate demand for the engraver's work but will make samples of his engraving more valuable in later years.

Until just recently it has been hard to affix a firm money value to engraving. American engravers, in particular, were plagued by pricing competition

Three superb metal engravings supplied by the Pachmayr Gun Works of Los Angeles. These three deep-relief scenes were done on Winchester Model 94 rifles.

from Europe. Like any other product involving a high degree of skill and artistic craftsmanship, the money value is established by the lowest bidder. Master engravers in France, Italy, Germany, Austria, and Belgium could turn out fine engraving a lot cheaper than American engravers simply be-

Outstanding engraving, checkering, and stock carving as supplied by the Winchester factory. The rifle is a Model 94 .30/30 carbine.

cause of a much lower cost of living and a favorable (to Americans) dollar exchange. But by the beginning of the 1970s this situation had begun to change rapidly. European inflation and the floated dollar have put European prices up to the level of the best U.S. artists.

The work of modern engravers is distinguishable from that of past generations in a number of ways. First of all, it is simply better. This observation, it must be understood, is not intended as a criticism of the work of past masters but merely points up the fact that each generation of craftsmen improves on the skill of the past. Just as surely, future engravers will be better than those of today.

The improved technique of today's masters is probably most evident in the area of animal anatomy. Even as recently as the first half of this century, most attempts at engraving animals resulted in stiff, unlifelike profiles that were little more than caricatures of the real thing. This was due in large measure to the simple fact that engravers didn't always have a clear idea of what a certain animal looked like or how it moved. Modern engravers have a limitless source of photographs and firsthand observations to draw from.

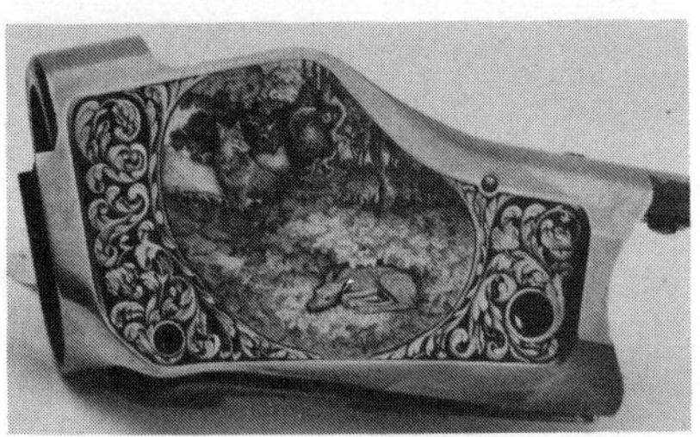

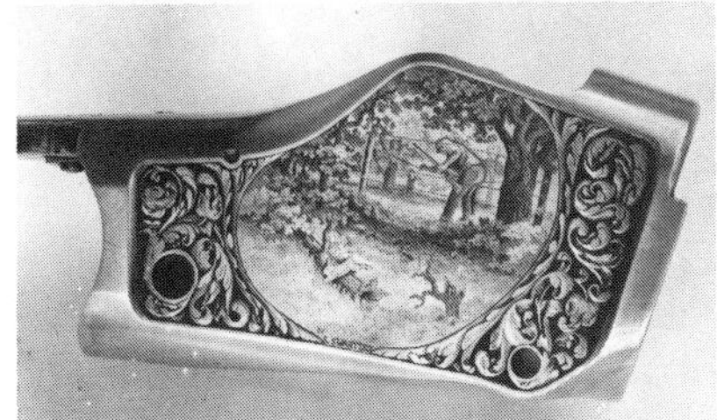

This extremely attractive and interesting layout for a Winchester High Wall receiver was done by Bob Swartley of Napa, California. Extremely delicate cutting is a hallmark of the Swartley style.

Also they receive the benefits of better instruction in the subtleties of anatomy. Today, when an engraving expert praises the animal engraving of a nineteenth-century master such as, say, L. D. Nimschke, what he is actually applauding is Nimschke's achievements in *relation* to other engravers of his day. By modern standards it may appear pretty poor.

Another, and probably the most significant, feature of modern engravers is their ability to work in such a variety of styles. This is especially true of

Magnificently executed engraving job by Franz Marktl. Young Marktl, who was trained in Austria, now lives and works in the U.S. The rifle is a short Mauser.

American engravers. Under the traditional European apprentice system an engraver was more likely to learn only a basic scroll or two, an oakleaf pattern, and perhaps a stag-and-hound design. The scrollwork, in particular, was often so highly characteristic of a local system of instruction, or apprenticeship, that other engravers or engraving experts could identify the town or village of its origin.

I've proved this to my own satisfaction by showing samples of engraving to various European engravers whom I've met on my travels. Quite often I've received correct answers not only as to where the engraver in question was schooled but also who his instructor was. Often I've gotten a chuckle out of the way engravers tend to judge engraving along nationalistic lines. Handed a sample of Italian work, for example, a German engraver might say, "This is not German engraving and it is not so good." Or, shown a German sample an Italian might say, "These coarse lines and ugly oak leaves come from Germany—where else?"

American engravers frequently learn their craft by self-instruction, working with other engravers (such as at a sporting arms plant) and studying samples and photographs of the work of other engravers. Some American engravers, as a matter of fact, have joined the ranks of the world's finest artists with no formal instruction whatever. What's more, by having exposed themselves to such a broad variety of engraving styles and techniques, several are able to perform in an amazingly wide spectrum of styles.

As it so happens this trend is also developing outside the U.S. The European apprentice system is dying out in many areas and students of engraving are more at liberty to pursue a great range of styles. This, as I'm sure they realize, will be necessary if they expect to be able to meet the demands of the modern customer.

Sadly, for those who have been promising themselves a first-rate engraving job, the improved quality and versatility of the newer breed of artists is raising the price of engraving. The customer is buying not only the engraver's skill and time but also his years of schooling. Some engravers quote a flat fee for a specific amount of coverage, and others charge an hourly rate for "however long it takes." The last hourly quote I got from a top-of-the-stack engraver was $18 per hour, and it would soon be, I was told, raised to $20. Twenty dollars is certainly not an unreasonable hourly rate these days, especially when one considers what some plumbers, union tradesmen, and even garbage collectors make, but nonetheless an elaborate engraving job can add up to a lot of hours.

One of the best pricing schedules I've ever seen worked out for engraving is that of Frank Hendricks of San Antonio, Texas. Hendricks took up engraving while stationed in Germany with the Air Force. Exposed to first-rate German instruction, Frank learned well and is now one of the very top engravers in the world. His languidly graceful African cats, in particular, are without peer. Hendricks meets the client more than halfway by furnishing a detailed catalog of the styles and patterns he offers with a firm pricing for a specific coverage of each style or pattern. This way the customer can "compose" the combination which bests suits his taste and can accurately calculate what it will cost.

The more common pricing arrangement for engraving is a more or less general estimate by the engraver on what a specific job will cost. Naturally, gold and silver inlays add considerably to the cost of an engraving job, but by the same token engraving jobs which include a number of finely done inlays tend to appreciate faster than plainer work.

Though engraving is deeply couched in tradition, the more modern breed of artists are creating patterns which are distinctly contemporary. This does not mean that modernistic designs are used but that the work often has a distinctly up-to-date flair. This is especially noticeable on some of the patterns seen on the more modern rifles, which, in fact, feature highly distinctive configurations of their own. An excellent example is the Frank Hendricks engraved Champlin rifles. Rather than trying to "hide" as much of the rifle as possible with profuse coverage, Hendricks designed the engraving so as to embellish and even emphasize the naturally graceful lines of the Champlin action and trigger-guard assembly. This effect is especially striking when the metal is "frost" nickel-finished and the engraving darkened for bolder contrast.

This points up another characteristic of modern engraving—the increased emphasis on attractive layout and pattern design. Just covering a firearm with engraving, even good engraving, is not enough to qualify an engraving job as "good" these days. The top artists execute their work in a highly balanced pattern intended to create a harmonic balance between the mutual lines of the gun and the engraving itself. Engraving that clashes with the gun can never be better than second-class, no matter how well executed, and even engraving which draws too much attention to itself and not the overall unit is not in the best taste.

There was a time, not too long ago, when metalsmiths, stockmakers, and engravers all seemed to be fighting for attention on custom firearms. Everything seemed to clash and the complete unit was somehow uncomfortable to look at. The trend is very much in the opposite direction these days, with the best examples of custom rifles looking like action, barrel, stock, *and* engraving were designed as an artistically balanced unit.

Recently a representative from the famed English firm of Holland & Holland unveiled for me their last ever double-barreled rifle to be chambered for the behemoth .600 Nitro Express round. The price, which was hinted to be somewhere in the neighborhood of £25,000, included a large amount of the hard-to-get .600 ammo, which is nearly equal, no doubt, to the value of the rifle. Since the rifle was to be the last ever of that caliber I would have supposed it to be a bastion of the traditionally conservative English gunmaking with lots of beautifully executed but quietly understated scroll engraving. But not so! Instead it was embellished with extraordinarily deeply cut forms of game animals, troops of baboons racing up the barrel and—horror of horrors—deep-bosomed native lasses. Jolly olde Englande will never be the same again once word of that rifle gets around. English engraving is usually strong on scroll, but they don't tend to do so well on their animals or any deep-relief sculpting. But to the credit of Holland I'll say one thing: the work on this .600 was mighty good.

By and large, so-called "factory" engraving, the work provided by arms manufacturers on their custom-order and top-grade models, does not com-

An example of the best in factory engraving. This work, done in Belgium, is on a Grade V Browning BAR.

pare well with the best free-lance engraving. Over the years manufacturers have occasionally engaged the services of a top-line artist for extra-special projects, but most work is done "in house." In generations past the best engravers in the business worked for such firms as Colt and Winchester, probably because the jobs offered security, but this is no longer the case.

The best factory engraving seen today is on the shotguns of Armi Famars, Fabbri, and top grade Brownings. Browning engravers, by the way, form a hierarchy in the plant with the top-of-the-line models such as the Diana and Midas over-and-unders being engraved by really first-class artists—so good, in fact, that they are allowed to sign or otherwise identify their work. The "best" grade British guns are, as always, engraved in impeccably cut arabesque scroll. The work is wonderful but when you've seen one you've seen them all.

The work done by American factories is always done in amply skilled, workmanlike fashion but generally lacks the detail and dazzle of fine free-lance work. But, in fairness, it must be pointed out that these engravers are given little incentive and must do a specified amount of work in a given time, and I'm sure that doing the same pattern over and over eventually numbs one's artistic fervor.

Yet, modern American factory engraving is especially notable for a couple of interesting economic traits. The first of these, which has come about only recently, is a *relative* decline in cost. Only a few years ago factory work, regardless of relative quality, was considerably more expensive than that of independent engravers. The independents were, no doubt, compelled to hold their prices down because of competition from abroad and also because they felt they were competing with the factories for a share of the market. And then too, they worked on a direct basis which didn't include a couple of dealer markups.

But here of late the independents have raised their prices to a level which makes factory work a lot more affordable, by contrast, to the average Joe. By and large this puts the quality of factory engraving more in balance with what it's worth compared to the better free-lance work. But there is, as mentioned above, a second economic trait peculiar to factory engraving. That is the way *original* factory engraving adds so much to the collector's value of a gun. Collectors put a heavy emphasis on all features being factory-original. Even third-rate work will eventually be worth more than the very best engraving done after the gun left the shop. And it doesn't take all that long for an engraved gun to become a collector's piece. For example, Model 70 rifles manufactured and engraved as recently as the 1950s are now bringing many times their original prices.

Perhaps the most notable change of all, as far as modern engraving goes, is, believe it or not, the customers. For one thing they are becoming increasingly difficult to please. No longer can an engraver scratch a few circles on a gun and expect the customer to go away smiling. Guided by ever increasing exposure to good engraving, customers are not only becoming more specific in their requests but better judges of the final product.

When a customer shells out several hundred dollars for a gold inlay of a running antelope, it had better look like an antelope, and it had damn well better look like it's running.

Index

Note: References in *italics* refer to illustrations.